Jesus & Moses in India

By Asad Farooq

Tomb of Moses, Capital of Kashmir, India
(Photo by Ms. Suzanne Olsson)

iUniverse, Inc.
Bloomington

Jesus & Moses in India

iUniverse books may be ordered through booksellers or by contacting:

iUniverse
1663 Liberty Drive
Bloomington, IN 47403
www.iuniverse.com
1-800-Authors (1-800-288-4677)

ISBN: 978-1-4502-8261-1 (sc)
ISBN: 978-1-4502-8263-5 (dj)
ISBN: 978-1-4502-8262-8 (ebk)

Printed in the United States of America

iUniverse rev. date: 4/20/2011

"And it will be righteousness for us, if we are careful to do all this commandment before the Lord our God, as he has commanded us."
(Deuteronomy 6:25)

"For I say unto you, That except your righteousness shall exceed the righteousness of the scribes and Pharisees, ye shall in no case enter into the kingdom of heaven." (Matthew 5:20)

Jesus said about the followers of his Second Coming:

"I will give you the wisdom to know what to say. None of your enemies will be able to oppose you or to say that you are wrong." (Luke 21:15 CEV)

"O mankind, We have created you from a male and a female; and We have made you into tribes and sub-tribes that you may recognize one another. Verily, the most honorable among you, in the sight of God, is he who is the most righteous among you. Surely, God is All-knowing, All-Aware" (Qur'an 49:13-14)

Love for All; Hatred for None

In the eyes of God we are all one.

Contents

1. Why did the Jews crucify Jesus?. 1

2. Clues in the Bible: Jesus was alive when taken down from the
   Cross. 8

3. Prophecy of Prophet Isaiah (Part 1). 31

4. Prophecy of Prophet Isaiah (Part 2). 36
   The Marriage of Jesus 39
   Brothers & Sisters of Jesus. 40

5. Paul versus Jesus 44

6. Why Jesus was considered god?. .49
   Six signs of a false messiah or a prophet. 50
   Socrates and the Poison. 53
   What are Stigmata?. 56
   Similarities between Jesus Christ and Lord Krishna. 58
   Similarities between Jesus & Buddha. 60
   Similarities between Jesus & Horus. 62
   Similarities between Jesus & Osiris 63
   Similarities between Jesus & Dionysus 64
   Similarities between Jesus & Apollonius of Tyana 65
   Similarities between Jesus & Attis of Phrygia. 66

7. Crucifixion cross examined by Four Gospels 67

8. Jesus went to Heaven. 74

9. Kashmir the "Promised Land". .81

10. Tomb of Moses in India 86
    Temple of Solomon. 94
    Tombs of the Israeli Prophets 96

11. Tomb of Jesus 106

12. Adam & Eve 112

13. The Original Sin 115

14. Noah and the Flood 122

15. Could a man (Jesus) be God? 128

Jesus and God 131

16. "Son of God" 139

17. Miracles of the People 153

18. God's promise to Ahmad. 162

19. Psalms or the Fifth Gospel? .169

20. The Book of Psalms. 186
    Wife of Jesus 197

21. The Second Coming of Jesus Christ 202
    What is Rapture?. 207
    A thief in the night 209
    Will the World End in 2012? 214

22. The Holy Ghost (Part 1) 222
    Harsh Punishments of the Qur'an. 237
    Fatwa on Your Head?. 242
    Moses & Muhammad 247
    Jesus & Ahmad 247
    Why do the Muslim women wear head Coverings? 259

22. The Holy Ghost (Part 2) 276
    What did Christians lose? 276
    Who are Double Christians? .289
    John the Baptist and the Gospel of Barnabas. 294
    "For unto us a child is born" .302
    Jesus the king of peace. 305

23. Islam in the Bible 311
    Why do Muslims kill other Muslims? 337

24. Jesus in the Qur'an 340
    Jesus: A Mystery?. 348
    Which of the Following Statements are we supposed to
      follow?. 353

List of a few books written Jesus in India. 357

Summary. 359

Biblical References. 363

Index. 383

Preface

By seeking to remove any misconceptions among Judaism, Christianity and Islam, this book attempts to unite the world's three most dominant religions, to bridge the differences, and to establish the link of all three religions back to our honorable patriarch Abraham.

Years of research supported by hard facts is presented in this book. At times, the reader may find that the writer is being impudent towards other religions. However, this is not at all the intention. The writer has only attempted to present facts and the content of this book should not be taken as an attempt to prove any religion or any holy scripture to be false.

This book highlights the fact that many misconceptions surrounding Christianity were caused by people who came many years after Jesus of Nazareth. Although many references from the Torah, the Gospels, the Qur'an and the books of the prophet Ahmad, have been used, this book does not represent any particular religion. The writer has tried his best to make sure that every concept introduced should come from the Bible. Although this book cites other references, nearly every concept is verified from the Bible first and then supported by other sources.

Acknowledgments

I would like to express my gratitude to a few people for helping me write this book; without whose help and support, I would not be able to accomplish my goal. First, I give great thanks to my mother Suraiya Sultana Farooq Sahiba for her prayers and full support. I also thank Saba, Rija and Amber for their full support. Special thanks to Amir Idllbi Sahab, Salahuddine Iddlbi, Seema Farooq Sahiba and Anas Ahmad for their great support. Special thanks to M. Arshad Sahab for his full support, initial editing and assistance for this book. Special thanks to M. Amjad Sahab, Faizan, Naumaan, Robina F., Rizwana M., Ather, Jamal, Omar, Mutahar, Shazal, Aslam, Anwer Sahibaan, M. Asim, Mazhar-Ul-Haque Sahab, Shahida Mazhar Sahiba. Brishna Khan, Arham Farooq, M. Akram Sahab. My heartfelt thanks go to my religious teacher Younus Farooq Sahab (My Father). Thanks to Dr. Hamid-Ur-Rehman Sahab, Shamshad Ahmad Nasir Sahab, Dr. Fida-Ul-Haque Sahab, (of FNH Foundation), Shakeel Ahmad Munir Sahab, Anwer Mehmood Khan Sahab, Dr. Aslam Daud Sahab of Canada. Aftab Ahmad Sahab, Mahmood Khan Sahab, Dr. Farid Ahmad Sahab, Mr. Abid Idllbi , Farooqi Anwar Sahab, Nuzhat Hafiz Sahiba, Qudsia Ahmad Sahiba, Muzaffar Ahmad Zafar Sahab, Khalid Hamidi Sahab, Tariq Hamidi, Noman Hamidi. Ajmal Shahid Sahab, Ather Shahid, Asim Ansari Sahab, Ramzan Jatala Sahab, Rehan Hamidi, Saud Saeed Sahab, Saim Hamidi., Saleem Javed Q., Asif Hussain, Naeem A.Mughal, Sajid Rizvi, Ahmad Hasan, Abid Alam, Muhammad Ashraf Sahab, Brother Johnny, Mr. Robert Marquez of El-Rancho Elementary, Manuel Ferrell, Brenda Avila, Angela Cuellar, James Cuellar, Veronica Cuellar, Jerome Egan, and Rhonda Peterson, who encouraged me to write this book. Very special thanks to Ms Suzanne Olsson for amazing pictures and Mr. George Cardiel for his support.

Dedication

I would like to dedicate this book to my beloved mother Mohturma Suraiya Sultana Sahiba, a very pious lady; she is the greatest mother on earth. I also would like to dedicate this book to my father Mohtarum Muhammad Younus Farooq Sahab: a great man, a beloved father, and a great teacher of religion.

1. Why did the Jews crucify Jesus?

According to *Ahmad*, there exist two factual reasons as to why the *Jews* wanted to crucify *Jesus*:

First Reason:

When the *Jews* were waiting for the *Messiah*, they developed a perception that *Elijah* had ascended up to the heaven with his body and the chariot he was riding on. It even says in the *Bible*,

> *"And it came to pass, as they [Elijah & Elisha] still went on, and talked, that, behold, there appeared a chariot of fire, and horses of fire, and parted them both asunder; and Elijah went up by a whirlwind into heaven."*[1]

The prophecy about *Elijah's Second Coming* in the book of *Malachi*, states that he will come before the *Messiah*. Therefore, the *Bible* says:

> *"Look, I am sending you the prophet Elijah before the great and dreadful day of the LORD arrives."*[2]

This led to the expectation within *Judaism* that *Elijah* would return bodily. *Jews* honestly and vigorously believed that if our book of *God* is telling us that *Elijah* will come from heaven first and then the *Messiah* will come then this is the way it supposed to happen. Subsequently, the *Jews* were very disappointed by the proclamation of *Jesus* being the promised *Messiah*.

---

[1]   Please see *2 Kings 2:11*
[2]   Please see *Malachi 4:5* New Living Translation copyright © 1996, 2004

1

They were probably thinking if *Jesus* is the promised *Messiah*, then where is *Elijah*? They asked *Jesus'* disciples this question, which is evident in the *New Testament* as follows:

1. *"Then his disciples asked him, 'Why do the teachers of religious law [Jewish Rabbis] insist that Elijah must return before the Messiah comes?' Jesus replied, 'Elijah is indeed coming first to get everything ready. But I tell you, Elijah has already come, but he wasn't recognized, and they chose to abuse him. And in the same way they will also make the Son of Man suffer.' Then the disciples realized he was talking about John the Baptist"* (Matthew 17:10 to 13 NLT).

2. The disciples inquired, *"Why say the scribes that Elias must first come?' And he answered and told them, 'Elias verily cometh first, and restoreth all things; and how it is written of the Son of man, that he must suffer many things, and be set at nought. But I say unto you, That Elias is indeed come, and they have done unto him whatsoever they listed, as it is written of him"* (Mark 9:11-13).

3. Jesus said: *"And if ye will receive it, this is Elias, [John the Baptist] which was for to come"* (Matthew 11:14).

4. The *Bible* says: *"he [John the Baptist] shall go before him [Jesus] in the spirit and power of Elias, to turn the hearts of the fathers to the children, and the disobedient to the wisdom of the just; to make ready a people prepared for the Lord"* (Luke 1:17).

The *Jews* have the same conception of *Elijah's* arrival--that he would come from the sky with the angels on his right hand and left hand and the whole world would see this magnificent day—as did all the *Christians* and the *Muslims* about the arrival of their messiah too. According to these verses, *Jesus* basically told the *Jews* that *Elijah* would never come from heaven because he never went to heaven with his body. *Jesus* probably intended in this verse that if the *Jews* are waiting for the *Second Coming* of *Elijah* then *John the Baptist* is his *Second Coming*. The *Jews* were furious at *Jesus* at that time because nobody saw *John the Baptist* coming down from heaven as the *Jews* were expecting. *John the Baptist* was not the *Elijah* in any sense according to them; the name of his parents was different, his name was different, and he was totally a different man as far as they were concerned. The *Jews* probably felt deceived by these two cousins (Jesus & John the Baptist). One says he is the *Messiah* and when they asked him about *Elijah* he says his cousin is the *Elijah*. On the other hand, *Jesus* did not even bother to explain why *John the Baptist* is *Elijah*. This basically denotes that their concept of *Elijah* ascending to heaven is not based on facts. That is why *Jesus* also articulated:

1. *"And no man hath ascended up to heaven, but he that came down from heaven, even the Son of man..." (John 3:13).*

2. *"...flesh and blood cannot inherit the Kingdom of God. These perishable bodies of ours are not able to live forever"* (I Corinthians 15:50).

That was one of the main reasons that the *Jews* rejected and crucified their *Messiah* (Jesus). He was the only one who could have given them the guidance from *God*.

Now the *Christians* are going to make the same error today that the *Jews* made *2000* years ago and reject the *Messiah* just because they wanted *Elijah* to come their way from heaven and they did not accept the way *God* sent him. They are still waiting for *Elijah* and the *Messiah*. *Elijah* never came their way and it has been about *3000* years. It has been all of these years and the *Jews* still could not comprehend that their perception was wrong. Now *Christians* are waiting for the *Second Coming of Jesus* the same way that the *Jews* were waiting for *Elijah*. The *Christians* deem that *Jesus* went to heaven with his body and will come back in the clouds with the angels on his right hand and left hand and *"every eye shall see and every knee shall bow."* But *Jesus* told them in very clear word:

"You will no longer see me at all until you say blessed is 'He' who comes in the name of the Lord."[3] This basically means *Christians* will not be able to see *Jesus* until they accept the one who will come after him, the *'Comforter'* or, in *Greek, 'Parakletos.'* I will enlighten my readers in detail who *Parakletos* is in the chapter titled *The Holy Ghost*.

As I have mentioned earlier, it is written: *"No man has ascended up to heaven but he that cometh down from heaven even the Son of man..."*[4] This basically means even *Jesus* did not come from heaven and he was born on earth in the womb of *Mary*. Therefore, how can we construe from this that *Jesus* went to heaven with his body when he himself is denying that. To clarify further, the *Bible* also said: *"Flesh and blood cannot inherit in the kingdom of God"* The *Jews* made an error and could not understand how a "mere man" (John the Baptist) could come instead of *Elijah*, so they rejected the messiah of the age. During that time, *Jesus* could not give adequate proof to the *Jews* of how *John the Baptist* is *Elijah*. In present time *Ahmad* is not recognized in

---

3 Please see *Matthew 23:39*
4 Please see *John 3:13*

3

1. Why did the Jews crucify Jesus?

the same way *John the Baptist* was not recognized, and still *John the Baptist* is not recognized, by the *Jews* as the *Second Coming of Elijah.*

Second Reason:

The *Jews* were told in the old scriptures that only when they are in distress and misery will the *Messiah* come and liberate them from all of their tribulations. The *Jews* might have thought that the *Messiah* was going to be a great warrior with a big army; he will fight and kill their oppressors, and will set the *Jews* free. The *Bible* does not articulate that the *Messiah* will be a great warrior. When the *Jews* came under the *Romans*, they knew this was the time for the *Messiah* to appear; however, to construe that he will bring a big army and fight and defeat the *Romans* was a man-made perception. But in my opinion, it was only natural for them to believe this way, because if they thought that the *Messiah* is going to liberate them from the biggest and most powerful rulers of the time, then he must be a great warrior and he must have a big force to fight the *Romans* and set the *Jews* free.

Consequently, *Jesus* comes and says 'I am the Messiah.' He is all alone, does not possess any army, any weapons, or any power. He exhorted them, *"whoever slaps you on your right cheek, turn the other to him also" (Matthew 5:39 NKJV)*. *Jesus* was a very humble, very peaceful man. He did not believe in hostility or in bloodshed. When the *Jews* heard his words *"whoever slaps you on your right cheek, turn the other to him also"* they immediately went against *Jesus* and sought to stop him and his teachings. They probably thought if they accept this peaceful teaching then they will never be able to fight against the *Romans* and they will remain under slavery forever. This notion is even articulated in the *New Testament* in these words:

> *"If we let Him alone like this, everyone will believe in Him,*
> *and the Romans will come and take away both our place and*
> *nation."*[5]

The *Jews* saw *Jesus* with abhorrence and they wanted to impede his teachings and influence. The *Jews* knew that the easiest way to kill *Jesus* was by knife or sword as they knew he did not have any guards or weapons; but they would still have to contend with *Jesus'* believers, who would still see him as a hero, a martyr, and the true messiah. Furthermore, his teachings would continue to gain more converts, while the *Jews* would continue losing their members to this false messiah (God forbid). Therefore, the *Jews* got together to make a malicious plan to not only stop his teachings but to also bring all

---

[5]   Please see *John 11:48 NKJV*

4

their lost *Jews* back to *Judaism*. The resolution was to prove from the *Bible* that he is a false messiah. But how would they do that? They had realized that more and more *Jews* were converting into *Christianity* simply because *Jesus* had fulfilled many *Biblical* prophesies and showed many miracles and wonders. He looked pious, clement, showed wisdom, spoke eloquently, and appeared to be a good contender for the messiah. However, *Jesus* did not fit the description of what the *Jews* thought their messiah would be like.

About a century after *Jesus* there was a man named *Simon Bar Kokhba*, or *Bar Kochba*, who embodied the beliefs that were counter to *Jesus*. He had a belligerent nature and talked against the *Romans*. He offered the *Jews* liberation from the *Romans* in the way that they had anticipated from their messiah. He was successful in vanquishing the *Romans* in *Judea* and gained many followers. Things changed when *Bar Kokhba* called himself the *Messiah*. For this action, *God* punished him as the *Romans* putting *Bar Kokhba* and his followers to the sword; men, women, and children were killed. The *Jews* were decimated and the few who survived fled to other countries to save their lives.

Unfortunately, they could not put their foot into *Jerusalem* for almost two thousand years. After *Bar Kokhba's* defeat the *Jews* should have realized that this is a punishment from *God* for rejecting *His* true *Messiah* (*Jesus*) and for believing that *Bar Kokhba* was the true messiah. If we presume for a second that *Jesus* was not the true messiah (God forbid), and if the real messiah of the *Jews* comes today the way they are anticipating, then one serious question arises: what would he do? Since the *Jews* are not under the slavery of *Romans* or any others for that matter, who would the messiah set the *Jews* free from?

Revisiting the topic under discussion, the *Jews* were very bewildered and they wanted to find out if *Jesus* was the true messiah or not. *Scribes* and *Pharisees* came up with a clever plan to test *Jesus*: hang him on the cross. If he survives the cross somehow, then he is the real messiah and everyone will believe him. The *New Testament* records this view in these words:

> *"Likewise also the chief priests mocking said among themselves with the scribes, He saved others; himself he cannot save. Let Christ the King of Israel descend now from the cross, that we may see and believe."*[6]

If he dies then he becomes accursed of *God* and the *Jews* would know that he is not the true messiah. It is also written that "*for he that is hanged is*

---

6   Please see *Mark 15:31 & 32*

accursed of God."[7] His followers would realize that they had made a grievous mistake by accepting him as a true messiah, and they would all renounce *Jesus*. The *Jews*, consequently, would regain all their lost *Jews* back to *Judaism*.

Jesus never implied to anybody in the entire *New Testament* that his dying on the cross would bring any virtue to anyone, bring salvation for anyone or having faith in his accursed death will save them or gives them eternal life. Instead, he told his disciples to keep the commandments of the *Mosaic Law* if they want to earn eternal life. Thus, the *Bible* says:

"Behold a man came to Jesus and said 'Good master, what good thing I shall do, that I may have eternal life?' Jesus said why callest thou me good? There is none good but one that is God, but if thou wilt enter into life, keep the commandments."[8]

Unfortunately, this verse has been changed in most *Bibles*. Almost all the new *Bibles* read this verse as follows: *"Why do you ask me about what is good?"* Do you see the difference? The *King James Version* says: *"Why do you call me Good?"* But these new *Bibles* are saying *"Why do you ask me about what is good?"* Do you know why most of the new *Bibles* have changed the wording of this verse? *Ahmad* the *Second Coming of Jesus Christ* asked in one of his books how could the followers of *Jesus* call him *God*, when he does not even consider himself to be called good? The *Christian* scholars perhaps realized that this verse could raise a lot of questions so they changed it. *Jesus* could have advised his followers that if you want to earn eternal life just wait for my crucifixion and through the faith on my accursed death on the cross you will earn eternal life. Instead, the *Bible* says:

"Ye see then how that by works a man is justified, and not by faith only. For as the body without spirit is dead, so faith without work is dead also" (James 2:24 to 26).

This means that just having a faith is nothing, we have to have good works as well if we want to earn eternal life. According to *Ahmad*, these two reasons seem to play a vital role in the crucifixion of *Jesus*. The above two reasons are only a summary to various accounts, presented by *Ahmad*.

Please allow me to make one thing utterly clear once and for all: The *Romans* had nothing to do with the crucifixion of *Jesus*. Unless any *Jewish or Christian* scholar provides evidence to me from the *Bible* that *Jesus* was a criminal (God forbid), I could not find any credible reason to perceive

---

7   Please see *Deuteronomy 21:23*
8   Please see *Matthew 19:16*

that *Jesus* was crucified by the *Romans*. I acknowledge the fact that *Jesus* was crucified through the *Roman Government,* but that government had no interest in crucifying him. The *Bible* articulates:

> *"Why?" Pilate demanded. "What crime has he committed?" But the crowd only roared the louder, "Crucify him!"*[9] The *Bible* also clarifies that the *Jews* wanted him to be crucified.

> The *Bible* says: *"Pilate saw that he wasn't getting anywhere and that a riot was developing. So he sent for a bowl of water and washed his hands before the crowd, saying, "I am innocent of the blood of this man. The responsibility is yours!" And all the people yelled back, "We will take responsibility for his death-we and our children!"*[10]

I know that in the last fifty to sixty years because of the friendship with the *Jews* or for some political gains, some *Christian* scholars have been censuring the *Romans* for the crucifixion of *Jesus,* but this is absolutely erroneous. Until anyone can prove that *Jesus* stole something, killed someone, or broke any of the *Roman Laws,* and thus conclusively prove he was a criminal, we cannot blame the *Romans* at all. On the other hand, the *Jews* knew it was imperative for them to crucify *Jesus* and they took that responsibility very boldly: *"We will take responsibility for his death-we and our children!"*[11] By proving from the *Bible* that the *Jews* were responsible for the crucifixion of *Jesus,* not the *Romans,* I do not mean to inflict any detestation upon the *Jews* or to wreak havoc in society. All I mean is that the *Jews* of the time of *Jesus* were responsible for his crucifixion. To create any abhorrence for the *Jews* of today would be very unfair and an unethical act. That would be the same as if we started killing all men by declaring all men are sinful and should be chastised because of the sin of *Adam.* Punishing someone for the sins of someone else is a very grave sin in itself.

---

[9]   Please see *Matthew 27:23 NLT* Copyright © 1996, 2004
[10]   Please see *Matthew 27:24 & 25 NLT*
[11]   Ibid.

2. Clues in the Bible: Jesus was alive when taken down from the Cross

1) *Jesus* was on the cross for about *two hours*:

The *Christians* traditionally know that *Jesus* was on the cross for about six to nine hours. The *Gospel* of *Matthew* says: *"Now from the sixth hour there was darkness over all the land unto the ninth hour."*[12] It sounds like *Jesus* was on the cross for about nine hours. No healthy person dies in nine hours. According to the *Roman* history, people were usually hanged on the crosses for three days, and they still had not died. If someone did not die on the cross within three days, then the *Romans* would break the person's legs to make the person die. So how could *Jesus* die in just nine hours when we know that he was only thirty-three years old and a healthy man?

In the book *'Jesus in India,'* on page 25, *Ahmad* says that *Jesus* was on the cross for about two hours. I thought that it would be almost impossible to prove from the *Bible* that *Jesus* was on the cross for about two hours, while the whole *Christian* world thinks that it was about six to nine hours. But modern day versions of the *Bible* are also moving towards the *Ahmadiyya* view of the events that occurred. The new versions of the *Bible*, such as the *New Living Translation*, states:

> *"At noon, darkness fell across the whole land until three o'clock. At about three o'clock, Jesus called out with a loud voice..."* (*Matthew 27:45-46*).[13]

---

[12] Please see *Matthew 27:45*
[13] Please also see: *Contemporary English Version, Amplified Bible, English Standard Version, Worldwide English Bible, and Phillips Modern English Bible*

Which means the sixth hour to the ninth hour only denotes *12pm to 3 pm*. Not only that, the *Gospel* of *John* says:

> *"It was now about noon of the day of preparation for the Passover. And Pilate said to the people, "Here is your king!" "Away with him," they yelled. "Away with him--crucify him!" "What? Crucify your king?" Pilate asked..."[14]* This means *Jesus* was not crucified at noon, but he was ordered to be crucified at noon.

The book of *Matthew* says that when *Jesus* was ordered to be crucified the soldiers took him to a hall. It says:

> *"Then released he Barabbas unto them: and when he had scourged Jesus, he delivered him to be crucified. Then the soldiers of the governor took Jesus into the common hall, and gathered unto him the whole band of soldiers. And they stripped him, and put on him a scarlet robe. And when they had platted a crown of thorns, they put it upon his head, and a reed in his right hand: and they bowed the knee before him, and mocked him, saying, Hail, King of the Jews! And they spit upon him, and took the reed, and smote him on the head. And after that they had mocked him, they took the robe off from him, and put his own raiment on him, and led him away to crucify him"* (Matthew 27:26:31).

After *Jesus* has suffered from all this the guards take him to *Golgotha*, which was about *650* yards, or about half a mile, from the palace of the governor. *Jesus* was not only walking, he had to carry his own cross, which according to some accounts weighed about one hundred pounds. Even if it took him fifteen minutes in the common hall, and about thirty minutes to walk to the *Golgotha*, then actually *Jesus* was on the cross for barely two hours. 'About two hours' is not sufficient time for a young, healthy, and physically fit *Jesus* to die because of crucifixion. While evidence supporting the two hour claim did not exist in *Ahmad's* time, this evidence exists now in the form of changed wording in the *Bible*. If *Ahmad* was not from *God* then why the word of *God* has changed in his favor? It is imperative to present here some of the other changes which have occurred in the newer versions of the *Bible*. These changes transpired in the favor of *Ahmad's* proclamation, that *Jesus* was alive when he was taken down from the cross.

---

[14] Please see *John 19:14-15 New Living Translation*

King James Version or Old Bibles		New Bibles printed after Ahmad's proclamation
1	"He showed himself alive" (Acts 1:3).	"He was actually alive" (Acts 1: 3 New living Translation).
2	."The Lord is risen indeed, and hath appeared to Simon" (Luke 24: 34).	"And they learned from the group that the Lord was really alive and had appeared to Peter" (Luke 24: 34, Contemporary English Version).
3	"...Why seek ye the living among the dead?" (Luke 24: 5).	a) "Why are you looking in a tomb for someone who is alive?" (Luke 24: 5, New Living Translation). b) "Why are you looking in the place of the dead for someone who is alive?" (Luke 24: 5, Contemporary English Version)
4	"And Jesus cried with a loud voice, and gave up the ghost" (Mark 15: 37).	"And Jesus cried out with a loud voice, and breathed His last" (Mark 15: 37, New King James Version, NLT, NIV, ESV, NASB, RSV,).
5	"he was taken up; and a cloud received him out of their sight" (Acts 1: 9).	"a cloud hid him from their sight" (Acts 1: 9 NIV).
6	"So then after the Lord had spoken unto them, he was received up into heaven, and sat on the right hand of God" (Mark 16: 19).	Most *Revised Standard Version Bibles*, between *1946* to *1970*, do not usually contain 12 verses of *Mark* chapter 16 after verse 9 through 20. Nor do they say anything about *'Received up into heaven.'* These verses are not the part of two most authentic *Bibles, Codex Siniaticus* and *Codex Vaticanus*.

Is this a mere coincidence that the *Bibles* of today have changed in the favor of *Ahmad*? Have you ever seen a single example from the history of mankind that a man claims to be from *God*, and whatever he relates to them seems to be contradictory to the *Bible*, but then the word of *God* changed in his favor? Could that person be an imposter?

Please allow me to present some of the other changes which have occurred over the last hundred years or so which did not necessarily come into existence in the favor of *Ahmad's* proclamation, but these are new changes in the *Bible*.

This seems to me an attempt by the theologians to prove their orthodox view.

King James Version or other old Bibles	Newer Bibles
1	"...and the governor asked him, saying, Art thou the King of the Jews? And Jesus said unto him, Thou sayest" (Matthew 27: 11). Only two new version of the *Bibles* conveyed, what *Jesus* might have said: "...the governor, who asked him, "Are you the king of the Jews?" "Those are your words!" Jesus answered." (Contemporary English Version & New Century Version))	1. "...and the governor asked Him, Are you the King of the Jews? Jesus said to him, You have stated [the fact]." (Amplified Bible). 2. "...And the governor asked Him, saying, "Are You the King of the Jews?" Jesus said to him, "It is as you say." (New King James Version). 3. "the Roman governor. "Are you the King of the Jews?" the governor asked him. Jesus replied, **"Yes, it is as you say."** (New Living Translation). 4. "...Governor, who questioned him: "Are you the 'King of the Jews'?" Jesus said, "If you say so." (The Message, [Bible]).

2	The disciple asked *Jesus* why they could not cast out demons, *Jesus replied:* *"Howbeit this kind goeth not out but by prayer and fasting" (Matthew 17:21).*	This verse has been omitted by the following new versions. (I guess the Christians did not want to fast, so they conveniently deleted this exhortation of Jesus). 1. *New Living Translation* (NLT). 2. *New International Version* (NIV). 3. *English Standard Version* (ESV). 4. Morphological Greek New Testament (MGNT). 5. *The Message.* 6. *Contemporary English Version* (CEV). 7. *New International Reader's Version* (NIRV). 8. *Today's New International Version* (TNIV).
3	*"…and [Jesus] saith unto them,* *Peace be unto you" (Luke 24: 36).*	This verse either has been deleted by some new versions or changed into something else. Please read the following: Not mentioned (Revised Standard Version or RSV) 1. *"…Jesus appeared and greeted them"* (CEV). 2. *"…Peace (freedom from all the distresses that are experienced as the result of sin) be to you!"* (Amplified Bible).
4	*"And their words seemed to them as idle tales, and they believed them not" (Luke 24: 11).*	The whole verse #11 is not mentioned in 'Worldwide English' (New Testament). Instead, the verse # 12 is marked as verse #11.

5	*(For of necessity he must release one unto them at the feast.) (Luke 23: 17).*	This verse has been omitted by the following new versions: 1. *New Living Translation* (NLT). 2. *New International Version* (NIV). 3. *English Standard Version* (ESV). 4. Morphological Greek New Testament (MGNT). 5. *The Message.* 6. *Contemporary English Version* (CEV). 7. *New International Reader's Version* (NIRV). 8. *Today's New International Version* (TNIV).

Let us direct our attention to modern day viewpoints on the crucifixion of *Jesus*. Even today, in the *Philippines*, people volunteer themselves to be crucified every year in the memory of the event of the crucifixion of *Jesus Christ*. None of them have ever died. According to the history of crucifixion in the *Philippines*, the first crucifixion took place on *Good Friday* 1961. *Arsenio Añoza*, a faith healer, volunteered to be nailed on the cross in *Pampanga* province, during *sinakulo* (passion play). *Añoza* performed crucifixions annually on *Good Friday* between 1961 and 1976. On *Good Friday 1997*, in *San Pedro Kutud, San Fernando, Pampanga,* the historical epicenter of religious self-mortification in the *Philippines*, fourteen *Filipinos* were crucified for about an hour and a half. None of these people died. How could *Jesus* have died in about two hours from the crucifixion, when a modern man, who is much weaker than the men *2000* years ago, does not die in two hours?

2) *Jesus* gave up the ghost (Mark 15: 37):

The book of *Matthew* says: *"Jesus, when he had cried again with a loud voice, yielded up the ghost."* The *Greek* word which was originally used in this verse was "πνεύμα," pronounced *pneuma*, which means *"breath."* So the actual verse would be 'he took his last breath' [before fainting]. As *The New King James, NLT,* and *NIV Bibles* say: *'[Jesus] breathed his last'* (Mark 15:37). This verse says nothing about the death.

13

3) Jesus showed *Infallible proofs* (Acts 1:3):

> *"To whom also he shewed himself alive after his passion by many infallible proofs, being seen of them forty days…"* This is another perfect verse to prove that *Jesus* escaped the death. Here it says that *Jesus* proved to them in many ways that *he was alive.* He showed these signs for over a period of '*forty days'* while he was among them. *Jesus* tried his best for forty days to prove that he was alive. It is hard to believe that the followers would still construe that *Jesus* died on the cross (*Jesus in India* paraphrased).

4) God *heard* Jesus' prayer (Hebrews 5:7):

This is one of the most crucial verses of the *Bible* which proves beyond any reasonable doubt that *Jesus* escaped the death: This verse says:

> *"God had the power to save Jesus from death. And while Jesus was on earth, he begged God with loud crying and tears to save him. He truly worshiped God, and God listened to his prayers"*[15]

This means when *Jesus* was praying to *God*, crying and saying, *'Oh Father let this cup (the cup of death) away from me…'*[16] *God* heard his prayer and saved him from the accursed death of the cross. *Jesus* also says:

> *"What man is there of you, whom if his son ask bread, will he give him a stone? Or his son asks for fish, will he give him a serpent?"*[17]

When *Jesus* asked *God* to give him life, would *God* give him death? I have presented the verse from the *Contemporary English Version* to elucidate my point that *God* listened to the prayer of *Jesus* and saved him. The *Bible* also says that *God* would not hear the prayers of false prophets (Proverbs 15:29). But since we all know *Jesus* was not a false prophet, *God* must have listened to his prayers as the above verse proves.

5) Two *Angels* in White (John 20:12):

In the *Gospel* of *John*, it is stated:

---

[15]   Please see *Hebrews 5:7* Contemporary English Version Bible
[16]   Please see *Matthew 26:39*
[17]   Please see *Matthew 7: 9*

"two angels in white,' sitting, the one at the head, and the other at the feet, where the body of Jesus had lain" (John 20:12).

Some *Christians* contend that if *Jesus* did not die on the cross, and did not possess a *'new glorified body,'* then how was he able to roll over a stone that weighed almost a ton with his weak and wounded body? But they forget about the *'two angels in white.'* The fact is those two angels were two normal human beings clothed in white. As *Gospel* of *Luke* tells us: *"...behold, two men stood by them in shining garments" (Luke 24:4).* Even today if someone helps us, we call that person an angel. The *Bible* might be saying that those two men had an angelic character or they were angel in nature. If *Jesus* really had a glorified body, then what need did he have to move the stone anyway? He could have just walked out of the tomb without ever opening the door and making the *Jews* suspicious.

Jesus had an unpleasant experience with his followers in one point. *Judas* betrayed him for only thirty silver coins and *Peter* cursed him three times, *"Then he [Peter] began to curse and swear, saying, "I do not know the Man!" Immediately a rooster crowed"* (Matthew 26:74). That was one of the reasons perhaps that *Joseph of Arimathaea* did not want to utilize local help (local means, disciples of Jesus from Jerusalem) but he brought two of his *'Essene'* friends. These *Essene* friends were not the followers of *Jesus*. That was one of the reasons perhaps that none of the followers of *Jesus* were able to recognize them. Because of their courageous act, not knowing *Jesus* and still wanted to risk their lives by going against the *Romans*, they were rewarded in the *Bible* forever as *"angels."*

6) Why seek ye *LIVING* among Dead (Luke 24:5):

If you have had any prior bewilderment, this verse should clear it. Is there any doubt that the two angels asked the disciples why they were looking for an alive person among the dead people? *New Living Translation Bible* says: *"Why are you looking in a tomb for someone who is alive?"* Does this not mean that *Jesus* was alive? The people who gave *Jesus* first aide were telling the disciples first hand that *'Jesus was alive.'* Is that not enough to propose *Jesus* was alive?

7) Appearance like a *Gardener* (John 20:15):

The resurrection of *Jesus* mentioned in the *Bible* was not in a literal sense. Miraculous help of *God* could be considered resurrection also, but it was rather an escape from death. That seems to be the reason perhaps that instead of walking openly in public, *Jesus* probably put on a disguise. He changed his appearance so much that his own disciples, who were with him for three years, could not recognize him. And even the clothes he was wearing were not the kind of clothes *Jesus* would have worn normally. He might have borrowed the clothes from the gardener, so the people wouldn't be able to recognize him. That could be the reason that *Mary Magdalene* thought he was a *'gardener.'*

8) Do not cling (*hold tight*) me (John 20:17):

When *Mary Magdalene* finally recognized *Jesus*, and she sought to cling to him, *Jesus* said: *"Noli me tangere"*[18] or do not cling me, for I am not yet ascended to my father.*[19] According to the *Dead Sea Scrolls, Jesus* says: *'do not touch me that he is not yet cleansed from the effect of the sickness.'* Or perhaps, he was in pain because of having been on the cross for several hours. According to my research, in these verses, *Jesus* probably answered two issues. First, when he said: *"do not cling to me"* he probably meant 'I have pain in my body' or 'I can't take any clinging.' Second, *Jesus* probably answered to the astonishment of *Mary Magdalene* that, *'Yes, I am still alive,'* or *'Yes, I am not dead.'* The *Syriac Edition of New Testament* clears the picture even more. It says: *"I have not gone to my Father yet."*[20] So *"going to father"* meant "dying." Even today, we use the same terminology to tell little kids about the death of their loved one. When we think it is not appropriate to say your mom or dad has died, we just say 'they went to heaven.'

But if we take the *Gospel's* word literally, *"Do not cling me for I am not yet ascended to my father,"* then that would be a very odd thing for *Jesus* to say because if *Mary* could not cling to him while he was on earth, then how she was supposed to cling to him when he would have ascended up to his father? Was *Jesus* planning to take *Mary Magdalene* bodily with him to his father?

9) *Jesus* got *upset: Jesus eats* (Luke 24:37-43):

This incident shows very clearly that *Jesus* did not die on the cross. When *Jesus* came to meet his disciples, the *Bible* says:

> *"But they were terrified and frightened, and supposed that they had seen a spirit." Jesus said: Why are you troubled? And why do doubts arise in your hearts? Behold my hands and my feet, that it is I myself. Handle me and see, for a spirit does not have flesh and bones as you see I have." When he had said this, he showed them his hands and his feet. But while they still did not believe for joy, and marveled, he said to them, "have you any*

---

[18]   Please see *Jerome's Latin Vulgate 405 AD*

[19]   Please see *New King James Version* © 1982 by *Thomas Nelson, Inc*

[20]   Please also see *New Century Version*, and *Contemporary English Version*

food here?" And they gave him a piece of a broiled fish, and of an honeycomb. And he took it, and ate in their presence."

All that *Jesus* stated in the above verses shows that he had escaped the death miraculously, rather than dying and then coming back to life. By asking his followers, *'why doubts arise in your hearts?' Jesus* probably means how could you even think that he had died on the cross and became *'accursed of God.'* [21] How much clearer could he have said than this: *"spirit does not have flesh and bones as you see I have."* Is he trying to say that he has become a spirit when he is saying "I am not a spirit"? The question is why a spirit had fresh wounds like a mortal body?

After reading this verse, can we still construe that *Jesus* walked through walls when he is saying I am a normal flesh and bone person? Even after he showed them his hands and feet, they still thought that he was not a real man, but a spirit. Then he asked them, do you have any food? When, *'they gave him fish and honeycomb,' he ate in front of them.'* What was *Jesus* trying to prove by eating in front of his disciples? That he is a spirit? Or he ate to prove that he is a normal human being, who has flesh and bones like any normal human being, and has hunger to eat like any normal human being. This is very strange that the deceased is saying I am alive and well, but nobody wants to believe him? [22]

10) *Doors were shut,* Jesus entered the room (John 20:19):

Many *Christian* friends often ask me that if *Jesus* had not possessed a *glorious spiritual* body, then how did he enter the closed door rooms? Thanks to the discovery of the *Dead Sea Scrolls,* this enigma has been resolved. According to the *Dead Sea Scrolls,* the term *'doors being shut'* was used to articulate that it was not a general meeting. Not all the disciples were invited to the meeting, but the few trustworthy ones. In a general term it was a *closed door meeting.* When one reads the *Dead Sea Scrolls,* it becomes lucid that to enter into a *closed door meeting,* we need special permission, not a spiritual body. The *Bible* itself clarifies this mystery in these words:

"Many deceivers have gone out into the world. They do not believe that Jesus Christ came to earth in a real body. Such a person is a deceiver and an antichrist." [23]

---

[21] Please see *Deuteronomy 21:22*

[22] Excerpts from *Jesus in India* paraphrased

[23] Please see *2 John 1:7 New Living Translation*

11) *Dream* of Pilate's wife (Matthew 27:19):

[*Just then, as Pilate was sitting on the judgment seat, his wife sent him this message: "Leave that innocent man alone, because I had a terrible nightmare about him last night"* (NLT Bible). This dream was enough for *Pontius Pilate* to decide that *Jesus* was not only innocent, but he had to do something to save his life in order for him to be saved from the curse of *God*. *Pilate's* wife's dream was similar to a warning, which was given in a dream to *Joseph*, husband of *Mary*, when *Jesus* was a child. It says:

> *"Behold, an angel of the Lord appeared to Joseph in a dream, saying, "Arise, take the young child [Jesus] and his mother [Mary] flee to Egypt ...for Herod will seek the young child to destroy him"* (Matthew 2:13).

We all know that because of this dream of *Joseph, Jesus'* life was saved in his childhood. How can we imagine that *God's* warning for *Pilate*, through his wife's dream, would fail?][24]

Pontius Pilate did everything he could in his power to save the life of *Jesus* because of that dream. But at the same time he had to do everything secretly so he would not get caught helping *Jesus* and end up on the cross himself. He ordered the crucifixion on *Pass over Friday*, which he knew because of the *Jewish* law; *Jesus* would not be hanging on the cross for more than a few hours, following the *Sabbath*. Pilate also deliberately delayed the process of Crucifixion for *six hours*.[25] That was one of the reasons perhaps, *'Pilate was marveled if Jesus was already dead'* (Mark15: 44). Because he could not believe how someone could have died in just few hours. But the fact is *Jesus* did not because *God* saved him.

12) *Jesus'* sweat was great drops of *Blood* (Luke 22:44):

Jesus knew the meaning of dying on the cross. According to the *Old Testament*, if someone dies on the cross he becomes *'accursed of God'* (Deuteronomy 21:23). *Jesus* did not want to die on the cross and *become accursed of God*. That was the reason perhaps that *Jesus* uttered, *"My soul is exceeding sorrowful, even unto death"* (Matthew 26:38). Then he started to pray to *God* and said, *"O my Father, if it be possible, let this cup (cup of death) pass from me…"* (Matthew 26:39). According to the *Bible, Jesus* said the same prayer three times. And after each time, he went back to his disciples, and asked them to wake up and pray with him *(Matthew 26:40)*. The *Bible* says:

---

24   Bracketed text from *Jesus in India* paraphrased
25   Please see *John 19:14*

"And being in an agony he prayed more earnestly and his sweat was as it were great drops of blood falling down to the ground" (Luke 22:44).

According to the doctors, *'sweating blood'* is not a figure of speech; rather, it is a condition of extreme anxiety called *Hematohydrosis.*[26] In extreme fear of pain, or death, arteries burst and the blood seeps into the sweat glands and the sweating of blood occurs. This extreme anxiety shows that *Jesus* did not want to give his life on the cross willingly. A sacrifice is supposed to be something you do willingly. What we read here how *Jesus* was crying and praying to *God*, it does not sound like a willful act of sacrifice. As I mentioned above, every year three people volunteer themselves to be crucified just to feel what *Jesus* felt *2000* years ago. Why they do not cry and are extremely fearful?

13) An Angel *strengthened* Jesus (Luke 22:43):

When *Jesus* prayed to *God* to remove this cup *(the cup of Death)* from him, *Gospel of Luke* says: *'an angel appeared to Jesus from heaven, strengthening him.'* The question arises: what did the angel promise *Jesus* in order to strengthen him? Would that be something like Don't worry you will die? Or Don't worry, you won't die, and *God* will save you? If the angel was saying "Don't worry you will die," then it does not make any sense because *Jesus* was asking for life not death. But if the angel told him "Don't worry you won't die, *God* will save you," then it makes more sense, since that seems to be the reason that *Jesus* asks *God*, *"Eli, Eli, lama sabachthani," that is, "My God, My God, why have you forsaken me" (Matthew 27:46).* The angel who strengthened *Jesus* must have assured him that God will save him. If the angel had never assured him, then he would have never asked *God* in such distrust, *'Why have you forsaken me?* But *God* did not break His promise. *Jesus* was not dying, but rather, he was falling into unconsciousness.

14) *Jesus* drinks *vinegar* (*John* 19:30):

[In the book, *Where did Jesus Die* by *J.D. Shams. Mr. Shams* says that *Jesus* gave up the ghost right after drinking the vinegar, in spite of everything he was well conscious, and one should think that there must be something in the vinegar which killed him or fainted him. *Jesus* was talking to *God*, says: *"Father, forgive them; for they know not what they do" (Luke 23:34).* He tells a thief on his side, *"Today you will be with me in paradise" (Luke 23:43).*] (Bracketed text is paraphrased)

---

[26] Please see *Jesus: The Complete Story, The Last Days,* by the *Discovery Channel*

One of the followers of *Jesus* named *Nicodemus* was a physician. *Nicodemus* knew if he could mix *'Hyacine'*[27] in the vinegar, and give that to *Jesus* somehow, then that would make him unconscious. Then the followers of *Jesus* would be able to save the life of their beloved *Messiah*. *Hyacine* is a very strong anesthetic, it attacks the central nervous system, and it renders the person unconscious, as if he was totally dead. *Hyacine* is found in the roots of a plant called *Mandrake*. *Mandrake* was available before *Jesus* in the times of *Abraham (Genesis 30:14, 15 &16* and *Song of Songs 7:13)*. It was also available in the times of *Jesus*, and it is available even today. Therefore, the fainting of *Jesus* was mistaken for death.

15) *Graves* were opened and Saints arose (Matthew 27:52):

> *Matthew* says when *Jesus* gave up the ghost: *"And the graves were opened; and many bodies of the saints which slept arose, And came out of the graves... and went into the holy city and appeared to many."*

If we take this literally, then this should have been a big excitement in *Israel. Jews* should have reported it in every book written at that time. But in fact, this great event was not even mentioned by the other three *Gospels*. Therefore, *Mark, Luke,* and *John* were totally unaware of this enormous event. When these dead people would have entered in their respective homes, there must have been immense excitement everywhere. The *Jews* had an excellent opportunity to ask these saints, as well as their own deceased ancestors, who were brought back to life, whether *Jesus* who claimed to be *God*, is really *God*? Or whether he was lying about that? (God forbid). Since *Christians* deem *Jesus* as an incarnation of *God* (God forbid), then these dead people who came from *God* should have testified in his favor. Their testimony should have been sufficient to convert the whole *Israel* into *Christianity*.

But the fact is totally opposite to which *Christians* usually construe from this event. In fact, it was a dream of one of the disciples of *Jesus*. This disciple was given a glad tiding in a dream that *Jesus* would be saved from the cross and would go back home safely. When we read ancient books about the *Interpretations of Dreams,* we get a very interesting meaning of *graves being opened and their dead ones going to their homes.*[28] These books say that it means that the prisoner would be released from his bondage. He would be rescued

---

27   Please see *Jesus: The Complete Story, The Last Days,* by the *Discovery Channel*
28   Please see *Kitab T'atirul-Anam fi T'abirul-Manam* by *Qutbuz Zaman Shaikh Abdul Ghani Al-Nablisi,* page 289.

from the hands of his persecutors, and would go back home to his loved ones. (Bracketed text is excerpts from *Jesus in India* (Paraphrased))

16) Blood and Water *Gushed* out (John 19:34):

Gospel of *John* says: *'One of the soldiers stabbed him [Jesus] in the side with his spear. Blood and water **gushed** out' (John 19:34).*[29] We now know that dead bodies do not bleed. When the heart stops pumping, there is no circulation of blood. If there is no circulation of blood, then there is no *gushing* out of it either. But not only is this mentioned in the *Gospel*, it further states: *'And he that saw it bare record, and his record is true: and he knoweth that he saith true, that ye might believe.'*[30] Here we can see that the *Gospel writer* is trying to give us a clue that bares record that *blood and water gushed out*, this means *Jesus* was alive, and *his record is true*. So you might believe that *Jesus* was alive when he was taken down from the cross. The *gospel is telling the truth.*

17) Tomb door was *opened* (Luke 24:2):

It is traditionally known to the *Christians* that after the crucifixion *Jesus* was given a *new glorified body*. According to some of the accounts, *Jesus* walked through walls and entered rooms through closed doors. If *Jesus* was really given a new glorified body, then what was the reason for the door of the tomb being opened? That would be a very convincing sign of *Jesus'* new glorified body if *Jesus* would have walked out through the closed tomb door too. Then there is another strong point here: if he really died and came back to life then he should have walked through the cities of *Israel* with his hands raised like a winner. He should have called the *Jews* and the *Romans* and challenged them since they had tried to kill him. That would have been the biggest sign of his truthfulness, and the whole of *Israel* would have converted to *Christianity* right away. On the contrary, he hides from them, and put on a disguise that even his own disciples could not recognize.

18) Tomb was like a *Chamber*:

The tomb, in which *Jesus* was laid, was not the kind of tomb of what we have today. In today's tombs, we do not have room for people to enter and exit. The tomb mentioned in the *Bible* was a special tomb specially arranged for *Jesus* by his secret disciple *Joseph of Arimathaea*. The question is why would a rich and honorable man buy a grave in a graveyard for criminals? This means that he was guided by *God* to save the life of *Jesus*. In view of this fact, he knew

---

[29] Please see *John 19:34* in *The Message* (Bible) Copyright © 1993 by *Eugene H. Peterson*

[30] Please see *John 19:35*

after the fainting of *Jesus* with *Hyacine* that he would not have much time to carry wounded *Jesus* to a safe place. Buying a new tomb where nobody had been laid before, a tomb that was close to the *crucifixion site,* was not only an intelligent plan, but was also good for *Jesus'* health condition.

A first century Tomb

19) Disciples were *afraid* to tell anyone (Mark 16:8):

The book of *Mark* says that when *Mary Magdalene* and a few other disciples found out that *Jesus* was alive *"They did not tell anyone because they were afraid."* But the question that arises here is what was the reason for their fear? If *Jesus'* coming out alive from the tomb was a miracle, then they should have announced it far and wide so everyone could hear about it and see the greatest miracle of all times: a man dies and then he comes back to life. But we do not read that in the *Bible.* Instead, we read that *Jesus* puts on a disguise so elusive that his own followers were unable to recognize him. The disciples, who did find out that *Jesus* was alive and well, they were afraid to tell anyone because they feared that the *Jews* might catch *Jesus* and put him back on the cross.

20) Thomas puts his finger in the *wound* of *Jesus* (John 20:25-27):

When *Thomas* hears that *Jesus* is still alive, he says: *"Except I shall see in his hands the print of the nails, and put my finger into the print of the nails, and thrust my hand into his side, I will not believe."* *Jesus* says to *Thomas:* "Reach *hither thy finger, and behold my hands; and reach hither thy hand, and thrust it into my side; and be not faithless, but believing.*"[31]

The question is what did *Jesus* mean when he said *be not faithless, but believing?* Was *Jesus* trying to say that he had died and become a spirit—then why would a spirit have fresh wounds--or was he trying to say that he had escaped death and he is the same flesh and bone person as he was before?

It is imperative to mention what *Thomas* probably meant when he says: *"My Lord My God."* I have been told by my *Christian* friends that when *Thomas* called *Jesus "My Lord My God"* he meant *Jesus* is *God*. But in fact, when *Thomas* sees *Jesus'* nail prints and wounds on his side, *Thomas* says these words in disbelief. Even today when we see something shocking, like a tornado sweeping through a city, we say, Oh my *Lord*, or Oh my *God*. Does it mean we are calling that tornado *God* or are we saying those words in disbelief?

21) *Jesus* met his disciples in a village (Luke 24:13-29):

The *New Testament* tells us that the followers of *Jesus* saw him alive and well, after the crucifixion. Thus, the *Bible* says in *Luke:*

> *"...two of them (disciples) were traveling that same day to a village called Emmaus, which was seven miles from Jerusalem. ...while they conversed and reasoned, that Jesus himself drew near and went with them. But their eyes were restrained, so that they did not know him. And he [Jesus] said to them. What manner of communications are these that you have one to another, as you walk, and are sad? ...Cleopas answered and said to Him [Jesus], Are you the only stranger in Jerusalem, and have You not known the things which happened there in three days? ...*
>
> *They told Jesus...certain women of our company, who arrived at the tomb early, astonished us. When they did not find his body, they came saying that they had also seen a vision of angels who said he [Jesus] was alive... Then He [Jesus] said to them, "O foolish ones, and slow of heart to believe in all that the prophets have spoken! Then they drew near to the village where they were going, and he [Jesus] indicated that he would have gone farther. But they constrained him, saying, "Abide with us, for it is toward evening, and the day is far spent." And he went in to stay with them. ...He [Jesus] sat at the table with them, that he took bread, blessed and broke it and gave it to them"*[32]

---

[31] Please see *John 20:27*
[32] Please see *New King James Version*

23

In this incident, we learn three things: First, those two disciples were walking towards a village *seven miles from Jerusalem*. If *Jesus* had possessed a *'new glorious, spiritual body,'* then why did he have to walk seven miles? Why could he not just appear there? Second, the disciples were talking with *Jesus*, but they still did not recognize him. *Jesus* had probably put on a disguise so people would not recognize him. His disguise was so good that even his own followers could not recognize him. Then how could a non-believer recognize him? Third, the *Bible* says the disciples saw a vision of angels telling them *'Jesus was alive'*?

22) Disciples did not know *Jesus* would be *'raised'* from the dead (Matthew 20:19):

We read in *Matthew* that *Jesus* proclaimed: *"...he will be crucified and third day he shall rise again."* But somehow *Jesus'* followers did not know that *Jesus* had really said that. We read in one of the accounts that when they heard *Jesus* was raised from the dead the disciples thought it was an idle tale. The other verse says the disciples did not know the Scripture. Thus, the *Bible* says:

> A. *"It was Mary Magdalene, Joanna, Mary the mother of James...who told these things to the apostles. And their words seemed to them like idle tales, and they did not believe them"* (Luke 24:10-11).

> B. *"For as yet they did not know the Scripture, that he must rise again from the dead"* (John 20:9).

The *Christianity* is founded on the conviction that *Jesus* died on the cross and was raised the third day. If that was so significant to *Christianity*, one might think that *Jesus* would have told his disciples what was going to happen. It is a grave point to contemplate. There is another verse which says: *"...The Lord is risen indeed, and hath appeared to Simon"* (Luke 24:34). But after learning that *Jesus* did not die on the cross, the modern-day scholars have changed the wording. The new *Bibles* say now: *"And they learned from the group that the Lord was really alive and had appeared to Peter."*[33] But *Paul* made it easy for us by confessing that he had created the perception of *Jesus* rising from the dead: *"Remember that Jesus Christ of the seed of David was raised from the dead according to my gospel"* (2 Timothy 2:8). *Jesus* never said that he would rise from the dead. There is another verse in the *Bible* in which *Jesus* supposedly said: *"This cup is the new covenant in My blood, which is shed for you"* (Luke 22:20). When I started to research this verse, I could not find it in most older *Bibles*. No wonder the scholars have been bewildered about this verse for some five hundred years and

---

[33] Please see the *Contemporary English Version*

why the famous *Christian* artist *Leonardo Da Vinci* did not illustrate the cup or chalice of *Christ* in the renowned painting of the *Last Supper?* Perhaps, the verse was not added to the *Bible* until after *Da Vinci*'s time. It is worthy to note that after *Jesus* supposedly rose from the dead, he never mentioned a single time in the entire *New Testament* that he had died and had come back to life.

23) *There are some standing here, who shall not taste death* (Matthew 16:28):

[*Jesus* said: *"Assuredly, I say to you, there are some standing here who shall not taste death till they see the Son of Man coming in His kingdom."*[34] According to the *Christian* doctrine, *Jesus* died on the cross and then went to heaven. It has been *2000* years, and he has not come back yet. So the disciples who are mentioned above in the prophecy should be alive also, since *Jesus* has not come back yet.][35]

According to the *Dead Sea Scrolls*, *Jesus* did not die on the cross, and after the crucifixion took refuge in some nearby countries. He did come back many times to meet his disciples. The disciples mentioned above were still alive when he came back. All those disciples who saw *Jesus* supposedly in visions actually saw *Jesus* in person, but because of the fear of the *Jews*, they did not say it explicitly. *Jesus* travelled extensively all his life, according to the new research; being a great traveler he fulfilled another aspect of the word *Messiah*. I have provided evidence from the history of *Christianity* so that you may believe that he survived the crucifixion and went back to meet his disciples as he promised.

24) *Jesus* was in the tomb for merely *One & a half* days:

Christians traditionally know that *Jesus* was in the tomb for three days and three nights. Almost every *Christian* would tell you that *Jesus* rose from the dead on the third day. When I started counting hours, I realized that *Jesus* was in the tomb for only one and a half days. According to the *Gospels*, *Jesus* was on the cross between 12 noon to 3 o' clock.[36] Which means *Jesus* was placed in the tomb on *Friday* afternoon. From *Friday* afternoon until *Saturday* afternoon is *24* hours (one day). When the ladies came to the sepulcher on the first day of the week[37] in those days *Sunday* used to be the first day of the week unlike today when *Monday* is the first day of the week. The ladies came early in the morning on *Sunday*, so that makes a day and a half, not three days and three nights.

---

34   Please see *Matthew 16:28* New King James Version © 1982.).

35   Bracketed text excerpts from *Jesus in India* paraphrased

36   Please see *Matthew 27:46; Mark 15:33;* and *Luke 23:44* in the following *Bibles* for clarification, *New Living Translation, Contemporary English Version, New Century Version* and *The Message [Bible]*.

37   Please see *Matthew 28:1; Mark 16:2; and Luke 24:1*

Where did people get this notion about three days and three nights? I guess the scribes were trying to match three days and three nights of *Sign of Jonas*.

25) *Sign of Jonas* (Matthew 12:38-41):

Jesus predicted about the attempt of his enemies to crucify him on the cross, and his escape from death miraculously in these words: When some *scribes* and *Pharisees* came to *Jesus* and asked him:

> "*...we like to see a sign from you.' Jesus replied: "An evil and adulterous generation seeketh after a sign; and there shall no sign be given to it, but the sign of the Prophet Jonas: For as Jonas was three days and three nights in the whales' belly; so shall the son of man be three days and three nights in the heart of earth. The men of Nin-e-veh shall rise in judgment with this generation, and shall condemn it: because they repented at the preaching of Jonas; and, behold, a greater than Jonas is here.*"

Let's compare what happened to *Jesus* according to the prophecy of *Jonas*. *Jesus* said what happened to *Jonas* will happen to him as well. We believe *Jesus* is the true *Messiah*, and true prophet of *God*. According to the *Bible*, when a true prophet of *God* says something, it must come true[38] because he speaks the word of *God* and not his own.

Taken from King James version	*Commonly Known to Christians*
1. *Jonas* was in whale's belly for 3 days and 3 nights (Jonah 1:17).	
2. *Jonas* was in the whale's belly alive <u>not dead</u> (Jonah 2:2).	1. *Jesus was in the tomb for one & a half-day.*
3. *Jonas* prays to God (Jonah 2:1).	2. *Jesus was dead in the heart of earth.*
4. *Jonas* comes out of the whale's belly (Jonah 2:10), and goes back to his nation, and the whole nation repented [meaning believed Jonas] *(Jonah 3:10)*	3. *Jesus was dead & he was not praying.*
	4. *Jesus comes out from the heart of earth, goes to heaven, and sits on the right hand of God.*

---

[38]   Please see *Deuteronomy 18:22*

Please contemplate on this point, do these two incidents equate at all? There cannot be a comparison between a living man and a dead man. Then why did *Jesus* say what happened to *Jonas* will happen to *Jesus* too. Scholars usually contend that the three days of *Jonas* in the belly of the whale agrees with the three days of *Jesus* in the heart of earth. They further contend that the whole prophecy does not have to match. The reason that the scholars do not agree with the other parts of the prophecy is that they know it very well that it will prove the survival of *Jesus* and not his supposed sacrificial death on the cross. Unfortunately, the only part of the prophecy these *Christian* scholars try to match with *Jesus'* situation does not match with *Jonas's* either. This means when they say *Jesus* stayed in the heart of the earth for three days and three nights, just as *Jonas* was in the whale's belly for three days and three nights even that does not match with any of the three *Gospel* accounts. For instance, the *'Sign of Jonas'* prophecy is also mentioned in another chapter of the same *Gospel* of *Matthew*, but there he does not mention anything about three days and three nights. The *Bible* says:

> *"A wicked and adulterous generation seeketh after a sign; and there shall no sign be given unto it, but the sign of the prophet Jonas. And he left them, and departed"* (Matthew 16:4). The *Gospel* of *Luke* also mentions the prophecy of *Jonas* and says: *"For as Jonas was a sign unto the Ninevites, so shall also the Son of man be to this generation"* (Luke 11:30). But the *Gospel* of *Luke* does not mention anything about *'three days and three nights'* either. *Mark* and *John* do not even mention the *Sign of Jonah* at all.

[The fact is three days and three nights was not even mentioned in the original prophecy. According to *Dr. James Deardorff, Professor Emeritus at Oregon State University*, the author of the books *'Jesus in India,'* and *'Celestial Teachings.'* Mr. *Deardorff* has also studied the document *'The Talmud of Immanuel,'* [*The Teaching of Immanuel or The Teaching of Jesus*]. This document was discovered in *1963* from *Jerusalem* and is in its original *Aramaic* language. In the *English* translation of this *Talmud* document, *Talmud 18:5* has been compared with the *KJV* of *Matthew 16:4*. The comparison as described by Dr. *Deardorff* is presented below.][39]

---

[39]   Bracketed text is reference from *Metaphoric light Literal darkness* by *Anwer Mahmood Khan*

Matthew 16:4 King James Version	**Talmud 18:5**
A wicked and adulterous generation seeketh after a sign; and there shall no sign be given unto it, but the sign of the prophet Jonas. And he left them, and departed.	*This wicked and unfaithful generation is seeking a sign; no sign shall be given to it except for the sign of Jonah, who disappeared **alive** into the belly of the fish, dwelled **alive** in its belly and emerged **alive** again into the light.*

What *Jesus* wanted to tell us perhaps, how *Jonah* survived the impossible ordeal. *Jonas* went in the whale's belly **alive**, dwelled *there **alive**,* and emerged **alive**. The original prophecy had nothing to do with three days and three nights. What really happened was explained by *Ahmad (the Second Coming of Jesus Christ)*. According to *Ahmad*, prophet *Jonas* was sent by *God* to a nation called *Nin'-e-veh (Jonah 1:2)*. Instead of going to *Nin'-e-veh*, *Jonas* tried to go to *Tar'-shish* and takes a ship from *Jop'-pa* to *Tar'-shish*. When he was on the ship, a big storm came and the people of the ship started to pray to *God* to save their lives.

One of the wise men said they would conduct a drawing to see who will be thrown into the ocean. *Jonas'* name came in the drawing and he was thrown into the ocean. As a punishment from *God*, a whale swallowed *Jonas*. Then *Jonas* realized that he made a great mistake and began to pray to *God* in the belly of the whale *(Jonah 2: 2)*. Because *Jonas* was a true prophet of *God* and a very righteous man, *God* forgave him and the *whale vomited him out on the dry land (Jonah 2:10)*. *God* asked *Jonas* to go back to his nation, where *God* originally sent him. Then *God* says: *Arise, go unto that great city, and preach unto it the preaching that I bid thee (Jonah 3:2)*. When *Jonas* went back to his nation, the whole nation repented [or believed him as a true prophet of God] *(Jonah 3:10)*.

Jesus experienced the similar tribulation. *God* sent *Jesus* to the lost tribes of the *'house of Israel,'* as *Jesus* mentioned in the *Bible*, saying: *"I am not sent but unto the lost sheep of the house of Israel."*[40] What does he do now? Instead, of going to the *'eleven lost sheep of the Israel,'* he goes to *one* known sheep of *Israel*. The tribe that was living in *Israel* was never known as the *'lost tribe.'* On the other hand, the eleven sheep of *Israel* were known as lost sheep due to the attack of the king of *Babylon*. The *Bible* tells us: *"...the people whom Neb-u-chad-nez'-zar* [the King of Babylon] *had carried away captive from Jerusalem to Babylon" (Jeremiah 29:1)*, they were called *the lost sheep of Israel*, because after they stayed in *Babylon (present-day Iraq)* for a long time, they migrated

---

[40]   Please see Matthew 15:24

from *Babylon* to the nearest country *Persia*, (present-day *Iran*) which is at the border of *Iraq*.[41]

Nobody knew except *Jesus*, where they went from *Babylon*. They went to *Kashmir* the *Promised Land*. But *Jesus* does not go there. As a warning from *God*, he was put on the cross. Being on the cross *Jesus* realized that he made a huge mistake. Then he started to pray to *God*. *Jesus* says in *Psalms*: *"But thou hast cast off and abhorred, thou hast been wroth [angry] with thine anointed [Your Messiah]" (Psalms 89:38).* This is one of the crucial reasons that the book of *Psalms*, which was mainly written by *Jesus*, was not included in the *New Testament*. Simply, because *Jesus* was not only praying to *God* according to the *Psalms*, but also asking for *God's* forgiveness about his mistake. Why *Christian* scholars who portray *Jesus* as *God* would include in the *Bible* the verse which says *Jesus* was asking for forgiveness? But nowadays, dozens of *Bible* publishers have integrated *Psalms* after the *Book of Revelation* as a part of *The New Testament*.

Since *Jesus* was a true prophet of *God*, and a very righteous man, *God* exonerated him. With the help of *'hyacine mixed vinegar,'* he faints and was taken down from the cross alive. *Jesus* is also showing his gratitude to *God* throughout the book of *Psalms* for the forgiveness *God* had granted him. Please remember that angels never make mistakes, but men do. I am talking about mistakes and not sins. *Jesus* made a mistake, but he could not commit any sin because he was the *Messiah*. After he lived in the midst of his followers *'for forty days,'*[42] *Jesus* took refuge in nearby countries and then at last, went to the *lost tribes of Israel*. Upon the arrival of *Jesus*, the *Kashmiris* by and large became *Christian*. That is how this prophecy was fulfilled. The fact is that it is almost impossible for anyone to escape alive after a whale has swallowed him. In the same manner, it is almost impossible for a man to escape a crucifixion when the whole of *Israel* is watching. Please remember that the only sign *Jesus* promised to show was the *Sign of Jonah*. Please contemplate on this point, that why did *Jesus* pick an allegory of a man who endures an ordeal but he does not die as his only sign?

26) I have other *sheep* (John 10:16):

There is another prophecy of *Jesus* which gives us an analogous message. *Jesus* says *"And other sheep I have, which are not of this fold: them also I must bring, and they shall hear my voice; and there shall be one fold and one shepherd."*[43]

---

[41] Bracketed text is excerpts from *Jesus in India*, paraphrased
[42] Please see *Acts 1:3*
[43] Please see *John 10:16*

This prophecy tells us in clear words that *Jesus* is talking about preaching to another nation, *which are not of this fold* and that whole nation would believe him. *Jesus* also says:

> *"I am not sent but unto the lost sheep of the house of Israel"*
> *(Matthew 15:24).*

If we put these two verses together, this means that *Jesus* was talking about other *Jewish tribes* who were living in foreign lands, but he was not talking about *Gentiles*. As most scholars contend about this prophecy that *Jesus* was talking about other *non-Jewish* nations (Gentiles) who were living in other parts of the world. According to the *Old Testament*, there were 12 tribes of *Israel*. It says: *"...there was none left but, the tribe of Judah only."*[44] The other eleven are considered *'lost'* because no one knew, with the exception of *Jesus*, that they were living in *Kashmir, India*. Even the book of *Jeremiah* talks very clearly about the lost sheep of *Israel* in these words:

> *"My people hath been lost sheep: their shepherds have caused them to go astray, they have turned them away on the mountains: they have gone from mountain to hill, they have forgotten their resting place" (Jeremiah 50:6).*

If *Jesus* did not preach to them as well, then he preached to only one tribe? Is that what he was promising in this prophecy? If *Jesus* did not go to the *Kashmir, India,* then where did he go?

According to my research all the *Bibles* from thirty to seventy years old, do not even mention that *'Jesus went to heaven'* at all. The *New King James Version Bible* says in a foot note about the 12 verses of *Mark* that *"Verses 9-20 are bracketed in NU-Text as not original. They are lacking in Codex Sinaiticus and Codex Vaticanus..."* These verses comprise *Mark 16:19* which says, *'Jesus went to heaven.'* The *Bible* did not say explicitly where *Jesus* went. The followers of *Jesus* were afraid that the *Jews* and the *Roman* authorities could find out that *Jesus* had escaped the cross. The disciples could be persecuted for helping *Jesus* escape the capital punishment.

---

[44] Please see *II Kings 17:18*

3. Prophecy of Prophet Isaiah (Part 1)

Jesus' migration was also foretold in Isaiah:

God told us about the migration of *Jesus* long before his birth:

Command To Leave Babylon [Israel]
"Leave the city of Babylon! [Israel] Don't touch anything filthy. Wash yourselves.
Be ready to carry back everything sacred that belongs to the LORD. You won't
need to run. No one is chasing you. The LORD God of Israel will lead and protect
you from enemy attacks."

The Suffering Servant

"The LORD says: My servant will succeed! He will be given great praise
and the highest honors" (Isaiah 52:11,12 &13 Contemporary English Version ©
Copyright 1995 by American Bible Society). A footnote says in The Living Bible:
"The Servant of the Lord, as the term is used here, is Messiah, our Lord Jesus. This
was the interpretation of this passage by Christ himself, and the writers of the New
Testament and orthodox Christianity ever since" (The Living Bible, Paraphrased
Copyright© 1971).

Please remember that the original *Hebrew* and *King James Versions* do not
mention anything about *Babylon*. There is no record of *Jesus* living in *Babylon*
before crucifixion. But traveling through *Babylon* after the crucifixion is
inevitable from the history. It is interesting to note that a sect of *Christianity*
has been discovered in *Herat, Afghanistan*, whose leader *Abba Yahyah* claims
that they were taught *Christianity* originally by *Jesus* himself, while he was

migrating from *Palestine* to *India*.[45] The migration had to have occurred after the crucifixion, as *Jesus* himself predicted his migration in the *"Sign of Jonas."* Another evidence that this prophecy is about *Jesus* and no one else is that when you read the heading for *Isaiah* chapter 52 in the *Douay Rheims Version Bible*, it says: *"...Christ's kingdom shall be exalted."*[46] Which means beyond the shadow of doubt, this prophecy is about *Jesus* and no one else.

Jesus was commanded by *God* in *Isaiah* to leave *Israel*. The same exhortation is mentioned in *'Hadith, Muslim's* holy book (*Sayings of Muhammad*) over *1400* years ago. *God* commands *Jesus* in these words: *"O Jesus, move from one place to another lest thou shouldst be recognized and persecuted"*[47] Perhaps, this is the very reason that *Jesus* disguised himself so well that his own disciples could not recognize him.

There is another *Hadith* about the travels of *Jesus*. It says: *"The Holy prophet Muhammad declared that the most favored in the sight of Allah [God] are 'Gharib (poor or innocent),' [Someone] asked what was meant by 'Gharib,' he [Muhammad] answered: People like Jesus, the Messiah who flee from their country to save their faith" (Kunzul-A'maal Volume 6).*

As I mentioned earlier, *Jesus* was given great praises and the highest honors in *Kashmir*. This is a great favor of *God* on *Jesus*, that when he came to *Kashmir*, thousands of *Jews* who were waiting for the *Messiah* believed in *Jesus*. [The currency of that time, which was in coins, had *Jesus'* name on it. Another coin was found which has a picture of an *Israelite*, which could be the picture of *Jesus*. These coins were traced back to the time of *Jesus*. They were found in *Punjab, India* more than *100* years ago.] This also proves about *Jesus'* stay in *Kashmir*. Since we know that kind of honor was never given to *Jesus* in *Israel*, that is the reason perhaps, *Jesus* says: *"A prophet has no honor in his own country" (John 4:44).*[48] The language written on that coin is not in *Hebrew* or *Greek*, but in *Pali*, one of the languages spoken in *Northern India*, particularly in *Kashmir*. According to this, *Jesus* did not die until he got *Kingly Honor* in this world, just as prophet *Isaiah* prophesied: *"The LORD says: My servant will succeed! He will be given great praise and the highest honors"(Isaiah 52:13).* As the *Qur'an* also mentions: *"Jesus, son of Mary, honored in this world and in the hereafter" (Aal-e-Imran 3:45-46).*][49]

---

45 *Among the Dervishes* by *Omar M. Burke* on page # 107
46 Please see *Douay Rheims Version Bible* Copyright © 1971
47 Please see *Kunzul-A'maal* Volume 2, page # 34
48 Please also see *Matthew 13:57; Mark 6:4; Luke 4:24*
49 Bracketed text is excerpts from *Jesus in India* paraphrased

[The story of the wise men from the *east* who visited *Jerusalem* at the birth of *Jesus* (who evidently were *Israelites*), because no nation besides them expected the appearance of the messiah and because of their saying: *"Where is he that is born King of the Jews? for we have seen his star in the east..." (Matthew 2:2)*. This statement contains a hint that *Jesus* would be honored by those sheep who were living in the *Eastern* countries. If they were not *Jews*, then why were they excited about the *King* of the *Jews*?][50]

But to say that the wise men followed the star from *East* all the way to *Jerusalem* and arrived exactly at the door of *Mary* and *Joseph* is not a credible story. Most scholars of today reject this story as a fairy tale. *Mr. Jonathan Reed*, Professor of religion at *University of La Verne*, says that *Matthew* was trying to match the incident of star of *Bethlehem* to the star of *Augustus*. According to *Mr. Reed*,

> *"When Augustus saw a comet on the sky, he made the claim that that was his father Julius Caesar, and the comet was his soul taking his place amongst the gods. He minted coins with the picture of Julius Caesar on one side and the star on the other side. He even began to refer to himself 'Divi Filius,' the 'Divine Son.' He spread the message of his divinity all over the empire."*

According to *Mr. Reed:*

> *"This is the message the Christians challenged with the message that Jesus is son of God.* Furthermore, they say that *'the star of Bethlehem may have been Matthew's answer to Caesar's comet; if one celestial sign made Augustus the son of a god another could do the same for Jesus."* Mr. Reed* further says: *"What Matthew is trying to say is that no this poor lowly Jewish peasant is in fact the son of God not this high & mighty imperial Lord."*

This seems to me that the story of three wise men following the star has neither spiritual value nor historical background. Likewise, the incident of *King Herod's "Slaughter of the Innocents"* has no historical evidence. Even the other three *Gospels* do not find that incident worth mentioning it. Most scholars of today utterly reject this event as an attempt to parallel *Jesus* with *Moses*. As we all know that the pharaoh ordered all the male children to be tossed in the river *(Exodus 1: 22)* and *Moses* was saved by the grace of *God*. According to *Mr. Reed:*

---

50   Bracketed text is excerpts from *Where did Jesus die?* By *J. D. Shams* paraphrased

"There are a lot of ancient historians that talk about Herod the great, and one of them is the Jewish historian Josephus, who tells in great detail of some of the maniacal acts of Herod the great, but the 'slaughter of the Innocents,' as reported in the Matthew is no where mentioned in Josephus."

According to the historians, the *Gospel writers* seem to relate every major event in the life of *Moses* with *Jesus* to establish that *Jesus* is as big a figure as *Moses*. Nowadays, new efforts have been made to prove the story of the *Slaughter of the Innocent,* by collecting a few bones of children scattered around *Israel* and placing them in an old grave. I do not know what they are trying to prove because the fact is that there is not a shred of evidence in history that this incident ever happened. According to *Dr. Daniel Smith Christopher,*[51] even the Twelve disciples of *Jesus* are paralleled by the *Gospel* writers to equivalent the Twelve tribes of *Moses*.

Revisiting the topic under discussion, *Jesus* also hinted the same parable. *Jesus* says: [*"How think ye? if a man have an hundred sheep, and one of them be gone astray, doth he not leave the ninety and nine, and goeth into the mountains, and seeketh that which is gone astray? And if so be that he find it, verily I say unto you, he rejoiceth more of that sheep, than of the ninety and nine which went not astray"* (Matthew 18:12-13).

Jesus also says: *"A prophet is not without honour, save but in his own country, and in his own house"* (Matthew 13:57). This means that *Jesus* would not be honored in his own country of *Israel*. If *Jesus* died on the cross and went to heaven, does that mean that *Jesus* was never honored anywhere? If the above parable is correct, if it is true that *Jesus* was a good shepherd. If it is correct that eleven tribes of *Israel* were lost and were scattered abroad by foreign powers, as divine punishment for their turning away from the right path. The *Bible* says: *"Therefore the LORD was very angry with Israel, and removed them out of his sight: there was none left but the tribe of Judah only"* (2Kings 17:18). If it is true that *Jesus* was *sent to the lost sheep of the house of Israel,* (Matthew 15:24), and if it is true that *Jesus* promised to preach to the *other sheep also* (John 10:16), then it was, undoubtedly, his foremost duty to go in search of these lost sheep of the house of *Israel,* and rejoice after finding them. *Jesus* was the true *Messiah,* and beloved of *God*. He could not neglect the duty imposed upon him by *God*.][52]

---

[51]   *Dr. Daniel Smith Christopher*, Professor of *Biblical* Studies at *Loyola Marymount University*

[52]   Bracketed text is excerpts from *Where did Jesus die?* By *J. D. Shams* paraphrased

The *Gospel of Philip* says: *"Those who say that the Lord died first and (then) rose up are in error, for he rose up first and (then) died"* (Gospel of Philip 63:31).

4. Prophecy of Prophet Isaiah (Part 2)

Part 2 (53:9-11)

The prophecy of *Isaiah* foretells the crucifixion of *Jesus*, his escape from the cross, him having children, and living a long life. The prophecy says:

> (a) *"And he [God] made his grave with the wicked, and with the rich in his death... Yet it pleased the Lord to bruise him [nailed on the cross], he had put him to grief [unconscious on the cross]. When you shall make him an offering for sin..."*

> (b) *"Now the servant will live to see his own descendants"*

> (c) *"he will have a multitude of children, many heirs. He will enjoy a long life, and the LORD's plan will prosper in his hands."*

All I have done is combined three versions of the same prophecy to clarify these verses. I have not changed anything. Part A is from the *King James Version*, Part B is from *Contemporary English Version* and Part C is from *New Living translation*.

Since this is very important prophecy about *Jesus*, you will see many different interpretations. I personally checked fifty-seven different translations from *Bibles* that are up to one hundred years old, and found this prophecy to some extent different in many versions. In this prophecy of *Isaiah*, first it says that *'he made his grave with the wicked,' and with the rich in his death.'* It denotes that when *Jesus* was crucified, he was treated like a criminal, and he

36

was given a provisional grave to stay, in a place called *'Golgotha'* meaning *'a place of a skull.'*[53] *Golgotha* was commonly known to the *Jews* and the *Romans* as a graveyard for criminals or sinners. When *Jesus* actually died long after the crucifixion, his *'long life'* also fulfilled the other part of the prophecy: *'He will enjoy a long life.'* This fact clearly indicates that *Jesus* was not going to die at the young age of thirty-three. But in fact, he died at the age of *120* years in *Srinagar, the Capitol of Kashmir, India.* The second part of the prophecy *'and with rich in his death'* was also fulfilled when *Jesus* died in his old age in *Kashmir.* At the time of his death, he had thousands of followers and he used to be treated like a king according to the history. The *king of Kashmir*, who accepted *Christianity*, must have given his beloved *Messiah* a *Royal Funeral.* His tomb is no ordinary tomb either. It has all the looks of a *royal tomb*, which elucidates *'and with rich in his death.'*

A portion of the prophecy says: *"When you shall make him an offering for sin, he shall see his seed."* By reading with some attention, you will notice that it sounds abrupt, or out of line. The reason is that the verse "חיי" = *"Chayay"* meaning *"he shall live"* has unfortunately been deleted in most *Bibles.* I was able to find this verse in the *Bible*, mentioned above. Is it not interesting that it was prophesied long before *Jesus* was born that *'Jesus* will live or survive' the crucifixion? It also says in the *Jewish Torah' (Bible)* that *he shall see to the full [age].*[54] The *Hebrew* word used here is "שבע," = 'Saba' could also be "שיבה" = *'Seybah'* which means *'long life,'* or *'full age.'* As you can see that *'long life,'* was used by *New Living Bible* also. If the original *Hebrew* word was not *'Seybah,'* then why *NLT Bible* used it?

According to the *Genesis 6:3*, a man's full age is *120 years.* Amazingly, this is the exact age of *Jesus* mentioned in the holy book of *Muslims*, called *'hadith' (traditions of Muhammad).* Hadith says: *"Jesus son of Mary lived up to the age of 120 years."*[55] These *Hadith* were compiled some *1400 years* ago. Even if we do not comprise these two verses of *Isaiah, 'He shall live'*, and *'he shall see to the full [age],'* as most of the *Bible* scholars have done, we still have the full message that *"When you shall make him an offering for sin he shall see his seed, he shall prolong his days."* One *Bible* says that *"he will have a multitude of children, many heirs. He will enjoy a long life." (New Living Bible).* Please see on the next page this prophecy of *Isaiah* which was revealed to Prophet *Ahmad.*

---

[53] Please see *Matthew 27:33*
[54] Please see *Online Jewish Bible*, www.MechonMamre.org, Isaiah 53:11
[55] Please see *Kunzul-Amaal* Vol. 6 page #120

4. *Prophecy of Prophet Isaiah (Part 2)*

4. Prophecy of Prophet Isaiah (Part 2)

This is the **original** prophecy of *Isaiah*, which God revealed to Ahmad in Hebrew. God taught him it's meaning. This is a very special prophecy, because it was first revealed to *Isaiah* about 2,744 years ago. Then it was revealed to Jesus about 2004 years ago. When Jesus said: ' *believe in all that the prophets have spoken' (Luke 24:25)*. He meant that he survived the crucifixion for the fulfillment of the prophecy of *Isaiah*. Then the same prophecy was revealed to Ahmad *(Second Coming of Jesus Christ)* over one hundred years ago, in these words:

English	Phr	Strong's	Hebrew	Tense
for he was cut off	Phr	[01504]	גָּזַר gazar	Tense
out of the land	Phr	[0776]	אֶרֶץ 'erets	
of the living:	Phr	[02416]	חַי chay	
And he made	Phr	[05414]	נָתַן nathan	Tense
his grave	Phr	[06913]	קֶבֶר qeber	
with the wicked,	Phr	[07563]	רָשָׁע rasha'	
and with the rich	Phr	[06223]	עָשִׁיר 'ashiyr	
in his death;	Phr	[04194]	מָוֶת maveth	
when thou shalt make	Phr	[07760]	שׂוּמָה suwm	Tense
his soul	Phr	[05315]	נֶפֶשׁ nephesh	
an offering for sin,	Phr	[0817]	אָשָׁם 'asham	
he shall live		[02425]	חָיָי chayay	
he shall see	Phr	[07200]	רָאָה ra'ah	Tense
[his] seed,	Phr	[02233]	זֶרַע zera'	
he shall prolong	Phr	[0748]	אָרַך 'arak	Tense
[his] days,	Phr	[03117]	יוֹם yowm	
He shall see	Phr	[07200]	רָאָה ra'ah	Tense
of the travail	Phr	[05999]	עָמָל 'amal	
of his soul,	Phr	[05315]	נֶפֶשׁ nephesh	
[But] he shall see	Phr	[07200]	רָאָה ra'ah	
to the full [age]	Phr	[07646]	שָׂבַע saba'	

◄ This verse is missing in most of the Bibles, but I found it in the Contemporary English Version © 1995 by American Bible Society

The above quoted prophesy of Ahmad is from his famous book "*Tuhfa-e-Gularvia*". This book was published in September of 1900 in Qadian, Punjab, India.

There is another evidence that has been discovered. This one is written in one of the historical books of *India*. It says *"...Jesus travelled further and reached Kashmir. Dr Jyotsna writes [Kadambani, Dec. 1990] that there are even now some people who claim to be the descendents of Jesus Christ in Kashmir Valley. It seems that during his second visit to Kashmir, he met a Shaka, or Hindu King, of India. Jesus seems to have died in Sri-Nagar in his old age and a tomb in Rasaballa [Roza-Bal] is regarded as his, which is visited and worshipped even now by Hindus and Christians of Kashmir."*

The Marriage of Jesus

The marriage of *Jesus* which was prophesied by *Isaiah* is confirmed by the book of *Revelation* in these words: *"Let us be glad and rejoice, and give honour to him: for the marriage of the Lamb is come, and his wife hath made herself ready. And to her was granted that she should be arrayed in fine linen, clean and white: for the fine linen is the righteousness of saints And he saith unto me, Write, Blessed are they which are called unto the marriage supper of the Lamb. And he saith unto me, These are the true sayings of God."*[56]

All *Christians* unanimously believe that in the entire *Bible*, on every instance the word *Lamb* is mentioned, it is about *Jesus*. If you look up this word *"Lamb,"* = ἀρνίον = "arnion" in *Greek* or type *"G721"* in the search area of the famous *Bible* website called BlueLetterBible.org, it says: *"Lamb i.e. Christ."* *Jesus* had to survive the crucifixion in order for him to get married and have children, because according to the *Bible, Jesus* had no children prior to the crucifixion. He had to survive in order for him to live a long life, because the *Bible* says he was only thirty-three years old when he was put on the cross. These prophecies of *Isaiah* and *Revelation* about the wife and children of *Jesus* were confirmed by the *Qur'an* in these words:

> *"And, indeed, We sent Messengers before thee [Muhammad], and We gave them wives and children."*[57]

The first messenger this verse pertains to is *Jesus* because he is the only one who came right before *Muhammad*. *Isaiah* prophesied about *Jesus* approximately *742 years* before *Jesus* was born that 'he would have children.' How was *Jesus* supposed to have children, when he died unmarried? And how was he supposed to live long when he died at a young age? Have you ever contemplated that why only *Jesus* was prophesied in the *Bible* to have children?

---

[56]   Please see the book of *Revelation 19: 7-9*
[57]   Please see *Qur'an* Chapter *Al-Ra'd 13: 38-39*

We do not find any other prophecy about any other *Biblical* prophet that he would have children. Most of the prophets already had children, but they were not prophesied in advance for having the children. The reason seems to be that *God* knew *Jesus* would be worshiped as a god after the crucifixion. *God* sent prophecies about his wife and children, therefore, anyone who even tenuously thinks of worshipping a man, would think twice if he finds out that *Jesus* was married and he had children. That seems to be the reason; *God* sent prophecies about the *seed* of *Jesus* in four different books of the *Bible*, by four different prophets. *God* also knew that his disciples would believe that he actually died on the cross and '*became accursed of God.*' *Jesus* never said 'I am God.' Scholars often ignore a very crucial testimony of *Jesus*: he called himself the '*Son of Man*' 84 times in the *Bible*.

The *Bible* also talks very clearly about the brothers and sisters of *Jesus*. Anyone who thinks of him as *God* would think twice to venerate him as *God* if they found that that *Jesus* had regular brothers and sisters like everyone else.

Brothers & Sisters of Jesus

1. *"Is not this the carpenter, the son of Mary, the brother of James, and Joses, and of Juda, and Simon? and are not his sisters here with us..." (Mark 6:3).*

2. *"Mary the mother of James" (Luke 24:10). James* was the brother of *Jesus.*

3. *"Other of the apostles saw I none, save James the Lord's brother"* *(Galatians 1:19).*

4. *"While he yet talked to the people, behold, his mother and his brethren stood without, desiring to speak with him" (Matthew 12:46).*

Some *Christians* contend that brothers and sisters pertain to the disciples of *Jesus* only, but it does not mean his real brothers and sisters. But if you read the next verse from the *Bible*, you would know that this notion is erroneous. Because the next verse talks about *Jesus'* mother, brothers, and disciples separately.

5. *"After this he went down to Capernaum, he, and his mother, and his brethren, and his disciples: and they continued there not many days" (John 2:12).*

6. *"There came then his brethren and his mother, and, standing without, sent unto him, calling him. And the multitude sat about him, and they said unto him, Behold, thy mother and thy brethren without seek for thee And he answered them, saying, Who is my mother, or my brethren? And he looked round about on them which sat about him, and said, Behold my mother and my brethren! For whosoever shall do the will of God, the same is my brother, and my sister, and mother" (Mark 3:31-35).*

This denotes that his real brothers and sisters had no significance in his life, he esteemed only his disciples. But he did have real brothers and sisters. Then a serious question arises: what kind of god was *Jesus,* who had brothers and sisters? Let us see what the *Bible* says about worshiping a human being:

> *"Although they knew God, they did not glorify Him as God, nor were thankful, but became futile in their thoughts and their foolish hearts were darkened. Professing to be wise, they became fools, and changed the glory of incorruptible God into an image made like corruptible man... Therefore God also gave them up to uncleanness, in the lusts of their hearts... who exchanged the truth of God for the lie, and worshiped and served the creature [Man] rather than the Creator [God], who is blessed forever."*[58]

The above verses of the book of *Romans* clearly verifies that whoever worships a man instead of *God* is in a serious confusion. To clear these confusions in the time of the *Second Coming of Christ, God* revealed this prophecy of *Isaiah* to *Ahmad* (the 2nd *Coming of Jesus Christ*).

The scribes perhaps did not want to humble their deity *(Jesus)* by mentioning his marriage and the eventual raising of a family. But according to the *Dead Sea Scrolls, Jesus* was married to *Mary Magdalene* and had three children. The oldest of *Jesus'* son was called *Justus,* son of *Jesus. Mary Magdalene* was an expecting mother at the time of crucifixion and she migrated with *Jesus* in her pregnancy. This event was also hinted by the prophecy of *Isaiah* in these words:

---

[58]   Please see *Romans 1:21-25*

41

> *"Depart! Depart! Go out from there, Touch no unclean thing;*
> *Go out from the midst of her, be clean, You who bear the vessels*
> *of the LORD."*[59]

Some modern scholars deem *'Vessel of the Lord'* in this verse is referred to the holy child of *Jesus*. The marriage of *Jesus* with *Mary Magdalene* was also hinted by the *Gospel of Philip*. Recently, an article was posted on *Yahoo. com* by *James Polster*. Mr. *Polster* claims to have journeyed to *Kashmir, India* where he met with a man who is supposed to be the descendant of *Jesus Christ*. According to this article a man named *Sahibzada Basharat Saleem* claims to be the direct descendant of *Jesus Christ*. Mr. *Sahibzada Basharat Saleem* has a genealogy which links his ancestors back to *Jesus*.

There has been another discovery in *Egypt*, the *Gospel of Mary Magdalene*. This *Gospel* shows that *Mary Magdalene* was not only the most favorite disciple of *Jesus*, but she was also the symbol of wisdom. *Mary Magdalene* understood the message of *Jesus* more than any other disciple. She became the teacher and the woman in charge of the early *Christian* church. According to the modern scholars, she was falsely alleged as a prostitute to keep the women's role out of the church.[60]

The message given in the prophecy of *Isaiah 53:10* is an analogous message, which was mentioned in the book of *Job also*. In this prophecy, *Eliphaz, the Temanite* tells *Job* that this pain of yours is nothing to compare to a man (Jesus) who trusted *God* (even in his worst time, hanging on the cross), and *God* not only saved him, but also gave him many glad tidings for future. The prophecy says:

> *"Behold, happy is the man whom God corrected: therefore*
> *despise not your chastening of the Almighty: For he [God] bruises*
> *[him], but his hands make [him] whole [heal] (Job 5:17-18). In*
> *famine he shall redeem you from death: and in war from the*
> *power of the sword (Job 5:20). You shall know also that your*
> *seed shall be great, and your off spring as the grass of the earth*
> *(Job 5:25). You shall come to your grave in a full age, like as a*
> *shock of corn comes in, in his season" (Job 5:26).*

The scribes tried to paste this prophecy of *Job* on *Job* himself by appending in the *Bible*:

---

[59] Please see *Isaiah 52: 11, New King James Version*
[60] Please see documentary, *The real Mary Magdalene* by the *Discovery* channel.

"After this lived Job an hundred and forty years, and saw his sons, and his sons' sons, even four generations So Job died, being old and full of days" (Job 42:16-17).

First of all, if *Job* lived *140* years, this verse contradicted *Genesis 6:3*, where it says: *"... [man's] days shall be an hundred and twenty years."* Secondly, can a dead man write about himself? *"So Job died, being old and full of days."*

Similarly, could *Moses* write this about himself?:

"And he [God] buried him [Moses] in a valley in the land of Moab, over against Bethpeor: but no man knoweth of his sepulchre unto this day. And Moses [was] an hundred and twenty years old when he died: his eye was not dim, nor his natural force abated. And the children of Israel wept for Moses in the plains of Moab thirty days: so the days of weeping [and] mourning for Moses were ended" (Deuteronomy 34:6-8).

Could *Joshua* write about himself?

"And it came to pass after these things, that Joshua the son of Nun, the servant of the LORD, died, being an hundred and ten years old. And they buried him in the border of his inheritance..."[61]

Please contemplate on this point: every time an ancient scroll is discovered it refutes the beliefs of the *Christians* of today. The only reason we can think of it is that the people after *Jesus'* time started forgetting his real teachings and commenced their own teachings. This practice not only made the contradictions in the *Bible*, but also made new beliefs which were not taught by *Jesus*. This basically means that the *Christians* modified the *Bible* according to their beliefs instead of modifying their beliefs according to the *Bible*. Most of these contradictions and strange beliefs seem to be the inventions of the time of *Constantine*.

The *Qur'an* is the only religious book in the world that proclaimed emphatically over *1,400* years ago that *Jesus* did not die on the cross. If Prophet *Muhammad* and his book *Qur'an* were not from *God*, (God forbid) then how did he know something over *1,400* years ago, when most people in the world still do not know today?

---

[61] Please see *Joshua 24:29-30*

5. Paul versus Jesus

The scholars of our time, after learning that *Jesus* did not die on the cross, have began to wonder about *Paul*. They are still not sure whether he was the real follower of *Jesus* or not. According to them, *Paul* always contradicted *Jesus* and promoted his own doctrines. *Paul* was the first one who said *"Jesus died for our sins."* But *Jesus* never said he would die for people's sins. *Paul* was the first one who went against the words of *Jesus*. *Jesus* said: *"do not go to Gentiles" (Matthew 10:5)*. But *Paul* decided to *"go to Gentiles"* (Acts 13:46). *Jesus* said: *"Do not think that I came to destroy the law or the prophets... but to fulfill" (Matthew 5:17)*. But *Paul* said: *"Christ has redeemed us from the curse of the law, being made a curse for us."* [62]

In my opinion, *Paul* was a very devout *Jew* and he honestly believed that *Jesus* was a false messiah (God forbid). Therefore, *Paul* did not want *Christianity* to spread among the *Jews*. First, he openly tried to destroy *Christianity* by killing *Christians*. Thus, the *Bible* says:

> *"And that is just what I did in Jerusalem. On the authority of the chief priests I put many of the saints in prison, and when they were put to death, I cast my vote against them."* [63]

This strategy did not work because whenever he killed one *Christian*, more *Jews* would become *Christian*. *Christianity* was spreading too fast for him to stop. Then he changed his strategy by claiming to meet *Jesus* in a vision, when he was on the road to *Damascus*. Then he supposedly accepted *Christianity*. After meeting with *Jesus* in his vision, did *Paul* ever convey the message of *Jesus*? No, but he came up with his own version of *Christianity*

---

[62]   Please see *Galatians 3:13*
[63]   Please see *Acts 26:10-11*

to preach. What was the reason for him to do that? Probably, he wanted the *Jews* to abhor *Christianity*, and stay away from it. The *Jews* strongly believed in one *God*; *Paul* told them about three gods *(Trinity)*. It is manifested from the history pages that *Paul* initiated three gods, but it is also evident that this notion took a strong hold in *Christianity* around the era of *Constantine*.

The *Jews* were commanded by *God* to obey the *Law* of *Moses*. But *Paul* said the law is a curse and you don't have to obey it. The *Jews* strongly believed that whosoever dies on the cross becomes accursed of *God* and that person can never be from *God*. *Paul* said: *'Christ has redeemed us from the curse of the law, being made a curse for us.'* *Paul* knew very well that no *Jewish* person in his right mind would ever believe in an accursed messiah. The *Jews* believed in circumcision. *Paul* said: *'if you are circumcised, Christ shall profit you nothing.'* By turning *Christianity* upside down, he was very successful in keeping *Christianity* away from the *Jews* forever. As a result, thanks to *Paul's* subtle conspiracy, *Christianity* has spread in almost every nation of the world, except among the *Jews*. The *Jews* have accepted *Jesus* but very insignificantly as compare to other nations. Other nations accepted *Christianity* at some time in their totality.

Let us see what some of the *Christian* eminent scholars wrote about *Paul*:

> *"What is called Christianity today is largely a teaching of precepts artificially created by Paul, and should more correctly be called Paulinism. "Christianity" is the religion founded by Paul; it replaced Christ's Gospel with a Gospel about Christ.' In this sense, Paulinism corresponds to the misinterpretation and falsification of Christ's actual teachings in a manner initiated and organized by Paul. It has long been accepted by theological research that the Christianity of the organized Church, with its central tenet of salvation through the vicariously sacrificial death of Jesus, is based on misinterpretation. 'All the beautiful aspects of Christianity can be traced to Jesus, all the not-so-beautiful to Paul,' said the theologian Overbbeck"* (F. Overbeck, *Christentem und Kultur, published posthumously, 1919).*[64]

> *"Paul placed little emphasis on the actual words and teachings of Jesus, but was preoccupied with his own teachings. He put Jesus on a pedestal and made him into the Christ figure that Jesus never intended to be. Today a profound new understanding of*

---

[64]   Please see *Jesus lived in India* by *Holger Kersten*

> *Christianity is possible by rejecting all that is obviously bogus,*
> *and by turning to the true, undiluted teachings of Jesus and the*
> *real essence of religious faiths."*[65]

Mr. *Holger Kersten* further states:

> *"The theologian Grimm put it in a nut shell: 'However deeply*
> *these teachings may have come ingrained in Christian thought,*
> *they still have nothing to do with real Jesus (E. Grimm, 'Die*
> *Ethik Jesu,' 1917)."*

This is what *Paul* says about *Christian* faith: *"If Christ be not risen, then is our preaching vain, and your faith is also vain" (I Corinthians 15:14).* Then *Paul* says in *Timothy*: *"Remember that Jesus Christ of the seed of David was raised from the dead according to my gospel" (2 Timothy 2:8).* To me he is contemptuous towards *Christians* who believed him. First *Paul* says that if *Jesus* is not raised from the dead, your faith is vain. Bear in mind, he said *"Your Faith."* He did not say *"Our Faith"* is vain. Then he himself elucidated why *your faith is vain* because according to *Paul, Jesus* was raised from the dead, according to his gospel. Which means *Jesus* never said that. *God* never mentioned it anywhere. It is *Paul's* invention. But if you still believe it, your faith would be in vain.

Let us read some of the astonishing sayings of *Paul*:

a) *"And unto the Jews I became as a Jew, that I might gain the Jews; to them that are under the law, as under the law, that I might gain them that are under the law" (I Corinthians 9:20).*

b) *"For if the truth of God has increased through my lie to His glory, why am I also still judged as a sinner?" (Romans 3:7 NKJV).*

c) *"What I am saying with this boastful confidence, I say not with the Lord's authority but as a fool" (2Corinthians 11:17 English Standard Version).*

d) *"To my shame, I must say, we were too weak for that! But whatever anyone else dares to boast of –I am speaking as a fool…" (2Corinthians 11:21 ESV).*

---

[65]   Ibid.

e)   *"Are they ministers of Christ? (I speak as a fool)..."*
     (2Corinthians 11:23 KJV).

Is this the teaching *Christians* call the *Word of God*, without interpolation?
Paul said something in *Galatians* which would make you realize that why
some people think that he was against *Christianity* and wanted the *Jews* to
stay away from it. *Paul* says:

> *"Behold I Paul say to you, that if you are circumcised [Jew],
> Christ shall profit you nothing. For I testify again to every man
> that is circumcised, that he is debtor to do the whole law. Christ
> is become of no effect to you, whosoever of you are justified by
> the law; you are fallen from the grace."*[66]

In this verse, *Paul* is telling all the people that '*I Paul* say to you.' It means
evidently that these are the inventions of *St. Paul* and they have nothing to
do with the truth. *Paul* wants the readers to know that *Paul* is telling you,
not *God*, not *Jesus* but he is telling you. Then he says: "*if you are circumcised,
Christ shall profit you nothing*" this denotes that if you are a *Jew*, you would
not benefit from believing in *Jesus* as a messiah. "*For I testify again to every
man that is circumcised, that he is debtor to do the whole law.*"

This means if you are a *Jew*, you have to obey the whole *Law of Moses*.
"*Christ is become of no effect to you.*" This means that he is saying again that if
you are a *Jew, then* believing in *Jesus* would have no effect on you spiritually.
Then he addresses *Christians* by saying: "*whosoever of you are justified by the
law; you are fallen from the grace,*" which means if *Christians* try to obey the
law of *Moses*, you would be fallen from the grace of *God*. Another words *Paul*
is saying: 'don't obey the law, or the *Law of Moses* is not for the *Christians*.'
One may wonder why he is telling the *Jews* that you are '*debtor to do the whole
law*,' but he is telling the *Christians* to not obey the law?

[Compare the incident of *'Paul's Vision'* when he supposedly met *Jesus* the
first time on the road to *Damascus*. We read in *Acts 9:3-7*:

> *"And as he journeyed, he came near Damascus: and suddenly
> there shined round about him a light from heaven. And he
> fell to the earth, and heard a voice...And the men which
> journeyed with him stood speechless, hearing a voice, but seeing
> no man."*

But in *Acts 22:9 Paul* says:

---

[66]   Please see *Galatians 5:2-4*

> *"And they that were with me saw indeed the light, and were afraid; but they heard not the voice of him that spake to me."*

Paul says in *Acts* chapter 9 and chapter 22: *"...a great light shone round about me [only]."*

But in *Acts 26:13 Paul* says: *"...a light from heaven, above the brightness of the sun, shining round about me and them which journeyed with me."*

Paul says in *Acts 9:4 "And he [Paul] fell to the earth... And the men which journeyed with him stood speechless."*

But in *Acts 26:14* he says: *"...we were all fallen to the earth."*

Paul says in *Acts 22:10 "what shall I do, Lord? And the Lord said unto me, "Arise, and go into Damascus; and there it shall be told thee of all things which are appointed for thee to do."*

And one *Ananias* told him what he should do. But in *Acts 26: 16-18. Paul* says that *Jesus* told him what to do.][67]

It is very hard to believe that after reading these contradictory testimonies of *Paul* people still believed him that he was sent by *Jesus*. After these contradictory testimonies he told the disciples that all the law has been abolished, while *Jesus* said '*do not think I have come to abolish the law but to fulfill,* and disciples believed *Paul* over *Jesus*?

---

67   Bracketed text excerpts from the book *Where did Jesus die?* by *J.D. Shams* paraphrased

6. Why Jesus was considered god?

Unfortunately, some of the disciples did not know that *Jesus* had survived the crucifixion miraculously. There was a small group of people who knew *Jesus* had survived, but they could not openly announce this fact, because of the fear of retribution by the *Jews* & *Roman* authorities. Then are the ones (followers of Jesus) who thought he had died on the cross. But they started to think that how could we tell the world that *Jesus* was a true messenger of *God*, or a true messiah, when our own book is testifying against him as an accursed person, *For he that is hanged is accursed of God*. They had no choice but to depict him as a god, because the theory of a human accursed messiah would not work. Therefore, they started saying that *Jesus* willfully died on the cross, and became accursed for us to pay for our sins.

According to the history of *Christianity*, this idea did not take full hold in *Christianity* until over three hundred years later. The support of *Constantine* for *Christianity* was the crucial era when church leaders and bishops were compelled by *Constantine* to agree on one creed. Believe *Jesus* as *God* or not, they all had to agree on something. This denotes that *Constantine* evidently had no interest in *Christianity*. Otherwise, he should have insisted on truth and not just *agree on something*. Not only that, but *Constantine* was baptized just a few days before his death bed. This also shows that he had no interest in *Christianity*; all he wanted was to have one religion for the entire empire to keep the empire in one accord.

Some *Christian* scholars try to explain why *Constantine* wanted to be baptized just a few days before his death was to leave earth with a clean slate so he can enter the heaven easily. This seems like an attempt to prove that he was really interested in *Christianity*. In fact, no one knows when or how he or she is going to die. Maybe the *Emperors* get a week notices before they die but in reality it never happens. We never know when we are going to die of a heart attack, choking, being killed or when accidental death overtakes us. And why do the *Christians* baptize their children in early ages, when baptizing is supposed to take place a few days before death? Even the incident of *Constantine* to support *Christians* after his victory is not clear in history. Some accounts say that just before the battle, *Constantine* lifted up his eyes and saw a fiery cross on the sky. He won the battle and he attributed his victory to *Christianity* and he started supporting them. Some accounts say that *Constantine* saw *Jesus* on the sky and *Jesus* said *'in my name conquer,'* and he started supporting *Christians* henceforth. Which account is true?

Going back to the topic under discussion [Ahmad says:

> *"If those who agreed to call Jesus accursed had realized that what kind of demeaning title they are attaching with their beloved Messiah, they would have never used that title for him."*

The following are some of the popular meanings of *"Accursed of God"*: 1) *Enemy of God* 2) *God's hatred be on him* 3) *Bound to live in hell forever* 4) *He hated God* 5) *He denied God* 6) *Estranged from God.*][68]

That is the reason *Jesus* was crying and asking *God* *"to remove this cup [cup of death, or the death on the cross] from me…" (Luke 22:42). "And he was heard in that he feared" (Hebrews 5:7).* *Jesus* was a righteous man and not a sinner. He was a beloved of *God*, and not an enemy of *God*. This is the reason *Bible* says:

> *"No man speaking by the spirit of God call Jesus accursed"* *(1Corinthians 12:3).*

Six signs of a false messiah or a prophet

If *Jesus* had actually died on the cross then according to the *Bible* he fulfilled all six signs of a false messiah or a prophet. Some people say that these six signs are for the prophets, but *Jesus* was not the prophet, he was *Son of God* (God forbid). According to the *New Testament, Jesus* called himself prophet

---

[68] Bracketed text is excerpts from *Jesus in India*

5 times in the following verses, *Matthew 13:57, Mark 6:4, Luke 4:24, Luke 13:33* and *John 4:44.* On the other hand, other people called *Jesus* the Prophet in the following verses 8 times. *Matthew 21:11, Luke 7:16, 7:39 and 24:19 plus in the book of John 4:19, 6:14, 7:40* and *9:17.*

Bible tells us six signs of a false prophet as follows:

1. *He would be killed.*[69] The *Qur'an* also tells us the severity of attributing false statements towards *God* in these words:

   "And if he had fabricated against Us some of the sayings, We would certainly have seized him by the right hand, Then We would certainly have cut off his aorta. And not one of you could have withheld Us from him."[70]

   The book of *Psalms* also says: *"The LORD redeemeth the soul of his servants: and none of them that trust in him shall be desolate."*[71]

   Some people may say that *God* is talking about saving the soul of a prophet not the life of a prophet which means, a prophet could get killed. But if a person is already dead what is the meaning of saving his soul? We all know that all souls are already saved for the *Day of Judgment*, to judge by *God.* But if you look up this word in the original *Hebrew Bible* it says "נפש" = "*nephesh*" which also means *'life.'* This means that the *Bible* is talking about *"The Lord saves the lives of his servants [or Prophets.]"* The word used for desolate is אשם = "*asham*" which also means *'destroyed'* or *'wasted.'*

   This denotes that the *Bible* is talking about *"none of them that trust in him shall be destroyed [or wasted]."* According to these verses of the *Bible* and *Qur'an*, none of the true prophets of *God* have ever gotten killed by their enemies. If they did get killed then they were false prophets. The reason the *Bible* tells us about many prophets got killed because the scribes tried to justify *Jesus'* killing on the cross by his enemies. But in actuality, none of them ever got killed by their enemies. Is that possible that *God* would tell us how to recognize a true prophet, if a prophet dies a natural death, then he is definitely a true prophet, but if he gets killed by his enemy then he is definitely a false prophet.

---

69   Please see *Deuteronomy 18:20 in New International Version Bible*
70   Please see Qur'an, *Al-Haqqah 69: 44-48*
71   Please see *Psalms 34:22*

Then *God* sent his own son and let him be killed by his enemies. Why would *Christians* try to persuade the *Jews* that he was a true prophet, if he died on the cross? Perhaps that is the reason *St Paul* had to turn to *Gentiles*, because this notion would not work with the *Jews*.

2. *"For he that is hanged is accursed of God" (Deuteronomy 21:23)*.

3. *"God would not hear his prayer" (Proverbs 15:29)* Jesus did pray with strong cries and supplications if *God* still did not hear his prayer and he did die then according to this verse he was a false *Messiah* or prophet. *(God forbid)*

4. *"His life will be shortened" (Proverbs 10:27)*. Jesus was put on the cross just after three years of his ministry. If he died within three years as most *Christians* believe then according to the above verse, he was a false *Messiah* or *prophet. (God forbid)*

5. *"God will forsake him" (Jeremiah 23:31-39)*. If *Jesus* did die and *God* forsook him, then he was the false *Messiah* or prophet. *(God forbid)*

6. *"Behold, I will feed them [false prophets] with wormwood, and make them drink the water of gall" (Jeremiah 9: 15 & 23:15)*. This verse tells us that *God* will give the false prophets/messiahs gall to drink. If *Jesus* drinks gall then according to this verse he becomes false prophet/messiah. (God forbid)

    a. *"...for the LORD our God hath put us to silence, and given us water of gall to drink, because we have sinned against the LORD" (Jeremiah 8: 14)*.

    b. The book of *Psalms* says: *"They gave me also gall for my meat; and in my thirst they gave me vinegar to drink" (Psalms 69:21)*.

    c. According to the *Gospel of Matthew*, Jesus was offered gall. *"They gave him [Jesus] vinegar to drink mingled with gall: and when he had tasted [thereof], he would not drink" (Matthew 27:34)*. But the *Gospel of John* says that *Jesus* died right after he drank the vinegar. Therefore, it says: *"When Jesus therefore had received the vinegar, he said, It is finished: and he bowed his head, and gave up the ghost" (John 19:30)*.

If *Jesus* actually died right after drinking that gall mixed vinegar, then according to the above mentioned prophecy of *Jeremiah* he was a false prophet or messiah (God forbid). It is totally up to the reader to believe that *Jesus* died on the cross and fulfilled all six signs of a false prophet or messiah or he was miraculously saved from the cross and defeated all six signs.

According to the *Bible*, even the word *'die'* does not necessarily mean a real death. *Paul* says:

> *"I protest, brothers, by my pride in you, which I have in Christ Jesus our Lord, I die every day!"* (1Corinthians 15:31 ESV).

After reading the above verse can we honestly say that *Paul* literally dies everyday and comes back to life every day? The same applies to *Jesus*. When some of the *Gospel* writers wrote that *Jesus* died, they did not lie: they only meant he suffered. This notion can also be verified by reading all the prophecies about *Jesus*. None of the prophecies ever say he will die for any one. Even the prophecy of *Isaiah 53:10*, which I have presented earlier, does not say anything about dying, but it articulates about his suffering.

Socrates and the Poison

For instance, the story of Prophet *Socrates* taking the poison hemlock in 399 B.C.E. is nothing but a misconception. When the *Socrates* took the poison, it only meant that he accepted persecution over giving up his beliefs and renouncing of his religion. Although, the last moments of his life were described in detail by *Plato* in *Phaedo*. But that was nothing but a cover-up story by his followers, just like the story of all the true prophets of *God* including *Moses*, *Jesus* and *John the Baptist*, who were condemned to death by the tyrant rulers. But they all escaped with the help of *God*. As I have mentioned earlier, the true prophets of *God* neither get killed nor commit sins, like committing suicide in the case of *Socrates*. The *Qur'an* tells us about this view in these words:

> *"They [persecutors] said, "Burn him and protect your gods, If ye do (anything at all)!" We said, "O Fire! be thou cool, and (a means of) safety for Abraham!"* (Al-Anbiya 21:68-70).

In this verse the *Qur'an* tells us that when *Prophet Abraham* was thrown in fire, the fire became cool and it did not burn him. This verse of *Qur'an* is also using the similar metaphor as used by the followers of *Prophet Socrates*, as they mentioned that he took poison hemlock (persecution) instead of giving up his beliefs. In the similar way, the *Qur'an* is telling us that *Prophet Abraham* was thrown in the fire of persecution, but *God* made it cool or saved him from the evil plans of his persecutors.

Some people usually contend that if only false prophets could be killed and the true prophets should die of their old age then how did *John the Baptist* get killed by his enemy, *King Herod*? With the blessing of *God* even this enigma has been solved. Recently, a tomb has been discovered in the *Island of Patmos*, which is known to the local people as the tomb of *John the Baptist*, who according to them died in an advanced age. The discovery of the tomb of *John the Baptist* also encourages the theologians to reconsider who really wrote the *Book of Revelation*.

Traditionally, it was known as the book written by *John the Apostle*, but now it has been acknowledged by many modern scholars as the book written by *John the Baptist*. However, many theologians are confused about the first three chapters of the book of *Revelation*. They find that the first three chapters were written at a much later time. They contend that if they are written by *John the Baptist* he should have been dead by then. But if you read those first three chapters you would come to a conclusion that they were added much later than the rest of the book. In my opinion, these first three chapters were added around the 4th century C.E. According to the theologians, the whole book of *Revelation* was probably not written by *John the Apostle* because of the style of writing and the language, it is nothing like the book of *John*. According to *Dr. Alan Meenan*:

> *"The Greek of the Gospel is pure and simple Greek, the Greek*
> *of the book of Revelation is really quite atrocious."[72]*

Going back to the subject under discussion, the *Qur'an* tells us the survival of *John the Baptist* in a special way. The name *Qur'an* tells us of *John the Baptist* is *"YahYah,"* which means *"one who lived"* or *"one who survived."[73]* If *John the Baptist's* name was given at birth as *Yahyah*, 'one who survived' how could he have been killed? The *Qur'an* mentions the prophet *John the Baptist* many times, but it never mentions even a single time that *John the Baptist* got killed. The *Qur'an* says these honorary words for him:

---

[72] *Dr. Alan Meenan*, founder, *The Word is Out*. Please see the *National geographic* documentary, *Dooms Day: Book of Revelation*
[73] Please see Qur'an Ch. *Maryam 19:7-8*

> *"And peace was on him [John the Baptist] the day he was born, and the day he died, and peace there will be on him the day he will be raised up to life again."* [74]

One of the most fundamental beliefs in *Christianity* is that "*Jesus* died for their sins". The *Bible*, on the other hand, denies this concept. It reminds people of all eras by negating this concept in six different books through six different prophets.

1. *"But let every man prove his own work, and then shall he have rejoicing in himself alone, and not in another. For every man shall bear his own burden [sin]"* (Galatians 6:4-5).

2. *"Fathers shall not die for the children, neither shall the children die for the fathers, but every man shall die for his own sins"* (Deuteronomy 24:16).

3. *"The soul who sins is the one who will die. The son will not share the guilt of the father, nor will the father share the guilt of the son. The righteousness of the righteous man will be credited to him, and the wickedness of the wicked will be charged against him"* (Ezekiel 18:20 *New International Version* Bible Copyright 1984).

4. *"The LORD commanded, saying, The fathers shall not be put to death for the children, nor the children be put to death for the fathers; but every man shall be put to death for his own sin"* (II Kings 14:6).

5. *"The LORD commanded, saying, The fathers shall not die for the children, neither shall the children die for the fathers, but every man shall die for his own sin"* (II Chronicles 25:4).

6. *"But everyone shall die for his own iniquity: every man that eateth the sour grape, his teeth shall be set on edge"* (Jeremiah 31:30).

The *Bible* also says:

> *"Dear friends, if we deliberately continue sinning after we have received a full knowledge of the truth, there is no other sacrifice that will cover these sins"* (Hebrews 10:26 NLT).

---

[74] Please see *Maryam 19:15-16*

The *Qur'an*, also confirms the verses presented above in these words: "*...thou art not made responsible except for thyself...*"[75] I really wish if any *Christian* scholar from any part of the world could show me just one verse in the entire *Bible* in which *Jesus* said 'I am *God*,' or 'worship me.' Or if he or she could show me just one verse in which he ever said that his crucifixion would bring any salvation to *Christians*. Or if *Jesus* ever told his disciples to wait for crucifixion if they want to earn eternal life. On the contrary, *Jesus* always told his disciples that they should keep the commandments (Ten Commandments or the '*Law of Moses*'). If the followers of *Jesus* believed they would achieve salvation through his accursed death on the cross, then *Jesus* should have known about it too. The *New Testament* also says by the pen of *James*, the brother of *Jesus*:

> "*Seest thou how faith wrought with his works, and by works was faith made perfect? And the scripture was fulfilled which saith, Abraham believed God, and it was imputed unto him for righteousness: and he was called the Friend of God. Ye see then how that by works a man is justified, and not by faith only... For as the body without the spirit is dead, so faith without works is dead also.*"[76]

What are Stigmata?

After learning from me that *Jesus* did not die on the cross, my *Christian* friends often ask me if what I am saying is true and then there is no significance of the cross. If there is no significance of the cross then why are there so many people in the world who miraculously have stigmata? The *Stigmata* refers to the *Christ-like* marks on the skin. These marks are usually of the nail wounds and mostly they appear on the hands and the feet of the faithful. Sometimes we see that the people have a cross like wound appear on their forehead. I cannot really comment on something people claim to have received from *God*. Because it is between *God* and that person and I have no right to judge any one. But I can tell my readers a brief history of *Stigmatism* and let you decide what you think about it.

According to the history of the *Stigmatism*, it was started with the preacher called *St. Francis of Assisi* in *1224*. *Stigmata* is the plural of the *Greek* word

---

75 Please see *Qur'an Ch. 4 Al-Nisa:84-85*
76 Please see *James 2: 22 to 26*

στίγμα = '*Stigma,*' which simply means mark. *St. Francis* saw a vision in which he saw *Jesus* with his wounds. When he awoke he had the same marks of the crucifixion on his body. However, *Padre Pio* in *1911* had also reported these wounds and said to have bled almost a cup of blood for fifty years. He wore hand gloves all his life. But the *Church* not only tried to stop him from preaching, but they did not endorse his *Stigmata* until recently--almost 40 years after his death. Surprisingly, when he died he had no wounds on his hands or on his feet when the gloves were removed. *God* knows well what really happened.

After that many people came forward with similar signs. The most recent case of *Stigmata*, however, is more interesting than the rest of the cases. In *1992*, a *Catholic* Priest name *Fr. James Bruce*, purportedly had *Stigmata* but on his wrist unlike all other cases who had *Stigmata* on their palms. People were puzzled that why eight hundred years later the wounds were shifted from palms to the wrists. It came to the knowledge of the people that around that time a new research came to light which suggested that the palm is too fragile and soft to endure the body of a man. Therefore, *Jesus* would have been nailed to the cross through his wrist. You can put two and two together and find out why the wounds shifted from the palms to the wrists? What I thought after learning about this shift of wounds that either *God* gave them wrong wounds for eight hundred years or He gave *Fr. James Bruce* the incorrect wounds now. After all, out of all those dozens of *Stigmata* cases only two were certified or endorsed by the *Church* in eight hundred years.

Revisiting the topic under discussion about dying for the sins of the world. *Jesus* also says: *"For I say unto you, That except your righteousness shall exceed the righteousness of the scribes and Pharisees, ye shall in no case enter into the kingdom of heaven."*[77] If one could go to heaven just by faith in the accursed death of *Jesus* on the cross, then why did *Jesus* say that except your righteousness shall exceed the righteousness of the scribes and *Pharisees*, you cannot go to heaven? It does not only mean that you have to be righteous to go to heaven, but your righteousness should exceed the righteousness of the scribes and *Pharisees* in order for you to go to heaven. The *Qur'an* says that what the *Christians* believe is the belief of the previous religions. Hence it says:

"And the Jews say, "Ezra is God's son," while the Christians say, "The Christ is God's son." Such are the sayings which they utter with their mouths, following in spirit assertions made in earlier times by people who denied the truth!..."[78]

---

[77] Please see *Matthew 5:20*
[78] Please see Quran Ch. *Al-Taubah 9:29-30*

This means that the belief of *Christians* that *Jesus* is son of *God* is the belief adopted from the previous religions. This verse does not imply at all that the *Christianity* introduced by *Jesus* is false or the origins of *Christianity* are based on the assertions made by the other religions before them.

This verse only denotes to the beliefs of *Christians* around the time of the revelation of the *Qur'an* which was about 610C.E. were not based on the teachings of *Jesus,* but rather the teachings of either *St. Paul* or the product of *Nicene Creed.* These beliefs were held around 325C.E. and might be the innovations of scribes who came many years later. Let us look at the history pages to see how far we can substantiate the claim of the *Qur'an.* The *New Testament* articulates:

> *"Jesus replied, "The most important commandment is this: `Hear, O Israel! The Lord our God is the one and only Lord"* *(Mark 12:29 NLT).*

The *Jewish Encyclopedia* says about the early *Christians:* "*Ebionites… Judeo-Christians sect in Palestine, fl. 2ⁿᵈ-4ᵗʰ cents. Its members observed the Mosaic Law (e.g. circumcision, Sabbath) but rejected sacrifices; they believed in Jesus as the Messiah, though denying his divinity and opposing Pauline doctrine…"*[79]

The first reference is from the *Bible* and then the second reference from the history of *Christianity* written by the *Jews.* Let us see if the claim of the *Qur'an* can be verified by the scriptures of the religions that existed before *Christianity.* Let us start with *Lord Krishna,* who existed about 2000 years before *Christianity,* and was indeed archetypical of *Christ* like figures:

Similarities between Jesus Christ and Lord Krishna

- ❖ *Christ and Krishna were called both a God and the Son of God*

- ❖ *Both was [were] sent from heaven to earth in the form of a man*

- ❖ *Both were called Savior, and the second person of the Trinity.*

---

[79] Please see, *The New Standard Jewish Encyclopedia,* Fifth Edition, By Doubleday & Company, Inc. Copyright © 1959-1977 by Encyclopedia Publishing Company, LTD. ISBN 0-385-12519-4 pg. #586

❖ *They both had adoptive human fathers, who were carpenters*

❖ *Both men were born of virgins and in a stable*

❖ *A spirit or ghost was their actual father [part of Trinity].*

❖ *Both were visited at birth by wise men and shepherds, guided by a star.*

❖ *Angels in both cases issued a warning that the local dictator planned to kill the baby and had issued a decree for their assassination. The parents fled. Mary and Joseph stayed in Muturea; Krishna's parents stayed in Mathura.*

❖ *Christ's other name was Yashuwa. Krishna's other name was Yeshva.*

❖ *[Christ was also called Iesous (Jesus in Greek)][80]. A title of Krishna was Iesus.*

❖ *Both Yeshua and Krishna withdrew to the wilderness as adults and fasted.*

❖ *Both were god-men: being considered both human and divine.*

❖ *They were both considered omniscient, omnipotent, and omnipresent.*

❖ *Both celebrated a last supper. Both forgave [their] enemies.*

❖ *Both descended into Hell and were resurrected. Many people witnessed their ascensions into heaven.*

❖ *Christ's birthday is celebrated on December 25th. Krishna's birthday is also celebrated on December 25th.*

Author *Kersey Graves* (1813-1883), a *Quaker* from *Indiana*, compared *Jesus Christ's* and *Krishna's* life. He found what he believed were 346 elements in common within *Christian* and *Hindu* writing

---

[80]   Bracketed text added by the Author

Similarities between Jesus & Buddha

❖ *Both Jesus and the Buddha were born of royal blood lines and of ritually pure and chaste women (Mary or Maria and Maya).*

❖ *Both were born of Virgins.*

❖ *Those births were celebrated by celestial beings, and drew wise men from afar to behold both infants and bestow them with precious gifts.*

❖ *Both went to their temples at the age of twelve, where they are said to have astonished all with their wisdom.*

❖ *Both began their ministries at about age 30.*

❖ *Both fasted for forty days in which each was tempted by a devil to abandon the spiritual path for worldly things.*

❖ *Both reportedly walked on water, and each helped a disciple to do so through concentration or faith; and in both cases the disciple started to sink until assisted by the Master.*

❖ *Both reportedly worked miracles of multiplying food, each healed a blind man with moisture from his own body and calmed a dangerous and threatening storm.*

❖ *Both men then took on the role of itinerant spiritual master and teacher, living off the hospitality of the villagers they visited.*

❖ *Both formed a smaller group of close disciples that included an inner circle.*

❖ *Both commanded their disciples to live simply and traveling light to their disciples.*

❖ *Both taught in indirect and sometimes puzzling ways, including parables, metaphors, similes, and other comparisons.*

❖ *Neither attempted to make the spiritual path sound easy: both said that their followers must give up security and worldly things and break family ties.*

❖ *Both commended returning hatred with love, anger with kindness, aggression with non-violence, and stinginess with generosity.*

❖ *Both delivered a memorable sermon from a high place.*

❖ *Both strove to establish a kingdom of heaven on earth.*

❖ *The deaths of both were cosmic events, accompanied by earthquakes. In dying, both reportedly conquered death [or resurrected] thus a symbol of the death of each subsequently took on a positive meaning and became emblematic for the religion that he inspired. Both men were venerated as gods after their deaths.*

Both Jesus & Buddha had parallel titles:

❖ Both were called 'Light.'

❖ Both were called 'Prince.'

❖ Both were called 'King.'

Not only the profile of *Buddha* matches with the profile of *Jesus*, but also the teachings of *Buddha* match with the teachings of *Jesus*. Please read the following:

❖ Both said: *'Love your enemy.'*

❖ Both said: *'Meek shall inherit the earth.'*

❖ Both said: *'If someone slaps you on one cheek: turn another.'*

❖ Both said: *'Provide neither gold, nor silver, nor brass in your purses.'*

❖ Both said: *'Righteousness is a safe treasure, which no one can steel.'*

❖ Both said: *'Do to others, as you wish to be done by them.'*

❖ Both said: *'It easier for a camel to go through the eye of a needle than for a rich man to enter the Kingdom of God.'*

There are so many similar teachings of Buddha, but I chose to present ones which were popular about *Jesus* and *Buddha*.

Similarities between Jesus & Horus

❖ *Both were born of virgins.*

❖ *Both were only begotten sons of the God.*

❖ *Both had mothers with similar names: Jesus: Miriam or Mary; Horus: Isis or Meri.*

❖ *Both were of royal descent.*

❖ *Both were born in a cave. Both births were announced by angels. Both births were witnessed by shepherds.*

❖ *Both births were later witnessed by a group of three: For Jesus; three wise men; For Horus: three solar deities.*

❖ *Both were threatened to be killed by Kings: Jesus was threatened by Herod; Horus was threatened by Herut.*

❖ *There is no information on either man between the ages of ten and thirty.*

❖ *Both men were baptized at the age of thirty.*

❖ *Both were tempted by Satan on high mountains. Both resisted temptation.*

❖ *Both had close band of twelve disciples.*

❖ *Both walked on water, cast out demons, healed the sick, restored sight to the blind.*

❖ *Both stilled the sea by his power. Both raised the dead.*

❖ *Both delivered a sermon on the mountain.*

❖ *Both were crucified and accompanied by thieves. Both crucifixions are doubtful by many.*

❖ *Both descended into Hell; resurrected after three days.*

❖ *Both resurrections were announced by women.*

❖ *Both men's birthdays are celebrated on December 25th.*

Please see the website for the details about similar teachings by both men. (Paraphrased by the author) http://www.religioustolerance.org/chr_jcpa5.htm

Similarities between Jesus & Osiris

❖ *Both were known to their followers as Sons of God, savior of mankind, god made men.*

❖ *Both were born of Virgins.*

❖ *Both were born in caves.*

❖ *Both births were prophesied by stars.*

❖ *Both at a marriage ceremony performed the miracle of converting water into wine.*

❖ *Both had followers who were born-again through baptism in water.*

❖ *Both rode triumphantly into a city on a donkey. Tradition records that the inhabitants waved palm leaves.*

❖ *Both had 12 disciples.*

❖ *Both died as a sacrifice for the sins of the world.*

❖ *Both were hung on a tree, stake, or cross.*

❖ *Both after the death, descended into hell.*

❖ *Both returned to life, on the third day after their death.*

❖ *Both were visited by three of their female followers to the cave where they were laid.*

❖ *Both ascended to heaven after resurrection.*

<u>*Commonly known Titles for both men:*</u>

❖ *God made flesh.*

6. Why Jesus was considered god?

❖ *Savior of the world.*

❖ *Son of God.*

Commonly known beliefs for both men:

❖ *"God made man" and equal to the Father.*

❖ *They will return in the last days.*

(Please see *The Jesus Mysteries, by Timothy Freke and Peter Gandy,* pages #60-61, Published by *Harmony Books* New York, ISBN# 0-609-60581-X) Paraphrased by the Author

Similarities between Jesus & Dionysus

❖ *Both were known to their followers as Sons of God, savior of mankind, god made men.*

❖ *Both were born of Virgins.*

❖ *Both were born in caves.*

❖ *Both births were prophesied by stars.*

❖ *Both at a marriage ceremony performed the miracle of converting water into wine.*

❖ *Both had followers who were born-again through baptism in water.*

❖ *Both rode triumphantly into a city on a donkey. Tradition records that the inhabitants waved palm leaves.*

❖ *Both had 12 disciples.*

❖ *Both died as a sacrifice for the sins of the world.*

❖ *Both were hung on a tree, stake, or cross.*

❖ *Both after the death, descended into hell.*

❖ *Both returned to life, on the third day after their death.*

❖ *Both were visited by three of their female followers to the cave where they were laid.*

❖ *Both ascended to heaven after resurrection.*

<u>*Commonly known Titles for both men:*</u>

❖ God made flesh.

❖ Savior of the world.

❖ Son of God.

<u>*Commonly known beliefs for both men:*</u>

❖ *"God made man,"* and equal to the Father.

❖ They will return in the last days.

(Please see *The Jesus Mysteries, by Timothy Freke and Peter Gandy,* Published by Harmony Books New York, ISBN# 0-609-60581-X) Paraphrased by the Author

Similarities between Jesus & Apollonius of Tyana

❖ *Both were known to their followers as God, savior of mankind, god made men.*

❖ *Both births were announced by angels.*

❖ *Both were born of virgins.*

❖ *Both started their ministry at the age of 30.*

❖ *Both performed miracles.*

❖ *Both healed the sick and raised the dead.*

❖ *Both preached the message of peace and love.*

❖ *Both ascended up to heaven.*

Similarities between Jesus & Attis of Phrygia

❖ *Both were the Divine Son and the Father.*

❖ *Both men's birthdays are celebrated on December 25. (Though, evidently, both were not originally born on December 25th.)*

❖ *Both were born of the Virgins.*

❖ *Both were considered the saviors*

❖ *Both were slain for the salvation of mankind.*

❖ *Both men's bodies were eaten by their worshippers as the bread (bread and wine of Christianity).*

❖ *Both were crucified on Friday, on a tree, from which his holy blood ran down to redeem the earth.*

❖ *Both descended into the underworld [Hell].*

❖ *Both were resurrected three days later, on March 25 (as tradition held of Jesus) as the "Most High God."*

In fact, there are almost a dozen people who have similar profiles as *Jesus* does. After reading all of the above references, is it not evident that the testimony of the *Qur'an* is true when it says:

> *"Such are the sayings [of Christians] which they utter with their mouths, following in spirit assertions made in earlier times by people who denied the truth..."? (Al-Taubah 9:29-30).*

7. Crucifixion cross examined by Four Gospels

Let us compare the incident of crucifixion depicted by each of the four *Gospels*:

1. What were the last words of Jesus on the cross?			
By Gospel of Matthew	By Gospel of Mark	By Gospel of Luke	By Gospel of John
"My God, My God, Why have you forsaken me?" Jesus, when he had cried again with a loud voice, yielded up the ghost *(Matthew 27:46)*	*"My God, My God, Why have you forsaken me?" ...and Jesus cried with a loud voice, and gave up the ghost* *(Mark 15:34)*	*"Father, into thy hands I commend my Spirit" and having said thus, he gave up the ghost* *(Luke 23:46)*	***"It is finished"*** *he [Jesus] bowed his head and gave up the ghost* *(John 19:30)*

2. What was the last commandment of Jesus for his disciples?			
By Gospel of Matthew	By Gospel of Mark	By Gospel of Luke	By Gospel of John
"Go ye therefore, and teach all nations, baptizing them in the name of the Father, and of the Son, and of the Holy Ghost" (Matthew 28:19)	"Go ye into all the world, and preach the gospel to every creature" (but this verse is not found in older Bibles and specially two most reliable manuscripts such as Codex Sinaiticus & Codex Vaticanous) (Mark 16:15)	"And now I will send the Holy Spirit, just as my Father promised. **But stay here in the city** until the Holy Spirit comes and fills you with power from heaven." (Gospel of Luke says totally opposite to what Matthew & Mark had said). It says very clearly, "**stay in Jerusalem**") (Luke 24:49)	"If I will that **he tarry till I come**, what is that to thee? follow thou me" (John 21:23)
What did Jesus really say 'go to all nations' or 'to stay here in Jerusalem and wait'?			

3. Where did Jesus go after his last commandment?			
By Gospel of Matthew	By Gospel of Mark	By Gospel of Luke	By Gospel of John
(not mentioned in Matthew)	"...he was received up into heaven" (this verse is not found in most Older Bibles) (Mark 16:19)	"...and carried up into heaven" (this verse is not found in most, Old Bibles) (Luke 24:51)	(not mentioned in John)

4. Where did Jesus meet his disciples the last time?			
By Gospel of Matthew	By Gospel of Mark	By Gospel of Luke	By Gospel of John
*"Then the eleven disciples went away into **Galilee**, into a mountain where Jesus had appointed them"* *(Matthew 28:16)*	*"But go your way, tell his disciples and Peter that he goeth before you into **Galilee**: there shall ye see him..."* *(Mark 16:7)*	*"And he lead them out as far as to **Bethany**, and he lifted up his hands, and blessed them ... and carried up into heaven"* *(Luke 24:50-51)*	*"After these things Jesus shewed himself again to the disciples at the sea of **Tiberias**..."* *(John 21:1)*

5. What did the centurion say when he saw Jesus give up the Ghost?			
By Gospel of Matthew	By Gospel of Mark	By Gospel of Luke	By Gospel of John
"Truly this was the Son of God" *(Matthew 27:54)*	*"Truly this man was the Son of God"* *(Mark 15:39)*	*"Certainly this was a righteous man"* *(Luke 23:47)*	(not mentioned in John)

6. Who came first to the sepulcher, and when?			
By Gospel of Matthew	By Gospel of Mark	By Gospel of Luke	By Gospel of John
"In the end of the Sabbath, as it began to dawn toward the first day of the week, came Mary Magdalene and the other Mary to see the sepulchre" *(Matthew 28:1)*	*"And when the Sabbath was past, Mary Magdalene and Mary the mother of James and Salome... very early in the morning the first day of the week... at the rising of the sun"* *(Mark 16:1-2)*	*"Now upon the first day of the week, very early in the morning... It was Mary Magdalene, and Joanna and Mary the mother of James, and other women..."* *(Luke 24:1 & 10)*	*"The first day of the week cometh Mary Magdalene early, when it was yet dark"* *(John 20:1)*

7. How many angels, and where did they sit or stand?			
By Gospel of Matthew	By Gospel of Mark	By Gospel of Luke	By Gospel of John
"And, behold, there was a great earthquake: for the angel of the Lord descended from heaven, and came and rolled back the stone from the door, and sat upon it" *(Matthew 28:2)*	*"And entering into the sepulchre, they saw a young man [a man, not an angel] sitting on the right side, [inside the tomb, not outside] clothed in a long white garment..."* *(Mark 16:5)*	*"...behold, two men stood by them in shining garments"* *(Luke 24:4)*	*"...she stooped down, and looked into the sepulchre, And seeth two angels in white sitting, the one at the head, and the other at the feet, where the body of Jesus had lain"* *(John 20:11-12)*

8. Who delivered the message of Jesus?			
By Gospel of Matthew	By Gospel of Mark	By Gospel of Luke	By Gospel of John
An angel told women: *"Go quickly, and tell his disciples that he is risen from the dead"* *(Matthew 28:7)*	A young man told them *"he is risen... But go your way, tell his disciples..."* *(Mark 16:6-7)*	*Luke* does not tell us if two angels gave them any message for disciples.	*John* says Jesus himself gave *Mary Magdalene* the message for disciples. *(John 20:17)*

9. Where did Jesus meet his disciples first?			
By Gospel of Matthew	By Gospel of Mark	By Gospel of Luke	By Gospel of John
*"Then the eleven disciples went away into **Galilee**, into a mountain where Jesus had appointed them"* *(Matthew 28:16)*	(No city is not mentioned in *Mark*)	*Luke* says Jesus first appeared to eleven in ***Jerusalem***. *(Luke 24:33-44)*	(No city is mentioned in *John*)

10. What was written on the cross?			
By Gospel of Matthew	By Gospel of Mark	By Gospel of Luke	By Gospel of John
"THIS IS JESUS THE KING OF THE JEWS" *(Matthew 27:37)*	*"THE KING OF THE JEWS"* *(Mark 15:26)*	*"THIS IS THE KING OF THE JEWS"* *(Luke 23:38)*	*"JESUS OF NAZARETH THE KING OF THE JEWS"* *(John 19:19)*

I am not trying to imply here that *Jesus* was a false *Messiah* or the *Bible* is not the book of *God*. The only thing I am trying to establish here is the fact that none of the four *Gospel* writers were the disciples of *Jesus*. The first *Gospel*, the *Gospel* according to *Matthew*, says:

> *"And as Jesus passed forth from thence, he saw a man, named Matthew, sitting at the receipt of custom: and he saith unto him, Follow me. And he arose, and followed him."*[81]

If *Matthew* was talking about himself then why he did not explicitly say that *Jesus* saw me and asked me to follow him? We read in *Matthew* 10:2-4 and Luke 6:13-16 the list of the twelve disciples of *Jesus, Mark* and *Luke* are not even mentioned in that list. Please see it for yourself and match it with your own *Bible*. I am not writing this to allege false accusations against *Christianity*. The only reason I am mentioning this is to indicate the misconceptions of *Christianity*. These misconceptions occur in every religion. It does not necessarily mean that the religion under discussion is a false religion; it only means that over a period of time people usually construe in a way which was not meant initially.

List of Disciples	List of Disciples
According to Matthew	According to Luke
1. Simon, who is called Peter	1. Simon, (whom he also named Peter,)
2. Andrew his brother	2. Andrew his brother
3. James the son of Zebedee	3. James
4. John his brother	4. John
5. Philip	5. Philip
6. Bartholomew	6. Bartholomew
7. Thomas	7. Matthew
8. Matthew the publican	8. Thomas
9. James the son of Alphaeus	9. James the son of Alphaeus
10. Lebbaeus, whose surname was Thaddaeus	10. Simon called Zelotes
11. Simon the Canaanite	11. Judas the brother of James
12. Judas Iscariot	12. Judas Iscariot

---

[81] Please see *Matthew 9:9*

If you notice above, some of the names of the disciples do not even match in these two *Gospels*. *Luke* says in his own *Gospel*:

> *"Even as they delivered them unto us, which from the beginning were eyewitnesses, and ministers of the word."*[82]

This verse tells us in lucid words that *Luke* heard from people and he himself was not the disciple of *Jesus*. According to *Paula Fredriksen*, Professor of Scripture, *Boston University*:

> *"Originally all these Gospels circulated anonymously, there were no names attached to them until almost 200 [years]. And the Christian theologian who came up with the idea having a New Testament was roundly condemned as a heretic."*[83]

She also said in another documentary:

> *"they [Gospel writers] can't be writing history the way we would expect history to be written by a modern author. They are doing something else, and what is intriguing and difficult about what they produce is that it contains a mix of both fiction and fact."*[84]

The reason for writing different accounts out of the documentaries is that I am trying to enlighten my readers to see that almost 80% of the concepts I have mentioned in my book have already been talked about on *History, Discovery,* and *National Geographic* Channels. These channels are discussing these issues over and over. But most people do not pay attention to them. But when we draw attention to our *Christian* brothers to enlighten them, they get very upset and say, "what do you know about our history or The *Bible*?" But as I have mentioned, these issues have been discussed almost daily by your own scholars on your own national TV channels. These are not accusations raised by us; yes, it is true that these issues were introduced by *Ahmad* the first time about 120 years ago. But the *Christians* used to express their amusement about these issues at that time. *Ahmad* had prophesied that there will be a time when many honest *Christian* scholars would confer these issues candidly. Now you can see and hear with your own eyes and ears on your own radio and national *Television* channels these issues discussed almost every day.

---

[82]   Please see *Luke 1:2*
[83]   Please see documentary *Did Jesus die?* By BBC FOUR London
[84]   Please see *National Geographic* documentary, *Tomb of Jesus*

Even if we presume for a moment that they were the disciples of *Jesus*, then according to their own testimony they all fled to save their own lives. Thus the *Bible* says: *"Then all the disciples forsook him, and fled."*[85] None of the *Gospel* writers were present at the time of crucifixion. None of them was an eyewitness to the crucifixion of *Jesus*. According to the *National Geographic* documentary titled *Tomb of Jesus:*

> *"The Gospels are not eye witness accounts, they were written some 40 years after Jesus' death and it is important to remember they were written to glorify his life not simply record it."*

As I have presented above, all four *Gospel* writers were reporting different accounts, and, many times, were even contradictory to each other. It is plausible that the *Gospel* writers heard from the people who were not sure about what happened, either. Especially when the *Bible* says it was dark and no one could see anything clearly. The *Bible* says: *"And when the sixth hour was come, there was darkness over the whole land until the ninth hour"* (Mark 15:33). How could anyone see a ghost leaving a body anyway? What happened to *Jesus* after he rose from the dead? The *Bible* says he went to heaven. Let us see if the *Bible* actually says that.

---

[85] Please see *Matthew 26:56 & Mark 14:50*

73

8. Jesus went to Heaven

According to the *Gospel* of *Mark Jesus went to heaven [bodily]*,[86] *and sat at the right hand of God. Luke* also says *"Jesus went to heaven [bodily]."*[87] These are the only two verses in only two out of four *Gospels* which say that. If it was such a magnificent moment in the history of *Christianity*, would not the other two *Gospels* have revealed it also? Not only that, but this glorious moment is not recorded in any history book of that time. The book of *Acts* says something similar:

> *"And when he had spoken these things, while they beheld, he was taken up; and a cloud received him out of their sight."*[88]

It sounds like *Jesus* went somewhere, but consider this verse in a real life context. A man asks you to meet him on a mountain and for a little while he converses with you. Then after he is done talking with you he starts ascending on the mountain. The clouds are low and he disappears in the clouds. Would it not seem like he is being received by the clouds? But does this mean that he went to heaven with his body? Can clouds lift up a man? Clouds are no more than a mere moisture we all know that. Since *Christians* have been reading this all their lives, they presume that it has been in the *Bible* since the day the *Bible* was written. If this is true, then *Jesus* has been alive for over *2000* years. This concept is absolutely inconsistent with what is written in the *Old Testament*. The book of *Genesis* says:

---

86   Please see *Mark 16:19*
87   Please see *Luke 24:51*
88   Please see *Acts 1:9*

"And the LORD said, My spirit shall not always strive with man, for that he also [is] flesh: yet his days shall be an hundred and twenty years" (Genesis 6:3).

I started to think why is this major difference in the two books from the same *God*? I am talking about the *New* and the *Old Testaments* of the *Bible*. According to my research, almost every *Bible* in the country which contains footnotes about *Mark 16:9-20* refers to the passage as being doubtful or not being found in the ancient manuscripts. The *Bibles* that do not contain any footnotes at all do not say anything about *Mark 16: 9-20*. Not all the *Bibles* contain the verse of *Luke 24:51* that *"Jesus went to heaven."* The *Bibles* which do not have footnotes still put *Mark 16:9-20* in double brackets. Some explain the reason in the *"Preface"* that *the verses in the double brackets are doubtful.* Some put double brackets on these verses, and do not mention anything at all.

Not all *Bibles* have 12 verses of *John 7:53 to 8:11* either. These *Bibles* include one by *Zondervan*, which is the world's largest *Bible Publishing Company*. It is the number one publishing brand of the CBA (*Christian Booksellers Association*) *Bible* market, capturing nearly forty six percent of the *Bible* market. It has held numerous top ten positions on the *CBA* best selling lists since *1995* (According to *Book Industry Trends 2001*). In addition, *Oxford University Press, Thomas Nelson, Harper Collins, Catholic Bible Press, Tyndale House Publishers, Inc., World Bible Publishing Inc.,* and *The New Jerusalem Bible,* write analogous notes for these twelve verses of *Mark*, twelve verses of *John, Luke* 24:51, and twenty other verses of the *New Testament.*

| 1. **American Bible Society** (RSV)

Division of Christian Education of the National Council of the Churches of the Christ in the United States of America.

TRANSLATED FROM THE ORIGINAL TONGUES, BEING THE VERSION SET FORTH. 1611, REVISED A.D. 1881-1885 AND A.D. 1901, COMPARED WITH THE MOST ANCIENT AUTHORITIES AND REVISED A.D. 1952 | All *Bibles* published by *American Bible Society* (A.B.S) until 1970 do not have *Mark 16:9-20* at all.

These *A.B.S. Bibles* do not have verse *24:51of Luke*: *"Jesus went to heaven."*

They also do not have 12 verses of *John 7:53 to 8:11*. These *A.B.S. Bibles* also do not have 20 Verses that are found in *New Bibles*. These 20 verses are as follows: Matthew 12:47, Matthew 17:21, Matthew 18:11, Matthew 21:44, Matthew 23:14, Mark 7:16, Mark 9:44, Mark 9:46, Mark 11:26, Mark 15:28, Luke 17:36, Luke 22:20, Luke 23:17, Luke 24:12, Luke 24:40, John 5:4, Acts 8:37, Acts 24:7, Acts 28:29 and Romans 16:24. These Bibles also do not have the famous verse of *Luke 22:20*, either: *"This cup which is poured out for you is the new covenant in my blood"*. |
| 2. **Oxford University Press Inc.**

Revised Standard Version

Copyright ©1962 | All *Bibles* published by *Oxford* until 1970 do not have *Mark 16:9-20* at all. These *Oxford Bibles* do not have verse 24:51 of *Luke* either.

They also do not have 12 verses of *John 7:53 to 8:11*. These *Oxford Bibles* also do not have 20 Verses that are found in *New Bibles*. These 20 verses are as follows: Matthew 12:47, Matthew 17:21, Matthew 18:11, Matthew 21:44, Matthew 23:14, Mark 7:16, Mark 9:44, Mark 9:46, Mark 11:26, Mark 15:28, Luke 17:36, Luke 22:20, Luke 23:17, Luke 24:12, Luke 24:40, John 5:4, Acts 8:37, Acts 24:7, Acts 28:29 and Romans 16:24. These Bibles also do not have the famous verse of *Luke 22:20* |

3. ***Thomas Nelson & Sons Inc.*** Revised Standard Version (RSV) (New York) Copyright© 1946	All *Bibles* published by *Thomas Nelson & Sons* until *1970* do not have *Mark 16:9-20* at all. These *Thomas Nelson Bibles* do not have verse 24:51 of *Luke* either. They also do not have 12 verses of *John 7:53 to 8:11.* These *Thomas Nelson Bibles* also, do not have 20 Verses that are found in *New Bibles.* These 20 verses are as follows: Matthew 12:47, Matthew 17:21, Matthew 18:11, Matthew 21:44, Matthew 23:14, Mark 7:16, Mark 9:44, Mark 9:46, Mark 11:26, Mark 15:28, Luke 17:36, Luke 22:20, Luke 23:17, Luke 24:12, Luke 24:40, John 5:4, Acts 8:37, Acts 24:7, Acts 28:29 and Romans 16:24. These Bibles also, do not have the Luke 22:20
4. ***Zondervan** / Harper & Row* (Now known as Harper Collins). Revised Standard Version New York, N.Y. Copyright ©1952	All *Bibles* published by *Zondervan* until *1970* Do not have *Mark 16:9-20.* These *Zondervan* Bibles do not have verse 24:51 of *Luke.* They also do not have 12 verses of John 7:53 to 8:11. These *Zondervan Bibles* also, do not have 20 Verses that are found in *New Bibles.* These 20 verses are as follows: Matthew 12:47, Matthew 17:21, Matthew 18:11, Matthew 21:44, Matthew 23:14, Mark 7:16, Mark 9:44, Mark 9:46, Mark 11:26, Mark 15:28, Luke 17:36, Luke 22:20, Luke 23:17, Luke 24:12, Luke 24:40, John 5:4, Acts 8:37, Acts 24:7, Acts 28:29 and Romans 16:24. These Bibles do not have *Luke 22:20.*

5. The Mac Arthur Study Bible *New **King James Version*** Published by Word Bibles Copyright 1997 ISBN# 0-8499-1222-9	It mentions *Mark 16:9-20* in a footnote: *"The external evidence strongly suggests these verses were not originally part of Mark's Gospel. While the majority of Gr. manuscripts contain these verses, the earliest and most reliable do not."* *John 7:53-8:11 is mentioned* in a footnote: *7:53-8:11 are bracketed by NU-Text as not original.*
6. ***The New Jerusalem Bible*** (Saints Devotional Edition) Published by Doubleday (A division of Random House Inc.) New York, N.Y. Copyright 2002 1ˢᵗ Edition ISBN# 0-385-50066-1	*Mark 16:9-20* is mentioned in a footnote: *"Originally Mark probably ended abruptly on this note of awe and wonder. The next 12 verses, missing in some MSS, are a summary of material gathered from other N.T writings."* *John 7:53- 8:11* is mentioned in a footnote: *Many ancient MSS omit 7:53-8:11.*

This is a clear sign and support of *God* with *Ahmad* (*The Second Coming of Jesus Christ*). *God* promised *Ahmad* that He (God) would send signs after signs from heaven to prove that *Ahmad* is a true messenger of *God*, until the whole world would believe him as a true messenger, and the *Second Coming of Jesus Christ*. *Ahmad* proclaimed that *God* revealed to him that *Jesus* was not the son of *God*, he did not die on the cross, and he did not go up to heaven bodily. Further elaborating on this subject, *Ahmad* said since *Jesus* did not go to heaven bodily, he is not coming back from heaven, bodily, either. All those who are alive (Ahmad said this about 120 years ago) will die but they will never see *Jesus* coming down from heaven. Generations after generations will pass but no one will see *Jesus* coming down from heaven. Now with the blessing of *God* it has become apparent from the *Bible* that the original text of the *New Testament* never mentioned anything about *Jesus'* bodily ascension to heaven.

Now *Christians* are very upset at *Ahmad* when he articulated that *"Jesus never went to heaven according to your own Bible*, and he is not coming back, either." *Ahmad* said: *"I am the Second Coming of Jesus Christ."* Now the question is where did *Jesus* go after crucifixion? If he did not go to the heavens (bodily) then where did he go? There are two probable explanations that came to light about the verse *'Jesus went to heaven.'* The question is what was heaven considered to be in the time of *Jesus*? According to the *Dead Sea Scrolls*, in the time of *Jesus* earth was divided into three parts. The 1ˢᵗ part was flat earth for the ordinary people. The 2ⁿᵈ part was hills for the priests and the 3ʳᵈ part was high mountains for the high priests. This 3ʳᵈ part was also called heaven. Therefore, according to this terminology, *Jesus* went to heaven to live in the high priests' area. The second reason it says in the *Bible* that *'Jesus went to heaven'* is because when *Jesus* went to live in *Kashmir, India*, that area was considered heaven on earth because of its beautiful snow covered mountains and abundance of natural resources.

But why *India*? Why not someplace else? Because, *Kashmir, India* is the *"Promised Land"* mentioned in the *Bible* for thousands of years. Almost all major *Biblical* prophets went and lived there in different eras. The *Christians* of the time of *Ahmad* contended that *India* is thousands of miles away from *Jerusalem*. How could *Jesus* have travelled so far? *Ahmad* replied to them in one of his books and asked them: which is farther, *India* or heaven? He further said that the *Christians* believe that *Jesus* went to heaven in his mortal body, and that to them was logical, but to travel to *India*, only a few thousand miles away, is impossible? Recently, a documentary titled *'Jesus in India,'* narrated by *Mr. Edward T. Martin*, appeared on *the Sundance Channel*. Mr. *Martin* says that *India* is about *4000* miles from *Jerusalem* to *Srinagar*. The ancient route (the Silk Route), could be covered in one year walking about 10 miles a day.[89] Apart from this, it is an established fact that *St. Thomas* traveled to *India* and founded a church there. If this is not true that he went to *India* and died there then why did Pope *John Paul II*, in his visit to *India*, on February 5ᵗʰ *1986* visited the tomb of *St. Thomas* and offered prayer there? The question is if *St. Thomas* could go to *India* then why *Jesus* could not go there? Let's read the following chapter for further detail.

---

[89] Excerpts from *'Jesus in India,'* a documentary by *Paul Davids*, paraphrased

8. Jesus went to Heaven

who was crucified. He has risen, he is not here; see the place where they laid him. ⁷ But go, tell his disciples and Peter that he is going before you to Galilee; there you will see him, as he told you." ⁸And they went out and fled from the tomb; for trembling and astonishment had come upon them; and they said nothing to any one, for they were afraid.ᵏ

Please see in this Bible, Mark Ch. 16 ends at Verse No. 8 (RSV Bible © 1946)

THE GOSPEL ACCORDING TO

LUKE

1 Inasmuch as many have undertaken to compile a narrative of the things which have been accomplished among us, ² just as they were delivered to us by those who from the beginning were eyewitnesses and ministers of the word, ³ it seemed good to me also, having followed all things closelyᵃ for some time past, to write an orderly account for you, most excellent Thē·oph'i·lŭs, ⁴ that you may know the truth concerning the things of which you have been informed.

5 In the days of Her'ŏd, king of Judea, there was a priest named Zech·a·rī'ăh,ᵇ of the division of A·bī'jăh; and he had a wife of the daughters of Aaron, and her name was Elizabeth. ⁶And they were both righteous before God, walking in all the commandments and ordinances of the Lord blameless.

⁷ But they had no child, because Elizabeth was barren, and both were advanced in years.

8 Now while he was serving as priest before God when his division was on duty, ⁹ according to the custom of the priesthood, it fell to him by lot to enter the temple of the Lord and burn incense. ¹⁰And the whole multitude of the people were praying outside at the hour of incense. ¹¹And there appeared to him an angel of the Lord standing on the right side of the altar of incense. ¹²And Zech·a·rī'ăh was troubled when he saw him, and fear fell upon him. ¹³ But the angel said to him, "Do not be afraid, Zech·a·rī'ăh, for your prayer is heard, and your wife Elizabeth will bear you a son, and you shall call his name John. ¹⁴ And you will have joy and gladness, and many will rejoice at his birth; ¹⁵ for he will be great before the Lord,

ᵏ Other texts and versions add as 16.9-20 the following passage:
⁹ *Now when he rose early on the first day of the week, he appeared first to Mary Magdalene, from whom he had cast out seven demons.* ¹⁰ *She went and told those who had been with him, as they mourned and wept.* ¹¹ *But when they heard that he was alive and had been seen by her, they would not believe it.*
¹² *After this he appeared in another form to two of them, as they were walking into the country.* ¹³ *And they went back and told the rest, but they did not believe them.*
¹⁴ *Afterward he appeared to the eleven themselves as they sat at table; and he upbraided them for their unbelief and hardness of heart, because they had not believed those who saw him after he had risen.* ¹⁵ *And he said to them, "Go into all the world and preach the gospel to the whole creation.* ¹⁶ *He who believes and is baptized will be saved; but he who does not believe will be condemned.* ¹⁷ *And these signs will accompany those who believe: in my name they will cast out demons; they will speak in new tongues;* ¹⁸ *they will pick up serpents, and if they drink any deadly thing, it will not hurt them; they will lay their hands on the sick, and they will recover."*
¹⁹ *So then the Lord Jesus, after he had spoken to them, was taken up into heaven, and sat down at the right hand of God.* ²⁰ *And they went forth and preached everywhere, while the Lord worked with them and confirmed the message by the signs that attended it. Amen.*
Other ancient authorities add after verse 8 the following: *But they reported briefly to Peter and those with him all that they had been told. And after this, Jesus himself sent out by means of them, from east to west, the sacred and imperishable proclamation of eternal salvation.*
ᵃ Or *accurately*   ᵇ Greek *Zacharias*
16.7: Mk 14.28; Jn 21.1-23; Mt 28.7.   1.2: 1 Jn 1.1; Acts 1.21; Heb 2.3.   1.3: Acts 1.1.
1.4: Jn 20.31.   1.5: Mt 2.1; 1 Chron 24.10; 2 Chron 31.2.
1.9: Ex 30.7.   1.11: Lk 2.9; Acts 5.19.
1.13: Lk 1.30, 60.   1.15: Num 6.3; Lk 7.33.

This is a real picture of a 50 years old Bible, which ends at verse 8 in Mark chapter 16

9. Kashmir the "Promised Land"

In the *Old Testament, Kashmir* is often referred to as '*the land of east*' and the inhabitants as '*the children of east*.' *India* is in the eastern part of the world, so therefore, it would not be farfetched to imagine that the *Bible* is talking about *India*. I will try my best to prove from the *Bible* and from the history of *India* that *India* is the *Promised Land* mentioned in the *Bible* and it is not an assumption. Let me present to you with a few *Biblical* references about the *land of east*:

1. *"Then Jacob continued on his journey and came to the land of the eastern peoples" (Genesis 29:1).*

2. *"...Abraham gave gifts, and sent them away from Isaac his son, while he yet lived, eastward unto the east country" (Genesis 25:6).*

3. *"And Solomon's wisdom excelled the wisdom of all the children of the east country, and wisdom of all the Egypt" (1Kings 4:30).*

4. *"Job ...so that this man was the greatest of all the men of the east" (Job 1:3).*

5. *"Behold, therefore I will deliver thee to the men of the east for a possession" (Ezekiel 25:4).*

Not only is the east or land of the east mentioned in the *Bible*, but also the name '*INDIA*' itself is mentioned in the *Bible*. The book of *Esther* mentions *India* in these words:

i) *"Now it came to pass in the days of Ahasuerus, this is Ahasuerus which reigned from **India** even unto Ethiopia over an hundred and seven and twenty provinces" (Esther 1:1).*

ii) *"Then were the king's scribes called at that time...and the deputies and the rulers of the provinces which are from **India** unto Ethiopia..." (Esther 8:9).*

The question arises, was *India* only mentioned in the *Bible* by its name, or there are other cities of *India* mentioned also? The miracle of *God* is that there are thirteen cities which are stated in the *Bible* and most of the cities still have the same names, even after three to four thousand years. According to a modern book,[90] over 320 names of cities, tribes and people in *Hebrew* can be found in *India*, besides these thirteen major names of the cities in *India*.

1. ***Cabul*** [Hebrew כבול present day Kabul] (1Kings 9:13[*mentioned 2 times*]) most of us know that *Kabul* is the *Capital of Afghanistan*. According to the history of *India*, *Afghanistan* used to be a part of *India*.

2. ***Hazeroth*** [Hebrew חצרות present day Hazara] (Numbers 33:17 [*mentioned 6 times*]) used to be in *India* but is now in *Pakistan*, after *India Pakistan* separated in *1947*.

3. ***Kohath*** [Hebrew קהת present day Kohath] (Numbers 3:27 [*mentioned 32 times*]) Major city in *Northern Pakistan*.

4. *Kibro**Thhatta**avah* [Hebrew קברות התאוה present day Thhatta] (Numbers 11:35 (*mentioned 5 times*)) another major city in *Pakistan*. Perhaps people did not like a long name, so they shortened it to *Thhatta*.

5. ***Pashur*** (Hebrew פשחור = Pashchuwr) [present day Peshawar] (Jeremiah 38:1 (*mentioned 14 times*)) Major city of *Pakistan*.

6. ***Chebar*** (Hebrew כבר = Khabour) [present day Khebar, or Khyber a common name in Afghanistan] (Ezekiel 1:3 [*mentioned 8 times*]) also mentioned in the *Bible* as *Habor* (1Chronicles 5:26 [*mentioned 3 times*])

---

[90] Please see *Jesus in Heaven on Earth* by *Khwaja Nazir Ahmad* ISBN: 0913321605

7. ***Ham*** [Hebrew חם present day Ham] 2nd son of Prophet *Noah*. (Psalms 105:27 (*mentioned in the Bible 17 times*)) A city of *India* in *Srinagar, Kashmir*.

8. ***Cherith*** (Hebrew כרית = Kheroth or Herat). (1Kings 17:3(*mentioned 2 times*)) A major city in *Afghanistan*.

9. ***Habor*** [Hebrew חבור present day Bokhara] (2 Kings 17:6 (*mentioned 3 times*)) A major city in *Afghanistan*.

10. ***Halah*** [Hebrew חלח present day Balakh or Balkh] (2Kings 17:6 (*mentioned 3 times*)) A city of *Afghanistan*.

11. ***Tibhath*** [Hebrew טבחת present day Tibet] (1Chronicles 18:8).

12. ***Laadah*** (Hebrew לעדה It could be pronounced as *Ladah* or *Ladakh*, because of the '*kha*' or '*ha*' sound at the end) [present day Ladakh] (1Chronicles 4:21). Just like *Chanukah*, it could be pronounce as *Chanukah, Hanukah* or *Khanukah*. The name of the son of *Shelah* the grandson of *Judah*.

13. ***Lasha or Lasa*** [Hebrew לשע, pronounced as Leh'-Shah] present day Lhasa or Lasa] the capital of *Tibet*. (Genesis 10:19)

When I read the names of these thirteen cities in the *Bible*, I wanted to find out what *Encyclopedias* of the *Bible* say about them. I was surprised to find that the *Encyclopedias* of the *Bible* do not even mention most of the cities mentioned above (At least these cities are not mentioned in many different One-Volume encyclopedias I looked at). Ironically, out of thirteen names, only one or two names are mentioned in some of the *Encyclopedias* and in front of these names it says *"Unknown location."* Is it really possible that all major *Bible Encyclopedia* publications such as *Oxford University Press*, the *Lions Publication*, the *Eerdmans Publishing Company*, and *The Reader's Digest Association, Inc.*, forgot to mention these cities? They all did not know the location of these names? *Eerdmans*[91] claims that they have mentioned all of the places of the *Bible* from A to Z accurately. These cities do not come between A and Z? It is plausible that these *Encyclopedia* publications knew very well where these cities are, but they do not want to talk about them?

The question is if *Jews* were the only *Chosen People* of *God*, then why were they thrown out of *Israel* seventeen times? Another question is if *Palestine* is the *Promised Land* for the *Jews*, then why they could not live in their *Promised*

Land? After the *Jews*, the *Christians* should be the *"Chosen people of God"* because they accepted the messiah which was rejected by the *Jews*. Then why they could not live in the *Promised Land* which is supposed to be the gift of *God* for accepting his beloved son, as well? The *Christians* lived in the supposed *Promised Land* for barely 300 years out of 2000 years of the history of *Christianity*.

Please contemplate on this point: if the *Muslims* are the followers of a man who according to you is not from *God* (God forbid), then why have the *Muslims* been living in your *Promised Land* longer than the *Jews* and the *Christians* have lived there? The *Muslims* have been living in the *Promised Land* of the *Jews* and the *Christians* for 1,221 years to be exact. According to your *Bible*, only righteous people can live in the *Promised Land*, thus, the *Bible* says:

> "*The righteous shall inherit the land, and dwell therein forever*" *(Psalms 37: 29).*

This verse of *Psalms* was confirmed by the *Qur'an* in these words:

> "*And already have We written in the Book of David, after the exhortation, that My righteous servants shall inherit the [Promised] land.*"[92]

If the *Muslims* are sinners, infidels and not from *God* then why would *God Almighty* allowed them to live in the land of righteous people for that long? If one may say that, yes, *Christians* lived there for only 300 to 400 years, but when *Jesus* returns we will live there forever. But the intricate problem is according to your own belief; when *Jesus* returns, he will not touch the ground (Rapture), he will meet all of his faithful in mid air and take them back to the heaven and the earth will be completely destroyed. Therefore, when will he have time to live and rule *Israel* forever? I apologize to say this but there is a big inconsistency in this belief.

Similarly, the *Jews* believe that the *Temple Mount* is the place where *God* actually lived. But strangely enough, mortal men evicted their *God* in 74 C.E. The only house of *God* on earth (*Temple Mount*) was utterly destroyed by the *Romans*. If *God* could not protect his own house, then how is he supposed to protect the *Jews?* The *Jews* also believe that the *Ark of the Covenant* was so powerful that it could destroy many armies at once. But when the enemy came to pick up the *Ark of Covenant*, the *Jews* had to hide it somewhere. Why?

---

[92]   Please see Quran Ch. *Al-Anbiya' 21 : 105-106*

Why could not the *Ark of Covenant* protect itself? They hid it so well that for thousands of years they still cannot find it.

The *Christians* believe that wherever *Moses* walked he had a cloud over him to protect him. If this was the case then why did *Moses* have to run away from his country to *Midian,* when *Pharaoh,* a mere man, tried to kill him? The *Bible* says:

> *"Now when Pharaoh heard this thing, he sought to slay Moses. But Moses fled from the face of Pharaoh, and dwelt in the land of Midian..."*[93]

Why that cloud could not protect him and why the non-believers could not see that heavenly sign and accepted him as a special prophet? But the strangest thing of all is the *Christians* believe that *Jesus* is the most special person in the world and he was the son of *God* (God forbid). If this is the case, then why there was no cloud over him to protect him from those who persecuted him so severely? My dear readers, I am not trying to make fun of your beliefs. The only thing I am trying to point out is that these beliefs are man-made beliefs. That is why they are inconsistent and appear to be contradictory, but *God's* words cannot contradict.

---

[93] Please see *Exodus 2:15*

10. Tomb of Moses in India

Where is the tomb of *Moses*? It's an intricate question. This is hard to believe that the *Jews* love Prophet *Moses* more than anything in the world and they would die for him. But at the time of his death--which was the most crucial time of his life, all of his followers left him alone and let him die alone. This is quite unlikely to have happened. This story of *Moses* is similar to the story of *Jesus*. According to my research, towards the end of his life, Prophet *Moses* was also ordered by the king to be killed. Because of this threat, *Moses* had to leave *Israel* in secrecy, but he did not leave alone; he was accompanied by a few of his devout followers. Just like *Jesus*, *Moses* was also afraid of his followers to leak out the news of his escape. Some *Jews* may say that our people in the time of *Moses* were very devout and very trustworthy people they may wonder why do I presume that they were not trustworthy. Let us turn to the *Bible* and see what *Moses* said about his own followers. He said:

> *"For I know thy rebellion, and thy stiff neck: behold, while I am yet alive with you this day, ye have been rebellious against the LORD; and how much more after my death?...For I know that after my death ye will utterly corrupt [yourselves], and turn aside from the way which I have commanded you; and evil will befall you in the latter days; because ye will do evil in the sight of the LORD, to provoke him to anger through the work of your hands."*

Please see also *"They have corrupted themselves, their spot is not the spot of his children: they are a perverse and crooked generation."*[94] Now you may

---

[94]   Please see *Deuteronomy 31:27 & 29 & Chapter 32:5*

understand why *Moses* could not have announced his departure, when he left *Israel* to go to *Kashmir, India.*

Prayer flags at the edge of Moses' grave.
Pictures by Suzanne Olsson

(It is an old Indian custom to put prayer flags on spiritual people's graves. Unfortunately, not much of Moses' grave can be seen.)

The notion that *Moses* travelled to *India* and his tomb is in *Kashmir* might sound like breaking news, but in fact this news is about *345* years old. In *1664*, a *French* Physician name *Francois Bernier* (1625-1668) had an opportunity to be a personal physician of *Mughal Emperor Aurangzeb. Bernier* was asked by *Aurangzeb* to write about *Kashmir*. During his travels in *Kashmir, Dr Bernier* wrote a book, in his book[95] he writes:

> *"There are, however, many signs of Judaism to be found in this country [India]. Their countenance and manner, and that indescribable peculiarity which enables a traveller to distinguish the inhabitants of different nations, all seemed to belong to that ancient people [Jews]. You are not to ascribe what I say to mere fancy, the Jewish appearance of these villagers having been remarked by our Jesuit father, and by several other Europeans, long before I visited Kachemmire.*
>
> *A second sign is the prevalence of the name of Mousa, which means Moses, among the inhabitants of this city, notwithstanding they are all Mahometans.*
>
> *A third is the common tradition that Solomon [King David's son] visited this country, and that it was he who opened a passage for the waters by cutting the mountain of Baramoulay [Baramula].*
>
> *A fourth, the belief that Moses died in the city of Kachemire, and that his tomb is within a league of it. And a fifth may be found in the generally received opinion that the small and extremely ancient edifice seen on one of the high hills was built by Solomon; and it is therefore called the Throne of Solomon to this day."[96]*

Some *Christians* and *Jews* ask that if *Moses'* tomb in *Kashmir* is the real tomb then why is that tomb not tended by *Jews* or *Christians*, but by the *Muslims?* As I have mentioned earlier, *Muhammad* and *Ahmad* are mentioned by *Moses* and *Jesus* so clear that those who got the real message from them embraced *Islam* instantaneously. These *Jewish* and *Christian* cities and holy sites became the property of *Muslims* after they had accepted *Islam*. The *Jews*

---

[95] Please see *Travels in the Mogul Empire* by *Dr. Francois Bernier* 2nd Edition Published by Low Price Publications Delhi, India on page #430, ISBN 978-81-7536-458-5

[96] Please see *Travels in the Mogul Empire,* by *Francois Bernier* on page #430

and the *Christians* can argue and say that the references I have provided are misinterpreted by *Muhammad & Ahmad,* but they cannot deny the history; the areas which once belonged to them (*Palestine* and other holy sites of the *Jews* and the *Christians*) have belonged to *Muslims* for the last thousand years. Did the *Muslims* get these areas by force, as some contend, or did they get these areas just by absorbed into the *Islam*? If these areas were taken by force then why did they not acquire them back when they had regained the power in those areas? And why the majority of people in those areas are still *Muslims,* why they did not renounce *Islam* after gaining power?

Going back to the topic of ascension, people usually send the bodies of their religious leaders to the heaven when they feel that the people who have rejected them could harm their bodies. Anyone can send anyone to heaven, it's easy, just say that my neighbor went to heaven (bodily), my priest went to heaven (bodily) or anybody went to heaven bodily. The *Qur'an* says no one can ever come back. All of those who have been considered to have gone up to heaven, none of them has ever come back. Let me give you few examples to make it easy. According to the various religions, tribes and people, *Enoch, Elijah, Elisha, Lord Krishna, Buddha, Horus, Mithras, Dionysus, Osiris, Apollonius, Jesus, Mary and Baba Nanak,* all have supposedly gone to heaven bodily. But in *6000* years of the history of mankind, no one can deny that none of them has ever come back. Thus the *Qur'an* says:

1. *"But there is a ban on any population which We have destroyed: that they shall not return" (21:95-96 Translation by Yusuf Ali).*

2. *"Until, when death comes to one of them, he says: "O my Lord! send me back to life In order that I may work righteousness in the things I neglected." - "By no means! It is but a word he says."- Before them is a Partition till the Day they are raised up" (Al-Mu'minun 23:99-100 translation by Yusuf Ali).*

3. *"See they not how many generations before them we destroyed? They will not return to them" (Ya-Sin 36:31- 32 Yusuf Ali).*

Even *Jesus* denied of anyone's bodily ascension in these words: *"And no man hath ascended up to heaven, but he that came down from heaven, even the Son of man..."*[97] The perfect example is about *Baba Guru Nanak,* the founder of the *Sikh* religion. When he died, there was a quarrel at his death. The *Muslim* followers said that *Guru Nanak* was a *Muslim* saint and he should be buried. On the other hand, there were some *Hindu* followers who claim that

---

[97] Please see *John 3:13*

Guru Nanak was a *Hindu* saint and he should be cremated. To solve this bitter dispute, a *Muslim* wise man sent *Guru Nanak's* body to a secured place. Then he called the followers of *Baba Nanak* and said why should we decide what to do with the body? Why should we not ask his body what we should do with it? Everybody agreed but when they entered the room where the body was laid, there was nothing there. Then the wise man said I guess *Baba Nanak* neither wanted to be buried nor he wanted to be cremated, so his body went to heaven. Problem solved and everybody went home happily. But in the time of the *Second Coming of Christ* (Ahmad) most famous peoples tombs which were concealed for thousands of years have been discovered. Among those are the tombs of *Jesus, Moses, Aaron, Solomon, Mary mother of Jesus, Mary Magdalene, John the Baptist,* and *Baba Guru Nanak.*

According to my research, *Moses* lived in the *Promised Land* for a long time until he died there. I know some people might say our *Bible* says *Moses* could not enter *Promised Land.* But the problem is that the *Bible* also says many other things which did not turn out the way we construed they would. It does not mean that the *Bible* is wrong; it only means we did not comprehend these things correctly.

There is a *Hadith* by *Prophet Muhammad* which talks about the tomb of *Moses.* It says:

> *"When Moses' death drew nigh he asked God that he should be allowed to go to within a stone's throw from the Promised Land, and there he died." Abu Hurairah,* the reporter of the prophecy, said that the holy prophet added, *"If I were there I would have shown his sepulcher, situated near the roadside, at the foot of a russet hued hillock."*[98]

According to this *Hadith, Moses'* tomb should be a stone's throw away from the *Promised Land* and it should be situated near roadside at a foot of a reddish colored hill. Those who have visited this tomb describe the area in the exact same manner. As we now know that *Kashmir* is the *Promised Land, Hadith* makes this statement more credible.

People are often bewildered between the *'Holy Land'* and the *'Promised Land.'* The *Holy Land* is *"Palestine."* But if the *Promised Land* is equivalent to the *Holy Land,* then why do *Moses* and his followers had to look for it for forty years? *Palestine* is never known in the history as a lost state. Why *Moses* and almost a million people with him were unable to find the *Promised Land*

---

[98]   Please see *Sahih-Ul-Bukhari*, Vol. 2, page #191 *Egypt* 1932

in forty years while according to the *Bible* the route between *Palestine* and the *Egypt* is a very common route and the *Palestinians* used to go to *Egypt* frequently and the *Egyptians* used to go to the *Palestine* prevalently.

Hence the *Bible* says:

1. *"And there was a famine in the land: and Abram went down into* **Egypt** *to sojourn there..." (Genesis 12:10).*

2. *"And Joseph was brought down to* **Egypt**; *and Potiphar, an officer of Pharaoh..." (Genesis 39:1).*

3. *"And Israel dwelt in the land of* **Egypt**, *in the country of Goshen..."* *(Genesis 47:27).*

4. *"Now these are the names of the children of Israel, which came into* **Egypt**; *every man and his household came with Jacob...." (Exodus 1:1).*

5. *"And Joseph's ten brethren went down to* **buy corn in Egypt**" *(Genesis 42:3).* Please contemplate on this point that *Joseph's* brothers went to *Egypt* just to buy corn. This shows quite clearly that in those days traveling to *Egypt* from *Palestine* or returning from *Egypt* back to *Palestine* was so simple and easy that people would travel to *Egypt* just to buy corn?

While the distance between *Palestine* and *Egypt* is only about 250 to 260 miles, why was it a mystery of a lifetime for *Moses* and his followers? This means that if the *Israelites* would have walked only ten miles a day, they would have entered in the supposed *Promised Land* in about twenty-five days. Let us make it easier for the *Israelites*. Let us say, if they would have walked only five miles per day they would have entered the *Promised Land* in about fifty days. If *Palestine* is the *Promised Land*, then why did it take them forty years to find it? In forty years, they would have walked about 72,000 miles if they would have walked only five miles per day. Did you know that to go around the globe is just about 25,000 miles? This means that the *Israelites* would have circled around the globe almost three times in forty years. Not only is the story of the lost *Promised Land* a mystery, but there lies an enormous dilemma.

The scholars of today contend that it is impossible to feed about a million people who left *Egypt* with *Moses*. Thus the *Bible* says:

> *"That night the people of Israel left Rameses and started for Succoth. There were about 600,000 men, plus all the women*

and children. And they were all traveling on foot. Many people who were not Israelites went with them, along with the many flocks and herds.[99]

According to a *Rabbi*,[100] if those *Jews* who were over a million in number had just held hands in straight line they would have entered the *Promised land [if Palestine was the Promised Land]*.

Mr. Holger Kersten, the author of the book *Jesus lived in India*, did profound research on the subject of the *Tomb* of *Moses* in *India*. I am presenting you only a short summary. Please read pages 53 to 55 of his book for the detailed account. [*Bible* talks about *"The Promised Land"* and the death of Prophet *Moses*. The areas mentioned in the *Bible* about the *Promised Land* and the death of *Moses* are located in *Kashmir India*. Which means the tomb of *Moses* should be there also if he had died in that area. The *Bible* says:

> *"Then Moses climbed Mount Nebo from the plains of Moab to the top of Pisgah... Then the Lord said to him [Moses] "This is the land I promised on oath to Abraham, Isaac and Jacob when I said, I will give it to your descendants. I have let you see it with your eyes, but you will not cross over into it." And Moses the servant of the Lord died there in Moab, as the Lord had said. He buried him in Moab, in the valley opposite Beth peor, but to this day no one knows where his grave is"]*[101]

According to *Mr. Kersten*, this seems quite odd that *Moses* wrote about his own tomb, *"to this day no one knows where his grave is."* This verse indicates that the writer of this book *Deuteronomy* was not *Moses*, but someone else. Also it is very hard to believe that nobody would have prepared for his funeral or marked his burial site, even with such fame *Moses* had. On the contrary, in *Kashmir India*, where all these four places are located, there is a tomb which is known to the local people as *"Tomb of Moses."* The people, who are called *Rishis*, have been taking care of this *Holy Tomb* (*Tomb of Moses*) have never left its site. This makes a lot of sense, and that is what we expect from the followers of *Moses* that they would take good care of the tomb of this great legend, a hero and a *Holy* prophet of *God*, who set them free from the slavery of the barbaric *Pharos*. Beside these four places, *Moab, Mount Nebo, Pisgah* and *Beth peor,* there are three other places that are mentioned in the *Bible* that are also in *India: Abarim, Heshbon,* and *Haran,* the *Bible* says: On that

---

[99]   Please see *Exodus 12:37 & 38 NLT*
[100] I regret that I could not find his website again to present it for reference
[101] Please see *Deuteronomy 34:4 (paraphrased)*

same day the *Lord* told *Moses*, *"Go up into the Abarim Range to Mount Nebo in Moab* (Deuteronomy 32: 48 & 49). Another verse says *"...and were in the valley near Beth peor east of the Jordan, in the land of Sihon king of the Amorites, who reigned in Heshbon* (Deuteronomy 4:46). *Haran* is also mentioned in *Genesis* as the birthplace of Prophet *Abraham*[102] which is also located in the city of *Srinagar,* capital of *Kashmir.*

1. *Moab*----------is mentioned in the Bible 168 times.

2. *Nebo* ------------is mentioned in the Bible 13 times.

3. *Pisgah*------------is mentioned in the Bible 5 times.

4. *Beth peor* --------is mentioned in the Bible 4 times.

5. *Abarim*----------- is mentioned in the Bible 4 times.

6. *Heshbon*--------- is mentioned in the bible 38 times.

7. *Haran* is mentioned in the *Old Testament* 19 times

Same *Haran* is mentioned in the *New Testament* as *Charran* 2 times

*Crossing Jhelum River in the Himalayas at **Beth-Peor**, or **Bandipore**, before entering the forest. (Picture by Suzanne Olsson)*

---
102 Please see *Genesis 11:31*

Temple of Solomon

The *Temple of Solomon* in *Kashmir* was built about *1000 BC*. This is the time when *Solomon* of the *Bible* would have existed. If this temple is that old then it could be the temple the *Jews* have been looking for. I would earnestly urge *Jewish* people to please at least look into it. They might also find in *Kashmir* the *Ark of the Covenant* they have been looking for. The *Temple of Solomon* being in *India* is not a new concept; rather, it is about 344 years old. *Mr. Francois Bernier* visited the *Kashmir* in *1665* and wrote about the *Temple of Solomon*. He says in his book:

> "*A third [evidence] is the common tradition that Solomon [King David's son] visited this country, and that it was he who opened a passage for the waters by cutting the mountain of Baramoulay [Baramula]... And a fifth [evidence] may be found in the generally received opinion that the small and extremely ancient edifice seen on one of the high hills was built by Solomon; and it is therefore called the Throne of Solomon to this day.*"[103]

About Solomon's Temple (by Ms Suzanne Olsson)

"The original temple was built at least 3,000 years ago facing east and was called by several ancient names, including Jayeshthegvara [Sanskrit word for Zoroastrian]. Historically there has always been close links [a common origin] between Zoroastrianism and Hebrew-ism, which is why the original temple name was 'Solomon.' Solomon and Hiram Abiff came here every three years to maintain this temple. The Rajatarangini tells how the Hebrews guarded their borders carefully, protecting the Kashmir Valley for thousands of years. It was in 1848 that the name was changed by Hindus to Shankacharaya Hill, in an effort to reclaim the 4 aspects of the 'old' Hinduism from India. No credit is given to the temple's ancient history or builders."

---

[103] Please see Chapter *Tomb of Moses* for further details.

"Solomon's Temple in Kashmir (left) is older than Tomb of Absalom (Son of King David) in Jerusalem (right) although the styles are similar. Picture on left, "wings" similar in design to description of Ark of the Covenant. Could this once have served as a hiding place for the Ark?"[104]

---

[104] Please read the research in *Jesus in Kashmir, The Lost Tomb* by *Ms Suzanne Olsson*, to find out more.

Tombs of the Israeli Prophets

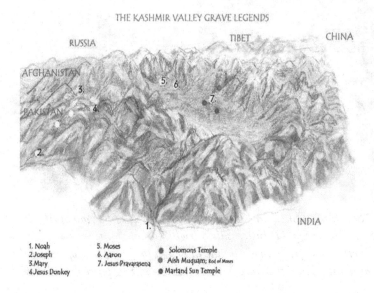

Map: *Tombs of Prophets of Israel in Kashmir, India (by Ms. Suzanne Olsson)*

1) NOAH-MANU:

This grave is located in *Tanda*, a small village a few miles north of *Sialkot*. It is one of a series of Barrow style graves on a hillside, each about 30 feet or 98.4 meters in length (also known as tumulus or kurgan style graves). A local historian, *Mohammed Zaman Khokhar* thoroughly researched these graves for years. He wrote a book in six volumes (published in 2000) *"The Ten Yard Graves of the Beloved of Pakistan."*

2) JOSEPH (Father of Jesus)

In *Pashtun*, the predominant local population and language, *Joseph* becomes *Yusaf,* thus the name *Yuz Asaf*, as 'son of *Joseph'* links *Joseph* the father with *Jesus*, his son buried nearby in *Srinagar*. Several years ago *Pakistan* TV aired a documentary film about this grave. It is alleged to be the grave of *Joseph*, father of *Jesus*. The documentary was made by a local independent film crew based on the legends surrounding this grave. Since then, the film had been forgotten and is now lost. Efforts are underway to relocate the site and include this grave in the project.

3) MARY (Mother of Jesus)

The grave of *Mary* is well known. It has been written about extensively around the world. It is situated on a hilltop in the *Himalayan* Mountains, in an area known as the *Punjab (Rawalpindi)*. The name of the town is now *Murree*. It was originally known as *Mari*, named after *Mary (Hazrat Mariam in the Quran)*. Local residents have always supported efforts to locate this grave and move it to a safer location. The site has been disturbed several times by construction and by bomb attacks against the transmission tower on the hilltop.

Tomb of Mary in the City of Murree or city of Mary,
Pakistan. (Photo by Ms Suzanne Olsson)

5) Aaron (Brother of Moses)

This is a barrow-type grave called a cairn. Built above-ground of rocks, it is situated on the site of the *Fourth Buddhist Council in Harwan, Kashmir*. The name *Harwan* is derived from the name *Aaron* (Aaron-Haroon-Harwan). The area has been set aside and maintained as a historic Park by *India* and the *State of Kashmir*. *Aaron's* grave is located half-way up the hill and the foundations of his home are still visible. An etched stone once marked his grave and identified him, but this has disappeared, probably carted to archives in *New Delhi* for safe keeping. *Aaron* was the ancestor grandfather of *Mother Mary*, and *Jesus* may have inherited this land from his mother and he may have been present as an elderly advisor during the *Fourth Buddhist Council*. Research-author *Aziz Kashmiri* mentioned there is also a grave for *Tanook* (Tanuk), a grandson of *King David*, somewhere in the region.

The site of Aaron's old homestead and grave in Harwan, Kashmir: Buddhist residences from Fourth Buddhist Council are visible ruins beyond. (photo by Suzanne Olsson)

6) Tomb of MOSES:

This grave of *Moses* is also in the *Himalaya* mountains of *Kashmir*, in an area known as *Bandipore*. Some efforts have been made to associate this name with the *Biblical* burial site of *Moses* called *Beth-Peor*. *Beth* (Hebrew: home-place) Peor (Hebrew: opening in the mountains, a pass).

> *"Moses was buried not far from there "in a valley in the land of Moab, opposite Beth Peor, but no one knows his grave to this day"* (Deuteronomy 34:6).

There are perhaps three or four different locations associated with the grave of *Moses*. In the *Himalayan* mountains are two sites associated with *Moses*. The grave located in *Bandipore* is a *kistvaen-type grave* located on a forested

Himalayan mountain just on the border with *Skardu*, (also known as Azad Kashmir, one passes through here following the *Old Silk Road* as it eventually leads to *Kashgar*, and to the grave of *Bibi Injeel*. The description of her grave is in the *China* section below.

Me: wearing black burkha at Moses' grave. It is pure magic up here. As difficult and dangerous a passage this was, I feel privileged to be on this journey. (Suzanne Olsson)

7) JESUS (Yuz Asaf-Issa)

Jesus is believed by many to have survived the crucifixion and later journeyed along the *Old Silk Road*, settling in *Kashmir*, where he died of old age. The reason he chose this location is because his ancestors (including those listed above) had been coming here for generations, and he was following their custom. He came here to die and be buried among them, as his mother had before him.

There are several families which belief that *Yuz Asaf* is their ancestor, and some of these families possess ancient scrolls with their genealogy. *Bashrat Saleem* had given several interviews about his claims before his death, but there was only mild interest in his family scrolls at the time. Now with the great advances made in DNA testing, the *Shaheen* family and others are keen to know who *Yuz Asaf* really was, and if he is indeed their ancestor as they believe. If proven true, then any search for a so-called 'Grail child' may lead to *Kashmir*, and may be full of unexpected surprises.

Yuz Asaf is buried in the *Khanyar* district of *Srinagar*, in a tomb known as *Roza Bal*. The original burial place may be a cave or stone room carved out in the ground, with a simple shelter built over it to hold the false casket that was once full of artifacts associated with *Jesus-Yuz Asaf*. Ever since the site was first recorded in circa 112 AD, it has attracted visitors from around the world who believed since ancient times, even before the advent of *Islam* in the region, that this was the grave of the prince, *Yuz Asaf* (which means *son of Joseph*). It is primarily for the claims of the local families that DNA will be gathered.

An old picture of the tomb of Jesus (photo by JD Shams)

8) BIBI INJEEL:

Bibi Injeel translates to '*the Lady from the Bible*' but no more is known about her. It is probably one of the *Marians*, perhaps *Magdalene*, or *Mary of Bethany*, or *Marjan* (wife of Yuz Asaf) or *Mariamne* who was married to *Moses*. *Bibi Injeel's* grave is above-ground and still visited by locals to this day. *Kashgar* (Kashi) is on the *Old Silk Road* at a major point where north-south-east-west traffic all converges. It was once an important hub of *Buddhism*, and later *Christianity* that spread all across *China* and the world from here. It is located in the region of the *Taklamakan* Desert where many *Tocharian* mummies have been discovered. Looking at the mummies, and at depictions of *Jesus*, one immediately sees a resemblance, which raised the prospect that *Jesus* and his family may be linked to the *Tocharian* mummies. This will be easy to prove because the DNA of *Tocharian* mummies has routinely been gathered for years. It is also possible that *Jesus* will be related to the nearby *Afghan Pashtuns* who have inhabited the area for centuries and claim their ancestry from dispersed *Jewish* tribes, the so-called *"Lost Tribes of Israel."*

[There is another verse in the *Bible* which talks about the same area as the *Promised Land* also. The *Bible* says: *"Then the Lord said to Moses, "Go up this mountain in the Abarim range and see the land I have given the Israelites"*(Numbers 27:12). Another verse talks about the similar promise. It says: *"Not one of you will enter the land I swore with uplifted hand to make your home…"As for your children that you said would be taken as plunder, I will bring them in to enjoy the land you have rejected"* (Numbers 14:30 & 31).][105]

---

[105] Bracketed text is the summery of the book *Jesus lived in India*, by *Holger Kersten* (*paraphrased*)

the leader's portion was kept for
him.
When the heads of the people
assembled,
he carried out the LORD's righteous

Your enemies will cower before you,
and you will trample down their
high places. ª"

The Death of Moses

34 Then Moses climbed Mount
Nebo from the plains of Moab to
the top of Pisgah, across from Jericho.
There the LORD showed him the whole
land—from Gilead to Dan, ²all of Naphtali, the territory of Ephraim and Manasseh, all the land of Judah as far as
the western sea,ᵇ ³the Negev and the
whole region from the Valley of Jericho,
the City of Palms, as far as Zoar. ⁴Then
the LORD said to him, "This is the land I
promised on oath to Abraham, Isaac
and Jacob when I said, 'I will give it to
your descendants.' I have let you see it
with your eyes, but you will not cross
over into it."

⁵And Moses the servant of the LORD
died there in Moab, as the LORD had
said. ⁶He buried himᶜ in Moab, in the
valley opposite Beth Peor, but to this
day no one knows where his grave is.
⁷Moses was a hundred and twenty
years old when he died, yet his eyes
were not weak nor his strength gone.
⁸The Israelites grieved for Moses in the
plains of Moab thirty days, until the
time of weeping and mourning was
over.

⁹Now Joshua son of Nun was filled
with the spiritᵈ of wisdom because Moses had laid his hands on him. So the
Israelites listened to him and did what
the LORD had commanded Moses.

¹⁰Since then, no prophet has risen in
Israel like Moses, whom the LORD knew
face to face, ¹¹who did all those miraculous signs and wonders the LORD sent
him to do in Egypt—to Pharaoh and to
all his officials and to his whole land.
¹²For no one has ever shown the mighty
power or performed the awesome
deeds that Moses did in the sight of all
Israel.

DEUTERONOMY 4:44

Introduction to the Law

⁴⁴This is the law Moses set before the
Israelites. ⁴⁵These are the stipulations,
decrees and laws Moses gave them
when they came out of Egypt ⁴⁶and
were in the valley near Beth Peor east of
the Jordan, in the land of Sihon king of
the Amorites, who reigned in Heshbon
and was defeated by Moses and the Israelites as they came out of Egypt.
⁴⁷They took possession of his land and
the land of Og king of Bashan, the two
Amorite kings east of the Jordan. ⁴⁸This
land extended from Aroer on the rim of
the Arnon Gorge to Mount Siyonᵇ (that
is, Hermon), ⁴⁹and included all the Arabah east of the Jordan, as far as the Sea
of the Arabah,ᶜ below the slopes of Pisgah.

DEUTERONOMY 32:48

Moses to Die on Mount Nebo

⁴⁸On that same day the LORD told Moses, ⁴⁹"Go up into the Abarim Range to
Mount Nebo in Moab, across from Jericho, and view Canaan, the land I am
giving the Israelites as their own possession. ⁵⁰There on the mountain that
you have climbed you will die and be
gathered to your people, just as your
brother Aaron died on Mount Hor and
was gathered to his people. ⁵¹This is
because both of you broke faith with me
in the presence of the Israelites at the
waters of Meribah Kadesh in the Desert
of Zin and because you did not uphold
my holiness among the Israelites.
⁵²Therefore, you will see the land only
from a distance; you will not enter the
land I am giving to the people of Israel."

ª29 Or *will tread upon their bodies*   ᵇ2 That is, the Mediterranean   ᶜ6 Or *He was buried*
ᵈ9 Or *Spirit*

11. Tomb of Jesus

Jesus went to *India* to join the lost sheep of the house of *Israel*. As *Jesus* promised,

> *"I have other sheep also, which are not in this fold. I must lead them as well and they will listen to my call, and there will be one flock and one shepherd" (John 10:16).*

The following page contains the pictures of the two articles which were published in two world famous news agencies, such as *CNN* and *Washington Times*, about the tomb of *Jesus* and *Moses* in *India*.

CNN World News had a head line in its *July 26ᵗʰ 1997 edition*, which says: *"Muslim cleric claims Moses' tomb is in India."* In this article it says that a man watches over a tomb which he believes is the tomb of Prophet *Moses* and he claims that he has been taking care of this tomb since his childhood, a tradition which goes back in his family for generations. *Mr. Bashir A. Reshi* says he never had any suspicion that this tomb belongs to prophet *Moses*. The tomb of *Jesus* is also in *Kashmir* according to a local scholar, *Mr. Aziz Kashmir*. This article quotes *Qur'an Chapter 23; verse 50-51* where it says that *'God gave refuge to Jesus & Mary on a high place having pastures and springs.'* At the end of the article it says according to the *Kashmiri* traditions, *Jesus* came to *Kashmir*, where he married and died at the age of *120.*[106] (Paraphrased by Author)

---

[106] I apologize to my readers that I cannot show you the full article, because of the Copyright by *CNN* and by *Washington Times*

The next article, *Jesus' tomb in Kashmir?* is from *'The Washington Times.'* This article says that *Jews* from *Israel* were flocking to *Kashmir* to see the graves deemed to be those of *Jesus and Moses.* More than 100 *Israelis* came to *Kashmir* after *Israel* inculcates its citizens to depart *India.* Furthermore, it says that *1,623 Jews* from *Israel* spent their holidays in *Kashmir* in the first eight months of *2004.* Over *12,000* visitors have come to *Kashmir* in 2004. The article also says that the *Israeli foreign ministry* made a statement in *2004* requesting all *Israelis* at present *in Kashmir* to leave as soon as possible. (Apparently, these *Jews* could not stay away from their beloved prophet's tomb. (Paraphrased by Author))

11. *Tomb of Jesus*

The edifice which contains the Tomb of Jesus, in Sri Nagar, Kashmir, India

ABOVE: The interior of the Roza Bal, showing the ornate wooden sepulchre which once covered the tomb.

Stone carved foot prints of Jesus depicts the marks of crucifixion (photo by Ms Suzanne Olsson)

The original part of Bhabishya Purana (Hindu Mythological Records) widely believed to have been written at around 115 AD, has also noted the meeting of Yisu Mashi [Jesus Christ] with Emperor Shalibahana, the grandson of Vikramaditya [Bhabishya Purana, Part 1, Chapter 20, p. 416, Shanskriti Sansthan, Barelly, India]. In Verse 21-24 it is stated that this king of India (Shalibahan) had conquered Huna Desha (Western Tibet) and met one hermit in the white robe in the mountains." He is said to have told the king that he was born the son of a virgin, his name is Isamasi [Jesus Christ], and is Prabakta (spokesman) and Son of God. After this meeting, this Hindu king seems to have patronized Jesus and helped him. (Please read the article published in *Nepalnews.com, Sunday Post, Sunday July 7th 2002). The above incident was also quoted by *Jeff Salz* on *Discovery Channel* documentary titled *Jesus in Himalayas*, and by *Edward T. Martin* in his documentary *'Jesus in India,'* on *Sundance Channel.*

Jesus is a true prophet of *God* and a humble *Messiah*, but not *God*, as *God's* final revelation, the holy book *Qur'an* told us one thousand and four hundred years ago. The *Qur'an* says: *"The Messiah, son of Mary, was only a Messenger."*[107] The *Qur'an* also told us over fourteen hundred years ago that *Jesus* did not die on the cross: *"for of a surety they killed him not."*[108] *God* miraculously saved his life and then the *Qur'an* says:

> *"God gave him refuge in a mountainous, peaceful, green valley watered by fresh springs"* (Al-Mu'minun 23:50-51).

According to *Jesus in India* by *Ahmad* (*The Second Coming of Jesus Christ*),

> *"The place where Jesus was crucified was called Golgotha which means, "a place of skull" (Matthew 27:33). This is very strange that, the place where the tomb of Jesus is found is in the city of Sri-nagar, (Capital of Kashmir), which literally means "a place of skull." 'Sri' means 'skull' and 'Nagar' means 'a place.'* Where *Jesus* was crucified the name of the place was a place of skull. After crucifixion *Jesus* traveled over *about 4000* miles, and lived, and died in a place called *'a place of skull.'* Apparently, this name was adopted by early Christians in the memory of the crucifixion of Jesus Christ. In another words, many evidences in *Kashmir* suggests the link of the *Israelites* and *Jesus* in Kashmir."

---

[107]   Please see Qur'an Ch. *Al-Maidah 5: 75-76*
[108]   Please see Qur'an Ch. *Al-Nisa 4:157-158*

Another interesting finding is the *DNA* test results of the *Beni Israel* (*descendants of Israel*). This *DNA* test was done by two *British* scientists, *Tudor Parfitt* and *Niel Bradman*,[109] to test for *Jewish* descent in *Kashmiri* people of *India* and people of *Afghanistan*. The tests came out conclusively that those tested are the descendants of the *Israelites*. These two scientists belong to *The Center for Genetic Anthropology in London*.

The Country *Afghanistan* seems to play a major role in the travel of *Jesus* to *Kashmir*. According to the books *Jesus in India*, by *Ahmad* and *Jesus lived in India*, by *Holger Kersten* it says:

1. *"In A Cyclopedia of Geography, by James Bryce F.G.S. (London, 1856), on page 11, it is stated that the Afghans trace their genealogy to Saul, the Israelite King, and call themselves the descendants of Israel"* (*Jesus In India* page #112).

2. *"In the book History of Afghanistan, by Col. G. B. Malleson, published in (London, 1878), on page #39, it is stated that Abdullah Khan of Herat, the French traveler Ferrier, and Sir William Jones, a recognized orientalist, agree that the Afghan people are descended from the Beni-Israel; they are the descendants of the Ten lost Tribes"* (*Jesus In India*, by *Ahmad* page #112).

3. *"The Lost Tribes" by Dr. George Moore, who found many Hebrew inscriptions on archaeological sites in India. Quite close to Taxila, now in Sirkap, Pakistan, a stone was dug up that bears an inscription in Aramaic, the language that Jesus spoke…"*[110]

Another piece of evidence from the history of *Kashmir* is that *'at the local temple [in Kashmir] called the Temple of Solomon, there used to be an inscription which told of Yuz Asaf's claim made about 50AD to be Jesus, a prophet from Israel."*[111]

---

[109] Please see *Wall Street Journal. May 11th 1998 edition*
[110] Please see *Jesus Lived in India* page #56
[111] Please see *BBC FOUR* documentary titled *'Did Jesus die?'*

12. Adam & Eve

According to Ahmad, *Adam was born in India.*[112] *Mr. Holger Kersten* also wrote a very detailed account on *Adam* in *India. India* was always mentioned in the *Bible*, particularly in *Genesis* to *Esther* in many different ways. According to the *Ahmadiyya* view about *Adam*, that he was not the first man on earth. Rather, he was the first prophet of *God* on earth. The prophets are sent to nations and not to an uninhabited world because the prophets of *God* are guidance for mankind and not just men. When the *Bible* talks about *Noah*, can we construe that *Noah* was the only man on earth at that time? When the *Bible* talks about *Abraham*, was he the only man on earth? But if you insist that the *Bible* says *Adam* and *Eve* were the first human beings on earth, then adherence to this belief would raise a few very serious questions.

a) According to *Genesis 1:1,* *"In the beginning God created the heaven and the earth."* According to the historians, *Adam* and *Eve* lived *6000* years ago. Can we construe from reading *Genesis 1:1* that the heaven was made by *God* only *6000* years ago? Since heaven is the throne of *God*, does it propose that the age of *God* is also *6000* years? The *Bible* says:

   "And he that shall swear by heaven, sweareth by the throne of God, and by him that sitteth thereon" (Matthew 23:22).

   While *Neanderthal* man lived about fifty thousand years ago. Did he live before *God* by almost 44 thousand years? Did *dinosaurs* and other animals live millions of years before *God*? (God forbid)

---

[112]   Please see *Tohfa-e-Gularvia,* published in *1900* by *Ahmad* p. #177

b) According to *Genesis 4:14*, after killing his brother *Abel*, *Cain* told *God*:

> *"I shall be a fugitive and a vagabond in the earth; and it shall come to pass, that every one that findeth me shall slay me."*

But the question is if *Adam* and *Eve* were the only couple on the face of earth and they had only two sons, then from whom *Cain* was running from? And who is *'everyone'*? There was no one according to your belief but three *Adam*, *Eve* and *Cain*, then who was there beside these three to kill *Cain*?

c) According to *Genesis 4:16*,

> *"And Cain went out from the presence of the LORD, and dwelt in the land of Nod, on the east of Eden."*

Who was *Nod*? And where did he and his land come from when *Cain* was the only child of the only couple on the entire face of earth?

d) According to *Genesis 4:17* *"And Cain knew his wife; and she conceived, and bare Enoch..."* The same question arises again where did the wife of *Cain* come from?

The only reason I am mentioning these verses is that the conception of *Adam* and *Eve* being the only two people in the entire world is not supported by the *Bible* itself. Not only that, but this view gives birth to so many wrong perceptions. They are not only disgraceful beliefs but they are also blasphemies against *God*. For instance, if *Adam* and *Eve* were the only couple on the face of earth then their two sons were also the only two male children on earth. How does humanity evolve from two brothers? To justify this, people have come up with another erroneous idea that *Adam* and *Eve* had a daughter also and *Cain* married his sister (God forbid) because he had no choice; there was no other girl available for him. Is *God* so feeble (God forbid) that *He* could create only one couple and two children? After that he ran out of all the resources to create more people. Therefore, he allowed brothers and sisters to get married with each other? But when the people multiplied throughout the world, then *God* thought that now it's forbidden for siblings to get married. Is that the conception of *God* some people have? If *God Almighty* can create a family of four, then why He could not create thousands of people at the same time? Is it not true that in our age thousands of babies are being born each day? According to an estimate almost every second a baby is born. Why *God* was not able to do that in the time of *Adam and Eve*? Is *He* more powerful now then he was *6000* years ago?

Then what was the real story of *Adam* and *Eve*? According to the *Ahmadiyya* view, *Adam* and *Eve* were just an ordinary couple living in an ordinary world until *God* appointed *Adam* as the first messenger to his nation. When *Adam* became the first messenger, there were thousands of people already living on earth at that time. *Eve* was not the first woman on earth who came out of *Adam's* rib. As the *Bible* tells us clearly:

> "So God created man in his own image, in the image of God created he him; male and female created he them" (Genesis 1:27).

According to the above verse, *God* created *Eve* the same way *He* created *Adam*. She was the *'first lady'* of *Adam* in the same way we call the president's wife the *'first lady.'* Does that mean that there is no other woman in the entire country besides the *'First Lady'*? How many *churches* have you seen that have the name *'First Assembly of God'* or *'First Church of Christ'*? And they are in every city and almost every other street.

13. The Original Sin

*G*od told *Adam* and *Eve* that there are some people in their family tree, (not a real tree as many would construe) who are not good people, and they (Adam and Eve) should not have anything to do with them. Those people, being sneaky and snaky, tried to convince *Adam* to become their friends. But since *Adam* was told by *God* not to do anything with them he refused to be their friend. When the people with a satanic mind realized that *Adam* is not going to budge, they decided to approach *Eve*. Since they knew man always listens to his wife, and it is very hard for any reasonable man to refuse his wife. They approached Eve and convinced her and deceived her into their malicious plan.

Being deceived by her relatives, *Eve* convinced her husband to be friends with them. That was one of the reasons perhaps that *God* commanded *Adam* to leave that area. Some people believe that *Adam* and *Eve* lived in heaven and they got thrown out from it. This notion of *Adam* and *Eve* living in heaven is not supported by the *Bible*. Thus the *Bible* says, *"and God said unto them, Be fruitful, and multiply, and replenish the earth..."*[113] This verse of the *Bible* is also supported by the *Qur'an* while it talks about *Adam* it says: *"I am about to place a vicegerent in the earth."*[114] Another interesting point is *God* does not throw out people from heaven; once you live in heaven, you live there forever. If it was a real heaven, then why they were expelled?

The Bible says:

---

[113] Please see *Genesis 1:28*
[114] Please see Qur'an Ch. *Al-Baqarah 2:30-31*

> *"But of the tree of the knowledge of good and evil, thou shalt not eat of it: for in the day that thou eatest thereof thou shalt surely die" (Genesis 2:17).*

Satan, on the contrary, said to the woman: *"Ye shall not surely die" (Genesis 3:4).* It is very strange that *God* told *Adam* and *Eve* that if you eat from this tree *you shall surely die.* But *Satan* said *You shall not surely die.* They eat from that tree and *Adam* and *Eve* do not die. Does this mean *God* lied to them and *Satan* was telling them the truth? What kind of heaven was that where *God* lies and *Satan* tells the truth? There is no fruit of any tree on the face of earth that if you eat that fruit you will become wise or one would know right from wrong. The story of *Adam* and *Eve* is a very simple and very ordinary story of a prophet who was rejected by his people. *Adam's* enemies not only rejected him but also they tried to destroy him—in the same way that *Jesus* was not only rejected by his nation (Israel) but they tried to destroy him.

What was the story about *Adam* and *Eve* getting punishment from *God* after they ate from the tree? The *Bible* says:

> a) *"And the LORD God said unto the serpent, Because thou hast done this, thou art cursed above all cattle, and above every beast of the field; upon thy belly shalt thou go, and dust shalt thou eat all the days of thy life."*
>
> b) *"Unto the woman he said, I will greatly multiply thy sorrow and thy conception; in sorrow thou shalt bring forth children; and thy desire shall be to thy husband, and he shall rule over thee."*
>
> c) *"And unto Adam he said, Because thou hast hearkened unto the voice of thy wife, and hast eaten of the tree, of which I commanded thee, saying, Thou shalt not eat of it: cursed is the ground for thy sake; in sorrow shalt thou eat of it all the days of thy life; Thorns also and thistles shall it bring forth to thee; and thou shalt eat the herb of the field."*
>
> d) *"In the sweat of thy face shalt thou eat bread, till thou return unto the ground; for out of it wast thou taken: for dust thou art, and unto dust shalt thou return."*[115]

God told *serpent,* *"upon thy belly shalt thou go."* According to the *Christian* concept, *Adam* and *Eve* committed the sin. The same sin transferred into the generations of *Adam.* Everybody was born in that sin until *Jesus* paid the price of the sin committed by *Adam.* First of all, this conception of *Adam's*

---

[115] Please see *Genesis 3:14-19*

sin transferred into everybody is a hypothesis which is not backed up by the *Old Testament*. As a matter of fact, the *Old Testament* strongly prohibits this type of concept. It reminds people of all ages by negating this concept in six different books through six different prophets in six different eras in these words:

1. *"But let every man prove his own work, and then shall he have rejoicing in himself alone, and not in another. For every man shall bear his own burden" (Galatians 6:4-5).*

   This verse of the *New Testament* is also supported by the *Qur'an* in these words:

   "He who follows the right way follows it only for the good of his own soul; and he who goes astray, goes astray only to his own loss. And no bearer of burden shall bear the burden of another. And We shall never punish until We have sent a Messenger" (Qur'an 17:15-16).

2. *"Fathers shall not die for the children, neither shall the children die for the fathers, but every man shall die for his own sins" (Deuteronomy 24:16).*

3. *"The soul who sins is the one who will die. The son will not share the guilt of the father, nor will the father share the guilt of the son. The righteousness of the righteous man will be credited to him, and the wickedness of the wicked will be charged against him"* (Ezekiel 18:20 *New International Version* Copyright© 1984).

4. *"But everyone shall die for his own iniquity: every man that eateth the sour grape, his teeth shall be set on edge" (Jeremiah 31:30).*

5. *"...the LORD commanded, saying, The fathers shall not die for the children, neither shall the children die for the fathers, but every man shall die for his own sin" (2 Chronicles 25:4).*

6. *"...the LORD commanded, saying, The fathers shall not be put to death for the children, nor the children be put to death for the fathers; but every man shall be put to death for his own sin" (2 Kings 14:6).*

Please remember these verses are talking about sins and wickedness, but these verses are not talking about crimes, as most *Christians* would construe from them. They usually tell me that fathers should not be punished for the crimes of sons, or the sons should not be punished for the crimes of fathers.

But as you can see, *God* is talking very clearly about sins, not the crimes. But if it is true that the sin transferred into all the generations of *Adam*, and everybody was born in that sin until *Jesus* paid it off with his blood, then why do the snakes in *Christian* countries still walk on their bellies? Why they do not have legs now, since that sin has been paid in full? According to the common justice system in the world, once someone pays off his or her punishment the criminal gets liberated.

But according to this concept, *God* is such an unfair and unjust *God* (God Forbid). First he kicks *Adam* and *Eve* out of heaven, but He was not pleased with their punishment. Then he transfers the sin into all generations. From *Adam* till *Jesus* in about 4000 years, millions of people were born in that sin. Thousands of Prophets of *God* are born in that sin and died in their sin (God forbid). People had no free will; they were just born sinners. Because they were born in sin, *God* sent them all to hell. But this was not enough to please *God*. He took His own innocent son, who never committed any sin, and killed him on the cross. This was not enough to make *Him* happy either; hence, he kept the original punishment still in effect.

This means that the punishment of *God* which was imposed on *Adam*, *'In the sweat of thy face shalt thou eat bread.'* *Christians* who believe that *Jesus* paid the full price still have to work hard to make their living. After *Jesus* paid the price in full, they should have received their paychecks at home and not have to work hard to earn it. Then the *Christian* women should not have to go through the labor pains any more since *Jesus* paid the price in full. But they still do. And the serpent, as I have stated above, should have legs after the crucifixion of *Jesus*, but they still walk on their bellies. Is that a picture of a just and fair *God*?

The fact is that *Adam* was a farmer, even before he got that punishment. The *Bible* says: *"Then the LORD God took the man and put him into the garden of Eden to cultivate it and keep it"* (Genesis 2:15 NASB). What do we call the man who cultivates the ground? A farmer, right? Thus, the punishment had nothing to do with it. *Adam* was a farmer to begin with; he worked hard to make his living even before his punishment. Therefore, the new research shows that thousands of people lived before *Adam*. Especially the men of *Neanderthal*, who believe to have lived *50,000* years ago. Do you think that they got their paychecks at home and they did not have to work? I doubt it. Since *Adam* and *Eve* were not even born until 44,000 years later, the men of *Neanderthal* should not be under the sin of *Adam* and *Eve?* Right?

After we have examined the other aspects of the punishments of women and serpent, it is apparent that there was no original sin to begin with and *Jesus* did not die to pay the price of it, either. But if you still persist that *Adam* did commit a sin and that sin was transferred into all generations, and all men who were born, they were born in that sin. Then why does the *Bible* call many prophets righteous and many prophets perfect? Please read the following verses:

1. *Abraham* was " PERFECT" (Genesis 17:1).

2. *Noah* was " PERFECT" (Genesis 6:9).

3. God called *Job* " PERFECT" 4 times in his book (Job 1:1 - 1:8 - 2:3 - 8:20).

God called the following people *Righteous.*

a) *Mel-chis'-e-dec* was *"King of Righteousness"* (Hebrews 7:2).

b) [Zacha-ri'-as and his wife] both *"Righteous" before God, walking in all the commandments and ordinances of the Lord blameless* (Luke 1:6).

c) *Simon was "Righteous"* (Luke2:25).

d) *Abel was "Righteous"* (Hebrew 11:4).

After reading above verses from the *Bible*, is it not obvious that *God* did not stop men from becoming righteous or perfect, and please remember above is the validation from *God Almighty* that these people were righteous and perfect, not just a mere claim of a faithful. If you still insist that *Adam* did commit the sin and because of his sin everybody was born in that sin. Consequently, the lineage of man became sinful by nature: every male is a born sinner. And perhaps *God* came up with a perfect plan, instead of just forgiving a *4,000* year old sin of *Adam. God* brought his own son, who was innocent, most righteous, most perfect and then *He* killed him on the cross to be just and fair.

I ask my *Christian* friends that if everybody is a born sinner, then was *Mary*, the mother of *Jesus*, a sinner too? She had the same sinful blood as her father and mother and then when *Jesus* was born he was born with the same sinful blood too? (God forbid). But they contend that *God* had sanctified *Mary* that's how she was able to be free of sins and became the mother of *Christ*. Evidently, *God* could sanctify people and he did sanctify *Mary*, but *God* could not sanctify *Adam, Noah, Abraham, Moses,* etc, and millions of people between *Adam* and *Jesus* who were all born in sin (God forbid). Then He sent his own innocent son and killed him on the cross, but He could not sanctify other people?

But the question is could this concept be backed up by the *Bible*? May be not; rather, the *New Testament* totally denies this concept in these words:

a) "*And Adam was not the one deceived; it was the woman who was deceived and became a sinner.*"[116]

b) *The Qur'an* also clarifies that *Adam* was not the sinner in these words: "*And certainly We gave a commandment to Adam before, but he forgot; and We did not find in him any determination [intention of disobeying]*"[117]

The *New Testament and Qur'an* both clarifies this *6000* years old mystery and vindicates *Adam*. Who was the original sinner then? The woman, correct? Then according to this notion, the genealogy of woman is corrupted, every woman is born in sin. Consequently, when *Jesus* is born of a woman, is he a born sinner also? (God Forbid)

If you say, well these are your words the *Bible* does not say that. Let us see what the *Bible* says about '*born of a woman*':

1. "*What is man, that he should be clean? And he which is born of a woman, that he should be righteous?*" (*Job 15:14*).

2. "*How then can man be justified with God? or how can he be clean that is born of a woman?*" (*Job 25:4*).

According to the *Christian* conception of the original sin transferring into generations, we are given a grotesque picture of *Jesus,* unfortunately. According to the above verses, if *Jesus* was born without a man he becomes the only man on earth who is 100% a sinner (God forbid). If he would have born of a father and a mother, then he would only be 50% sinner like any other man. What I mean is that since *Jesus* was born without the father then he had only the corrupted blood of a woman according to the above verses. Then he was born with 100% sinful blood. According to the *Christian* belief of original sin, *Jesus* had no good blood at all. (God forbid) We do not believe *Jesus* was born with 100% sinful blood. All I am trying to do is to make you realize

---

[116] Please see *1 Timothy 2:14, New International Version (NIV)* © Copyright 1973, 1978, 1984 by *International Bible Society*

[117] Please see *Qur'an Ch. Ta Ha 20: 115-116*

that believing in *"Original Sin,"* creates much more turmoil in *Christianity*, rather than making *Jesus* a hero who died for the whole world and washed the sins of the world with his blood and cease the original sin.

14. Noah and the Flood

It is surprising that not only does the history of *India* indicate an enormous deluge, but it is also recorded in their religious book called *'Vedas.'* According to the book titled *India: A history*, by *John Keay*[118] it says:

> ["*...the earliest of several accounts, the Flood which afflicted India's people was a natural occurrence. Manu, Noah's equivalent, survived it thanks to a simple act of kindness. And, amazingly for a society that worshipped gods of wind and storm, no deity receives a mention. When Manu was washing his hands one morning, a small fish came into his hands along with the water. The fish begged protection from Manu saying 'Rear me. I will save thee.' The reason stated was that the small fish was liable to be devoured by the larger ones, and it required protection till it grew up. It asked to be kept in a jar, and later on, when it out grew that, in a pond, and finally in the sea. Manu acted accordingly.*
>
> *[One day] the fish forewarned Manu of a forthcoming flood, and advised him to prepare a ship and enter into it when the flood came. The flood began to rise at the appointed hour, and Manu entered the ship. The fish then swam up to him, and he tied the rope of the ship to its horn [perhaps it was a swordfish], and thus passed swiftly to the yonder northern mountain. There*

---

[118] Bracketed text excerpts from *India: A History* by *John Keay*, Copyright © *Atlantic Monthly Press*, New York. Chapter One, *The Harappan World*, pg. #1&2, *First American Edition*, ISBN 0-87113-800-X

Manu was directed to ascend the mountain after fastening the ship to a tree, and to disembark only after the water had subsided. Accordingly he gradually descended, and hence the slope of the northern mountain is called Manoravataranam, or Manu's descent. The waters swept away all the three heavens, and Manu alone was saved." Such is the earliest version of the Flood as recorded in the Satapatha Brahmana, one of several wordy appendices to the sacred hymns known as the Vedas which are themselves amongst the oldest religious compositions in the world. Couched in the classical language of Sanskrit... Some historians have dated the Indian flood very precisely to 3102 BC..."]

This matches with the *Biblical* flood very well, it is interesting to note that the *Qur'an* also talks about the deluge of *Noah,* but in the entire *Qur'an* it never says that the deluge of *Noah* came to the whole world. On the contrary, it articulates that the flood of *Noah* destroyed the nation of *Noah.*

1. The *Qur'an* says: *"And the people of Noah, when they rejected the Messengers, We drowned them, and We made them a Sign for mankind. And We have prepared a painful punishment for the wrongdoers" (Chapter 25:37-38).*

2. The *Qur'an* also says: *"And We destroyed the people of Noah before them; they were a disobedient people" (Chapter 51:46-47).*

3. *"And He (God) destroyed the people of Noah before them - verily, they were most unjust and most rebellious" (Chapter 53:52-53).*

The *Bible* does not explicitly say where the flood of *Noah* came. But in *India,* not only there is a written record that there was a huge deluge around *Kashmir,* but physical evidence also exists which proves it. I would like to clarify a couple of mystifications about the incident of *Noah's* flood. Firstly, people usually say that the age of *Noah* was 950 years. But the *Bible* says: *"...his [man's life] days shall be an hundred and twenty years" (Genesis 6:3).* Therefore, according to the *Bible,* the maximum age of any human being should be 120 years. Why the age of *Noah* surpassed the possible maximum age of a human being? According to the *Ahmadiyya* view, *Noah's* 950 years mentioned in the *Bible* is not the age of his life, but rather, it is the age of *Noah's Law* of his book (Shariah). Secondly, people are often confused about this verse of the *Bible* where it says:

> *"And of every living thing of all flesh, two of every sort shalt thou bring into the ark, to keep them alive with thee; they shall be male and female" (Genesis 6:19).*

It sounds like *God* told *Noah* that every kind of animal lived on earth at that time, he needed to bring them to the ark. But according to the historians, thousands of animals lived in that era. If *Noah* would have attempted to congregate all of those animals to get them on the ark, this action would have taken him many years to do that. Even his ark would not have adequate room to accommodate all those thousands of animals. According to the *Ahmadiyya* view on *Noah's ark, God* told *Noah* to bring a pair of all domestic animals, such as chickens, cows, goats, horses or donkeys. The reason for bringing these animals was not to preserve wild life as people usually infer from this verse, but rather, it was advised to do that so *Noah* and his followers could survive for a few months consume those animals. *Noah* and his followers could use the milk of cows, use chicken to eat, use horses or donkeys to ride around after the deluge recedes, etc.

I would like to mention about the city of *Ham*. The city of *Ham* (also known as *Koh-I-Hama* or *Mount Ham*) in the district of *Handwara, Kashmir,* is known to be driven from *'Cush.'* the grandson of *Noah*. The *Bible* articulates:

> *"These are the families of the sons of Noah, after their generations, in their nations: and by these were the nations divided in the earth after the flood" (Genesis 10:32).*

This means that after the flood, the sons of *Noah* gave their names to the areas they lived in. If they lived in *Israel*, as most people assert, then the cities with their names should be in *Israel* too. I acknowledge the fact that some of these names may be found in *Israel* also, but these names were adopted by the *Hebrews* after *Noah's* people had left *India* and resided in *Israel*. Likewise, the names *China Town, Japan Town* and *India Town* are also in *America*. But this does not mean that these names were originally *American* names which were adopted by others. The next chapters will further clarify this view unambiguously. If it is true that the *Tomb of Moses* is in *India*, then *Kashmir* was the *Promised Land*, and if *Kashmir* was the *Promised Land* then the flood of *Noah* also came in *Kashmir*.

The *Qur'an* says:

"And We made his offspring the survivors. And We left (this blessing) for him among generations to come in later times" (Qur'an Al-Saffat 37:77-79).

Is it a mere coincidence that even today there is a small tribe in *Kashmir* called *'Hanjis,'* also known as *'the people of the Boat'?*[119] This usually refers to the *Noah's Ark* and the descendants of *Noah*. Are there any claimants of *Noah's* descendants in any other part of the world? And if they do exist in other parts of the world, could they substantiate their claim? Even the tomb of *Noah* is in *Kashmir India*, Ms Suzanne Olsson writes:

"This grave [the grave of Noah/Manu] is located in Tanda, a small village a few miles north of Sialkot. It is one of a series of Barrow style graves on a hillside, each about 30 feet or 98.4 meters in length (also known as tumulus or kurgan style graves). A local historian, Mohammed Zaman Khokhar thoroughly researched these graves for years. He wrote a book in six volumes (published in 2000) "The Ten Yard Graves of the Beloved of Pakistan."[120]

According to the book, *Jesus lived in India* the description of the *Garden of Eden* which is mentioned in the *Bible* has many clues as to where this mystery garden could be situated. The *Bible* says:

"Now the Lord had planted a garden in the east, in Eden... A river watering the garden flowed from Eden; from there it was separated into four headwaters. The name of the first is the Pishon; it winds through the entire land of Havilah."

Havila was the son of *Cush*, who was the son of *Ham*, who was the son of *Noah*. The *Bible* further says:

"Where there is gold. (The gold of that land is good; aromatic resin [good pearls] and onyx are also good there.) "The name of the second river is the Gihon; it winds through the entire land of Ethiopia." (Genesis 2:12-13NIV -UK).

When you read this verse that *'Gihon' winds through the land of Ethiopia,"* you might think that if this river is compassing the *land of Ethiopia*, then this theory is totally wrong simply because *Ethiopia* is in *Africa*, and there is

---

[119] Please see the book *"Geography of Jammu and Kashmir State,"* by *Professor Majid Hussain*, Copyright © 1987 by *Rajesh Publications* New Delhi at page #40).

[120] Please see www.jesus-kashmir-tomb.com by *Ms. Suzanne Olsson*

no way the river of *Gihon* could run from *India* all the way to *Africa*, which are thousands of miles apart. But when you look up the name *'Ethiopia'* in a *Hebrew Bible*,[121] it does not say *'Ethiopia'* but it says *'Cush.'* Therefore, this theory is not incorrect after all. According to *Mr. Kersten*, *'Cush'* is the father of *Havila* and son of *Ham*, who is the second son of *Noah*. The name of *Kash-mir* is supposedly driven from two words: *'Cush'* and *'mir.'* *'Cush'* was the grandson of *Noah*, and *'Mir'* means *'valuable,'* which again pertains to the *Promised land,'* or the *'Valuable land.'* Therefore, the ancient name of *Kashmir* would originally be *'Cushmir'* which later on became *'Kashmir.'* So the second river was not compassing the land of *Ethiopia* but the *'land of Cush'* or *Kashmir*. The *Garden of Eden* which *God* is talking about has four clues for us to determine where this land could be: *East, Four headwaters, Gold,* and the *'Land of Cush.'*

The *Old Testament (Torah)* says in *Genesis* that four rivers came out from the *Garden of Eden*. The only place in the world where there are four rivers flowing together is in *India*, which evidently turned into five rivers after the deluge. The name of that area became the name of five rivers *Punjab*. *'Punj'* means 'five' and *'ab'* means water.

There are four main reasons as to why the flood of *Noah* may not be for the whole world:

1. *God* does not punish the whole world for the sins of one nation. If the nation of *Noah* were disobedient people who rejected him, then why would *God* drown the whole world for that?

2. According to *Mr. Plimer* a famous geologist *"If the flood of Noah came in the whole world and the whole world was drowned in water then the atmosphere would have changed. The air would have so much moisture in it that the people who survived (Noah and his family) would have drowned just by breathing the air. The atmospheric pressure would have crushed people's lungs."*[122]

3. According to the geologists, *"the earth does not contain enough water to drown the whole world. According to them, in order to drown the whole planet to the top of the Himalayas would need five times more water than what is available in the whole world."*[123]

---

121 Please see also *New King James Version by Thomas Nelson © 1984).*
122 Please see the *Discovery Channel* documentary, titled *Noah's Ark the true Story*
123 Ibid

4. Geologist *Ian Plimer* also says: *"A great flood would leave a signature; it would be a very very large signature apparent all over the world. There is no such signature, there is no evidence. In fact, there is only overwhelming evidence to the contrary."*[124]

According to the new research, *Adam* was the first prophet of *God*, sent to the nation of *India,* and then *Noah and Abraham* were also born there. *Moses* went to *India* to search for *the Promised Land* and some of the other prophets even died there as well. Two thousand years ago, the last *Israeli* prophet, *Jesus,* went to *India* and died there. Then the last messiah, who is supposed to be the prophet for the whole world, would appear from *India* also to complete the circle of 6,000 years. *Jesus* foretold the advent of his *Second Coming* in *India* in these words:

> *"For as the lightning cometh out of the **east**, and shineth even unto the west; so shall also the coming of the Son of man be"* (Matthew 24:27).

Please remember that in this prophecy *Jesus* is not talking about literal light: he is talking about the *'Spiritual Light'* which denotes to the *'teaching of Messiah'* which will start spreading from the *East* and then it will reach to the *West.*

Most of the religions of the world are waiting for the final prophet towards the end of the world. The last prophet is supposed to convert every other religion to his own religion. According to my *Jewish* friend *they also* have the similar belief; it may not be the belief of every *Jewish* sect. The *Christians* assert very openly that the *Second Coming* of *Jesus* will convert the whole world into *Christianity. Muslims* are proclaiming that their *'Mahdi,' (divine reformer)* when he comes, will convert the whole world into *Islam. Buddhists* are saying the *Second Coming* of *Buddha* will convert every religion into *Buddhism. Hindus* are saying the same about *'Krishna.'* Now contemplate on this point: how is this supposed to happen? How is it that every religion will convert every other religion into their religion? The truth is that only one man will come and he will convert the whole world into his religion. Otherwise, it is impossible for six different final prophets to come and convert the whole world into one religion.

---

[124] Ibid

15. Could a man (Jesus) be God?

According to the history of *Christianity*, *Constantine* became the *Emperor of Rome* in 312 C.E. In *Constantine's* era, two men fought furiously on the subject of who was *Jesus*, prophet or god? *Arias*, who believed that *Jesus* was the highest created being but he was not god. *Athanasius*, a bishop from *Alexandria*, disagreed. *Athanasius* believed that *Jesus* was both man and god. According to this, *Constantine* summoned all the bishops from all over the empire and held a conference in his seaside resort in *Nicaea*. In this council, this question was discussed was *Jesus* a man or a god? At this conference it was decided that *Jesus* is both man and god. This is known as the *Nicene Creed*.

According to this history, *Jesus* was not considered god until almost *300* to *400* years after his death. This notion that *Jesus* did not ask people to call him god is also mentioned in the *Qur'an* in a special way. It says:

> *"And when Allah will say, 'O Jesus, son of Mary, did you say to men, 'Take me and my mother for two gods beside Allah [God]?' he [Jesus] will answer, 'Holy art THOU, I could never say that which I had no right. If I had said it, Thou wouldst have surely known it. Thou knowest what is in my mind, and I know not what is in Thy mind. It is Thou alone Who art the Knower of all hidden things 'I said nothing to them except that which Thou didst command me - Worship Allah, my Lord and your Lord. And I was a witness over them as long as I remained among them, but since Thou didst cause me to die, Thou, hast been the Watcher over them, and Thou art Witness over all things; 'If*

Thou punish them, they are Thy servants; and if Thou forgive them, Thou surely art the Mighty, the Wise."[125]

According to the above verse of the *Qur'an*, the belief that *Jesus* is god was not introduced in *Christianity* until after his death, and the history of *Christianity* corroborates this claim.

God tells us in the *Bible*: *"God is a Spirit."*[126] On the other hand, *Jesus* said:

"Look at my hands. Look at my feet. You can see that it's really me. Touch me and make sure that I am not a ghost, because ghosts don't have bodies, as you see that I do!"[127]

Another words, *Jesus* is telling us clearly that he cannot be *God* because he is not a *Spirit*. Not only that, the *Bible* tells us:

"...and there is no God else beside me; a just God and a Saviour; there is none beside me. Look unto me, and be ye saved, all the ends of the earth: for I am God, and there is none else. I have sworn by myself, the word is gone out of my mouth in righteousness, and shall not return, That unto me every knee shall bow, every tongue shall swear" (Isaiah 45:21-23).

Unfortunately, *Christians* all over the world say that every knee shall bow and every tongue shall swear for *Jesus*. But these words should be applied to the *God Almighty ONLY*, not for a man. *Jesus* was born after *Isaiah*. How could these verses be applied to *Jesus* if he came after prophet *Isaiah*, when *God* says there is no *God* after Him?

God also tells us in the *Old Testament*:

"Thou shalt have none other gods before me "Thou shalt not make thee any graven image, or any likeness of anything that is in heaven above, or that is in the earth beneath, or that is in the waters beneath the earth."[128]

If you read this verse in *Hebrew*, it does not say 'earth beneath,' it only says earth. That means according to these verses men should not make any graven image, or any likeness of anything that is in heaven above, or *that is in*

---

[125] Please see Qur'an *Ch. Al-Mai'dah 5:116-117*

[126] Please see *John 4:24*

[127] Please see *Luke 24:39 NLT*

[128] Please see *Deuteronomy 5:7-9*

the earth. Jesus walked on earth. Is it not obvious from the verse quoted above that no man should be worshiped beside God? That is the reason perhaps that the scholars have added the word earth beneath so that the people could worship *Jesus.* But the *Bible* takes that mystery out, too.

a) The *Bible* says: "*God is not a man, that he should lie, neither the son of man, that he should repent…*"[129] The first message we get from this verse is '*God is not a man.*' The second message is that *God* is not the son of man, either.

b) The *Bible* also says: "*for I am God, and not man.*"[130]

c) The *Qur'an* says: "*Indeed, they are disbelievers, who say, 'Allah, He is the Messiah, son of Mary,' whereas the Messiah himself said, 'O Children of Israel, worship Allah [God] Who is my Lord and your Lord*" *(Al-Mai'dah 5:72-73).*

This means *Jesus* always referred everything to *God Almighty*, but he never said I am *God* or worship me. According to the *Christian* belief, *Jesus* is not only a man, but he is the only perfect man. Surprisingly, even this claim of *Christians* is not mentioned in any of the four *Gospels*. Even if we assume *Jesus* was the only perfect man, then according to the above verse of the *Bible, Jesus* cannot be *God*. Then it says *God* is not son of man, either. Ironically, *Jesus* called himself '*son of man*' 84 times in the four *Gospels. Jesus* then cannot be *God.*

God also tells us:

1. "*And he [God] said, Thou canst not see my face: for there shall no man see me, and live*" *(Exodus 33:20).*

2. Even the *New Testament* says: "*No man has seen God at any time*" *(John 1:18 & 1John 14:12).* How the *Jews* saw *Jesus* and they were still be able to live and persecute him, put him on the cross and watched him?

3. *God* says: "*For thou shalt worship no other god: for the LORD, whose name is Jealous, is a jealous God*" *(Exodus 34:14).*

4. *God* also says: "*Ye are my witnesses, saith the LORD, and my servant whom I have chosen: that ye may know and believe me, and understand that I am he: before me there was no God formed,*

---

[129] Please see *Numbers 23:19*
[130] Please see *Hosea 11:9*

neither shall there be after me' I, even I, am the LORD; and beside me there is no saviour" (Isaiah 43:10-11).

Jesus came after prophet *Isaiah*, then how *Jesus* could be *God*? When *God* said there shall be no *God* after me? *Isaiah* also articulates *beside me there is no saviour*. The *Christians* call *Jesus* their personal *Lord* and *Savior* when the *Bible* says there is no other god or savior besides the *God Almighty*?

Jesus and God

If *Jesus*, *God* and *Holy Spirit* are one, (God forbid) then a few questions arise:

1. If *Jesus* and *God* are one then, was *God* in the belly of *Mary* for nine months? And after *God* (*Jesus*) was born, six ordinary people [brothers and sisters of *Jesus* (Matthew 12:47)] were also born in the same womb where *God* was conceived? (God forbid).

2. If *Jesus* and *God* are the same, then who was the *God* before *Jesus'* birth? If you say that was his father then you believe in two *Gods*: one who always had been there since the creation of the heavens and the earth and *Jesus* who was born *2000* years ago.

3. If *Jesus* and *God* are the same then why *Jesus* was a follower of *John the Baptist*? Why *God* was baptized by a mere man and *God* became follower of a mere man?

4. If *Jesus* and *God* are the same, then did *Satan* tempt *God*? The *Bible* says:

    "Let no man say when he is tempted, I am tempted of God: for God cannot be tempted with evil..." (James 1: 13).

But the *Gospel* says *Jesus* was tempted by *Satan*. It says:

"the devil taketh him [Jesus] up into an exceeding high mountain, and sheweth him all the kingdoms of the world, and the glory of them; and saith unto Jesus, I will give you all the land And saith unto him, All these things will I give thee, if thou wilt fall down and worship me" (Matthew 4:8-9).

131

5. If *Jesus* and *God* are the same, when *Jesus* was on the cross is that mean *God Almighty* was on the cross? And according to the *Christian* belief, *Jesus* went to hell for three days. Did *God* go to hell for three days? (God forbid). *God Almighty* who is the most perfect could go to hell as the sinners go to hell?

6. If *Jesus* and *God* are one, then when the *Romans* spitted on *Jesus'* face, (Matthew 27:30) did they spit on *God's* face? (God forbid) Could anyone do that?

7. If *Jesus* and the *Holy Spirit* are the same, then did *Jesus* impregnate his own mother?

8. *Jesus* always worshipped *God*. Did *God* ever worship *Jesus*?

9. If *God* and the *Holy Spirit* are one (part of Trinity) Did *Jesus* ever worship the *Holy Spirit*? Or did the *Holy Spirit* ever worship *Jesus*?

10. *Jesus* is a perfect man. Is *God* a perfect man too? If they are same and equal in every way, then why not?

11. The *Bible* says: *"Put not your trust in princes, nor in the son of man, in whom there is no help"* (Psalms 146:3). *Jesus* calls himself the *Son of Man* eighty four times. Should anyone trust him or try to get help from a man?

12. If *Jesus* is *God* (God Forbid) then why did he kill thousands of people in the *Old Testament*? And why is he still killing millions of people all over the world? What happened to the *'God is love'* or *'Prince of peace' Jesus?*

    i) Nation of *Noah* was destroyed.

    ii) Nation of *Lot* was destroyed.

    iii) Nation of *David* which killed 70 thousand people *(2Samuel 24:15)*

    iv) Thousands of *Jews*, men women and children were killed in 74 AD

13. If *Jesus* is *God*, then why did he say, *'I am a jealous god,'* seven times in the *Old Testament*? Why did *Jesus* say, *"I am a terrible god"*? What happened to the *"Prince of Peace" Jesus?*

If you say when *Jesus* was manifested in flesh then he became peaceful, then two questions arise:

i) Was *Jesus* the same god of *Old Testament,* or not? If you say yes, then it does not matter if he became flesh or not: he killed thousands of people and he cannot be *"Prince of Peace."*

ii) If you say he was not the same god but he was His son, then there are two gods? One is jealous, terrible, full of vengeance (God forbid) and who killed millions of people. The other is the *"Prince of Peace God."* How do you explain if they are one?

Jesus taught his disciples about one *God,* as I mentioned earlier, but *Christians* preach about two gods. According to the *Christian* doctrine, when *God* says in *Genesis Let us make man.*[131] *God* was referring to *God* and *Jesus.* Does this mean there are two gods? When it says in *Mark,* *"So then after the Lord had spoken unto them, he was received up into heaven, and sat on the right hand of God."*[132] Does this mean there are two gods, one on the right hand and one on the left hand?

The book of *John* says:

"In the beginning was the Word, and the Word was with God, and the Word was God. The same was in the beginning with God."[133]

According to the *Christian* doctrine, *Jesus* was with *God* always and he was with *God* even in the creation of heaven and earth (God forbid). Does this not mean that there are two gods? *Christians* all over the world pray to *Jesus.* When we asked them why do they pray to a man when they should pray to *God, Christians* respond that they pray to *God* in the name of *Jesus* because *Jesus* said when you need anything ask *God* in my name and *God* will give you that. But the strange thing is when *Jesus* needed *God* to hear his prayer in the worst time of his life, the night before crucifixion in the garden of *Gethsemane Jesus* cried and begged *God* to save his life. He even sweats blood, but *God* did not hear him, *God* forsook *Jesus* and let him die. *Jesus* even mentions it by reminding all *Christians* that *God* did not hear him when *Jesus* said on the cross *"O' God O' God why have you forsaken me?"* (Matthew 27:46). Then how can *Christians* ask in *Jesus'* name and think *God* will hear them when *God* did not even hear his own son, according to *Christian* belief?

---

[131] Please see *Genesis1: 26*
[132] Please see *Mark 16:19*
[133] Please see *John 1:1*

The *Book of Romans* tell us that those who worship man besides *God* are in serious confusion. Not only that, this book tells us the punishment of *God* for those who worship man:

> "*Because that, when they knew God, they glorified [him] not as God, neither were thankful; but became vain in their imaginations, and their foolish heart was darkened. Professing themselves to be wise, they became fools, And changed the glory of the uncorruptible God into an image made like to corruptible man, and to birds, and fourfooted beasts, and creeping things. Wherefore God also gave them up to uncleanness through the lusts of their own hearts, to dishonour their own bodies between themselves: Who changed the truth of God into a lie, and worshipped and served the creature [man] more than the Creator [God], who is blessed forever.*"

The following passage is taken from *The Message* [Bible] for easy understanding:

> "*Worse followed. Refusing to know God, they soon didn't know how to be human either--women didn't know how to be women, men didn't know how to be men. Sexually confused, they abused and defiled one another, women with women, men with men--all lust, no love. And then they paid for it, oh, how they paid for it—emptied of God and love, godless and loveless wretches. Since they didn't bother to acknowledge God, God quit bothering them and let them run loose. And then all hell broke loose: rampant evil, grabbing and grasping, vicious backstabbing. They made life hell on earth with their envy, wanton killing, bickering, and cheating. Look at them: mean-spirited, venomous, fork-tongued God-bashers. Bullies, swaggerers, insufferable windbags! They keep inventing new ways of wrecking lives. They ditch their parents when they get in the way. Stupid, slimy, cruel, cold-blooded. And it's not as if they don't know better. They know perfectly well they're spitting in God's face. And they don't care--worse, they hand out prizes to those who do the worst things best!*"[134]

---

[134] Please see *Romans 1:21 to 32, The Message* [Bible] Copyright © 1993 by *Eugene H. Peterson*

Is this not the picture of today's many western countries? Unfortunately, many western countries have become victim of this misconception. *Homosexuality* is at its peak in the *west*, while the *Old Testament* says:

> *"The penalty for homosexual acts is death to both parties. They have committed a detestable act and are guilty of a capital offense."[135]*

Children are more disobedient to parents in many *western* countries than in non-western nations. People usually insult each other by saying, *"you are acting like my mother,"* or *"you are turning into your mother."* As if being a mother is a hideous thing. These people even make fun of *Mother Teresa* in their movies and television programs. *Mother Teresa* was a symbol of love, peace, and advocate for the poor and helpless. In most *Muslim* countries, we honor women by awarding them as *"mother."*

Adultery, fornication, prostitution, pornography, nudity, nude colonies, offensive scenes on TV, child abusers, child molesters, serial killers, serial rapists, alcoholics and drug users are more common in many *western* countries than in non-western nations. I am not saying that the *Muslims* are angels, but at least they are not as active as many westerners. Is this occurrence is due to a misconception of idol worshipping, or worshipping a man (Jesus) instead of *God*, or believing in three *Gods* (Trinity)? According to the verses of the *Bible* presented above, it seems quite obvious that this demeanor is the result of idol worshipping.

Ironically, the *Muslims* are usually blamed for bombing, terrorizing and destroying the world peace. But a question arises: who have killed more people in just the last hundred years, *Muslims* or someone else? Who fought the *First World War*, in which about eight million people were killed? Who fought in the *Second World War*, in which about 62 million people were killed? Was there any *Muslim* country involved in the first or the *Second World War*s at all? Who killed thousands of *Jews* in the *Holocaust*? Some of the accounts claim there were six million *Jews* killed. Was it the *Muslims* who killed them? Who bombed the *Japanese* cities of *Hiroshima* and *Nagasaki* that killed about 220 thousand people? Who attacked on *Vietnam* that killed about 1.5 million people? Who attacked *Iraq,* where, so far, over 1.2 million (reported by ORB) people have been killed? Who attacked *Afghanistan* where over *20,000* people have been killed and they are still being killed every day? The estimated number of people who have been killed according to the above wars and

---

[135]   Please see *Leviticus 20:13 New Living Translation* Copyright © 1996 by *Tyndale Charitable Trust*

attacks in just the last 100 years is about 75 million. Were they all killed by the *Muslims*?

I am not trying to start abhorrence towards anyone, or any religion for that matter. But the reason I am mentioning all this is because many good hearted *Jews* and *Christians* have started detestation against the *Muslims* just because they see on TV all the negative campaign against us. I have been told by many people that the *Muslims* are the only threat to the world peace, and if they are wiped out, the world will be a better place to live. But the *Muslims* are not the biggest threat to the world peace. Who is inventing most of the world's life destroying weapons, such as bombs, atom bombs, nuclear bombs, tanks, machine guns, missiles, rocket launchers, etc.? Are they *Muslims* or someone else? Yes, I agree that the *Muslims* buy and use these weapons also when they are attacked, but who is inventing them? Can you name any weapon which was originally invented by the *Muslims*? Even the sword, which is one of the simplest weapons to make, was not invented by the *Muslims*.

On the contrary, the *Christians* are very proud of their inventions. Most of my *Christian* friends say look, almost every major invention is conceived by the *Christians* and the *Muslims* have invented nothing. But I usually ask them what is the result of these inventions, are they bringing mankind closer to *God* or are they making them astray from the path of *God* and righteousness? Let me give you a very minute example about one of the simplest inventions, the television. If you have watched the TV programs from the 1940's and 50's, try to compare how they used to be so clean in their language and decent in their attire. How badly the world has become corrupted regarding vulgar language and nudity in just fifty to sixty years? You decide after watching today's shows has the world gotten closer to *God*, or most of these inventions have taken us away from *God*? Bombs and nuclear weapons which have destroyed many nations and killed thousands of people and still destroying many are they invented by *Muslims*? By destroying the world with these deadly weapons, would that bring us nearness to *God*?

Some *Christian* scholars openly say that the *Muslims* are terrorists and they were predicted in the *Bible* as an *Antichrist*. But if you read those verses which talk about the *Antichrist* you will come to know who the real *Antichrist* is. The *Bible* says:

1. *"And who is the great liar? The one who says that Jesus is not the Christ. Such people are **antichrists**, for they have denied the Father and the Son"* (1John 2:22).

2. *"And every spirit that confesseth not that Jesus Christ is come in the flesh is not of God: and this is that spirit of **antichrist**, whereof ye have heard that it should come; and even now already is it in the world" (1John 4:3).*

3. *"For many deceivers are entered into the world, who confess not that Jesus Christ is come in the flesh. This is a deceiver and an **antichrist**" (2John 1:7).*

According to the above verses, *antichrist* is he who denies Father and the Son, (God and Jesus), as two separate beings. Also he who does not believe *Jesus* as a flesh and bone person is *antichrist*. This means all those who believe *Jesus* was a spirit (part of Trinity) *Holy Spirit and God* are one, the same is an *antichrist*. Or those who claimed to be *Christ*-like (Christians) but they do act totally against his peaceful teaching are *Anti-Christians or Antichrists*. After reading the above verses of the *Bible*, how could anyone even tenuously think that the *Muslims* are the *antichrists* when we do believe *Jesus* and *God* are two separate entities? We also believe *Jesus* was a normal flesh and bone person, but was not spirit and definitely was not *God* either. The *Bible* also talks about the mark of the beast in regards to the *Anti-Christ*. It says:

"And no one could buy or sell anything without that mark, which was either the name of the beast or the number representing his name."[136]

Some scholars suggest that the mark of the beast is nothing but the *Social Security Number.*[137] This seems quite plausible; in today's western world, we cannot buy or sell anything without the social security number. But strange enough, most *Muslim* countries still do not have any concept of a social security number. And they are definitely not the ones who came up with that system.

It does not mean that *Christianity* is false or all *Christians* are bad. I am talking about only those who either invent these life destroying objects or help others to make them. I must admit that most *Christian* governments have established a high level of justice system in the world. For instance, in *India* over *100* years ago *Muslims* were able to worship their *God* because of the *British Empire's* justice system. Before, they were attacked severely by *Hindus* and *Sikhs*. That was a great favor of *British Empire's* on all the *Muslims* of *India*.

---

[136] Please see *Revelation 13:17 NLT*

[137] Please see *National Geographic Channel* documentary titled *Doomsday: Book of Revelation*

Hindu women were burnt alive after their husbands had died in observance of their religious rite called *"Suttee."* But when the *British* came, they banned these rituals. This was indeed a great favor on all the *Hindu* women of *India*. Today, most *Christian* countries are the refuge for all those who are banned in their own countries.

I have come from a so-called *Muslim* country, where I was not even allowed to be called *Muslim* or to practice my faith. But living in *America*, I am free to profess and practice my faith. I am not against the *Christians* or the *Jews* or the follower of any religion, since, my holy book (Qur'an) tells us that *God Almighty* is *God* of the whole of mankind and not for just the *Muslims*. The *Qur'an* tells us emphatically, that any country you live in you should be loyal to that country, it does not say anywhere that the *Muslims* should be loyal to only *Muslim* countries. Thus, the *Qur'an* says:

> *"O ye who believe! obey Allah, and obey His Messenger and those who are in authority among you. And if you differ in anything among yourselves, refer it to Allah and His Messenger if you are believers in Allah and the Last Day. That is best and most commendable in the end"* (Qur'an 4:59-60).

In this verse the *Qur'an* does not say at all that obey who are in authority among you if it's a *Muslim* authority. This means we should be loyal to any country in which we reside, *Muslim, Christian, Jewish, Hindu country*, it does not matter. We should always obey *the Law of the Land*.

My only point is that the *Bible* tells us that worshiping a man or three gods (Trinity), which is openly breaking of the first commandment, is the cause of all the main moral problems in the *Christian* world. Most *Muslims* still believe in one *God*; they cannot come under the punishment of the above verse. Especially, when the *Muslims* are the copiers in most inventions and not the inventers themselves.

16. "Son of God"

King James Version							
1	Son of Man (Matthew 8:20)	22	Son of Man (Matthew 24:30)	43	Son of Man (Mark 13:34)	64	Son of Man (Luke 17:30)
2	Son of Man (Matthew 9:6)	23	Son of Man (Matthew 24:37)	44	Son of Man (Mark 14:21)	65	Son of Man (Luke 18:8)
3	Son of Man (Matthew 10:23)	24	Son of Man (Matthew 24:39)	45	Son of Man (Mark 14:21)	66	Son of Man (Luke 18:31)
4	Son of Man (Matthew 11:19)	25	Son of Man (Matthew 24:44)	46	Son of Man (Mark 14:41)	67	Son of Man (Luke 19:10)
5	Son of Man (Matthew 12:8)	26	Son of Man (Matthew 25:13)	47	Son of Man (Mark 14:62)	68	Son of Man (Luke 21:27)
6	Son of Man (Matthew 12:32)	27	Son of Man (Matthew 25:31)	48	Son of Man (Luke 5:24)	69	Son of Man (Luke 21:36)
7	Son of Man (Matthew 12:40)	28	Son of Man (Matthew 26:2)	49	Son of Man (Luke 6:5)	70	Son of Man (Luke 22:22)
8	Son of Man (Matthew 13:37)	29	Son of Man (Matthew 26:24)	50	Son of Man (Luke 6:22)	71	Son of Man (Luke 22:48)
9	Son of Man (Matthew 13:41)	30	Son of Man (Matthew 26:24)	51	Son of Man (Luke 7:34)	72	Son of Man (Luke 22:69)
10	Son of Man (Matthew 16:13)	31	Son of Man (Matthew 26:45)	52	Son of Man (Luke 9:22)	73	Son of Man (Luke24:7)
11	Son of Man (Matthew 16:27)	32	Son of Man (Matthew 26:64)	53	Son of Man (Luke 9:26)	74	Son of Man (John 1:51)
12	Son of Man (Matthew 16:28)	33	Son of Man (Mark 2:10)	54	Son of Man (Luke 9:44)	75	Son of Man (John 3:13)

13	Son of Man (Matthew 17:9)	34	Son of Man (Mark 2:28)	55	Son of Man (Luke 9:56)	76	Son of Man (John 3:14)
14	Son of Man (Matthew 17:12)	35	Son of Man (Mark 8:31)	56	Son of Man (Luke 9:58)	77	Son of Man (John 5:27)
15	Son of Man (Matthew 17:22)	36	Son of Man (Mark 8:38)	57	Son of Man (Luke 11:30)	78	Son of Man (John 6:27)
16	Son of Man (Matthew 18:11)	37	Son of Man (Mark 9:9)	58	Son of Man (Luke 12:8)	79	Son of Man (John 6:53)
17	Son of Man (Matthew 19:28)	38	Son of Man (Mark 9:12)	59	Son of Man (Luke 12:10)	80	Son of Man (John 6:62)
18	Son of Man (Matthew 20:18)	39	Son of Man (Mark 9:31)	60	Son of Man (Luke 12:40)	81	Son of Man (John 8:28)
19	Son of Man (Matthew 20:28)	40	Son of Man (Mark 10:33)	61	Son of Man (Luke 17:22)	82	Son of Man (John 12:23)
20	Son of Man (Matthew 24:27)	41	Son of Man (Mark 10:45)	62	Son of Man (Luke 17:24)	83	Son of Man (John 12:34)
21	Son of Man (Matthew 24:30)	42	Son of Man (Mark 13:26)	63	Son of Man (Luke 17:26)	84	Son of Man (John 13:31)

According to the above chart, *Jesus* called himself '*Son of Man*' 84 times in four *Gospels*. Let us see what the *Bible* says about "*Son of God*"?

1	Son of God (Matt 4:3)	DA	12	Son of God (Mark 5:7)	DA	23	Son of God (John 3:16)	JS
2	Son of God (Matt 4:6)	DA	13	Son of God (Mark 15:39)	NP	24	Son of God (John 3:18)	JS
3	Son of God (Matt 8:29)	DA	14	Son of God (Luke 1:32)	NP	25	Son of God (John 5:25)	JS
4	Son of God (Matt 14:33)	DA	15	Son of God (Luke 1:35)	NP	26	Son of God (John 6:69)	DA
5	Son of God (Matt 16:16)	AG	16	Son of God (Luke 4: 3)	DA	27	Son of God (John 9:35)	JS
6	Son of God (Matt 26:63)	DN	17	Son of God (Luke 4: 9)	DA	28	Son of God (John 10:36)	DN
7	Son of God (Matt 27:40)	DA	18	Son of God (Luke 4:41)	DA	29	Son of God (John 11:4)	JS
8	Son of God (Matt 27:43)	DA	19	Son of God (Luke 8:28)	DA	30	Son of God (John 11:27)	DA
9	Son of God (Matt 27:54)	NP	20	Son of God (Luke 22:70)	DN	31	Son of God (John 19:7)	NP

10	Son of God (Mark 1:1)	NP	21	Son of God (John 1:34)	NP	32	Son of God (John 20:31)	NP
11	Son of God (Mark 3:11)	DA	22	Son of God (John 1:49)	DA			

LEGEND: DA=JESUS DIDN'T ANSWER AG=AGREED DN=DENIED NP=NOT PRESENT JS=JESUS SAID

According to the first chart, *Jesus* calls himself the *Son of Man* eighty-four times. In the second chart, the *Bible* used the term '*Son of God*' for *Jesus* thirty-two times in four *Gospels*. But out of *thirty-two* times, *Jesus* actually called himself *Son of God* only *five* times. The *twenty seven* other times are when other people called him *Son of God*. It is very strange that in *Matthew*, *Mark* and *Luke*, *Jesus* did not call himself *Son of God* more than one time. However, only *John* reports that *Jesus* called himself *Son of God* five times. Ironically, when the *Jews* found out that *Jesus* is calling himself *Son of God*, the *Jews* asked *Jesus* about it, and he denied. They surrounded *Jesus*, picked up stones, and wanted to stone him to death. *Jesus* asked:

> "*Many good works have I shewed you from my father; for which of those works do you stone me? The Jews answered him, saying, For a good work we stone thee not; but for blasphemy; and because that thou, being a man, makest thyself God, Jesus answered them, Is it not written in your law, I said, Ye are Gods? If he called them gods, unto whom the word of God came, and the scripture cannot be broken; Say ye of him, whom the Father hath sanctified, and sent into the world, Thou blasphemest; because I said, I am the Son of God?*"[138]

This was the best time for *Jesus* to say 'if you want to stone me, then go ahead and stone me that is what I am: I am *God*, or the *Son of God*.' But instead, what does he tell them? *Jesus* tells them is it not written in your law about *Moses*, when *God* told *Moses*, "*You are god to pharaoh*."[139] If *God* called *Moses* "god," on whom the word of *God* came, '*and the scripture cannot be broken*' (which means this was not a blasphemy to call *Moses* god?) Then why do you think I blasphemed if I said I am son of *God*? Does not that make me the *son of Moses*? The above reference of *Exodus 7:1*, '*You are god to Pharaoh*' has been deleted by the *Contemporary English Version*. It says:

> "*The LORD said: I am going to let your brother Aaron speak for you. He will tell your message to the king, just as a prophet*

---

[138] Please see *John 10:31-36*
[139] Please see *Exodus 7:1*

speaks my message to the people." This version also does not say that *"Aaron will be your prophet."* It only says, *Just as a prophet.*

As I have mentioned earlier, other people called *Jesus Son of God* twenty seven times in four *Gospels.* Out of twenty seven times, *Jesus* was asked fifteen times, are you *Son of God?* But *Jesus* did not answer. When *Jesus* was called son of *God* eight times out of other twelve times, *Jesus* was not even there. Therefore, he did not even know what someone was calling him in his absence. Out of the other four times when *Jesus* was called *Son of God, Jesus* denied it three times. That leaves us only one time in all of *Matthew,* and five times in the *Gospel of John.* In *Matthew, Jesus* did not say explicitly as he said in *John,* but *Jesus* seems to be agreeing with *Simon,* when *Simon* said to *Jesus* that you are *"Son of living God,"* and *Jesus* said:

> *"blessed art thou, Simon Bar-jo'-na: for flesh and blood hath not revealed it unto thee, but my Father who is in heaven."*[140]

But if you insist that even if *Matthew* says only one time, and *John* says five times that *Jesus* was *Son of God,* then he is *Son of God,* and we will take him as *Son of God* or *God's* only begotten son. However, the question is, was *Jesus* the only *Son of God?* Or did *God* call other people son of *God* too? Let us see what the *Bible* says about it.

'Son of God'

1. *"Thus saith The Lord Israel is my Son even my First born"* (*Exodus 4:22*).

2. *"I am a Father to Israel and Ephraim is my First born"* (*Jeremiah 31:9*).

3. *"Solomon is my Son and I will be his Father* (*I Chronicles 28:6*).

4. *"Adam which was the Son of God"* (*Luke 3:38*).

According to this verse of *Luke* every prophet of *God* was the *Son of God,* since the whole world is descendants of *Adam* we all are sons of *God.* (Please see genealogy of *Jesus* by *St. Luke*)

---

[140] Please see *Matthew 16:13-17*

5. *"...what manner of love the Father hath bestowed upon us, that we should be called Sons of God" (I John 3:1).*

6. *"For as many as are led by the Spirit of God they are the Sons of God" (Romans 8: 14).*
   Which means the door to become Son of God is still open to anyone.

7. *"The Spirit itself beareth witness our spirit that we are Children of God" (Romans 8:16).*

8. *"He that overcometh shall inherit all things and I will be his God and he shall be My Son" (Revelation 21:7).* Which means the door to become son of God is still open to anyone.

9. *"...Sons of God came to present themselves before the Lord" (Job 1:6).*

10. Generations of *Adam* are called the *Sons of God (Genesis 6:2).*

11. *"Blessed are the peacemakers for they shall be called the Children of God" (Mathew 5:9).*

12. *"Ye are the Children of the Lord your God" (Deuteronomy 14:1).*

13. *"Israel was a child, then I loved him and called him My Son" (Hosea 11:1).*

14. *"I have said, Ye are gods and all of you are Children of most High" (Psalms 82:6).*

15. *"For ye are all the Children of God by faith in Christ Jesus" (Galatians 3:26).*

16. *"But as many as received him to them gave he power to become Sons of God" (John 1:12).*

According to the above verses of the *Bible, God* himself called two prophets *First born sons.* Is *God* lying about the sons of *God,* and *two first born sons,* or did the *Bible* make a mistake? The truth is that *Son of God, First born son,* and *Only begotten son,* mean only that person is beloved of *God,* or he is a righteous man. Accordingly, any righteous man is *Son of God.* A *Christian* friend of mine said that when it says in the *Gospel of John* "*word was made flesh.*"[141] This means *God* became flesh. Whereas, *Jesus* totally denies that by saying:

> "*That which is born of the flesh is flesh; and that which is born of the Spirit is spirit.*"[142]

It means very clearly that a flesh cannot become spirit, and spirit cannot become flesh. They are not interchangeable.

When *Mary* conceived, she was told by the prophets about the child:

> "*...and they shall call his name "EM - MAN' -U -EL," which being interpreted is, God with us*" (Matthew 1:23).

Many *Christian* friends told me that in this verse, when the *Bible* says about *Jesus* that '*God with us*' this means when *Jesus* is with us, it means *God* is with us. That is true because *Jesus* is a messenger of *God*, and he is a true *Messiah* of his age. Accordingly, whenever a true messenger of *God* comes, it means help and blessings of *God* comes with him. A true messenger of *God* comes in reality as if *God* came Himself. But if I say, I will be with you does that mean that I am you? Saying *Jesus* is *God* is nothing but a blasphemy against *God*. As I have mentioned in the above verse, *Jesus* denied that kind of blasphemy.

[In another verse the angel of the Lord says to *Mary*:

> "*The Holy Ghost shall come upon thee, ...that holy thing which shall be born of thee shall be called the Son of God*" (Luke 1:35).

How much clearer *Bible* could have said than this that he would not really be *God*, but he will just *be called Son of God*. Do you see the difference between "*he **will be** God,* or *he will be **called** the Son of God*?" Otherwise, the *Bible* could have said in clear words that the son who will be born of thee will be *God*.][143]

Assuming something that the *Bible* is not saying is a blasphemy itself against *God*. Ironically, *Mary* who was told by the angel of the *Lord* that your son will be called the *Son of God* never believed her son was *God* and never followed him. On the other hand, the *Christians* of today believe *Jesus* was god and they worship him instead of *God*. Therefore, the *Bible* says:

---

141   Please see *John 1:14*
142   Please see *John 3:6*
143   Bracketed text is reference provided by *M. Asim*

*"Jesus answered, "Who is my mother and who are my brothers?"
Then he pointed to his disciples and said, "These are my mother
and my brothers! Anyone who obeys my Father in heaven is my
brother or sister or mother."[144]*

This clearly means his mother was not the follower. Another strange thing is that *Christians* say that *Mary* was sanctified by *God and* that is why she became the mother of *Jesus*. But what kind of sanctification is that if she did not even believe her own son and could not be his follower?

Jesus said, *"The first of all the commandments is ...The Lord our God is one Lord" (Mark 12:29).* All the prophets of *God* in the *Old Testament* always insisted on *"One God."*

When *Messiah* was prophesied in the *Old Testament*, none of the prophecies ever mentioned that the *Messiah* would be *God.* Even in the *New Testament, Jews* asked *John the Baptist*: *who are you...? ...he confessed...I am not the Christ? ...Are you Elias? ...Are you that prophet?[145]* It shows clearly that the *Jews* were waiting for either *Christ, Elias,* or *that prophet,* but in no case they were waiting for *God* almighty to come *Himself,* or even *His* son.

There is another conversation mentioned in the *New Testament* that talks about a rich man who dies and goes to *hell* and after he sees people being tormented, he sees *Lazarus* who was a poor man in the bosom of *Abraham.* He asks *Abraham* if *Lazarus* can go back and warn his brothers about false practices of men and burning in hell for that. The answer of *Abraham* in that conversation is *"they have Moses and the prophets let them hear them."* If *Jesus* was *God* or son of *God* (God forbid) then why did *Abraham* not tell him that they have *God* or the son of *God* among them and let them hear *God* or the son of *God?* The *Bible* says:

*"Then he [the rich man] said, I pray thee [Abraham] therefore,
father, that thou wouldest send him [Lazarus] to my father's
house For I have five brethren; that he may testify unto them,
lest they also come into this place of torment Abraham saith unto
him, They have Moses and the prophets; let them hear them And
he said, Nay, father Abraham: but if one went unto them from
the dead, they will repent And he said unto him, If they hear not
Moses and the prophets, neither will they be persuaded, though
one rose from the dead" (Luke 16:27-31).*

[144] Please see *Matthew 12: 48 to 50, Contemporary English Version*
[145] Please see *John 1:19-21*

The *Christians* all over the world claim that they believe in one *God*. But when we ask them then what is *"Trinity"* they try to explain that there are three gods in one *God*. According to them, there is *God* the father, which is almighty *God*, then *God* the son *Jesus*, and then god the *Holy Spirit*. All three are one *God*. Another words, they try to explain that *Almighty God* and *Jesus* are one entity. While the *Bible* denies this view clearly, all over in the *New Testament* we find so many verses where *Jesus* is talking to *God*, praying to *God*, and asking his disciples to pray to *God*.

I really wish anyone in the whole *Christian* world could show me only one verse of the *Bible* where *Jesus* said I am *God*, or pray to me. If *Jesus* and *Father* are the same and equal (God forbid), then why did *Jesus* worship his *Father*, but Father never worshiped *Jesus*? Can anyone show me just one verse? *Jesus* always said, whatever you need, pray to *God* and *'you will receive it*.[146] *Jesus* also said *"I ascend unto my Father, and your Father; and to my God and your God."*[147] When *Jesus* said my *Father* and your *Father*, my *God* and Your *God*, *Jesus* cleared the picture, that being the *Son of God* disciples and *Jesus* have no difference, both are not only *Sons of God*, but also both have the same father (*God*). As a result, the people of our time would not have any confusion, as to who is son of *God*, only *Jesus* or we all are sons and daughters of *God*.

Let me include a few sayings of *Jesus*, about *Jesus* and *Father (God)* that shows how he clearly states that *Father* and he are two separate beings and not just one:

1. *Jesus* said to the *Jews*: *"It is also written in your law, that the testimony of two men is true. I am one that bear witness of myself, and the father that sent me beareth witness of me" (John 8:17-18).*

2. *Bible* says: *"He that abideth in the doctrine of Christ, he hath both the Father and the Son" (2John 1:9).*

3. *Jesus* said: *"And he that sent me is with me: the Father hath not left me alone; for I do always those things that please him" (John 8:29).*

4. *Jesus* said: *"If I judge, my judgment is true; for I am not alone, but I and the Father that sent me" (John 8:16).*

5. *Jesus* said: *"My Father is greater than I" (John 14:28).*

---

[146] Please see *Luke 11:10*
[147] Please see *John 20:17*

6. *Jesus* said: *"Ye shall be scattered, every man to his own, and shall leave me alone: and yet I am not alone, because the Father is with me" (John16: 32).*

7. *Jesus* prays to *God*: *"Father, if thou be willing, remove this cup (cup of death) from me" (Luke 22:42-44).* In this prayer, whom *Jesus* was praying to if he is *God* himself? *(God forbid)*

8. *"He [Jesus] went out into a mountain to pray, and continued to pray all night in prayer to God" (Luke 6:12).*

9. *Jesus* said: *"I can of mine own self do nothing; as I hear, I judge: and my judgment is just; because I seek not mine own will, but the will of the Father, which has sent me" (John 5:30).*

10. *Jesus* said: *"My doctrine is not mine, but his that sent me" (John 7:16).*

I understand that there are some verses of the *Bible* which kind of confuse people, especially this one where *Jesus* said:

"...I am in the Father and the Father in me. The words that I speak, I speak not of my self: but the Father that dwelleth in me, he doeth the works."[148]

But people forget that *Jesus* said for his disciples *"It is not you that speak, but the Spirit of your Father, which speaketh in you."*[149] When *Jesus* said *"I am in my Father and the Father is in me,"* people usually construe from this that *Jesus* is saying that the *Father* is *Jesus* and the *Jesus* is father. But they do not take time to read ten more verses in the same chapter. Where *Jesus* said about his disciples that *"I am in my father, and you [Disciples] in me and I in you" (John 14:20),* would that mean that *Jesus* is his disciples and the disciples are *Jesus*? Since *Jesus* is considered *God*, then according to this verse *God* is disciple and the disciples are *God*? Therefore, everybody is *God*? Even *Jesus* showed his frustration with his disciples that his disciples try to pretend that they do the will of *Jesus*, but their heart is far away from him. *Jesus* said:

"These people draw near to Me with their mouth, And honor Me with their lips, But their heart is far from Me. And in vain they worship Me, Teaching as doctrines the commandments of men."[150]

---

[148] Please see *John 14:10*
[149] Please see *Matthew 10:20*
[150] Please see *Matthew 15:8-9*

The *Qur'an* also gives us a similar message, where it seems as if *Qur'an* is saying *Muhammad* is *God* (God forbid). It says:

1. *"...And thou threwest not [the dust on the enemy] when thou didst throw, but it was Allah Who threw it..." (Al-Anfal 8:17-18).*

2. *"Verily, those who swear allegiance to thee indeed swear allegiance to Allah. The hand of Allah is over their hands..." (Al-Fath 48:10-11).*

In these verses, the *Qur'an* is also articulating that what *Muhammad* did was in reality done by *God*. But this is the blessing of *God* that none of the *Muslims* ever construed from these verses that *Muhammad* was *God* (God forbid). Did you know that *Buddha, Krishna, Rama, Zoroaster, Confucius* and many more who never claimed originally that they were god, but they were worshipped as god after their demise? They were all sent by *God* as prophets. In the similar manner, *Jesus* never claimed to be *God* but he was worshipped as god, after his demise.

May *God* give us strength to recognize the one and only ONE *God,* the creator of universe, who does not need any help from any man. Our *God* who does not need any son, who does not need any wife to make divine babies. May we worship Him alone, and not a man. Therefore, the *Bible* says

> *"If you do at all forget the Lord thy God, and walk after other gods, and serve them, I testify against you this day that you shall surely perish. As the nations which the Lord destroyeth before your face, so shall you perish; because you would not be obedient unto the voice of the Lord thy God" (Deuteronomy 8:19 to 20).*

When *God* said *"you shall perish,"* this does not mean only death, because we all have to die anyway, but it means "eternal death." May *God* help us to stay away from hell fire. *Jesus* mentions the hell fire in these words:

> *"And there will be great weeping and gnashing of teeth, for you will see Abraham, Isaac, Jacob, and all the prophets within the Kingdom of God, but you will be thrown out" (Luke 13:28).*

This means even *Christians* can be thrown out of the *Kingdom of God,* not because they are bad people but because they took man as *God. Jesus* also articulated:

"Don't be afraid of those who want to kill you. They can only kill your body; they cannot touch your soul. Fear only God, who can destroy both soul and body in hell" (Matthew 10: 28 NLT).

The *Christians* all over the world claim that *Jesus* was the ONLY perfect man who ever existed. But strange enough, *Jesus* is perfect was never mentioned by any of the four *Gospel* writers. It was only mentioned in one of the letters of *Paul*, which was his personal opinion, rather than *God* calling *Jesus* perfect. As I have mentioned previously in the chapter titled *"the Original Sin,"* God called three prophets perfect and four prophets righteous. But none of the four *Gospel* writers ever wrote about *Jesus* that he was perfect.

Even if we assume for a moment that *Jesus* was perfect, then the *Christians* should contemplate on this issue that in what aspect he was perfect?

1. Was he a perfect son? He cannot be. He had no father, and he never respected his mother (according to the *Christian* belief). He often called his mother *"woman"* which is considered even today to be a very disrespecting act. If a man cannot respect his own mother, how can he teach us to respect our mothers or anyone? Perhaps, this is the reason most people of *Christian* countries have become victim of this misconception and they do not respect their parents.

2. Was he a perfect father? He cannot be because he had no children, (according to the *Christian* belief). Therefore, he had no chance to demonstrate if he was a perfect father or not.

3. Was he a perfect brother? He cannot be because he never recognized his own brothers: *"Who is my mother? and who are my brethren?"* (Matthew 12:48).

4. Was he a perfect husband? He cannot be because he had no wife (according to the *Christian* belief).

5. Was he a perfect ruler? He cannot be because he had no government.

6. Was he a perfect citizen? He cannot be because he was condemned to death by his government.

7. Was he a perfect teacher? Yes? Then why did he say: *"I have yet many things to say unto you, but ye cannot bear them now" (John 16:12).* This means he was unable to teach everything to his

disciples what they supposed to know. *Jesus* only had twelve disciples and out of those twelve one sold him for thirty silver coins (*Judas Iscariot*) and another disciple, *Peter,* cursed him to save his own life (Matthew 26:74). The rest of the disciples ran away to save their lives when *Jesus'* life was in danger. Was he able to teach his disciples how to obey him perfectly?

8. Was he a perfect *Messiah?* He cannot be because he died an accursed death (according to the *Christian* belief).

9. Was he a perfect *Prophet?* He cannot be because most of his prophecies were not fulfilled. (most *Christians* do not deem him as a prophet, they worship him as a god) (God forbid).

10. Was he a perfect *God?* (God forbid) He cannot be because he was half man and half god, according to the *Christians* belief, 50% purity cannot be considered as perfect.

11. Was he a perfect man? He cannot be because he was half god and half man, according to the *Christians*.

12. Was he a perfect *Savior?* He cannot be, because neither he could save the world from sinning, nor he could save his own life.

In what respect he was perfect? Ironically, *Christians* insist very strongly that *Jesus* had no worldly father or physical father, but at the same time they claim emphatically and proudly that *Jesus* was the descendant of *King David.* After a quick look at the next chart you will notice that the scribes did not do a good job pasting this belief on *Jesus. Matthew* starts *Jesus'* lineage from *Abraham* to *Joseph* (husband of mother Mary) and shows forty generations. While *Luke* tries to start with *God* and goes all the way down to *Joseph* with seventy six generations. But if you notice *Luke* reports from *Abraham* to *Joseph* (husband of Mary) and shows fifty five generations.

This means between *Matthew* and *Luke*, there is a difference of fifteen generations from *Abraham* to *Joseph* reported by two *Gospels. Matthew* says that *Jesus* was a descendant of *King David* through his son *Solomon.* On the contrary, *Luke* says that *Jesus* was the descendant of *King David* through his son *Nathan.* How could one man be descendant of two brothers? *Matthew* reports the name of *Joseph's* father was *Jacob.* On the contrary, *Luke* reports that the name of *Joseph's* father was *Heli.* At the end, I would like to draw your attention to the fact that these *Gospel* writers came many years after *Jesus.* This is the reason perhaps they had no basic knowledge of his life.

Genealogy according to (Matthew 1:1-16 NIV)		Genealogy according to (Luke 3:23-38 NIV)			
1	Abraham	1	God	41	Jonam
2	Isaac	2	Adam	42	Joseph
3	Jacob	3	Seth	43	Judah
4	Judah	4	Enosh	44	Simeon
5	Perez	5	Kenan	45	Levi
6	Hezron	6	Mahalalel	46	Matthat
7	Ram	7	Jared	47	Jorim
8	Amminadab	8	Enoch	48	Eliezer
9	Nahshon	9	Methuselah	49	Joshua
10	Salmon	10	Lamech	50	Er
11	Boaz,	11	Noah	51	Elmadam
12	Obed,	12	Shem	52	Cosam
13	Jesse,	13	Arphaxad	53	Addi
14	**King David.**	14	Cainan	54	Melki
15	Solomon[i]	15	Shelah	55	Neri
16	Rehoboam,	16	Eber	56	Shealtiel
17	Abijah,	17	Peleg	57	Zerubbabel
18	Asa,	18	Reu	58	Rhesa
19	Jehoshaphat,	19	Serug	59	Joanan
20	Jehoram,	20	Nahor	60	Joda
21	Uzziah,	21	Terah	61	Josech
22	Jotham,	22	**Abraham**	62	Semein
23	Ahaz,	23	Isaac	63	Mattathias
24	Hezekiah,	24	Jacob	64	Maath
25	Manasseh,	25	Judah	65	Naggai
26	Amon,	26	Perez	66	Esli
27	Josiah,	27	Hezron	67	Nahum
28	Jeconiah	28	Ram	68	Amos
29	Shealtiel,	29	Amminadab	69	Mattathias
30	Zerubbabel,	30	Nahshon	70	Joseph
31	Abiud,	31	Salmon	71	Jannai
32	Eliakim,	32	Boaz	72	Melki

33	Azor,	33	Obed	73	Levi
34	Zadok,	34	Jesse	74	Matthat
35	Akim,	35	**King David**	75	**Heli**[ii]
36	Eliud,	36	Nathan[iii]	76	Joseph
37	Eleazar,	37	Mattatha	77	Jesus
38	Matthan,	38	Menna		
39	**Jacob,**[iv]	39	Melea		
40	Joseph, the husband of Mary (mother of Jesus)	40	Eliakim		

Some modern scholars try to resolve this intricate problem by asserting that *Matthew* tried to show the genealogy of *Jesus*, while *Luke* shows the genealogy of his mother *Mary*. This is the reason they say these two genealogies do not match. While anyone with even a little wisdom or common sense knows that genealogy cannot be traced through the mother.

---

i   Matthew tells us that Jesus was the descendant of King David through his son Solomon.

ii Luke Says Joseph's father's name was Heli. But Matthew tells us the name of Joseph's father was Jacob.

iii Luke tells us that Jesus was the descendant of King David through his son Nathan.

iv. Matthew tells us that the name of Joseph's father was Jacob. But Luke Says Joseph's father name was Heli.

17. Miracles of the People

My *Christian* friends usually tell me that one of their reasons to believe *Jesus* is *God* is that he performed the miracles no man can even imagine being able to perform. Miracles, such as, raising the dead to life, giving sights to the blind, walking on water, etc. A question would be what is a miracle? Is it an act of *God* which shows us that *God* broke his own laws to show that miracle? A second question is would *God* break his own laws? A good law maker does not break his laws: he leaves room to bend them.

For instance, if a man who lives in a jungle, who never knew about the magnetic field, sees a man who is doing tricks with magnets, with small metal objects sticking on the magnet, it's a miracle for that man who never knew about the magnetic field. But is it really a miracle? Did *God* break his own law to do that miracle or was it a phenomenon, the man from jungle was not familiar with? If a person takes a radio to the people who did not know about the radio, is it a miracle for them that a box is talking? Is this really a miracle? In our understanding, a miracle is a phenomenon unknown to the people at the time it occurred. This means no law of *God* was broken, but we just did not know how it occurred. Yes, it is a miracle in the case of prophets and righteous people that *God Almighty* used that law at the time the prophets or the righteous people of *God* needed them most.

For example, the miracle of *Prophet Moses* parting the *Red sea,* or the *Sea of the Reeds*, and saving his people, but the *Pharos* were drowned in the same water. The fact is that when *Moses* came to the sea with his followers it was early in the morning. The *Bible* says:

"And it came between the camp of the Egyptians and the camp of Israel; and it was a cloud and darkness to them."[151]

God showed his miracle by sending a wind which made the water receded, which is in fact an everyday phenomenon. It says in the *Bible*:

"And Moses stretched out his hand over the sea; and the LORD caused the sea to go back by a strong east wind all that night, and made the sea dry land, and the waters were divided."[152]

In modern and scientific language, we call this phenomenon a *low tide*. When the Pharos came, they went in water probably thinking that if *Moses* and his people can go in this low water then why cannot they do that too? But when Pharos started chasing them, within hours the water started to rise and because of a *high tide* they drowned. Yes, it was a miracle that the low tide and the high tides occurred when *Moses* needed them most, but no law of *God* was broken to perform this miracle.

Moses & his followers walked on the seashore, while it was A low tide. (Sketch by Amber & Rija).

---

151   Please see *Exodus 14:20*
152   Please see *Exodus 14:21*

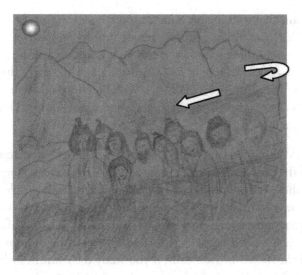

Pharaohs followed the same path & same seashore but unfortunately for them
that high tide had already begun & consequently, they drowned before they
could catch Moses.
(Sketch by Rija & Amber)

Walking on Water

What about *Jesus* raising the dead? The fact is that *Jesus* brought back people
from the dead, who were spiritually dead. *Jesus* gave them new life with his
spiritual teachings. The same applies to giving sight to the blind. *Jesus* gave
spiritual sight to those who were spiritually blind and living in darkness. Is it
not a saying *'O, I see'* for *O' I understand?* Does this mean a person was blind
and now all of a sudden he or she has started to see? What about walking on
water? The *Qur'an* tells us that *God's* throne is on water:

> *"And He it is Who created the heavens and the earth in six*
> *periods, and His throne rests on water..."*[153] The book of
> *Revelation* also gives us a parallel message: *"And the angel*
> *showed me a pure river with the water of life, clear as crystal,*
> *flowing from the throne of God..."*[154]

---

[153] Please see Qur'an Ch. *Hud 11:7-8*
[154] Please see *Revelation 22:1 NLT*

155

This means that walking on water denotes to *walking on the straight path, walking on God's path, to be on the right path* or *walk on the ways of God*, etc. Therefore, if *Jesus* walked on water, it connotes that he was from *God* and he walked the ways of *God*. Prophet *Buddha* also walked on water. This means he was from *God* also. But if you insist that *Jesus* literally walked on water then show me a *Christian* who also can walk on water since *Jesus* said his followers can show these miracles also.

The world famous evangelist, *Mr. Billy Graham*, visited some *African* countries in the early *1960s*. According to many *Christians*, wherever he goes he converts thousands of people into *Christianity*. He heals people of all kind of diseases some of his followers believe (including my friend who told me about him) that he even raises the dead. My question is to his faithful followers that if he is such a great miracle performer, then why he did not accept the challenge of the *Ahmadis*? Ironically, if you study the countries where he was very successful in converting, they were mostly *Christian* countries. Some contend that those are *Catholic* countries, but my point is *Christian, Catholic* or *Protestant*, they all are followers of *Jesus*. But when *Mr. Graham* visited in some *Muslim* dominated countries, he was not successful at all. *Mr. Graham's* biographer, *Mr. William Martin* writes in his book titled *A Prophet with honor*. While *Mr. Graham* never claimed to be a prophet. *Mr. William Martin* writes in the chapter titled *"From VICT'RY UNTO VICT'RY."*

> *"But in Kaduna Kano and Jos, all in the Islam-dominated northern part of the country, he not only attracted modest crowds but stirred strident criticism and resistance from Muslims, who, by his [Mr. Graham's] estimate, were winning ten converts from tribal religions for every one converted to Christianity... They [Muslims] disagreed, however, with his claims for the deity of Christ and resented the straightforward criticism of Islam in his sermons. They were also disappointed when he [Mr. Graham] declined a challenge to debate of their scholars on theological doctrine or even to meet privately with Muslim leaders...*
>
> *...Muslims in Sudan managed to rescind Graham's invitation to preach in that country, apparently because they feared he might disrupt proper observance of Ramadan, the sacred month during which Muslims severely restrict normal activities. The most explicit and memorable Muslim challenge, however, came in Kenya, where Maulana Sheikh Mubarak Ahmad, chief of the Ahmadiyya Muslim Mission in East Africa, hurled a challenge reminiscent of that proposed by the prophet Elijah in*

his famous contest on Mount Carmel with the priests of Baal (1Kings18:20-40).

In a letter to Graham, the Muslim leader proposed that thirty individuals--ten Europeans, ten Asians, and ten Africans, all certified by the director of medical services of Kenya to be incurable by scientific medicine--be assigned by lot into two groups and that he [Mr. Mubarak Ahmad] and Graham, together with a small band of associates, beseech God to heal the group assigned to them "to determine as to who is blessed with the Lord's grace and mercy and upon whom His door remains closed." If Graham declined, [Mubarak] Ahmad argued, "[I]t will be proved to the world that Islam is the only religion which is capable of establishing man's relationship with God."A group of American Pentecostals cabled him to "accept the challenge; the God of Elijah still lives," but Graham neither picked up the gauntlet nor offered any comment to the press."[155]

This basically means he did not accept the challenge at all. What kind of preacher and healer was *Mr. Graham*, who could raise people from dead but he could not pray to heal them and could not accept the challenge from the people he believes are not from *God*.

According to the history of prophets, nobody has ever accepted a prophet of *God* based on the miracles. On the contrary, when the people see anything done unusual by any prophet, they usually call those prophets magicians and they angrily walk away from them. If *Jesus* showed all those miracles then why no one believed him because of those miracles? Can you name even one disciple from the *New Testament* who became the follower of *Jesus* because he had seen the miracles of *Jesus*? *Jesus* started his ministry with twelve disciples. He lost one (Judas of Iscariot) but there is no evidence from the *Bible* if any of his disciples was added in the group of *Jesus'* followers just because he had seen those miracles. Then what was the purpose of those miracles if no one would believe them anyway? I have also stated that *Krishna, Buddha, Osiris, Dionysus, Horus, Apollonius, Mithras* and many more showed exactly the same miracles and according to the *Christians* they were all false deities. If the false deities could show the similar miracles as demonstrated by *Jesus* then how could the *Christians* convince us that *Jesus* was a true deity? And what is the purpose of his miracles anyway?

---

[155] Please see the book, *A prophet with honor; The Billy Graham story*, by *William Martin* on pages 259-260, published by *William Morrow and Company*, Inc. New York, ISBN# 0-688-06890-1

As I have mentioned earlier, when a few *Pharisees* came to ask *Jesus* to show them a sign, *Jesus* says:

> "An evil and adulterous generation seeketh after a sign; and there shall no sign be given to it, but the sign of the prophet Jonas."[156]

Jesus himself denied all those miracles by saying there will be no sign given to them. Why did he not say look at all of his signs or ask people who saw his signs. He raised people from dead, he gave sight to the blind people, he walked on water, he fed *5000* people with only five small fish. Instead, he said there will be no sign given. *Jesus* made clear not to be confused by his signs by saying the following:

> "He that believes on me, the works that I do shall he do also; and greater works than these shall he do."[157]

This means if *Jesus* raised the dead literally, then anyone who believes in *Jesus* should be able to raise the dead literally too. If *Jesus* walked on water literally, then anyone who believes in him should also be able to walk on water literally too. If *Jesus* fed 5000 people with only five small fish, then anyone who believed in him should be able to do so. Right? *Jesus* says "*and greater works than these shall he do.*" This means any *Christian* should be able to do greater miracles than the miracles performed by *Jesus*. Let me elucidate, when I show this commandment of *Jesus* to my *Christian* friends, they usually say that yes, if you have a perfect faith in *Jesus* you can perform all these miracles just like *Jesus* did. But *Jesus* never said you need to have perfect faith, in order to perform these miracles.

As a matter of fact, *Jesus,* at another occasion, says:

> "for verily I say unto you, If ye have faith as a grain of mustard seed, ye shall say unto this mountain, Remove hence to yonder place; and it shall remove; and nothing shall be impossible unto you."[158]

This means you can have as little faith as possible and still you can perform his miracles. *Jesus* also says "*even false prophets will show great signs and wonders.*"[159] If false prophets can show the same signs and wonders as *Jesus*

---

[156] Please see *Matthew 12:38-39*
[157] Please see *John 14:12*
[158] Please see *Matthew 17:20*
[159] Please see *Matthew 24:24*

did, then what is the purpose of his signs to begin with? If you still think that *Jesus* is the only one who walked on water, raised the dead, and gave sight to the blind then please read the following list of other people who performed similar miracles:

1. *"Elisha walked on water"* (2 Kings 2:14).

2. *"Elijah went up to heaven in a chariot of fire and horses of fire"* (2Kings 2:11).

3. *"Paul raised a dead man to life"* (Acts 20:9 to 12).

4. *"Elijah raises a dead child alive"* (1 Kings 17:21 to 22).

5. *"Elisha raises a dead child alive"* (2 Kings 4:32 to 35).

6. *"Elisha cures Naaman of leprosy"* (2 Kings 5:1 to 14).

7. *"Elijah heals a blinded army and restores the eyesight of its men"* (2Kings 6:20).

8. *"A dead man's body touches Elisha's bones, the man comes to life and stands up on his feet"* (2Kings 13: 21).

9. *"Moses makes darkness for three days"* (Exodus 10:22).

10. *"Moses makes sea to go back by a strong wind and makes sea a dry land"* (Exodus 14:21).

11. *"Moses turned water throughout the land of Egypt into blood"* (Exodus 7:17 to 20).

12. *"Joshua* ordered the sun and moon to stay still *'and the sun and moon stopped'"* (Joshua 10:13).

13. *"The priests make the whole nation pass Jordan by making a dry passage in Flooded River"* (Joshua 3:17).

14. *"Ezekiel raises up a slain army, from dry, scattered bones into life"* (Ezekiel 37:10).

15. *"Four men were thrown into fire and were not burnt"* (Daniel 3:25).

16. *"Paul cured a cripple"* (Acts 14:8-10).

17. *"Ananias restored eyesight of Paul" (Acts 9:17-18).*

18. *"Phillip healed palsies and lamed" (Acts 8:5-7).*

The *Qur'an* gives us a very interesting insight in regards to the miracles. I will present the summary of a few verses. It says when a prophet comes and claims that *God* has spoken to him and he is the messenger of *God*, people immediately reject that prophet and say that he is just an ordinary man and as a matter of fact he is worst among us. We have power, we have money and we are majority in number. He (the claimant) is poor, he has no status, and only a few and weak people follow him--*Jesus* was accused by the *Jews* that only few illiterate, weak and poor fishermen accepted him--why he does not show us great signs and wonders as our earlier prophets have shown? And on this excuse most people reject that prophet.

But those few who believe that prophet, they believe not because of his signs or wonders, but they believe that prophet because of his righteousness. After the demise of that prophet a few hundred years later, the believers of that prophet falsely attribute great signs and wonders to that prophet. When a new prophet comes, the same cycle starts all over again; people say to the new prophet, 'you are an ordinary man and we see nothing special in you or in your followers. Why do you not show us great signs and wonders as our earlier prophets have shown?' Then they reject that prophet as a liar and imposter. This cycle of "show us a sign like the great signs of our earlier prophets" does not seem to be ever ending.

We should stop and think what are we doing? We always reject a prophet because we think he is an ordinary man and we see nothing special in him. After we accept that prophet, we attribute false signs to him. Then we reject the new prophet based on those false signs we attributed to the earlier prophets. *Prophet Muhammad* was rejected by *Christians* because he did not show great signs and wonders like *Jesus*. But *Jesus* was rejected by the *Jews* because *Jesus* did not show those great signs and wonders like those of *Moses*. Now *Prophet Ahmad* (the Second Coming of Christ) has been rejected by *Christians* and *Muslims* because he did not show great signs and wonders as *Jesus* and *Muhammad* showed. The concept of "show us a sign like the great signs of our earlier prophets" is a summary of verses of the *Qur'an*. It does not say in a sequence as I have presented, please review the following verses of the *Qur'an*:

1. *"The chiefs of (Noah's) people, who disbelieved, replied, 'We see thee nothing but a mortal like ourselves, and we see that none have*

followed thee but those who, to all outward appearance, are the meanest of us. And we do not see in you any superiority over us; nay, we believe you to be liars" (HUD 11:27-28).

2. *"But now when the truth (Muhammad) has come to them [Jews] from US, they say, 'Why has he not been given the like of what was given to Moses?' Did they not reject that which was given to Moses before?' They said, 'Aaron and Moses are but two sorcerers who back up each other.' And they say, 'We reject the claim of both" (Al-Qasas 28:48-49).*

3. *"And they say, 'What sort of Messenger is this that he eats food, and walks in the streets? Why has not an angel been sent down to him that he might be a warner with him? 'Or a treasure should have been sent down to him, or he should have had a garden to eat there from.' And the wrongdoers say, 'You follow but a man bewitched"* (Al-furqaan 25: 7-9).

18. God's promise to Ahmad

God promised *Ahmad (the Second Coming of Jesus Christ)* that He would send signs after signs to prove that *Ahmad* is the true messenger of *God* and the *Second Coming of Jesus Christ. God* also revealed to him three major misunderstandings of the *Christian* belief, that is to say, 1) *Jesus* didn't die on the cross, 2) *Jesus* is not *God*, 3) *Jesus* did not go up to the heavens bodily. After *God's* promise with *Ahmad*, these incidents occurred, which proves the truthfulness of his revelation.

1. **Tomb of Jesus**: The *tomb of Jesus* was found in *Srinagar, Kashmir, India*. *BBC FOUR* London made a documentary titled *Did Jesus Die?* Which tells us a detailed account of *Jesus'* survival from the cross and his journey to *India*. Many books including *Jesus lived in India*, by *Holger Kersten, Roza Bal The Tomb of Jesus* by *Ms. Suzanne Olsson* and *Fida M Hassnain, Jesus in Kashmir: The Lost Tomb* by *Ms. Suzanne Olsson* and *Jesus & Moses are buried in India, by Gene D. Matlock,* talk about the life of *Jesus in India*.

2. **Shroud of Jesus**: The *shroud of Jesus* has been discovered. Surprisingly, it shows too much blood than what would bleed from a corpse, consequently, proving *Jesus* was alive when he was wrapped in it. (This comes from a book titled *Christ did not Perish on the Cross*, Published by the *Exposition Press Inc.* of *New York*). Maybe this is the reason *Christians* try their best to disprove the authenticity of the shroud. In their hearts they know it very well that it is the shroud of *Jesus;* this is the reason they

keep it very safe in a beautiful glass show case. But to keep their faith alive they reject it as a medieval forgery.

3. **Crucifixion: By an Eye Witness** A letter has been discovered which is believed to have been written about seven years after the crucifixion. In this letter, the disciple who wrote it says that he was an eye witness to the crucifixion of *Jesus Christ*. He clearly mentions that *Jesus* did not die on the cross and *Jesus* did not go up to the heavens bodily. (*Crucifixion: By an Eye Witness*, this letter was published by *Indo American Book Company*. Translated in *English* in 1907 ISBN #1-56459-853-5)

4. **Gospel of Philip:** The *Gospel of Philip* has been discovered. This Gospel says: *"Those who say that the Lord died first and then rose up are in error, for he rose up first and then died."* (*Gospel of Philip 63:31*)

5. **Life of Yuz Asaf:** A book has been discovered which talks about a prophet from *Israel*, named *Yuz Asaf*, and also talk about his book called *Injeel* (Gospel). The book *Injeel* is similar to the four *Gospels* with the exception of '*Trinity*.' There is no mention of three gods in one in *Injeel*. This means that a prophet of *Israel* went to *India* and lived there. The question is how many people we know who were prophets from Israel and brought a book called *Gospels* or *Injeel* . This book shows that not all of the scrolls of *The New Testament* portray *Jesus* as *God* or part of *Trinity*. (*Roohani Khazain* (Spiritual Treasures) *Vol. 17 pg.#100* or *Touhfa-e-Gulervia* by *Ahmad* pg. #14 paraphrased)

6. **Gospel of Mary Magdalene:** The *Gospel of Mary Magdalene* has been discovered. The Gospel says that *Mary Magdalene* was not only the most favorite of *Jesus*, but she was the symbol of wisdom. *Mary Magdalene* became the teacher and woman in charge of the early *Christian* church (Based on a documentary film by *Discovery Channel* titled *The real Mary Magdalene*).

7. **Gospel of Thomas:** The *Gospel of Thomas* has been discovered in *India*. It does not talk about the birth stories, *Jesus* being *God* (God forbid), dying of *Jesus* on the cross, or the miracle stories. It corroborates with the *Qur'an and* portrays *Jesus* as a prophet.

8. **Barbara Thiering**, **Ph.D.** *Barbara Thiering* has been a *Biblical* scholar, theologian, and the *Dead Sea Scrolls* expert for twenty

years. She is a professor at *Sydney University, Australia.* In her book, *Jesus and the riddle of the Dead Sea Scrolls, Dr. Thiering* writes that according to the study of the *Dead Sea Scrolls, Jesus* did not die on the cross and *Jesus* was just a man and not a *god.* She further states that *Jesus married Mary Magdalene and had three children.*

9. **The New Testament:** The oldest, most complete copy of The *New Testament* was found in *Syria.* It is known as the *'Syriac Edition'* and contains *Ahmad's* name in the *Gospel* of *John 18:37-38.* It does not say Comforter, it says Emeth or Ehmeth, which is also found in *Hebrew King James,* please type *"truth"* or type *"h571"* in search area of the on-line Bible website called blueletterbible. org.

10. **The discovery of tombs:** Many tombs have been discovered of the people who were known to have gone to heaven, such as, the *Tomb of Mary,* mother of *Jesus.* It was found in *Mari, Pakistan.* The city *Mary* was named after her in her honor of being the mother of *Jesus.* The *Tomb of Moses, Tomb of Aaron (brother of Moses), Tomb of Solomon* and the *Tomb of Mary Magdalene* are all in *India.* The *Tomb* of *John the Baptist* is purportedly has been discovered in the *Island of Patmos.* The Tomb of *Baba Guru Nanak* (founder of Sikh religion) has also been found.

11. **Old coins:** Two *old coins* were found in *India.* One has *Jesus'* name on it in *'Pali'* characters, and the other has a picture of an *Israelite* that could be a picture of *Jesus. Pali* is a language that is primarily spoken by *Kashmiris of India.* These coins show that *Jesus* visited *Kashmir,* it also shows that he received the highest respect before his death (*Jesus in India*).

12. **Golgotha:** The name of the place where *Jesus* was crucified is *"Golgotha,"* which means *"a place of a skull."* The tomb of *Jesus* is found in a city called *"Sri-nagar,"* which literally means *"a place of a skull"* (Matthew 27:33), (*Jesus in India*).

13. **Bodily Ascension and All RSV Bibles.** All *RSV Bibles* by *American Bible Society, Oxford University Press, Harper Collins, Thomas Nelson,* and *World Publishing Company* never mentioned the bodily ascension of *Jesus* to heaven until *1971.*

14. **Tomb of *Jesus***: *The Tomb of Jesus* found in *Kashmir* is of the same type as the one in which *Jesus* was placed in during a state of unconsciousness, after crucifixion. The tomb is older than the *Muslim Era*. The position of the tomb tells us that it does not belong to a *Muslim* because *Muslim* tombs are always positioned *north* and *south,* while this tomb is positioned *east* and *west,* exactly the way *Jewish* tombs are. *Hindus* do not bury, but cremate their dead ones. Therefore, it cannot belong to a *Hindu,* either.

15. ***Prophet Muhammad in the King James Bible:*** The name of Prophet *Muhammad* was found in the *Hebrew King James Version Songs of Solomon 5:16,* Please see *"altogether lovely"* in *Hebrew* Concordance you'll see מחמד *"Machmad."* You might think it says *Machmad* not *Muhammad,* but in *Hebrew* 'ch' is pronounced as 'kha' or 'ha' as throat clearing. As we see in *Chanukah* but we pronounce it *Hanukah.* Please see *Blue Letter Bible.org*

16. ***Jesus' words:*** A group of *200* mainline *Biblical* scholars from all over *America* concluded after six years of voting in *"Jesus Seminar"* that *80%* of words attributed to *Jesus* in the *Bible* are not his (*L.A times March 4th 1991*).

Seminar Rules Out 80% of Words Attributed to Jesus

■ Religion: Provocative meeting of biblical scholars ends six years of voting on authenticity in the Gospels.

By JOHN DART
TIMES RELIGION WRITER

The provocative Jesus Seminar on Sunday concluded six years of voting on what the Jesus of history most likely said, ruling out about 80% of words attributed to him in the Gospels and emerging with the picture of a prophet-sage who told parables and made pithy comments.

Virtually all of Jesus' words in the Gospel of John were voted down by scholars meeting in Sonoma, including a pulpit favorite, 3:16, "For God so loved the world that he gave his only Son. . . ."

Formed in part to counteract literalist views of the Bible, the Jesus Seminar, a 200-member group of mainline biblical scholars from all over the country, has stirred controversy since its first meetings in 1985. "Televangelists on talk shows say it's the work of the devil," said founder Robert Funk, a New Testament scholar who has published widely in Gospel studies.

The scholars have met twice a year examining either particular Gospels or types of sayings, basing their discussions on earlier scholarship and their own studies.

Many academic colleagues have criticized, among other things, the seminar's unconventional voting techniques—red and pink beads dropped into a ballot box for probable or possible authentic sayings.

Please see SEMINAR, A24

17. **DNA:** The DNA tests done by *British* scientists to test for *Jewish* descent in *Kashmiri* people of *India* and people of *Afghanistan* conclusively proves that they are descendants of the *Israelites* (*Wall Street Journal May 11ᵗʰ 1998*).

18. *The Jesus Conspiracy*: According to the book *The Jesus Conspiracy* by *Holger Kersten*, *"The director of the investigation of the shroud, Dr. Michael Tite, was given a bribe of one million pounds by the Vatican to manipulate the results of the Radiocarbon dating of 1988 to present the shroud as a medieval forgery... He further states, the discussions were rocking the Christian Church to its foundations."*

19. *Marham-i-Isa:* Or the '*Ointment of Jesus.*' In the very time of *Jesus*, a little after the event of the cross, a pharmaceutical work, '*Qarabadin-i-Rumi,*' was compiled in *Latin*. There was a mention of this preparation along with the statement that the preparation had been prepared for the wounds of *Jesus* by his disciples. With the help of this ointment, the wounds of *Jesus* healed up so

miraculously that he was able to walk about seventy miles on foot within a few days from *Jerusalem* to *Galilee* (*Jesus in India*). Thus the *Bible* says: *"Then said Jesus unto them, Be not afraid: go tell my brethren that they go into Galilee, and there shall they see me"* (Matthew 28:10).

20. **Jesus' words**: *Jesus* said: *For assuredly, I say to you,* you *will not have gone through the cities of Israel before the Son of Man comes* (Matthew 10:23). *Israel* became a state in *1948* then, where is the *Messiah*? Did *God* make a mistake that He let the *Jews* walk through the cities of *Israel* before the *Messiah* came? Or the *Messiah* is here, but people are just unable to recognize him?

21. **Scrolls:** *The Scrolls* of *Nag Hammadi* have been discovered.

22. **Hyacine:** A powerful natural anesthetic called *Hyacine* could be the cause for the fainting of *Jesus* on the cross. *Hyacine* grows in the roots of a plant called *Mandrake*. It was available in the time of *Genesis (Genesis 30:14-15-16; Song of Songs 7:13)* all the way up to the time of *Jesus*, and it is available even today. It was mixed with vinegar and offered to *Jesus* perhaps, when he was on the cross. That could be the reason for his fainting. (Based on a documentary by *Discovery Channel* titled *Jesus: The complete story, The Last Days*).

23. **Books:** Over twenty books have been written on the subject of *Jesus in India*. If the survival and travel of *Jesus* was an erroneous idea, then why more and more books and documentaries are coming out, mostly by *Christian* scholars?

24. **Sect of Christianity:** A Sect of *Christianity* has been discovered in *Herat, Afghanistan*, whose leader *Abba Yahyah* claims that they were taught *Christianity* originally by *Jesus* himself, while he was migrating from *Palestine* to *India*. (Please see the book *Among the Dervishes* by *O. M. Burke* ISBN: 0525473866 on page #107)

25. **Kurt Berna:** A *Catholic*, the first man to work on the shroud saw a vision in his wake in which *Jesus* appeared to him. According to *Mr. Berna, Jesus* told him that he never died on the cross, and was taken down from the cross alive but unconscious. *Berna* was imprisoned for this claim, but he never changed his statement.

26. ***Movies and documentaries:*** Many movies and documentaries have been aired about Jesus in India, these documentaries comprised of *Did Jesus Die,* by BBC four London, *Did Jesus Die,* by Australian Broadcasting Corporation, *Jesus in Himalayas,* by *Jeff Salz,* aired on *Discovery Channel, The Hidden Story of Jesus,* by Channel4 (UK), and *Jesus in India,* by *Edward T. Martin,* aired on *Sundance* Channel.

27. An *Old Testament* book, supposedly written by *King David* has raised many eye brows. This book tells us the survival of *Jesus* from the cross and living up to a ripe old age. Please see *Psalms or the fifth Gospel?*

Ahmad said over 120 years ago that *God* had promised him that many signs will come until his truth will be established on earth. If he is a liar (God forbid) then believe that liar whose prophecies have all been fulfilled. The question is why would *God* make his prophecies fulfilled if *Ahmad* is a liar? Another interesting point is there have not been any discoveries in the last fourteen hundred years which shook the foundation of *Islam.* No new theories have become popular in *Islam* that proves previous beliefs false. Yes, I am sure you might have heard from your priests that there are examples which prove *Islam* to be a false religion. But those are only allegations against *Islam* which have no basis at all. The question remains is why does almost every discovery made by *Christians* and *Jews* prove many of their beliefs to be in error? The answer lies in the statement of the *Qur'an* that *Jews* and *Christians* have changed their *Bible.* They do not like to admit this change, but I have written about it in the chapter titled *Bible vs. Qur'an.* Please review it and see for yourself. *God* did not misguide *Jews* and the *Christians* by saying something in one *Bible* and something else in another *Bible.* All these seemingly contradictions in the *Bible* are the creation of human hands and not by *God.*

19. Psalms or the Fifth Gospel?

Please compare the following verses of *Psalms* to the *New Testament*. They are almost identical to the *New Testament* verses. It might make you think whether the book of *Psalms* is supposed to be the fifth *Gospel* of the *New Testament* or not:

1) *"My God, my God, why have you forsaken me?" (Psalms 22:1).*
1) *"My God, my God, why have you forsaken me?" (Matthew 27:46 & Mark 15:34).*

2) *"They pierced my hands and my feet" (Psalms 22:16).*
2) *"They shall look on him whom they pierced" (John 19:37).*

3) *"…and in my thirst they gave me vinegar to drink" (Psalms 69:21).*
3) *"…I thirst. …they filled a spunge with vinegar …put it to his mouth…" (John 19:28-30).*

4) *"He keeps all his bones: not one of them is broken" (Psalms 34:20).*
4) *"A bone of him shall not be broken" (John 19:36).*

5) *"All they that see me laugh me to scorn: they shake the head" (Psalms 22:7).*
5) *"Those who passed by hurled insults at him, ' shaking their heads'" (Matthew 27:39 & Mark 15:29; NIV Bible).*

6) *"let him deliver him…" (Psalms 22:7).*
6) *"let him deliver him…" (Matthew 27:43).*

7) *"But when he cried unto him, He heard" (Psalms 22:24).*

169

7) "…strong crying and tears unto him that was able to save him, and was heard in that he feared" (Hebrews 5:7).

8) "They part my garments among them, and cast lots upon my vesture" (Psalms 22:18).
8) "They parted my garments among them, upon my vesture did they cast lots" (Matthew 27:35, Mark 15:24, and John 19:24).

9) "In my distress I called upon the Lord, and cried to my God: he heard my voice… Then the earth shook and trembled; the foundations also of the hills moved and were shaken, because he was wroth [angry]" (Psalms 18:6-7).
9) "…and the earth did quake and the rocks rent" (Matthew 27:51). God was angry, when the *Jews* tried to kill *Jesus* on the cross. But If *Jesus* died on the cross to please *God*, then *God* should be happy not angry.

10) "False witnesses are risen up against me" (Psalms 27:12 & 35:11).
10) "…many false witnesses came, yet found they none. At last came two false witnesses" (Matthew 26:60).

11) "All your garments are scented with myrrh and aloes and cassia" (Psalms 45:8).
11) "…Nicodemus, which at the first came to Jesus by night and brought a mixture of myrrh and aloes…" (John 19:39).

12) "…in whom I trusted, which did eat of my bread, hath lifted up his heel against me" (Psalms 41:9).
12) "…whom I have chosen: …he that eateth bread with me hath lifted up his heels against me" (John 13:18).

13) "Your God has anointed you. With the oil of gladness more than your companions" (Psalms 45:7).
13) "…thy God hath anointed thee with the oil of gladness above thy fellows" (Hebrews 1:9).

14) "They look and stare upon me" (Psalms 22:17).
14) "And the people stood looking on [Jesus]" (Luke 23:35).

15) "The king of earth set themselves, and the rulers take counsel together, against the Lord and against his anointed [Messiah]…" (Psalms 2:2)
15) "And the Pharisees went forth and straightway took counsel with the Herodians against him" (Mark 3:6).

16) "Lord said unto my Lord, sit thou at my right hand, until I make thine enemies thy footstool" (Psalms 110:1).

16) "Lord said unto my Lord, sit thou on my right hand, till I make thine enemies thy footstool" (Matthew 22:44; Mark 12:36; Luke 20:42; Acts 2:34-35 & Hebrews 1:13).

17) "The Lord is on my side; I will not fear: what can man do unto me?'"(Psalms 118:6).
17) "The Lord is my helper, and I will not fear what man shall do unto me?" (Hebrews 13:6).

18) "Then said I, Lo, I come: in the volume of the book it is written of me, I delight to do thy will, O my God" (Psalms 40:7-8).
18) "Then said I, Lo, I come (in the volume of the book it is written of me,) to do thy will, O God" (Hebrews 10:7).

19) "For thou wilt not leave my soul in hell" (Psalms16: 10).
19) "Because thou wilt not leave my soul in hell" (Acts 2:27).

20) "But the meek shall inherit the earth" (Psalms 37:11).
20) "Blessed are the meek: for they shall inherit the earth" (Matthew 5:5).

21) "Blessed be he that comes in the name of the Lord" (Psalms 118:26).
21) "Blessed is he that comes in the name of the Lord" (Matthew 21:9; Matthew 23:39 & Luke 13:35; NKJV).

22) "The stone which the builders refused is become the head stone of the corner" (Psalms 118:22).
22) "The stone which the builders rejected, the same is become the head of the corner" (Matthew 21:42).

23) "He will gnash with his teeth and melt away" (Psalms 112:10).
23) "...there shall be weeping and gnashing of teeth"(Matthew 25:30).

24) "I am counted with them that go down into the pit" (Psalms 88:4).
24) "And he was numbered with transgressors" (Mark 15:28 & Isaiah 53:12).

I have mentioned only *twenty-four* verses that are quoted in the *New Testament*. But the fact is that some *346* verses throughout the *Psalms* are quoted in the *New Testament*. Now the question is who wrote the *Psalms*? If it is true that the *Psalms* were written by *King David* and these were the prophecies about *Jesus*. Then contemplate on this point, if almost every major event of the life of *Jesus* was mentioned in the *Old Testament*, and in this case, in the *Psalms*, then don't you think that the *Jews* would have read it beforehand? If they would have seen everything mentioned in their book occurred in the same exact manner, don't you think that they would have accepted him instead of crucifying him mercilessly? The fact is that these *Psalms* were written by *Jesus* after the events had already taken place that is the reason *Jews* had no knowledge of them.

Was the Psalms really written by King David?

When I started to research about the *Psalms*, every clue indicated that it was not written by *David*. The research conclusively proves that almost 80% of it was written by *Jesus* himself. I know that it sounds a bit strange, but I have many pieces of evidence to prove it. Let us see what the most prominent *Bible* scholars say about the origins of the *Psalms*:

1. According to the book titled *The Oxford Companion to the Bible*: *"There is no hard evidence for the Davidic author ship of any of the Psalms. David's reputation as a musician (1Sam 16:23 & Amos 6:5) makes it reasonable to associate him with the Psalms, but it is not possible to prove authorship"* Copyright ©1993 by *Oxford University Press*. Edited by *Bruce M. Metzger* and *Michael D. Coogan*. On page #626; ISBN# 0-19-5046455:

2. According to the book titled *Family Guide to the Bible, A concordance and Reference Companion to the King James Version*.: *"Nearly half the Psalms have a heading attributing them to David, though he was probably not their author"* Copyright © 1984 by *Reader's Digest Association, Inc.* page #22; ISBN # 0-89577-192-6.

3. *"...Scholars now hesitate or refuse to date Psalms to the time of David [in general they were dated much later, some writers at the turn of the twentieth century even denying the possibility that any of the Psalms predated the Babylonian exile]."* Harper Bible Dictionary by *Paul J. Achtemeier* Copyright © 1996 by *Harper Collins*. On page #892-893; ISBN # 0-06-060037-3

4. According to the *Wikipedia Encyclopedia*: *"This is not intended to imply that David wrote all of the Zabur, [Psalms] because there were actually several prophets and holy men who contributed to the Zabur. However, Prophet David wrote more of the Zabur than anyone else. Other contributors include Musa, Uzair, Sulayman, Ethan,*

Heman, and Asaph. Many of the chapters state at the beginning who wrote that particular chapter." Wikipedia also says: *"Since the Psalms were written down in Hebrew not before the 6th century BCE, nearly half a millennium after David's reign (about 1000 BCE), they doubtless depended on oral tradition for transmission of any Davidic material."*

5. According to the *International Standard Bible Encyclopaedia*, *"In most cases it is plain that the editors meant to indicate the authors or writers of the Psalms. It is possible that the phrase "to David" may sometimes have been prefixed to certain Psalms, merely to indicate that they were found in a collection which contained Davidic Psalms. It is also possible that the titles "to Asaph" and' "to the sons of Korah" may have originally meant that the Psalms thus designated belonged to a collection in the custody of these temple singers. Psalms 72 may also be a prayer for Solomon rather than a Psalms BY Solomon.*

*At the same time, we must acknowledge, in the light of the titles describing the occasion of composition, that the most natural interpretation of the various superscriptions is that they indicate the supposed authors of the various poems to which they are prefixed. Internal evidence shows conclusively that some of these titles are incorrect. Each superscription should be tested by a careful study of the psalms to which it is appended. **The book is possibly more highly esteemed among Christians than by the Jews. If Christians were permitted to retain only one book in the Old Testament, they would almost certainly choose Psalms.** By 100 BC, and probably at a much earlier date, the Book of Psalms was completed and recognized as part of the Hagiographa, the 3rd division of the Hebrew Bible. ...It is the fashion among advanced critics to waive the titles of the Psalms out of court as wholly worthless and misleading."*[160]

A proof of this trend that the book of *Psalms* is more esteemed by the *Christians* than the *Jews* may be observed in the following *New Testament Bibles*, where only the *Psalms* was taken as more worthy to be read by the *Christians* than any other *Old Testament* book:

---

[160] Written by Sampey, John Richard. *Psalms, Book of, 1, International Standard Bible Encyclopaedia.* Edited by James Orr. Blue Letter Bible. 1913. 5 May 2003. 8 May 2004. <http://cf.blueletterbible.org/isbe/isbe.cfm?id=7145>

19. Psalms or the Fifth Gospel?

1) *Today's English Version* of the *New Testament and Psalms,* by *The Macmillan Company, New York,* Copyright © *1971* by *American Bible Society.*

Today's English Version
OF THE
New Testament
and Psalms

A TRANSLATION
MADE BY THE
AMERICAN BIBLE SOCIETY

THE MACMILLAN COMPANY

NEW YORK, NEW YORK

2) *New Testament, and Psalms* by *Thomas Nelson Inc. Nashville, New York* (pocket size).

3) *New Testament and Psalms, An Inclusive Version* by *Victor Roland Gold, and Jr. Thomas L. Hoyt, Oxford University Press 01 August, 1995 ~ ISBN: 0195284186.*

4) *Swahili, New Testament with Psalms,* Copyright © 1995 by *American Bible Society, ISBN: 9966400591.*

5) *New Testament Psalms (KJV)* Copyright © 1995 by *Broadman & Holman Publishers*; ISBN: 1558190449

6) *New Testament and Psalms,* Copyright © 2003 by *Cambridge University Press*; ISBN: 0521530040.

7) *The Orthodox Study Bible: New Testament and Psalms,* Copyright © 1993 by Thomas Nelson Publishers.

8) *New Testament and Psalms, Contemporary English Version* Copyright © 2002 by *American Bible Society*; ISBN: 1585165387

9) *The Niv Quiet Time Bible: New Testament & Psalms* Copyright © 1994 by *Intervarsity Press*

10) *Slim-Line New Testament with the Psalms-NRSV* Copyright © 1990 by *World Bible Publishing*; ISBN # 0529068354

In fact, there are over hundred *Bible* publishers who have appended *New Testament* with *Psalms* only. Why these *Bible* publishers only publishing the *Psalms* with the *New Testament*? Perhaps, they know it was written by *Jesus* and not by *David.*

Let us see what the *Bible* itself says about the different Chapters of the *Psalms.* If you look at the headings of the following *Bibles*: *New King James Version* Copyright © 1983 by *Thomas Nelson,* Inc., The Holy Bible *Douay Rheims Version* Copyright © 1971 by *Tan Books and Publishers, Inc. King James Version* Copyright © 1819 by *British and Foreign Bible Society,* and Holy Bible by *Society of St Paul* Copyright © 1958, you will find as follows:

1. Chapter 2 has a heading *'The Messiah's Triumph and Kingdom'* -------- in the New King James Version

2. Chapter 3 has a heading *'…the passion and resurrection of Christ'* -------- in the Douay Rheims Version

3. Chapter 4 has a footnote '...*Psalms thus inscribed to refer to Christ'* -------- in the Douay Rheims Version

4. Chapter 8 has a heading '...*the incarnation of Christ'* ----------- ------------ in the Douay Rheims Version

5. Chapter 9 has a footnote '...*the humility and sufferings of Christ'*----------- in the Douay Rheims Version

6. Chapter 13 has a heading '...*corruption of man before our redemption by Christ'*- in the Douay Rheims Version

7. Chapter 15 has a heading '*Christ's future victory and triumph...'* ----------- in the Douay Rheims Version

8. Chapter 16 has a heading '*The Hope of the Faithful, and the Messiah's Victory'* in the..."-----------NKJV

9. Chapter 20 has a heading '...*Christ's exaltation after his passion'* ---------- in the Douay Rheims Version

10. Chapter 21 has a heading '*Christ's passion: and the conversion of the Gentiles'*- in the Douay Rheims Version

11. Chapter 22 has a heading '*The suffering, Praise, and Posterity [future generations] of the Messiah'*------------------------------- --*in the* ---------- New King James Version

12. Chapter 23 has a heading '...*Christ's triumphant ascension thither'* ------ in the Douay Rheims Version

13. Chapter 34 has a heading '*David, in the person of Christ,'* ------- -------- - in the Douay Rheims Version

14. Chapter 39 has a heading '*Christ's coming, and redeeming mankind'*---- in the Douay Rheims Version

15. Chapter 40 has a heading '*The happiness of him that shall believe in Christ...'* - in the Douay Rheims Version

16. Chapter 44 has a heading '*The excellence of Christ's kingdom...'* ---------- in the Douay Rheims Version

17. Chapter 45 has a heading *'The Glories of the Messiah and His Bride'*-----------------------in the NKJV

18. Chapter 46 has a heading *'...the establishment of the kingdom of Christ'*- in the Douay Rheims Version

19. Chapter 47 has a heading *'The nations are exhorted cheerfully to entertain the Kingdom of Christ.'* In the 'King James Version' by -------------------------------- British and Foreign Bible Society © 1819

20. Chapter 49 has a heading *'The coming of Christ...'* --------------- ----------- in the Douay Rheims Version

21. Chapter 52 has a heading *'...corruption of man before coming of Christ'*-- in the Douay Rheims Version

22. Chapter 54 has a heading *'...it agrees to Christ persecuted by Jews,'* ------ in the Douay Rheims Version

23. Chapter 58 has a heading *'...it agrees to Christ and his enemies the Jews'* in the Douay Rheims Version

24. Chapter 59 has a heading *'...the church of Christ shall prevail'* ------------ in the Douay Rheims Version

25. Chapter 60 has a heading *'A prayer for the coming of the kingdom of Christ*- in the Douay Rheims Version

26. Chapter 67 has a footnote *'...St. Gregory understands it of Christ...'*----- in the Douay Rheims Version

27. Chapter 68 has a heading *'Christ in his passion...'* --------------- ----------- in the Douay Rheims Version

28. Chapter 71 has a heading *'A prophecy of the coming of Christ...'* ---------- in the Douay Rheims Version

29. Chapter 72 has a heading *'Glory and Universality of the Messiah's Reign'* in the ------------------ NKJV

30. Chapter 79 has a footnote *'...about Christ'* ----------------------- ------------- in the Douay Rheims Version

31. Chapter 84 has a heading *'The coming of Christ...'* ---------------------- in the Douay Rheims Version

32. Chapter 86 has a heading *'The Glory of the church of Christ'* ---------------- in the Douay Rheims Version

33. Chapter 87 has a heading *'...it agrees to Christ in his passion...'* ---------- in the Douay Rheims Version

34. Chapter 88 has a heading *'The perpetuity of the church of Christ...'* ------- in the Douay Rheims Version

35. Chapter 92 has a heading *'...the church of Christ'* ---------------------- in the Douay Rheims Version

36. Chapter 93 has a heading *'The Majesty, Power, and holiness of Christ's Kingdom'*--in the Eyre & Spottiswoode Bible

37. Chapter 95 has a heading *'...the coming of the Christ in his kingdom'* ---- in the Douay Rheims Version

38. Chapter 96 has a heading *'...the glorious coming and reign of Christ'* --- in the Douay Rheims Version

39. Chapter 97 has a heading *'...the victories of Christ'* ------------------------- in the Douay Rheims Version

40. Chapter 98 has a heading *'The reign of...Christ in his church'* ------------ in the Douay Rheims Version

41. Chapter 110 has a heading *'Announcement of the Messiah's Reign'* -------in New King James Version

42. Chapter 108 has a heading *'David, in the person of Christ,'* ------------------ in the Douay Rheims Version

43. Chapter 109 has a heading *'Christ's exaltation and everlasting priesthood'*- in Douay Rheims Version

44. Chapter 117 has a heading *'...the coming of Christ'* ---------------------- in the Douay Rheims Version

45. Chapter 118 has a heading *'...coming of Christ in his Kingdom'* --- British and Foreign Bible Society

(Some headings have been shortened by the author to fit in one line)

These 45 headings above show that these chapters are about *Jesus*. But unfortunately, most of the headings of these chapters have been taken out from various versions of the *Bible*. There are some chapters that have the heading *Psalms of Asaph* which is also a name of *Jesus*. This name was apparently adopted by *Jesus* after he left *Israel* in disguise. It is interesting to note that the same name is written on the tomb of *Jesus* in *Kashmir, India*. *'Yus Asaf'* which literally means *'Jesus the Gatherer.'* *'Yus'* is a shorten form of *'Yasu.'* This name is still in use by *Urdu* and *Arabic Bibles* for *Jesus*. *'Asaf'* in *Hebrew* is "אסף" = *'Acaph,'* which is pronounced as *'Asaph,'* meaning *'the gatherer'* (I Chronicles 16:5&6).

46. Chapter 50 has a heading *'A Psalms of Asaph'*---------------------
------------------- King James Version

47. Chapter 73 has a heading *'A Psalms of Asaph'*---------------------
------------------- King James Version

48. Chapter 74 has a heading *'Mas'-chill of Asaph'*---------------------
------------------- King James Version

49. Chapter 75 has a heading *'A Psalms or Song of Asaph'*------------
------------------- King James Version

50. Chapter 76 has a heading *'A Psalms or Song of Asaph'*------------
------------------- King James Version

51. Chapter 77 has a heading *'A Psalms of Asaph'*---------------------
------------------- King James Version

52. Chapter 78 has a heading *'Mas'-chill of Asaph'*--------------------
------------------- King James Version

53. Chapter 79 has a heading *'A Psalms of Asaph'*---------------------
------------------- King James Version

54. Chapter 80 has a heading *'...A Psalms of Asaph'*------------------
-------------------- King James Version

55. Chapter 81 has a heading *'A Psalms of Asaph'*---------------------
------------------- King James Version

56. Chapter 82 has a heading '*…A Psalms of Asaph*'------------------
------------------ King James Version

57. Chapter 83 has a heading '*A Song or Psalms of Asaph*'------------
----------------- King James Version

There are some other *Bibles* also, which have footnotes instead of headings that indicate the following chapters are about the *Messiah* (Jesus).

Taken from the *Holy Bible* published by *The Society of St. Paul*

1. Footnote says: chapter 17 is about Messiah

2. Footnote says: *"chapter 40 is about Messiah, and the writer of the Psalms says: 'thanks to God, to save him from death."* Please consider this, if this chapter is about Messiah then who was saved from death? *Jesus* or someone else?

3. Footnote says: chapter 61 is about Messiah	7) Footnote says: chapter 128 is about Messiah
4. Footnote says: chapter 69 is about Messiah	8) Footnote says: chapter 132 is about Messiah
5. Footnote says: chapter 89 is about Messiah	9) Footnote says: chapter 144 is about Messiah
6. Footnote says: chapter 127 is about Messiah	10) Footnote says: chapter 149 is about Messiah

---

Please contemplate on this issue, was there any other *Messiah* or *Christ* before *Jesus* in the entire *Bible*? Even the name '*Psalms*' is not a *Hebrew* word, but a *Greek* word. The *English* title '*Psalms*' derives from the *Greek* word '*psalmos*' which means *a song accompanied by stringed instruments.*[161] It is an established fact that *David* was born in *Bethlehem*, and he was one of the honorable patriarchs of the *Hebrews*, he had nothing to do with *the Greek*. There is no evidence that *David* even spoke any *Greek* at all. If *Psalms* were not written by *David*, then it must be written by someone who knew *Hebrew*, since the whole book of *Psalms* is in *Hebrew*. Who was the mystery man who knew a lot more about *Jesus* then he is mentioned in the *New Testament*?

The fact is if there is any book in the world which contains the original version of crucifixion and the life of *Jesus* it is the book of *Psalms*. If *Jesus* did not write it, then who wrote it? The book of *Psalms* says: "*…My God, my*

---

[161] Please see *The Modern language Bible* Copyright © 1969 by *Zondervan Publishing House*

God, why hast thou forsaken me?" (Psalms 22:1). We all know that these were the last words of *Jesus* on the cross. The part I am unable to comprehend is that where does it say in the *Bible* that *David* was crucified also, and his last word were similar to the last words of *Jesus*? The only difference in these two verses is that one is in *Hebrew* and the other is in *Greek*. עזב אל אל= "El, El, azab" which is written in the *Greek Bible* as *'Eli, Eli, lama sabachthani'* that is to say, *'My God My God why have you forsaken me?' (Matthew 27:46 & Mark 15:34)*. This is a historical fact that these *Hebrew* words were spoken by *Jesus*, and not by *David*. It is very strange that if *Jesus* spoke *Hebrew/Aramaic* all his life, then why are the original *Gospels* in *Greek* and not in *Hebrew/Aramaic*? This intricate problem could be solved by studying the history of *Christianity*. It says:

> *"In 325 C.E., the Nicene Council was held, where it was ordered that all original Gospels in Hebrew script should be destroyed. An Edict was issued that any one in possession of these Gospels will be put to death. In 383 C.E., the Pope secured a copy of the Gospel of Barnabas and kept it in his private library."*[162]

When you read the *Psalms*, you will notice that approximately 80% of the *Psalms* are written in first person singular. This means that if they are about *Jesus*, and they were written in first person singular, then they could most probably be written by *Jesus* himself. In the *New Testament*, it says: *'one of the soldiers pierced **his** side' (John 19:34)*. In *Psalms*, it says: *'They pierced **my** hands and **my** feet' (Psalms 22:16)*. The *New Testament* says: *'they filled a sponge with vinegar…and put it to **his** mouth' (John 19:29)*. The *Psalms* says: *'…and in **my** thirst they gave **me** vinegar to drink' (Psalms 69:21)*. Another proof that the *Psalms* were written after the crucifixion of *Jesus* and not before him is that most of the account of the crucifixion is written in past tense. If these verses were the prophecies of *David*, then these prophecies should have been in future tense, not in the past tense.

1. *'They **pierced** my hands and my feet' (Psalms 22:16)*.

2. *'…and in my thirst they **gave** me vinegar to drink' (Psalms 69:21)*.

In these eight verses of *Psalms* mentioned below, *Jesus* calls himself the *Messiah*. Then in the 9th and 10th verses, *God* calls *Jesus Messiah* too:

---

[162] Please see *www.Barnabas.net* for further detail

1. *"For a summit conference of the nations has been called to plot against the Lord and his Messiah, Christ the King"* (Psalms 2:2). (Please see *The Living Bible Paraphrased* by *Kenneth N. Taylor* Copyright © 1971 by *Tyndale House Publishers*).

2. *"Great deliverance giveth he to his king; and sheweth mercy to his anointed [His Messiah], to David, and to his seed for Evermore"* (*Psalms18: 50*). The original *Hebrew King James* says "משיח" = *'Mashiyach'* means *'Messiah.'* In all ten verses of *Psalms*, it does not say *'anointed'* in original *Hebrew*. (Please see *Hebrew King James Version* by *BlueLetterBible.org*).

3. *"Now know I that the Lord saveth his anointed [His Messiah]; he will hear him from his holy heaven with the saving strength of his right hand"* (Psalms 20:6).

4. *"The Lord is their strength, and he is the saving strength of his anointed"* [His Messiah] (Psalms28: 8).

5. *"Behold, O God our shield, and look upon the face of thine anointed [Your Messiah]"* (Psalms 84:9).

6. *"But thou hast cast off and abhorred, thou hast been wroth [angry] with thine anointed [Your Messiah]"* (Psalms 89:38).

7. *"Wherewith thine enemies have reproached, O LORD; wherewith they have reproached the footsteps of thine anointed [Your Messiah]"* (Psalms 89:51).

8. *"For thy servant David's sake turn not away the face of your anointed [Your Messiah]"* (Psalms 132:10).

Even *God* addresses to *Jesus* in the *Psalms* as a *Messiah*:

9. *"Saying, Touch not mine anointed [My Messiah], and do my prophets no harm"* (Psalms 105:15).

10. *"…I make the horn of David to bud: I have ordained a lamp for mine anointed [My Messiah]"* (Psalms 132:17).

These verses in the *'Latin Vulgate Bible,'* say *'Christos'* and *'Christi,'* which are *Latin* words for *'Christ'* (*Jesus*). The *'Latin Vulgate Bible'* was translated from the original languages into *Latin* by *St. Jerome* in 405 C.E. The question now arises that if the original *Hebrew 'Mashiyach' means 'Messiah,'* and the oldest *Latin* says *'Christ'* means *Messiah,* then why do the *English Bible* scholars translated it in *English* as *'anointed'*? I guess they want to hide the fact that these *Psalms* were written by *Jesus.*

In some verses of the *Psalms, Jesus* calls himself the *Son of man.'* As you know, *Jesus* called himself *Son of man* 84 times throughout the *New Testament,* too.

a)   *"...and the son of man, that thou visitest him?" (Psalms 8:4).*

b)   *"...upon the son of man whom thou madest strong for thy self" (Psalms 80:17)* (a footnote says: *"this verse is for Christ,"* in the *Douay Rheims Version*).

The book of *Matthews* contains 45 verses of *Psalms* as follows:

King James Version							
1)	Matthew 2:11 = Psalms 72:10	17)	Matthew 13:35 = Psalms 78:2	33)	Matthew 25:30 = Psalms 112:10
2)	Matthew 3:17 = Psalms 2:7	18)	Matthew 13:54 = Psalms 22:22	34)	Matthew 26:23 = Psalms41:9
3)	Matthew 4:6 = Psalms 91:11	19)	Matthew 14:33 = Psalms 2:7	35)	Matthew 26:50 = Psalms41:9
4)	Matthew 5:5 - Psalms 37:11	20)	Matthew 15:8 = Psalms 78:36	36)	Matthew 26:59 = Psalms 35:11
5)	Matthew 5:7 = Psalms 41:1	21)	Matthew 16:18 = Psalms 9:13	37)	Matthew 27:12 = Psalms 38:13
6)	Matthew 5:8 = Psalms 15:2	22)	Matthew 16:26 = Psalms 49:7	38)	Matthew 27:29 = Psalms 69:19
7)	Matthew 5:35 = Psalms 48:2	23)	Matthew 21:9 = Psalms 118:25	39)	Matthew 27:34 = Psalms 69:21
8)	Matthew 6:10 = Psalms 103:20	24)	Matthew 21:16 = Psalms 8:2	40)	Matthew 27:35 = Psalms 22:18
9)	Matthew 7:23 = Psalms 5:5	25)	Matthew 21:33 = Psalms 80:9	41)	Matthew 27;43 = Psalms 22:8
10)	Matthew 8:8 = Psalms 107:20	26)	Matthew 21:38 = Psalms 2:8	42)	Matthew 27:46 = Psalms 22:1
11)	Matthew 8:26 = Psalms 65:7	27)	Matthew 21:42 = Psalms 118:22	43)	Matthew 27:48 = Psalms 69:21
12)	Matthew 9:4 = Psalms 139:2	28)	Matthew 22:44 = Psalms 110:1	44)	Matthew 28:6 = Psalms 16:10

13)	Matthew 11:25 = Psalms 8:2	29)	Matthew 23:37 = Psalms 17:8	45)	Matthew 28:10 = Psalms 22:22
14)	Matthew 12:14 = Psalms 2:2	30)	Matthew 23:39 = Psalms 118:26		
15)	Matthew 13:15 = Psalms119:70	31)	Matthew 25:12 = Psalms 5:5		
16)	Matthew 13:32 = Psalms104:12	32)	Matthew 25:23 = Psalms 16:11		

Psalms is contained within other books, too.

Mark contains 28 verses, *Luke* contains 65, *John* contains 30, *Acts* contain 29, *Romans* contains 22, 1st and 2nd *Corinthians* combined contain 20 verses, *Galatians* contain one verse of *Psalms*, *Ephesians* contain 8, *Philippians* contain 4, 1st and 2nd *Timothy* contain 7 verses of *Psalms*, *Hebrews* contains 38 verses of *Psalms*. *James* contain 8 verses of *Psalms*, 1st & 2nd *Peter* 12 verses, 1st , 2nd & 3rd *John* 3 verses, and the *Revelation* contains 26 verses of *Psalms*.

None of the books of the *Old Testament* come close to *Psalms*, when we count the number of times has been quoted in the *New Testament*. What is the reason? What was so special about the book of *Psalms*? The specialty is that almost 80% of *Psalms* was written by *Jesus*, and not by *David*. Perhaps, that is the reason the *Gospel* writers quoted *Jesus* or *Psalms* more than any other book of the *Old Testament*. Unfortunately, these *Gospel* writers were not even well aware of the incident of the crucifixion or the basics of the life of *Jesus*.

20. The Book of Psalms

אל אל עזב =*El, El, azab?* that is to say,

My God, My God, why have you forsaken me? (Psalms 22:1)

This is a very interesting book, like the prophecy of *Isaiah 53*, and has many versions. Since, this book is very long and it is spread over 150 chapters, I will only mention those verses, which are the main parts in relation to the crucifixion and travels of Jesus. I would humbly suggest reading the whole book; it may astonish you.

> *1a) "I had fainted," 1b) "...unless I had believed to see the goodness of the Lord in the land of the living." (Psalms 27:13).*

1a) Jesus said, *"I had fainted,"*

How could *God* give us more explicit message than this in the *Psalms* that *Jesus* had only fainted, but he had not died on the cross? Unfortunately, this verse *I had fainted* has been deleted in the *New King James Version, Revised Standard Version* and *New American Standard Bible.* Yet, it still exists in *King James Version, American Standard Version* and in *Webster's Bible.* A serious question arises that if this verse relates to *King David,* then why did the *Christian* scholars omit it in the new *Bibles*?

This verse corroborates with the *Qur'an.* The *Qur'an* says that when *Jews* tried to kill *Jesus* on the cross:

> *"God made Jesus to appear to them like one crucified to death"* *(Al-Nisa, 4:157-159).*

186

In this verse of the *Qur'an*, *God* is telling us that *Jesus* (had only fainted) and he just appeared to be dead, but he was not dead.

1b) "I had believed to see the goodness of the Lord in the land of the living."

Perhaps, this verse is referring to the verse of *Isaiah 53:8* which says, *"For he was cut off out of the land of the living."* These two verses seem to corroborate with the verse of *Isaiah 53:9* *"He made his grave with the wicked and with the rich in his death."* This denotes that the way *God* told us about two graves, one in *Israel* and one in *Kashmir*. In the same manner *God* is apparently making two promises to *Jesus*, one is *'For he* [would be] *cut off out of the land of the living* in [*Israel*]. And at the same time, *God* is promising *Jesus* to give him prosperity, health, and long life *'in the land of the living'* in *Kashmir, India*.

2) "...You kept me alive" (Psalms 30:3).

This is an unambiguous message, *'You kept me alive.'*[163] *Jesus* was alive, when he was taken down from the cross, and he was alive when he was in the tomb. This verse corroborates with the *Qur'an*, it articulates: *"they [Jews] certainly did not kill him [on the cross]"* (*Al-Nisa 4:156-157*).

Some of my *Christian* friends contended that these two verses, *'I had fainted,'* and *'You kept me alive'* are not about *Jesus*. But the question is, if they are not about *Jesus*, then why they have been eradicated from the above mentioned *Bibles*? If these verses are about *King David*, then why *Christian* scholars need to worry about him? Whether, *King David* had fainted, or died or if he was kept alive, why would they change the *Bible* for someone they do not have much concern with? Another intricate question arises that when was *King David* crucified and when he was buried alive, can anyone provide a single reference from the *Bible* or the history of *Judaism*? On the contrary, we all know *Jesus* was crucified and he stayed in a provisional tomb.

In this verse, *'You kept me alive' Jesus* is apparently reminding us that his escape from the cross was the fulfillment of his prophecy, just as he predicted about the *'Sign of Jonas.' Jonah* was saved from the death and he was alive in the belly of the whale. *Jesus* is telling us in lucid words that he was alive in the heart of earth too. *Jonah* prayed from the belly of the fish, the *Bible* says: *"Then Jonah prayed unto the LORD his God out of the fish's belly"* (*Jonah 2:1*).

---

[163] Unfortunately, this verse also has been deleted in a few Bibles such as, *New International Version, Revised Standard Version, New Living Translation* and *English Standard Version*

Jesus is telling us in clear words that he prayed in the heart of earth too and *God* kept him alive.

> *3a)* "*I will extol you, O Lord; for You have lifted me up, And have not let my foes rejoice over me. 3b) O Lord: my God, I cried out to you, and you healed me. 3c) 'O Lord, You brought my soul up from the grave' 3d) that 'I should not go down to the pit' (Psalms 30:1-3). '...Your God has anointed you. With the oil of gladness more than your companions. All your garments are scented with myrrh and aloes and cassia' (Psalms 45:7-8). '...I shall be anointed with fresh oil' (Psalms 92:10).*

> *3a)* "*I will extol you, O Lord; for You have lifted me up, And have not let my foes rejoice over me.*" *(Psalms 30:1-3)*

In this verse, *Jesus* is apparently thanking *God* for saving his life from the accursed death (on the cross). *Jesus* is also thanking *God* for not letting his adversaries (Jews) to win in their malicious plan to crucify him, and laugh at him, as if he was a false messiah. (God forbid)

> *3b)* "*O Lord: my God, I cried out to you, and you healed me*" *(Psalms 30:1-3). ...Your God has anointed you. With the oil of gladness more than your companions. All your garments are scented with myrrh and aloes and cassia*" *(Psalms 45:7-8).*

This verse clearly indicates that *Jesus* was healed in the grave. The *Gospel* of *John* says:

> "*Nicodemus who came at night [Friday night] and brought a mixture of myrrh and aloes, about an hundred pound*" *(John 19:39).*

The *Dead Sea Scrolls,* clearly mentions that *Jesus* was given care in the grave by the *Essene* friends and he was healed up in there, thus, this verse entirely corroborates with the ancient documents. [There was a special ointment, which was prepared for *Jesus* by his disciples, and it was applied to *Jesus* for the first time, and no one else before him. That's why it is called *'Marham-i-Isa'* or the *'Ointment of Jesus.'* In the very time of *Jesus*, a little after the event of the crucifixion, a pharmaceutical work, the *'Qarabadin-i-Rumi,'* was compiled in *Latin.* In that compilation, there is a mention of this ointment along with the statement that *'the ointment had been prepared for the wounds of Jesus, by his followers.'*][164] This verse therefore says: *'I shall be anointed with fresh oil'* *(Psalms 92:10).* With the help of this ointment, the wounds of *Jesus* healed

---

[164] Bracketed text is excerpt from *Jesus in India*

up so miraculously that he was able to walk seventy miles on foot within few days from *Jerusalem* to *Galilee.*

In addition, the *Gospel of John* says: *"They took the body of Jesus, and wound it in linen clothes with spices, as the manner of the Jews is to bury" (John 19:40).* The scholars of today strongly suggest that that was not the custom of *Jews* to bury their dead ones. This denotes that those ointments were prepared to anoint *Jesus,* and not to embalm his dead body before burying him.

3c) "O Lord, You brought my soul up from the grave"

This verse could be the real meaning of resurrection. Even today, if someone experiences a near death experience, we say that 'he came back to life.' It does not mean that the person had really died, and then came back to life. It only means that the person was very close to death. According to the scholars who acknowledge the fact that *Jesus* did not die on the cross, usually say that if *Jesus* was crucified and *God* miraculously saved him then his disciples would have perceived his escape from death as a resurrection. They genuinely believed it as a miracle of *God,* it does not mean that they lied about it, or gave us incorrect information.

3d) "I should not go down to the pit"

In this verse, *Jesus* is apparently thanking *God* for not letting him go down to the pit. *'Pit'* here, it denotes to an 'accursed' death or *'hell.' Jesus* is obviously saying in this verse that he did not go down to the pit or hell. This is in sharp contrast to the common *Christian* belief that *Jesus* did go down to hell for three days and three nights, and *Jesus* did become accursed of *God* in order to save people from the fire of the hell. But the *New Testament* denies this conviction by saying: *"No one speaking by the Spirit of God calls Jesus accursed" (I Corinthians 12:3). Jesus* was a true *Messiah* and a true prophet he did not go down to the pit and certainly he did not stayed in the hell for three days.

4) *"Thou hast laid me in the lowest pit, in darkness, in the deeps. Thou hast put mine acquaintance far from me; thou hast made me an abomination unto them: I am shut up, I cannot come forth (Psalms 88:8).*

This is what *Jesus* probably prayed in the provisional grave. *Jesus* is apparently saying my friends or disciples have gone away, and I am helpless in this (grave) and cannot come out. As I mentioned in the *Sign of Jonas, Jonas* prayed in the whale's belly, he was alive in the whale's belly. *Jesus* had mentioned *Sign of Jonas* to the *Jews* as a token of his truthfulness. If *Jesus* was dead then that sign of *Jonas,* would not have matched with the situation of

Jesus at all. But as you can see in *Psalms*, just like *Jonas*, *Jesus* is praying to *God* from the heart of earth too.

> 5)   "*Let them be confounded and put to shame that seek after my soul: let them be turned back and brought to confusion that devise my hurt*" (*Psalms 35:4*).

This is the most crucial part of the prayer, where *Jesus* is apparently asking *God* to let the *Jews* be confounded. This is what exactly happened, the *Jews* planned to put *Jesus* on the cross, so they could kill him on the cross, and as a result, prove from the *Bible* that he was not the true messiah, but an imposter. In this verse of *Psalms*, *Jesus* seems to be asking *God* to put the *Jews* to the shame, (who wanted to kill him) by saving his life from the cross. Perhaps, *Jesus* wanted them to suffer the consequences for choosing the wrong method. The *Qur'an* says:

> "*Will you slay a man because he says, 'My Lord is Allah,' while he has brought you clear proofs from your Lord? And if he be a liar, on him will be the sin of his lie; but if he is truthful, then some of that which he threatens you with will surely befall you*" (*Al-Momin 40:27-28*)

This verse of the *Qur'an* is warning us that do not take matters in your own hand, if a man claims to be from *God*, let *God* punish him if he is a liar. But if he is really from *God*, then He will punish you for harming his prophet. In the next verse, *Jesus* is asking *God* a very strange thing. He says:

> "*let them turned back and brought to confusion that devise my hurt.*"

It seems as if *Jesus* is asking *God* not to show any more signs to the *Jews*. Let them be confused (about crucifixion), who are planning to harm him. It is interesting to note that the *Qur'an* gives us a similar message. Therefore, the *Qur'an* says:

> "*They [Jews] declared: We did kill the Messiah, Jesus son of Mary, the messenger of Allah; whereas they slew him not, nor did they crucify him upon the cross, but he was made to appear to them like one crucified to death; and those who have differed in the matter of his having been taken down alive from the cross are certainly in a state of doubt [confusion] concerning it, they have no definite knowledge about it, but only follow*

> *a doubt, and they killed him not for sure." (Qur'an, Al-Nisa 4:157-158).*

In this *Qur'anic* verse, *God* is articulating that the *Jews* did not kill *Jesus* on the cross, but he only appeared to be dead. It further states that the *Jews* are only confused about the crucifixion; they (Jews) did not kill *Jesus* for sure.

> 6) *"My tongue also shall talk of your righteousness all the daylong; For they are confounded, for they are brought to shame who seek my hurt"* (Psalms 71:24).

First, *Jesus* prayed to *God* to *"let them [Jews] be confounded and put to shame."* Then in this chapter, *Jesus* is thanking *God* and praising Him, and saying *"they are confounded and they are brought to shame."* It means beyond the shadow of doubt that it had already happened by the time the above words were spoken by *Jesus*. This verse is a great proof that these *Psalms* were written by *Jesus*, and written after the crucifixion, and not before that.

> 7a) *"You have delivered me from the strivings of the people; and you have made me the head of the heathen 7b) a people whom I have not known shall serve me, 7c) As soon as they hear of me they shall obey me: the strangers shall submit themselves to me"* (Psalms 18: 43-44).

> 7a) *"You have delivered me from the strivings of the people; and you have made me the head of the heathen."*

This verse also seems to be in connection with *Psalms 23:2 and 142:5*, and talking about the *Land of Kashmir, India*. Perhaps, in this verse, *Jesus* is thanking *God* for delivering him from the barbaric people who were trying their best to kill him on the cross. In the next verse, *Jesus* is saying, *"you have made me the head of the heathen."* According to the history, when *Jesus* went to *Kashmir*, to the *lost tribes of Israel*, a large portion of those *Jews* had lost *Judaism* and had become idol worshippers. They accepted *Jesus* as their *Messiah* and their spiritual leader.

> 7b) *"a people whom I have not known shall serve me."*

Perhaps, in this verse, *Jesus* is referring that his own people (*the disciples of Jerusalem*), the people, who he grew up with, and knew them very well, did not show faith in him. When he needed them most at the time of crucifixion, they fled to save their own lives. But when he went to the *'lost tribes of Israel'* in *Kashmir*, the people he did not even know, took care of him, and show faith in him.

191

7c) "As soon as they hear of me they shall obey me, the strangers shall submit themselves to me."

This verse seems to be corroborating with the prophecy of *Jesus* about preaching to another nations, as it is mentioned in the *Gospel* of *John* in these words:

> *"And I have other sheep, which are not of this fold: them also I must bring, and they shall hear my voice; and there shall be one fold, and one shepherd" (John 10:16).*

This verse is also mentioned in *Isaiah* in these words:

> *"He shall feed his flock like a shepherd: he shall gather the lambs with his arms, and carry them in his bosom, and shall gently lead those that are with young" (Isaiah 40:11).*

It is interesting to mention that the name written on the *tomb of Jesus* in *Kashmir, India,* is *'Yus Asaf'* which literally means *'Jesus the Gatherer.'* Just as the prophecy of *Isaiah* says, *"he shall gather the lambs with his arms."*

8) "Many are the afflictions of the righteous: but the Lord delivered him out of them all. He keeps all his bones: not one of them is broken. The Lord saves the life of his servants: and none of them that trust in him shall be desolate" (Psalms 34:19-22).

This verse, *"He keeps all his bones: not one of them is broken,"* clearly shows that this verse is about *Jesus.* We all know from the *Gospel* writings that *Jesus'* legs were not broken as compared to the thieves on his right hand and left hand sides, that their legs were broken. If *Jesus* would not have fainted by the mercy of *God,* his legs would have also been broken by the centurion, and he would have died miserably. If *Jesus* would have died then the next verse, *'The Lord saves the life of his servants'* would make no sense at all. This verse especially pertains to the prophets and the messengers of *God,* and not just to ordinary people. It means that *God* is promising to all true prophets that despite of troubles and afflictions, true prophets of *God* will always be saved from the human hands, that is to say 'the true prophets shall never be killed by their adversaries.' To clarify further that the *Hebrew* word '**עֶבֶד**'= *'Ebed,'* means *'servant,'* used in this context is for prophets and messengers of *God* only; I would present some of the verses of the *Old Testament,* where the word *servant* is used for the prophets:

i) "So Moses the servant of the LORD…" (Deuteronomy 34: 5).

ii) *"Surely the Lord GOD will do nothing, but he revealeth his secret unto his servants the prophets" (Amos 3:7).*

iii) *"And the LORD appeared unto him... I am with thee, and will bless thee, and multiply thy seed for my servant Abraham's sake" (Genesis 26: 24).*

Therefore, this promise that *'the Lord saves the life of his servants,'* also corroborates with the commandment of *God* in *Deuteronomy* about the prophets which says:

"But a prophet who presumes to speak in my name anything I have not commanded him to say, or a prophet who speaks in the name of other gods, must be put to death" (Deuteronomy 18: 20 NIV).

This means quite clear that all the true prophets of *God* have always been saved from the people. On the contrary, false prophets always have been killed. This means if *Jesus* was the true messiah then he must have survived the crucifixion. The *Qur'an* also confirms to this view in these words:

"and when I [God] restrained the children of Israel from putting thee [Jesus] to death when thou didst come to them with clear Signs" (Al-Mai'dah 5:110-111).

This seems to be a prophesy which was revealed to *Jesus*. In this prophesy, *God* is not only promising *Jesus* that if he would trust *God*, then his survival from the crucifixion would be inevitable. But at the same time, strengthening him with the examples of the previous prophets. These prophets are those who also trusted *God*, and *God* saved them all. a) *Abraham* was thrown in fire, but the fire could not burn him. b) *Joseph* was thrown in the well, but he did not die. c) *Jonah* was swallowed by a whale, but he still survived. d) *Moses* was chased by the barbaric army of pharos, but they could not kill him. Unfortunately, some of the scribes attached the killing of prophets in literal sense to justify the death of *Jesus* by his adversaries, the *Jews*. But *God* kept his promise that *'None of them that trust in Him [God], shall be desolate.'* Consequently, *Jesus* also survived just like other true prophets of *God*.

9) *"Surely goodness and mercy shall follow me all the days of my life: and I will dwell in the house of the Lord forever" (Psalms 23:6)."*

In this verse, *Jesus* is telling us with surety that prosperity and mercy of *God* will follow him his whole life. But if he died on the cross, then how would he prosper after death? How would he prosper his whole life, but he is very sure about prosperity, and mercy of *God* in these verses.

> 10) "...*I will fear no evil: For you are with me; your rod and your staff they comfort me*" (Psalms 23:4).

[It is interesting to note that in *Kashmir*, there is a '*staff*' which is considered the most valuable relic. According to the traditions, this was the *staff of Moses*, which was passed down to *Jesus*, on his arrival in *Kashmir*, as a symbol of *Mosaic heritage*. This staff is made of '*olive wood*' and is supposed to miraculously help in emergencies, especially in case of epidemics. The place where this staff is kept is called "*Aish Muqam*" which also refers to *Jesus*. '*Aish*' is said to derive from '*Isha*' or '*Isa*' [Jesus], and '*Muqam*' means '*a place of rest.*' According to the traditions, this is the place where *Jesus* used to withdraw for a while to devote himself to quite meditation.][165]

> 11) "*A seed shall serve him; it shall be accounted to the Lord for a generation*" (Psalms 22:30).

The *Dead Sea Scrolls* says that *Jesus* had a son, named *Justus, son of Jesus*. According to my research, *Justus* became the first successor after the death of *Jesus* in *Kashmir*. This verse of the prophecy was fulfilled in him.

> 12a) "*His soul shall dwell at ease; and his seed shall inherit the earth*" (Psalms 25:13). 12b) *His seed shall be mighty upon earth...*" (Psalms 112:2).

In this verse, it seems as if *God* is promising *Jesus* again that no matter what happens, you will have a prosperous life. In the next verse it says: "*his seed shall inherit the earth.*" There is a tribe in *Afghanistan*, called '*Isa Khel*' meaning '*family of Jesus.*' They are believed to be the descendants of *Jesus Christ*. Another family from *Kashmir* claims to be the descendants of *Jesus Christ*. Now we can see how this prophecy fulfilled, that even after *2000* years, there are still many people, who claim to be the descendants of *Jesus Christ*. ["*The word 'Afghan' appears to be of Hebrew origin; it is a derivative which means 'brave'. It appears that at the height of their victories they adopted this name for themselves*"][166]

> 12b) "*His seed shall be mighty upon earth...*" (Psalms 112:2).

---

[165] Bracketed text from *Jesus lived in India* by *Holger Kersten* page #222
[166] Bracketed text is excerpts from *Jesus in India* by *Ahmad* on page #80

As I have mentioned *Afghanistan*, plays a vital role in the travels of *Jesus*. Not to forget that this small nation became the reason for the downfall of *Soviet Union*, once the super power of the world. According to the *Psalms 'His seed shall be mighty upon earth.'* *Afghans* did become mighty on earth at one time when they were righteous.

13) "*With long life will I satisfy him, and shew him my salvation*" (*Psalms 91:16*).

God is making the same promise which he made through *Isaiah 53:10* that *Jesus* will live a *'long life.'* People usually tell me that if *God* promised *Jesus* long life, then belief that *Jesus* is alive for more than *2000* years, is correct. But they forget the verse of *Genesis 6:3* that a man cannot live more than *120 years.* A long life could also mean a full life which is *120 years* but it cannot be taken as, life after death. Perhaps, that is what *Jesus* is trying to say in the verse of *Psalms 89:48: What man is he that lives, and shall not see death?*

14) "*What man is he that lives, and shall not see death? Shall he deliver his soul from the hand of the grave?*" (*Psalms 89:48*).

Here *Jesus* is saying perhaps, that there is no man who can live forever, and not die. There is no man who can save himself from the grave: Everybody has to die. This means all those who are thinking *Jesus* is still alive, and has not died in *2000* years are making a grave mistake.

15) "*He made me to lie down in green pastures: He leads me beside the still waters. He restored my soul (Psalms 23:2). The Lord also will be a refuge for the oppressed, a refuge in times of trouble (Psalms 9:9). ...You are my refuge and my portion in the land of the living*" (*Psalms 142:5*).

These verses of *Psalms* are about the travel of *Jesus*. The *Qur'an* also gives us a similar message let me provide you with the additional meanings of the same words from the *Hebrew* lexicon, to prove that this verse of the *Bible* corresponds to the verse mentioned in the *Qur'an*, only the wording is different in the *Qur'an* and the *Bible*:

i) "נהל" this *Hebrew* word is *'Nahal'* which means *'lead,'* or *'Journey.'*

ii) "מנוחה" this *Hebrew* word is *'Manuwchah,'* which means still or *'resting place.'*

iii) "מים" this *Hebrew* word is *'Mayim'* which means *'still water,'* or *'water springs.'*

After the additional meanings of the same *Hebrew* words, let us review the verse of the *Bible*:

> *"He made me to lie down in green pastures He journeyed, to the resting place of water springs …a refuge in times of trouble."* Now let us match these verses with the verses of the *Qur'an*:

> *"God gave Jesus and his mother Mary refuge in a mountainous, peaceful, green valley, watered by fresh springs" (Qur'an 23:50-51).*

Surprisingly, we find similar message written in the *New Testament* in these words:

> *"For the lamb which is in the midst of the throne shall feed them, and shall lead them unto living fountains of waters: and God shall wipe away all tears from their eyes" (Revelation7:17).*

> 16) *"Your wife shall be as a fruitful vine by the sides of your house: your children like olive plants round about your table. Yes, you shall see your children's children, and peace upon Israel' (Psalms 128:3 & 6).*

If *Jesus* did live up to the age of 120 years, he must have seen his children and children's children in accordance with this verse. As many people have claimed to be his descendant, this prophecy apparently was fulfilled quite well.

> 17) *"Lover and friend has thou put far from me," (Psalms 88:18).*

Jesus probably meant only one, his most favorite disciple, *Mary Magdalene?* "רע" Rea = *Ra'-ah.* This *Hebrew* word means *'companion,' 'intimate'* or it could also mean *'intimate companion.'* In the time of *Jesus* and especially, in the *Jewish* areas people were not allowed to have close relationships with women. They would stone them to death for that kind of relationship. If *Jesus* and *Mary Magdalene* were close companions then most probably they were husband and wife. As the *Dead Sea Scrolls* tell us *Jesus* was married to *Mary Magdalene.*

> 18) *"Israel also came into Egypt; and Jacob sojourned in the land of Ham (Psalms 105:23). They showed his signs among them, and wonders in the land of Ham (Psalms 105:27). Wondrous works in the land of Ham and terrible things by the Red sea (Psalms 106:22). They joined themselves also unto Baal-pe'-or, and ate the sacrifices of the dead (Psalms 106: 28).*

Ham was the son of *Noah,* and *Cush* was the grandson of *Noah.* It is surprising that there is a city in *Kashmir,* known as *City of Ham* (also known as *Koh-i-Hama* or the *Mount Ham,* in the district of *Handwara).* This city was known in the *Biblical* times as the *'the land of Ham.'* Then there is *Kashmir,* this name is also known to have come from *Cush. Balpura (*also known as *'Baalpur')* is also a city in *Kashmir.* This city *'Baalpur'* is located in the district of *Awantipur,* which was known as *'Baal-peor,'* in the *Biblical* times. Basically, *Jesus* gave us a hint in above verses that in which foreign land he would be going after the crucifixion.

Wife of Jesus

According to the book *[Holy Blood Holy Grail,* the marriage of *Jesus* and *Mary Magdalene* is hinted quite well in the *Gospel* of *John.* The wedding, *Jesus* and his mother attended in *Cana,* was actually *Jesus'* own wedding. *Mary* (mother of Jesus) who not merely suggests to her son, but in fact orders him, to provide the wine. She behaves quite as if she were the hostess. Why would a guest worry about the vine running out in someone else's wedding? How can *Mary* (a guest) start ordering somebody else's servants? The servants promptly comply-quite as if they were accustomed to receiving orders from both *Mary* and *Jesus.* According to the *Gospel of John:*

> *"And when they wanted wine, the mother of Jesus saith unto him, They have no wine. ...His mother saith unto the servants, Whatsoever he saith unto you, do it" (John 2: 3-5).* The *Gospel* also says: *"Mary (Mary Magdalene) took a pound of costly ointment of pure nard and anointed the feet of Jesus and wiped his feet with her hair; and the house was filled with the fragrance of the ointment" (John 12: 3 RSV).]*[167]

---

[167]   Bracketed text excerpts from the book *Holy Blood Holy Grail,* by *Michael Baigent, Richard Leigh, and Henry Lincoln,* paraphrased

Matthew (RSV)	Mark (RSV)	Luke (RSV)	John (RSV)
"*...a woman came up to him with an alabaster flask of very expensive ointment, and she poured it on his head, as he sat at table*" (*Matthew 26:7*).	"*...a woman came with an alabaster flask of ointment of **pure nard**, very costly, and she broke the flask and poured it over his head*" (*Mark 14:3*).	" *And behold, a woman of the city, **who was a sinner**, when she learned that he was at table in the Pharisee's house, brought an alabaster flask of ointment*" (*Luke 7:37*)	"***Mary*** *took a pound of costly ointment of **pure nard** and anointed the feet of Jesus and wiped his feet with her hair; and the house was filled with the fragrance of the ointment*" (*John 12:3*)

This event, which is mentioned above in the four *Gospels*, is mentioned each time with a slight difference. The difference is *Matthew* and *Mark* says 'a women' it means no one knows who that woman was. *Gospel* of *Luke* says ' a woman, who was a sinner' (prostitute). But the *Gospel of John* revealed the secret by telling us that that woman was *Mary of Bethany*. According to the *Dead Sea Scrolls*, that *Mary* was *Mary Magdalene*. She anointed *Jesus* on the day of their wedding in accordance with a *Jewish* custom. If we take the *Gospel's* word for it, then how can a sinner (prostitute) anoint a righteous man like *Jesus*? Could righteous people get anointed by a prostitute? According to the book mentioned above that was the *Jewish* custom for women to anoint their husbands on the day of wedding. As we read in *Song of Solomon*: "*While the king was on his couch, my nard gave forth its fragrance*" (*Song of Songs 1:12RSV*). "*The Song of Solomon was the wedding liturgy of the David kings, a beautiful verbal accompaniment to the ceremonies.*"[168]

The marriage of *Jesus* is also written in the book of *Revelation* in these words:

> "*Let us be glad and rejoice, and give honour to him: for the marriage of the Lamb is come, and his wife hath made herself ready. And to her was granted that she should be arrayed in fine linen, clean and white: for the fine linen is the righteousness of saints And he saith unto me, Write, Blessed are they which are called unto the marriage supper of the Lamb. And he saith unto me, These are the true sayings of God*" (*Revelation 19: 7-9*).

---

[168] Excerpts from the book *Holy Blood Holy Grail*, by *Michael Baigent, Richard Leigh, and Henry Lincoln*, paraphrased

All the *Christians* unanimously believe that in the entire *Bible* whenever the word *Lamb* is mentioned, it is about *Jesus*. *Jesus* had to survive the crucifixion in order for him to have children, because according to the *Bible*, *Jesus* had no children before crucifixion. He had to survive in order for him to live a long life, because the *Bible* says he was only thirty-three years old when he was put on the cross. These prophecies of *Isaiah* & *Revelation* about the wife and children of *Jesus* is also corroborated by the *Qur'an* in these words:

> *"And, indeed, We sent Messengers before thee [Muhammad],*
> *and We gave them wives and children" (Al-Ra'd 13: 39-40).*

The verse applies to *Jesus* more than any other messenger, because he is the only one who came right before *Muhammad*.

Revisiting the issue of the *Psalms*, according to my research, 45 chapters of the *Psalms* have *Messiah* related headings, and are all about *Jesus*. There are 12 chapters that contain the heading *'A Psalms of Asaph'* are also about *Jesus*. Then there are some chapters that contain *Messiah* related footnotes that these chapters are about *Jesus*. Then there are hundreds of verses throughout *Psalms* that talk about a *Messiah*. All of these verses are also found in the *New Testament*, but there is no heading on those chapters, which indicate that they are about a *Messiah*. Then there are many chapters in the *Psalms* that talk about the future life of *Jesus*, but those verses are not quoted in the *New Testament*. Most of these prophecies about the future life of *Jesus* have been fulfilled, that's how we know they were the true prophecies about *Jesus*.

When you read the whole book of *Psalms*, you'll come to know that approximately 80% of the *Psalms* is about *Jesus*. This 80% includes hundreds of verses throughout the book, which have been repeated many times in the *Psalms* itself. Some whole chapters have been repeated in it. For example, chapter 53 repeated the whole of chapter 14. *Psalms* chapter 40 verses 14 through 18 exists separately as *Psalms* 70. *Psalms* chapter 108 verses 2 through 5 is composed of *Psalms* 57, verses 8 through 11. Then the other half of the *Psalms* 108 is composed of *Psalms* 60 verses 7 through 14. This denotes that the *Psalms* was originally a much smaller book than it has been stretched to. According to the *Hadith* (sayings of Muhammad), narrated by *Abu Hurairah:*

> *"The prophet (Muhammad) said the reciting of the Zabur (Psalms) was made easy for Daud [King David]. He used to order [his servants] that his riding animals be saddled, and*

> *[David] would finish reciting the Zabur [Psalms] before they were saddled.*"[169]

Why *God* specially revealed this revelation to *Muhammad*? Just to tell him that the *Psalms* was a short book? Or *God* wanted us to research that if *Psalms* of *David* was a short book, then who wrote the major part of it and why? I have tried my best to prove that the *Psalms* was mainly written by *Jesus*, could be the answer to the above question.

The *Jews* have been ridiculing *Jesus* for over *2000* years. They ask that if *Jesus* was the true messiah, then why *God* had never spoken to him. According to them, throughout the *Old Testament*, it is written that: *'God said to Moses, God said to Abraham, God said to Jacob, etc.* It proves that *God* talk to these prophets all their lives. But in the *New Testament*, it is never written anywhere that, *'God said to Jesus.'* Thus proves that *Jesus* was not from *God* and he was a false messiah (God forbid). But in the *Psalms*, you'll see that *God* is talking to *Jesus* throughout the book. *God* answered *Jesus'* prayers when *Jesus* prayed to *God*, *'O my God, I trust in you: let me not be ashamed, let not mine enemies triumph over me (Psalms 25:2).* In one verse, *God* is telling *Jesus*, *'...sit thou at my right hand, until I make thine enemies thy footstool' (Psalms 110:1).* Throughout the book of *Psalms*, *God* is not only talking to *Jesus*, but also giving him many glad tidings that have been fulfilled. The glad tidings about his future life, his wife, his children, and his successful life in a foreign land (*Kashmir, India*).

If the book of *Psalms* is really written by *Jesus* then a few questions arise, why it was not included in the *New Testament*, why it was appended in the *Old Testament*? And why *David* has been credited for this book? The answer to all these questions is very simple. As I mentioned above, in the *Psalms, Jesus* is telling us in clear words:

a) *"I had fainted [on the cross]" (Psalms 27:13).*

b) *"O Lord: my God, I cried out to you, and you healed me. 'O Lord, You brought my soul up from the grave' "You have kept me alive" (Psalms 30:2-3).*

c) *"Yes, you shall see your children's children, and peace upon Israel" (Psalms 128:3 & 6).*

---

[169] *Bukhari*, Volume 4, Book 55, Number 628, this *Hadith* was provided by *Omar Khan*

The *Psalms* have prophecies about *Jesus'* survival, the wife of *Jesus*, his children, and even grandchildren. How could the *Bible* compilers include these verses quoted above in the *New Testament* when they have been telling people for over *2000* years that *Jesus* died for our sins, and he was god?

The question remains; why *David* was credited for the *Psalms*? As I mentioned above, a reference from *'The Oxford Companion to the Bible,*

"David's reputation as a musician (1Sam 16:23 & Amos 6:5) makes it reasonable to associate him with the Psalms."

That is what the top scholars of *America* are saying about the origin of the *Psalms*. It is up to you to decide how you would like to take the book of *Psalms*? You could take it as the only original book written by *Jesus*. Or you can still consider it as a book of *King David* written about *Jesus*. But either way, you will have to believe that *Jesus* stated in this book that he had only fainted (on the cross), he was alive in the grave, and he was healed. After reading my research, you may not be able to say that he died on the cross, and came back to life.

This is very interesting that the *Christians* believe that *Jesus* walked on water; brought back many dead people to life, gave sight to blinds, and healed lepers. He was the son of *God*, and even he was *God* himself (God forbid). He created havens and earth, and he could do anything (God forbid). There is one thing that *Jesus* could not do for sure; most *Christians* agree on that, that *Jesus* could not write *Psalms*. Does it make any sense at all? While we all know for sure that *Jesus* could read, if he could read why he could not write? The *Bible* says:

"And he came to Nazareth, where he had been brought up: and, as his custom was, he went into the synagogue on the Sabbath day, and stood up for to read" *(Luke 4:16).*

21. The Second Coming of Jesus Christ

When the *Jews* were waiting for the *Messiah* they were told in the *Old Testament* that *Elijah* has ascended up to heaven with his body. It says:

"Behold, there appeared a chariot of fire, and horses of fire…and E-li'-jah went up by a whirlwind into heaven."[170] According to the traditions, supported by the verses of *Malachi,* where it says:

"Behold, I will send you Elijah the prophet Before the coming of the great and dreadful day of the Lord."[171]

The *Jews* have the same concept about the *Elijah* that he will come from the sky with the angels on his right hand and left hand and the whole world will see this glorious day. In the similar way, all the *Christians* and the *Muslims* are waiting for their *Messiah* that he will come from heaven with angels on his right hand and left hand and the whole world will see him. The disciples inquired *Jesus*:

"Why then do the scribes say that E-li'-as [Elijah] must come first?" Then Jesus answered and said to them, E-li'-as truly shall first come, and restore all things. But I say to you that E-li'-as is come already, and they [Jews] knew him not but have done unto him whatsoever they listed [wished]. Likewise shall also the Son of Man suffer of them. Then the disciples understood that he [Jesus] spoke unto them of John the Baptist" (Matthew 17:10-13; Matthew 11:14; Mark 9:12; Luke 1:17).[172]

---

[170] Please see *2Kings 2:11*

[171] Please see *Malachi 4:5*

[172] I apologize to my readers for the repeated mention of some accounts. In my opinion they are the demands of different chapters to contextualize the arguments and as not everybody reads a book cover to cover

This is the Picture of Ahmad (the Second Coming of Jesus Christ) His full name is given below:

Hazrat Mirza Ghulam Ahmad Qadiani, was born on February 14th 1835 and died 1908 Founder of the Ahmadiyya Muslim Jama'at The Promised Messiah and Imam Mahdi

203

Maulana Noor-Ud-Din 1ˢᵗ Successor of the Promised Messiah (Ahmad)

Mirza Bashir-Ud-Din Mahmood Ahmad 2ⁿᵈ Successor of the Promised Messiah

Mirza Nasir Ahmad, 3ʳᵈ Successor of the Promised Messiah

Mirza Tahir Ahmad, 4ᵗʰ Successor of the Promised Messiah

Fifth & the Current Successor of the Promised Messiah, Mirza Masroor Ahmad

The question is did *John the Baptist* come from the heavens? Nobody saw him coming from the sky. Everybody knew that *John the Baptist* was born to *Jesus'* aunt and he was cousin to *Jesus* then how anyone would have believed that *John the Baptist* came in the name of *Elijah*, and not *Elijah* himself came from heaven. Is it possible that someone could come in the name of someone else? The truth is that even today when someone is very brave person, we call him lion. Though lion is a totally different race, do we ever think that if someone has been called a lion, maybe he is becoming a lion, he is growing a tale, or his teeth are getting sharp and deadly? No, right? Because we use our common sense at that time and we know that that person has been called a lion just because he is very brave, *like a lion*.

The same way, how many people have been called *Hitler* just because they were very barbaric and ruthless people? We do not call them *like Hitler*, we just call them *Hitler*. Although, *Hitler* was his last name or family name, not even a title. But does it ever cross our mind that may be the original *Hitler*, who died long ago has came back to life? Then what about the *Messiah*? The *Messiah* was just a title given to *Jesus*, and it was not his personal name, and that title was passed down to another prophet of *God, Ahmad. Jesus* said: "... *whom the Father will send in my name.*"[173] *Ahmad* came in the name of *Jesus*, the *Messiah* for this *Dark Age*.

Another point we learn from this narrative that right after *Jesus* told them about the (Second Coming) of *Elias. Jesus* told them *"Likewise shall also the Son of Man suffer of them,"* this denotes that the way *Jews* did not recognize the *Second Coming of Elias* (John the Baptist), and rejected him, cursed him, called him a liar, imposter, and made him suffer many things. Likewise, people will do the same with the *Second Coming of Jesus* (Ahmad). *Jesus* mentioned this in the following verses also that he (Jesus) will suffer many things in his *Second Coming*:

1. *"For as the lightning, that lighteneth out of the one part under heaven, shineth unto the other part under heaven; so shall also the Son of man be in his day. But first must he suffer many things, and be rejected of this generation. And as it was in the days of Noe,[Noah] so shall it be also in the days of the Son of man"* (Luke17:24-25).

2. *"And he answered and told them, Elias verily cometh first, and restoreth all things; and how it is written of the Son of man, that he must suffer many things, and be set at nought"* (Mark 9:12).

---

[173] Please see *John 14:26*

My question is if *Jesus* supposed to come from the sky and according to some *Christian* traditions, he will not even touch the earth, but he will call from the sky, and all the true believers will be flying towards him (Rapture). Then how *Jesus* is going to suffer? Who would be powerful enough to go to sky and make *Jesus* suffer? According to the *Christian* traditions only believers will be flying that day. Then how the non-believers would be flying that day to go to the sky and make *Jesus* suffer? Another point is that *Jesus* said:

> "*For there shall arise false Christs, and false prophets, and shall shew great signs and wonders; insomuch that, if it were possible, they shall deceive the very elect" (Matthew 24:24).*

The question is again, that why we have to worry about false *Christs*, if *Jesus* supposed to come from the sky? Would false *Christs* and *false prophets* be coming from the sky too?

What is Rapture?

Many Christian friends ask me that if it is true that *Jesus* did not go to the heavens bodily, then why the *Bible* talks about the rapture, is that a misunderstanding too? First of all, the word rapture does not even exist in the *Bible*. In fact, the concept of rapture is barely one hundred and seventy-nine years old. The history of *Christianity* tells us that in *1830* a *British* preacher named *John nelson Darby*, started the concept of rapture. Though there is something mentioned in the *Bible* which could be identified with the concept of rapture. But that concept is more in a mystical sense than the literal sense. When *Jesus* was talking about the days of his *Second Coming* and he said:

> "*Then shall two be in the field; the one shall be taken, and the other left. Two women shall be grinding at the mill; the one shall be taken, and the other left*" (Matthew 24:40-41).

In the verse quoted above *Jesus* probably mean that in the time of his *Second Coming*, not everybody will accept him. If there are two people working in a field one will accept him and the other will be left as a non-believer. Two women will be grinding, one will be lucky enough to accept the *Second Coming of Christ* and the other will be left un-believer. This denotes that many people will hear the message of the promised messiah, but only few will be blessed enough to be his followers. As *Jesus* himself elucidated it in these words: *"... for many be called, but few chosen" (Matthew 20:16)*. But unfortunately, almost all the *Bible* translations have omitted this last part. I guess they could not fully comprehend it.

I am trying to draw your attention to the fact that when a prophet of *God* comes, he teaches his followers deep meanings. But after the demise of that prophet, those deep meanings stay very deep. This means that the followers forget the deep and profound meanings, and all they can understand is the only upper layer meanings. They always insist on the literal meanings of everything. Usually, they do not possess the wisdom to go deep down to the meanings giving by that prophet. That is the reason they end up with fairy tales, prophet flying, followers flying, dead are being raised, walking on water etc. When the new prophet brings back those profound meanings, the deep meanings then the followers of old prophet reject that prophet because they cannot comprehend them, they are usually very comfortable with the fairy tales and they do not desire to come out of it.

The truth is as *Jesus* said: *"No man has ascended up to heaven but he that cometh down from heaven even the Son of man..."(John 3:13)*. *Jesus* did not come, flying down from the sky, in his first advent. He was born in the womb of *Mary*, then how can he come in his *Second Coming* from the sky? The fact is that no prophet or messenger of *God* has ever come from the sky. Then how can we explain *"Every eye shall see and every knee shall bow"*? This is a time of science and knowledge, even if we assume for a second that it could happen, scientifically it is impossible, because the earth is not flat, it is round. Then even if *Jesus* came in a bright daylight from the skies of *America*, then in *Asia*, it would be nighttime and everyone would be sleeping. If he came from *Asian* sky then *Europeans* and *Americans* will be sleeping. Not only that, this concept contradicts the *Bible*, when it said:

> *"For yourselves know perfectly that the day of the Lord so cometh as a thief in the night" (Thessalonians5:2)*.

Please contemplate on this point, how he supposes to come? *"Every eye shall see and every knee shall bow"* that the whole world would see him, or he would come as *"a thief in the night"* and nobody would see him?

A thief in the night

A *thief in the night,'* has a special connotation to it, this denotes that when we are expecting someone, do we ever imagine that he or she would come from the window or he would jump from the wall to come in to our house? No, right? We expect the person to come from the front door. But the thieves always come unexpectedly and they come most of the times from unexpected ways. You would hardly see a thief knocking at the front door. *'A thief in the night'* means *Jesus* will not be coming in a way people will be expecting him. This means if people are expecting *Jesus* to come from the sky, then he would not come from the sky. If people are expecting him to come through a *Christian Church,* he will not be coming through a *Christian Church.* He will come totally unexpected way; he will be born on earth with totally different parents as *John the Baptist* was born on earth in the power and spirit of *Elijah* but with different set of parents, and he will come this time as a *Muslim.* I know it sounds a bit strange but *Jesus* himself prophesied about this transfer of the *Kingdom of God* in these words:

> *"Therefore say I unto you, **The kingdom of God shall be taken from you**, and given to a nation bringing forth the fruits thereof" (Matthew 21:43).*

Coming from the sky for anyone is totally baseless conception. Six thousand years of history of mankind is telling us that many people, prophets, messengers of *God,* saints and priests have been sent to the heavens bodily by their believers, but none of them has ever came back. But unfortunately, the *Jews* could not understand it, which was one of the main reasons perhaps that the *Jews* rejected the *Messiah* of their age. If *Jesus* could raise dead people then that was the perfect time for *Jesus* to show the *Jews* his truthfulness by raising dead *Elias* to life. The whole *Israel* would have believed *Jesus* and he would not have to go through, what he went through. But did he do that? No, because *Jesus* wanted the *Jews* to know the truth about *Elias.* The truth was *Elias* had died like a normal person, he never went to heaven bodily and he would never come from the heavens bodily either. *Jesus* did not even bother to explain to the *Jews,* as to how *John the Baptist* is the *Second Coming of Elias? Jesus* just said *John the Baptist is Elias.* When every *Jewish* person in *Israel,* knew that *John the Baptist* did not come from the heavens and he is definitely not the *Elias. Jesus* knew that their view about going to the heaven bodily and coming back from the heaven bodily was a base less claim. But the *Jews* lost all the blessings of *God* because of their erroneous belief.

Now the *Christians* are going to make the same mistake what the *Jews* made over *2000* years ago? When *Jesus* told them in clear words:

> *"For I tell you this, you will never see me again until you are* > *ready to welcome the one sent to you from God"*[174] *Jesus* also > said: *"Of righteousness, because I go to my Father, and ye see* > *me no more" (John 16:10).*

Jesus told them eloquently to his followers not to make the same mistake as the *Jews* did? Therefore, how could we assume *Jesus* went to heaven with his body when he himself is denying that? The *Bible* says: *'Flesh and blood cannot inherit in the kingdom of God' (1Corinthians 15:50).* So does it make any sense that *Jesus* said *"spirit does not have flesh and bones as you see I have" (Luke 24:39).* Then he said: *"Flesh and blood cannot inherit in the kingdom of God"* and then *Jesus* went to heaven? Is that possible that he could contradict himself so much?

Even after learning the serious mistake of the *Jews*, the *Christians* are making the same mistake today. History is repeating itself once again, but now *Christians* are waiting for the *Second Coming of Jesus* the same way what the *Jews* were waiting for *Elijah. Jesus* said:

> *"For I say unto you, Ye shall not see me henceforth, till ye* > *shall say, Blessed is he that cometh in the name of the Lord"* > *(Matthew 23:39).*

First we see from the history of mankind, who came after *Jesus* who is known to over a billion people as the prophet of *God? Muhammad* came after *Jesus*, even if you believe him a true prophet of *God* or not, but no one can deny the fact that he came after *Jesus*, and no one can change that. In this prophecy, *Jesus* gave us important news that do not look for him in *Christians*; he (Jesus) will not be coming in *Christians*. What I mean is that when *Jesus* said *'Ye shall not see me henceforth, till ye shall say, Blessed is he* means, first *Muhammad* will come and then if you believe in him then you will be able to recognize *Jesus*, because he will come from among the *Muslims*. To clarify further, *Jesus* said as I have mentioned earlier:

> *"Therefore say I unto you, The kingdom of God shall be taken* > *from you, and given to a nation bringing forth the fruits thereof"* > *(Matthew 21:43).*

---

[174] Please see *Matthew 23:39 & John 16:10, in The Living Bible*, paraphrased by *Kenneth N. Taylor* Copyright ©1971 by *Tyndale House Publishers*

This means that when the *Christians* will forget the teachings of *Jesus Christ*, instead of worshipping *God* they will start worshipping man (Jesus). Then the *Kingdom of God*, which denotes to the prophet hood, will be taken away from the *Christians* and will be given to the *Muslims*. *Jesus* further said in these words:

> *"Nevertheless when the Son of man cometh, shall he find faith on the earth?" (Luke 18:8).*

Jesus knew that when he will come again he will not find faith in his people. Then *God* will take away the good news from them and will give that good news to another nation (Islam) who will do the will of *God*. But when even the *Muslims* would forget the teachings of *Muhammad*, then the *Second Coming of Christ* would appear from among the *Muslims*. In the time of *Jesus*, the *Jews* were not as lucky as the *Christians* of today. In the time of *Jesus* there was no previous example that someone had come in someone else's name. Now by the grace of *God* in the time of *Second Coming* of *Jesus*, *Ahmad* gave us that previous example of *John the Baptist*, how he came in the name of *Elijah*.

According to my research and understanding of the scriptures, no true prophet of *God* has ever gotten killed. Otherwise, why would *God* tell us in the *Bible* that a false prophet will be killed but *He* would let the true prophets get killed also? The *Bible* says:

> *"But a prophet who presumes to speak in my name anything I have not commanded him to say, or a prophet who speaks in the name of other gods, must be put to death" (Deuteronomy 18:20 NIV).*

When the *Bible* talks about killing of prophets, it only means either people tried to kill prophets or their teachings were stopped or killed. For instance, if we say kill the engine. Does that mean we are asking to literally kill that engine or we mean stop the engine? In the same manner, many nations of many prophets killed their prophets meaning, they stopped their teachings. In a similar manner, the *Jews* of the time of *Jesus Christ* killed *Jesus*, in the sense of that they stopped his teaching brutally that he had to travel to other *Jewish* nations to start preaching again. Secondly, we read in *Matthew*, that *Jesus* said: *"your house [the house of Israel] is left to you, desolate."* What *Jesus* is trying to say here perhaps that because of the barbaric practice of the *Jews*, they tried to kill or tried to stone the prophets of *God*, *"your house [the house of Israel] is left to you, desolate."* This denotes that *Israel* will not receive any more prophets from *God*. This is not my assumption; the history of the

Jews and the *Christians* is telling us that no prophet ever came in *Judaism* or in *Christianity* after *Jesus*.

To elucidate *Jesus* mentioned:

> *"Kingdom of God shall be taken from you and given to a nation bringing forth the fruits thereof" (Matthew 21:43),* right after *Jesus* said '*your house is left to you, desolate."*

He also said, *you will never see me again.* If we put these three verses together we can get the whole picture. It means that not only *Israel* (Jews) will never receive any more prophets but also even *Jesus' Second Coming* will not appear from the *Christians* either. Therefore, according to the *Muslims*, when the kingdom of *God* was taken away from the *Christians*, it was given to the *Muslims*. *Muhammad* and *Ahmad* both were mentioned in the *Bible* by their names. But since some *Christian* scholars did not want people to know that they took out both names from the *Hebrew* and *Greek Bibles*. But all the prophecies in the current *Bibles* about *Muhammad* and *Ahmad* are still there. When the disciples asked *Jesus* about his *Second Advent*:

> *"Tell us, when shall these things be? And what shall be the sign of thy coming, and of the end of the world?" (Matthew 24:3).*

Jesus told them the following prophecies about his *Second Coming.* I will try to explain only the five main points of these prophecies in detail below.

1. *"Nation will rise against nation and kingdom against kingdom" (Matthew 24:7).*

2. *"Earthquakes in divers places" (Matthew 24:7).*

3. *"Pestilences" (Matthew 24:7).*

4. *"All these are the beginning of sorrows" (Matthew 24:8).*

5. *"Then shall they deliver you up to be afflicted, and shall kill you: and ye shall be hated of all nations for my name sake" (Matthew 24:9).*

6. *"And this Gospel of the kingdom shall be preached in all the world for a witness unto all nations" (Matthew 24:14).*

7. *"For as the lightning cometh out of the east, and shineth even unto west; so shall also the coming of the Son of Man be" (Matthew 24:27); (Luke17:24).*

8. *"the sun be darkened, and the moon shall not give her light"* (*Matthew 24:29*).

9. *"and the stars shall fall from heaven, and the powers of the heavens shall be shaken"(Matthew 24:29)*.

1) First World War

Why do we call the war of *1914* as *First World War* and not just a war? Simply, because it happened first time in the history of mankind, that nations rose against nations, just as *Jesus* prophesied. When *Ahmad* came he prophesied about the world war which took place after his prophecy, on *August 1st 1914*. When I told my *Christian* friends how this prophecy of *Jesus* was fulfilled in the time of *Ahmad*, he said in those days everybody knew about the world war, everybody knew it is going to happen any time. My question to those people was does it mean *Jesus* made a very childish prophecy that everybody knew about it already, and there was no significance in it? What was the purpose of that prophecy in the first place if anybody could have predicted it? Why it had to take place after *Ahmad*? Why *God*, who kept this world war not to occur for two thousand years, could not keep it from happening couple hundred more years and let *Ahmad's* prophecy go in vain?

2) Earthquakes

Earthquakes were mentioned in the *Bible* in 11 places, in conjunction with the *Second Coming of Christ* as follows: *1) Matthew 24:29; 2) Mark 13:25; 3) Luke21:26; 4) Isaiah 2:19; 5) Isaiah 2:21; 6) Isaiah 13:13, 7) Isaiah 29:6; 8) Joel 2:10 ; 9) Joel 3:16;10) Revelation 6:12; 11) Revelation 16:18.*

Ahmad the *Second Coming of Christ* predicted about these earth quakes which killed thousands of people in *India*. Some major news papers published the prophecies of *Ahmad* about these noteworthy earthquakes. *The Sunday Herald, Boston*, wrote: *"Great is Mirza Ghulam Ahmad, The Messiah: Foretold Pathetic end of Dowie and now He Predicts Plague, Flood and Earthquake."*[175]

---

[175] Please see: *The Sunday Herald--Boston*, June 23, 1907, Magazine Section, page 3. For a copy, contact *The Boston Public Library* Microfiche department

The Sunday Herald—Boston, June 23, 1907, Great
is Mirza Ghulam Ahmad, The Messiah...

Will the World End in 2012?

According to the prophecies of the *Bible*, the *Qur'an* and the books of Prophet *Ahmad*, the world is not going to end soon. As many people are predicting that the world will end 2012. I can guarantee people of the world that the predictions and prophecies of *Ahmad* are true. According to the *Bible*, the *Qur'an* and the books of *Ahmad*, the world will not end until they see *"New Heaven and New Earth."* All those who would read my book after 2012, might smile and say that the prophecies of *Ahmad* were true. Therefore, the *Bible* says:

> *"Then I saw a new heaven and a new earth, for the old heaven and the old earth had disappeared..."*[176]

This means that the world will not end until the people see the old and corrupted people of any religion replaced with new and righteous people. And this is only possible after the followers of the *Second Coming of Christ* (Ahmad's followers) become more in number than the *First Coming of Christ*

---

[176] Please see *Revelation 21:1 NLT*

(Jesus' followers). In my opinion, the world will not end until the '*Single Christians*' (followers of First Christ) become the followers of the *Second Coming of Christ* as well, and become "*Double Christians.*" *Ahmadis* all over the world are only 200 million, while the world population is about seven billion, so we have long ways to go to preach the *Gospel* of the *Second Coming of Christ* and the end of the world has long ways to come. The *Qur'an* also gives us a similar message, it says:

> "*On the day when this earth will be changed into another earth,*
> *and the heavens too; and they will all appear before Allah, the*
> *One, the Most Supreme*" (*Ibrahim 14:48-49*).

3) Pestilences: According to the prophecy of *Jesus Christ* about his *Second Coming,* the book of *Matthews* says, "*...and there shall be famines, and pestilences...*" (*Matthew 24:7*). *Ahmad* wrote a book titled *Kashtiye-Nooh* or the *Noah's Ark,* in *October 5th 1902*. In this book *Ahmad* predicted this *Biblical* prophecy about the famines and pestilences, and said that the people who believe in me will be saved in the same manner as the people who believed in *Noah* were saved from the worst deluge of the history. Thousands of people died in the pestilence predicted by *Ahmad.* But *God* kept his promise and saved all *Ahmadis,* the followers of *Ahmad.*

4) Come from East:

Jesus articulated, " *For as the lightning cometh out of the east, and shineth even unto west*" this denotes that *Jesus' Second Coming,* would appear from the *East* and his teaching would spread towards the *West.* In accordance with this prophecy, *Ahmad was* appointed by *God Almighty* in *1889,* to be the promised *Second Coming of Christ.* Who came from *India,* which is the eastern part of the world, and then his teaching started to spread towards the *West.* Coming of *Jesus Christ* from *India* is not only *Ahmadiyya* interpretation of the prophecies of *Jesus.*

Surprisingly, in 1875 a group of devout *Christians* from the west came to *India* and established a society called *Theosophical Society.* Its founder *Anne Besant* and the members of the society firmly believed that a messiah, a world teacher would come from the east, possibly from *India.* When they could not recognize the messiah, a world teacher (Ahmad), they picked up a young 14 years old *Hindu* boy name *Jiddu Krishnamurti.* They tried their best for 20 years to make him a messiah, but unfortunately, they did not know that *God* appoints prophets and messiahs and it is not in the power of men to do that. They even founded an organization called "*Order of the Star in the East,*" in

215

1925. In 1929, after the *Theosophical Society* nurtured *Mr. Krishnamurti* for 20 years, he announced that he is neither a messiah nor a prophet; and said do not rely on him.[177]

Is it easy to leave your country, your family, your friends, your language, your comfortable homes, your food, and your culture, your everything to look for the *Messiah*? If those people would not have believed with such a conviction that the messiah would come from the east especially from *India*, do you think they would have done all that? Did you know that a similar incident occurred after *Moses*? The *Jews* after receiving the prophecy:

> *"And he [Moses] said: "The LORD came from Sinai, And dawned on them from Seir; He shone forth from Mount Paran..."* (Deuteronomy 33:2).

Hundreds of *Jews* went to *Arabia* and settled around *Mt Paran* (an ancient name of Mecca), hoping to find *'that prophet'* (See also John 1:21) and become his followers. But unfortunately, when *Muhammad* did come fulfilling those prophecies they rejected him as a liar, as they rejected *Jesus* as a liar.

According to the book *The kingdom of the Cults*, it says:

> *"Following the chronology of Archbishop Ussher, and interpreting the 2300 days of Daniels as 2300 years, many Bible students of various denominations concluded that Christ would come back about the year 1843. Of this studious number was one William Miller, a Baptist minister... The great second advent movement which swept the United States in the 1840's..., who confidently taught in the year 1818, that in "about" twenty five years, i.e., 1843, Jesus Christ would come again."*[178] The book also says on page #413, 'Clearly it may be seen that although Miller popularized the 1843-1844 concept of Christ coming again, he was by no means alone. If we condemn him, we must also condemn a large number of internationally known scholars who were among the most highly educated men of their day..."*

According to the above references, many diverse sects of *Christianity* were honestly and earnestly waiting for the *Second Coming of Christ* in around *1840* and also expecting him to come from the *EAST*. *Ahmad* fulfilled both of these

---

[177] Please see *History* Channel's documentary titled *Jiddu Krishnamurti: The reluctant Messiah*

[178] Please see *The kingdom of the Cults*, by *Walter Martin*, published by *Bethany House Publishers* Copyright *1985*, Pages *411 & 413*

expectations, he was born in *1835* (scholars were off by merely five years) and he appeared from the *east*.

Prophecy of Prophet *Daniel: "Blessed is he who waits and arrives at the 1,335 days" (Daniel 12: 13 ESV)*. *God* revealed this prophecy of Prophet *Daniel* to *Ahmad;* he mentioned this prophecy in his book titled *Touhfa-e-Gulervia*, on page *#292 to 293*. According to this prophecy the *Messiah* supposed to come around the fourteenth century. As I have mentioned earlier, Prophet *Ahmad* came exactly the time when he supposed to have come.

5) Sun & Moon Eclipses:

This is one of the greatest prophecies of the *Bible* because this prophecy was not only told by *Jesus* but also told by many other major religions of the world. *Jesus* mentioned it three times in the following verses, such as *(Matthew 24:29, 2) Mark 13:24, 3) Luke 21: 25)*, but also it was told in the book of *Acts 2:20*. *John the Baptist* foretold this prophecy in the book of *Revelation 6:12*. And in the *Old Testament* it was foretold by *Isaiah, 13:10* & *Isaiah 60: 19*. By *Prophet Ezekiel 32:7*, by *Prophet Joel, 2:10, 2:31* and *Joel 3:15*.

This prophecy is also told in *Qur'an* in these words:

> *"When the eye is dazzled, And the moon is eclipsed, And the sun and the moon are brought together" (Al-Qiyamah 75:7-10)*.

This prophecy was told in the holy book of *Hindus, Mahatma Surdasji* has mentioned the prophecy that when *Kalki Autar* (similar term as Messiah) would appear, the moon and the sun would be eclipsed. He wrote: *"Both the moon and the sun will be eclipsed and there will be much violence and death"* (Sursagar). Perhaps, *Mahatma Surdasji* was also referring to the *Biblical* prophecy *'Nation will rise against nation,'* the *First World War* that killed about eight million people. The holy book of *Sikhs* tell us this prophecy in these words:

> *"When Maharaj will come as Nahkalank [Reformer], the sun and the moon will be his helper."*[179]

The books of *Hadith* also tell us about the sun and moon eclipses. This is a blessing of *God Almighty* that the *Hadith* tells us more in detail about the sun and moon eclipses. The more detail means harder to forge this prophecy. This *Hadith* is narrated *by Hadhrat Imam Muhammad bin Ali*, it says:

---

[179] Please see *Sri Guru Garanth Sahib*

*"There are two testimonies for our Mahdi (*another name for *messiah), which have never occurred since the creation of this universe and that is a lunar eclipse would occur on the first night (of the lunar eclipse dates) in the month of Ramadhan, and, the sun would be eclipsed in the middle (of the solar eclipse dates) of the same month (of Ramadhan)."*[180]

Please allow me to elucidate an important aspect of this prophecy, which has been twisted by many *Muslim* scholars, as a result, they make excuses not to recognize the messiah sent by *God*. They say that the prophecy says that *'the lunar eclipse would occur on the first night.'* But when it actually happened it occurred on the 13 of the month and not the first of the month as the prophecy says. The fact is that the moon of the first night is so tiny that it is hard to see it most of the times, now imagine if that tiny moon which is already hard to see gets eclipsed? Do you think anybody would be able to see that? Then why would *God* give us a sign which has been mentioned for thousands of years and through most major religions. But when it comes to pass, nobody would be able to see that. Would that be a good guidance of *God* to steer people away from recognizing the *Messiah*?

The moon eclipse had to occur on the thirteenth of the month, when the moon is full and it's easy to view. 13th of the month is in fact the first night of the full moon. Not only that the prophet who was *Arab* who knew *Arabic* language better than everyone else in that era, he said eclipse of *Qamar* (full moon). The *Arabic* word for the first night of the moon is *Hilal* (crescent) when the moon is tiny. Prophet *Muhammad* did not know if the eclipse of moon he was talking about or eclipse of *Hilal* (crescent) he was talking about?

The *Solar* and the *lunar* eclipses have occurred many times, but have they occurred before when the claimant of messiah was there? That's why the *Hadith* says *'which have never occurred since the creation of this universe.'* This denotes that without claimant, solar and lunar eclipses have no value at all. This means that if solar and lunar eclipses occurred before *Adam*, or few thousand years ago when nobody was waiting for the messiah, and nobody was claiming to be the messiah, then what was the significance of that occurrence? But it happened when the *Messiah* of the age "*Ahmad*" came about hundred years ago and he prophesized that because I am from *God* and I am not a false *Messiah* this sun and moon will eclipse and then it occurred in 1894 after he prophesied.

There is a certain criteria set by the wise people

[180] Please see *Sunan-Dar-Qutni*. Vol. 2, pg. 65 please see also *Akmal-ud-din*.

1. A claimant should be there

2. There should be sun & moon eclipses within the same lunar month

3. The Lunar month should be *Ramadhan* (the holiest month in the whole year for *Muslims*, also referred as the fasting month.

4. The lunar eclipse should occur on the 13th of *Ramadhan* and the solar eclipse should occur on 29th of the same month.

5. These eclipses should occur during the lifetime of a claimant after he has made the claim to be the *Promised Messiah*. (Excerpts from *"Eclipses and the Promised Messiah"* by Dr. *Muhammad Aslam Nasir Sahib* [Paraphrased]).

The *Christians* usually ask me that if it is true that your prophet *Ahmad* is the *Second Coming of Jesus Christ* then why the world is still in such turmoil, a lot of wars going on, a lot of destruction, a lot more immorality than ever before, and why the world of today is in worse condition than ever before? First, I usually ask them what kind of change in the world had occurred when *Jesus* came? Did other countries stop fighting just because a *Christian Messiah* had come? Did *Rome* stop crucifying people; stop charging too many taxes? Did immorality around the world stop, did the *Jews* stop persecuting *Christians*, and did the world become heaven to live after *Jesus*. No, right? Why not? according to your belief *Jesus* was *God* (God forbid) if your *God* could not bring about a change in the world and in the lives of non-believers then how could *Ahmad the Second Coming of Christ* do that while he only proclaims to be a mere prophet?

Let me present a scenario, this will tell you as to why a prophet cannot change the world, it doesn't matter how respected the prophet is. If a town or a city has a deadly plague, and thousands of people are dying and suffering so severely that there is a big chaos in that city. The government realizes the situation and sends the best doctor in that field. But when he arrives, the people reject him harshly. When he prescribes cautions how to safeguard yourselves from that plague people would not pay attention to that, when he gives medication to those who are suffering from that disease and people do not use those medications. Now contemplate on this issue, how those people are going to get better? The same applies in the case of a prophet. When *God* sees destruction, chaos, immorality, wars and bloodshed, then because of His mercy he sends prophets. But when the world rejects that prophet as a liar and imposter, and totally opposes his teachings, do you think they will become righteous, good and peaceful people after that? If not, then why not? The reason is that just by coming of any prophet cannot change anything, unless people believe in him to be the true prophet of *God* and listen to him, obey him and change their lives in accordance to his teachings. If the people do not take his advice how to stay away from sins, dishonesties, immoralities, and do not use his suggestions, how to become righteous people again, then how would that prophet benefit them? Today with the blessing of *God Almighty*, members of *Ahmadiyya Community* are about *200* million worldwide. Please visit www.alislam.org for further detail, and about the *Life of Ahmad*. The *Ahmadiyya* motto which is crucial in this age of darkness and abhorrence is as follows:

LOVE FOR ALL; HATRED FOR NONE

*Picture of Masjid Bait-Ul-Futuh, the Ahmadiyya Head Quarter,
London, England (Photo by Mazhar-ul-Haq Khan)*

22. The Holy Ghost (Part 1)

There are some prophecies in the *Bible*, which mention a prophet after *Jesus*. The *Christians* usually construe from these prophecies that *Jesus* was talking about a spirit, but if you study these prophecies little closely you'll comprehend that he was talking about a prophet not a spirit.

(Excerpts from Chapter 16)

Jesus said: [1] *"Nevertheless I tell you the truth; It is expedient for you that I go away: for if I go not away, the Comforter will not come unto you; but if I depart, I will send him unto you (John 16:7). [2] And when he is come, he will reprove the world of sin..." (John 16:8).*

[3]. *"I have yet many things to say unto you, but you cannot bear them now. Howbeit when he, the Spirit of truth, is come, [4], he will guide into all truth [5]: for he shall not speak of himself; but whatsoever he shall hear, that shall he speak: [6], and he will shew you things to come [7], he shall glorify me for he shall receive of mine, and shall shew it unto you" (John 16:12 to 14).*

(Excerpts from Chapter 15)

Jesus said: [8] *"but when the Comforter is come, whom I will send unto you from the father, even the Spirit of truth which proceedeth from the Father [9], he shall testify of me" (John 15: 26).*

(Excerpts from Chapter 14)

[10] *"If ye love me, keep my commandments And I will pray the Father, and he shall give you another Comforter, that he may abide with you forever..."*

[11] *"Even the Spirit of truth; whom the world cannot receive, because it seeth him not, neither knoweth him: but ye know him; for he dwelleth with you, and shall be in you" (John 14:15-17).*

[12] *"he shall teach you all things,* [13], *and bring all things to your remembrance, whatsoever I have said unto you" (John 14: 26).*

[14] *"Peace I leave with you, my peace I give unto you: not as the world giveth, give I unto you. Let not your heart be troubled, neither let it be afraid" (John 14:27).*

1st: If you notice the first prophecy *(John 16: 7)*, *Jesus* puts an extra emphasis on *'going away'* in a small verse, he mentioned *'going away'* three times. That was a tradition of many holy men whenever they wanted to emphasize on something they would say it three times. We see this trend in the *New Testament* as well, as *Jesus* asked his disciple *Simon*; *'Do you love me?'* And he said *yes*, then *Jesus* said *'feed my lamb' (John 21:15 to 17).* In these *verses*, *Jesus* repeated his question three times not because he had too much time, and nothing better to do, but because he wanted to make his point clear. The same way, he mentioned three times that 'I *go away*,' therefore, the people of our time would not make the mistake that whosoever is going to appear, would come after the death of *Jesus*, and not while he is still alive.

In all these prophecies, *Jesus* used the pronoun *'he'* instead of *'it,'* which shows quite clear that *Jesus* was talking about a *'man,'* and not a *'spirit.'* When I showed this prophecy of *Jesus* to my *Christian* friends, and I told them that in these verses *Jesus* is talking about prophet *"Muhammad"(The Founder of Islam)* because he came after *Jesus*, and all the glad tidings that are mentioned here, in all fourteen verses, they all were fulfilled in him. They said this is not true at all, because *Jesus* clearly said *"Spirit of Truth,"* he never said a prophet, especially if you say *Muhammad*; there is no way *Jesus* prophesized about him. Then I explained to them, how this prophecy was fulfilled in the person of *Prophet Muhammad*.

2) *"...Reprove the world of sin" (John 16:8).*

3) *"I have yet many things to say unto you, but you cannot bear then now" (John 16:12).*

4) *"...when he, the Spirit of truth is come he will guide you into all truth" (John 16: 13).*

5) *"He shall not speak of himself; but whatsoever he shall hear, that shall he speak" (John 16: 13).*

6) *"He shall shew you things to come" (John 16: 13).*

7) *"He shall glorify me, for he shall receive of mine, and shall shew it unto you" (John 16:14).*

8) *"but when the Comforter is come, whom I will send unto you from the father, even the Spirit of truth which proceedeth from the Father" (John 15:26).*

9) *"He shall testify me" (John 16:26).*

10) *"Comforter… he may abide with you forever" (John 14:16).*

11) *"   Even the Spirit of truth; whom the world cannot receive because it seeth him not, neither knoweth him: but ye know him; for he dwelleth with you, and shall be in you" (John 14:17).*

12) *"He shall teach you all things" (John 14:26).*

13) *"He shall bring all things to your remembrance, whatsoever I have said unto you" (John 14:26).*

14) *"Peace I leave with you, my peace I give unto you: not as the world giveth, give I unto you. Let not your heart be troubled, neither let it be afraid" (John 14:27).*

2nd: '**Reprove** *the world of sin.*' The meaning of '*reprove*' is the act of criticizing somebody for having done something wrong.[181] The question is how can a spirit criticize someone? If you say that I have *Holy Spirit* in me and if I criticize someone, it is same as *Holy Spirit* criticizing someone. But the problem is that your *Holy Spirit* is teaching you three gods which is utterly contradictory to the *One God* always taught by the *Old Testament*. If your *Holy Spirit* cannot even guide you towards *One True God*, then what else can you expect from it? Your *Holy Spirit* is teaching you man-god; could this be the teachings of the true *Holy Spirit*? Similarly, in these days, people do not even criticize their own children. When young girls get pregnant without marriage, all the criticism they get from their parents is, that we cannot afford you and your baby, go find another place to live. But the parents hardly tell their daughters that what you have done is fornication, and it is a serious sin

---

[181]   Please see *Encarta dictionaries of MSN.com*

against *God, worthy of death.*[182] The parents hardly tell young children that fornication is a sin and the fornicators will not go to the heavens.

Some *Christians* say that these laws were the laws of the *Old Testament* and they do not apply on them (Christians), but what about the *New Testament?* Does the *New Testament* say anything about it? The book of *Galatians* says:

> *"Now the works of the flesh are manifest, which are these; Adultery, fornication, uncleanness, lasciviousness..., as I have also told you in time past, that they which do such things shall not inherit the kingdom of God."*[183]

The book of *Corinthians* also commands us in the similar way:

> *"Know ye not that the unrighteous shall not inherit the kingdom of God? Be not deceived: neither fornicators, nor idolaters, nor adulterers, nor effeminate, nor abusers of themselves with mankind..."*[184]

When people cannot even reprove their own selves or their children for that matter, then how they are going to '*reprove the world of sin.*'? But when *Prophet Muhammad* came, he truly reproved the world of sin, and he brought the idol worshippers to *One God*, and strictly reinforced the laws against *fornication* and *adultery*, and made them pure with the *"Fiery Law."*[185] These *Biblical* prophecies corroborate with the *Qur'an*, it says:

"The Spirit of Truth (that had been promised to you) is come and falsehood is vanished" (Qur'an 17:82). This also substantiates the claim of *Muslims* that *Muhammad* is the '*Spirit of Truth.*'

> 3rd & 4th: *"I have yet many things to say unto you, but you cannot bear them now. But when he, the Spirit of truth come, he will guide you into all truth."*

Jesus mentioned above that he wanted to tell his disciples more about the *Kingdom of God*, but they were not ready. But when the *Spirit of truth* comes, he will tell them everything. Now my question is have you been told by the *Holy Spirit* something new, which was not told by *Jesus*, and it is not found in the *Bible?* The fact is, even if you find out something, which is true by every

---

182   Please see *Deuteronomy 22:20-21*
183   Please see *Galatians 5:19-21* NLT
184   Please see *I Corinthians 6:9*
185   Please see *Deuteronomy 33:2*

means, but it is not written in the *Bible*, and it is not told by *Jesus*, you would not believe that. If this perception is wrong about *Jesus*, that he did not bring complete teachings then please contemplate what *Jesus* said about a few very common issues in life?

1. What did *Jesus* say about brothers & sisters? (How should we treat them?)

2. What did *Jesus* say about sons & daughters? (How should we treat them?)

3. What did *Jesus* say about a marriage? (Should we marry or stay single? Why the early church especially *Paul* always preached celibacy?

4. What did *Jesus* say about a wife? (How should we treat her?)

5. What did *Jesus* say about wives? (How many wives, one can have? Many westerners, who make fun of *Islam's* permission of up to four wives, usually they have many girlfriends on the side)

6. What did *Jesus* say about divorced women? (Can she re-marry?)

7. What did *Jesus* say about men & women's equal rights? (Do they have equal rights in Christianity?)

8. What did *Jesus* say about women's rights of inheritance? (Do they have any rights in Christianity?)

9. What did *Jesus* say about relatives? (How should we treat them?)

10. What did *Jesus* say about guests? (How should we treat them?)

11. What did *Jesus* say about widowed women? (How should we treat them?)

12. What did *Jesus* say about orphans? (How should we treat them?)

13. What did *Jesus* say about Inheritance? (Who should get and what?)

14. What did *Jesus* say about entrust?

15. What did *Jesus* say about burying people? (*Jesus* did talk about burying people but he said a very strange thing he said: *"and let the dead bury their dead"* (Matthew 8:22). Is it possible?).

16. What did *Jesus* say about eating? (How should we eat, sit-down & eat or lie down and eat like *Jesus* used to eat? Anyway, is it healthy to eat lying down?)

17. What did *Jesus* say about washing hands before eating? (It did not bother him eating with dirty hands, *Jesus* said "...*but to eat with unwashen hands defileth not a man"* (Matthew 15:20).

18. What did *Jesus* say about cleanliness of a person?

19. What did *Jesus* say about use of alcohol? (How could he tell us not to use alcohol, when he drank himself and gave others to drink, according to a common *Christian* belief?)

20. What did *Jesus* say about Business? (How should we run it? Anyway we want? Or there are certain guidelines to run a business? Should we run it honestly or should we rip off people, lie & cheat?)

21. What did *Jesus* say about interest? (Is interest good or bad for people?)

22. What did *Jesus* say about Gambling? (Should a Christian gamble or not. Does the entire *Bible* say anything about gambling?)

23. What did *Jesus* say about a government? (How government should be run?)

24. What did *Jesus* say about people? (How they should react to a government? Should they be loyal to a government or they should revolt against it, if they please so?)

25. What did *Jesus* say about War situation? (How should we act in a war? Is it true that "everything is fair in love and War"?)

26. What did *Jesus* say about stealing? He did say not to steal but he himself stole corns from a corn field (God forbid). (please see Matthew 12:1 through 5)

27. What did *Jesus* say about the name of his religion? (Was that supposed to be Christianity? But that name was first introduced by *Paul* (Acts 11:26).

28. What did *Jesus* say about other religions? (How should we treat them?)

29. What did *Jesus* say about cleanliness in general?

30. What did *Jesus* say about thieves (what should be the punishment?)

This is strange that almost 100% of what *Muslims* believe comes from *Muhammad*. But almost 90% of what *Christians* believe comes from the people other than *Jesus*. This means *Paul, Peter & James etc*. When you try to find answers to the above questions please find the commandments by *Jesus* himself from four *Gospels* and not by *Paul, or Peter*, since *Jesus* was the *Messiah* and not the others. On the other hand, the *Qur'an* and the *Hadith* teach us answers to every question I have asked above. You be the judge as to whose teaching is complete?

The *Qur'an* also proclaims that the reason of *Qur'an's* revelation to *Muhammad* is to clarify many things which were disputed in the *Bible*, it says:

"Verily, this Qur'an explains to the Children of Israel most of that concerning which they differ" (Al-Naml 27:76-77).

When I showed this verse of *Qur'an* to my *Christian* friend he started laughing and said your prophet stole 90% from the *Bible*, how could *Qur'an* clarify anything? I am presenting below some of the examples, where *Qur'an* corrected the *Bible* according to our belief, but you be the judge.

Bible & Qur'an

1	Three Gods (Trinity)	The *Qur'an* says:
	(Matthew 28:19)	*a) "O People of the Book, (Christians) exceed not the limits in your religion, and say not of Allah anything but the truth. Verily, the Messiah, Jesus, son of Mary, was only a Messenger of Allah and a fulfilment of His word which He sent down to Mary, and a mercy from Him. So believe in Allah and His Messengers, and say not 'They are three.' Desist, it will be better for you. Verily, Allah is the only One God. Far is it from His Holiness that He should have a son. To Him belongs whatever is in the heavens and whatever is in the earth. And sufficient is Allah as a Guardian" (Al-Nisa 4: 171-172).*
		The *Qur'an* also says:
		b) "Say, 'He is Allah, the One" (Al-Ikhlas 112:1-2).
		To prove that what *Qur'an* says is also supported by the *Bible*. I will try to comprise verses from the *Bible*, if available.
		New Testament says: *"And Jesus answered him, The first of all the commandments is, Hear, O Israel; The Lord our **God is one** Lord" (Mark 12:29)*
2	*Jesus* is God (God forbid) (a common Christian belief)	The *Qur'an* says: *"Jesus is nothing, but a prophet"* (Al-Ma'idah 5:75-76).
		Jesus called himself prophet in the verses below:
		When a *Pharisee* came to *Jesus* and told him to run away from *Jerusalem*, because *King Herod* will kill you. *Jesus* said to him *"for it cannot be that a **prophet** should perish away from Jerusalem"* (Luke 13:31-33).
		*"And they were offended in him. But Jesus said unto them, A **prophet** is not without honour, save in his own country, and in his own house" (Matthew 13:57).*
		*"But Jesus said unto them, A **prophet** is not without honour, but in his own country, and among his own kin, and in his own house" (Mark 6:4 & John, 4:44).*

	Bible calls son of *Mary; Jesus*	The *Qur'an* calls him *Isa* All the old evidences show that the name of *Mary's* son was *Isa* not *Jesus*. Old *Tibetan* scrolls call him *Isa* Old *Hindu* book *Purana* talks about *Jesus* and calls him *Isa* [*Yeshua* is a *Hebrew* name which has been transliterated into *Greek* as *'Iesous'* (IhsouV: pronounced "ee-ay-SUS"). The English "*Jesus*" comes from the *Latin* transliteration of the *Greek* name into the *Latin 'Iesus.'*] If you take out *'s'* of the end it becomes *Iesu*. Which was the real name of *Jesus* mentioned in old scriptures *Isa* or *Iesu*. All *Arabic & Urdu Bibles* even today call him *Yesu*. (for bracketed text please see the website *www.thenazareneway.com* for a detailed account)
3	*Jesus* is son of *God* (God forbid)	The *Qur'an* says: *"God doesn't have a wife, how could he have a son?" (Al-An'am 6: 101-102)*. *"It does not befit the Majesty of Allah to take unto Himself a son. Holy is He. When He decrees a thing, He says to it, 'Be!', and it is" (Maryam 19: 35-36)*. *"And we believe that the majesty of our Lord is exalted. He has taken neither wife nor son unto Himself" (Al-Jinn 72:3-4)*.
4	According to the *New Testament, Jesus* was harsh towards his mother & often called her **'woman'** (John 2:4 & 19:26)	The *Qur'an* says: *"And He[God] has made me[Jesus] kind towards my mother, and has not made me arrogant and graceless" (Maryam 19:32- 33)*.
5	*Jesus* died on the cross and became accursed (Galatians 3:13)	The *Qur'an* says: *"Jesus definitely was not killed* (on the cross)*" (Al-Nisa 4:157-158)*. The *Bible* also says, when *Jesus* prayed to *God* in the garden of *Gethsemane*, to save his life, it says: *"God heard his prayer"* (Hebrew 5:7). That means he was saved from dying on the cross.
6	*Adam* was a sinner (a common Christian belief)	The *Qur'an* says: *"And verily, We [God] had made a covenant with Adam beforehand, but he forgot, and We found in him no resolve to disobey US" (TaHa 20:115-116)*. The *Bible* also says: *"And it was the woman, not Adam, who was deceived by Satan, and sin was the result" (1Timothy 2:14 NLT)*.

7	Every one inherited the sin of Adam (a common Christian belief)	The *Qur'an* says: *"thou art not made responsible except for thyself"* (Al-Nisa 4: 84-85). *"O ye who believe! take care of your own selves. He who goes astray cannot harm you when you yourselves are rightly guided..."* (Al-Maidah 5: 105-106). *"Who so does a good deed, does it for his own soul; and whoso does wrong, does so to its detriment"* (Al-Jathiyah 45:15-16). *Bible* also denies this belief in 6 different books through 6 different prophets. *"every man shall be put to death for his own sin"*(Deuteronomy 24:16, 2Kings 14:6, 2 Chronicles 25:4, Ezekiel 18:20, Jeremiah 31:30 & Galatians 6:5).
8	The *Bible* says: *God* rested the 7th day (Genesis 2:2)	The *Qur'an* says: *"And, verily, We created the heavens and the earth and all that is between them in six periods and no tiredness touched US"* (Qaf 50:38-39). *"Do they not realize that Allah, Who created the heavens and the earth and was not tired by their creation..."* (Al-Ahqaf 46:33-34).
9	The *Bible* says: *"There were about 600,000 men, plus all the women and children. And they were all traveling on foot. Many people who were not Israelites went with them, along with the many flocks and herds"* (Exodus 12:37).	The *Qur'an* says: *"Those (Israelites) who went forth from their homes and they were thousands"* (Al-Baqarah 2: 243-244). Scholars of today strongly suggest that it is impossible for *600,000* people plus all the women & children plus many non-Israelites plus all flocks & herds to make a long journey and wandered for 40 years. Please see also a similar view, *The History of the People of Israel,* by *Ernest Renan* on page 145, &1888. Also see the book *History of Palestine and the Jews.* by *John Kitto* on page #174.

10	The *Bible* says, *Abraham* lied about his wife *Sarah* and told the Pharaoh that she was his sister (a short summary of 7 verses of Genesis, Chapter 12 verses 13-19). The strange thing is that if the *Bible* is true about the lie of *Abraham* and the *Pharaoh* liked his wife *Sarah*, but *Sarah* was over 90 years old women, how could anyone fall in love with a woman who is that old?	The *Qur'an* says: *"Abraham was the most truthful man"* (*Maryam 19:41-42*).

11	The *Bible* is absolutely flawless, there are no interpolations whatsoever. (a common Christian & Jewish belief) The *Christians* & the *Jews* get very upset when we tell them that the *Quran* proclaims that they have changed their book. They say *Quran* is wrong because we never changed anything in our book, *Christians* claim that their *Bible* is flawless. But on the other hand, *Bible* itself accepts the proclamation of *Quran* in these words: *"The earth also is defiled under the inhabitants thereof; because they have transgressed the laws, changed the ordinance, broken the everlasting covenant"* (Isaiah 24:5). In addition to the verse above, the *Catholic Bibles* have apocrypha, a set of many books that are not part of *Christian Bibles*. These books are as follows: ***The Roman Catholic Apocrypha*** *Tobit* *Judith* *Wisdom* *Ecclesiasticus* *Baruch* *First Maccabees* *Second Maccabees*	The *Qur'an* says on many occasions that the *Jews* & the *Christians* have changed the *Bible*. *"Do you expect that they (Jews) will believe you when a party of them hear the Word of Allah [God], then pervert it after they have understood it, and they well know the consequences thereof"* *(Al-Baqarah 2:75-76).* *"There were some among the Jews who pervert words from their proper places..."* (Al-Nisa 4:45-46). *"...They [Children of Israel] pervert the words from their proper places and have forgotten a good part of that with which they were exhorted..."* (Al-Maidah 5:13-14). The *Qur'an* mentions that it is protected by *God* to be interpolated and also it says that no one can change the word of *God*, hence it says: *"Verily, We Ourself have sent down this Exhortation, and most surely We will be its Guardian"* (Al-Hijr 15: 9-10). *"...There is none that can change the words of Allah..."* (Al-An'am 6: 34-35). *"And recite what has been revealed to thee of the Book of thy Lord. There is none who can change His words, and thou wilt find no refuge beside Him"* (Al-Kahf 18: 27-28). The strange thing is that the book *Jews & Christians* consider from *God* changes almost every year, and the book they consider not from *God,* claims that no one can change it and this claim has been in effect for over fourteen hundred years. Some of my *Christian* friends contend that the *Qur'an* has been change and the example they give is that some *Qur'ans* start with 1st verse and the others start with 2nd verse. But this is not a change in the text, the text of all *Qur'ans* remains the same. I would consider a change if (God forbid) one *Qur'an* has more verses than the other *Qur'an*.	

Additions to *Esther*, this means six more chapters in *Esther* and the book *of Daniel*, have extra 2 chapters 13 & 14, in addition to the 12 chapters of *King James version*. *(Please see Catholic Bibles)*.

The oldest and the most reliable two *Bibles, Codex Sinaiticus* & *Codex Vaticanus*, do not even match entirely. If all the *Bibles* of today are the copies of those two oldest *Bibles* then what happened to the two books of *Old Testament* which are not included in today's *Bibles*, *'The Shepherd of Hermas'* and the *'Epistle of Barnabas.'* I am talking about differences of books not just the chapters or the verses. This oldest *Bible* (Codex Sinaiticus) has many other portions of books which are not included in today's *Bible*. They even have some pages missing, and some of the writings are considered by historians as written around 9th century, almost a millennia after *Jesus*. Even though this codex is believed to be 4th century *Bible* but some of the writings were added centuries after it was discovered. As I have mentioned earlier, there are *44* verses in some 30 to 40 years old *Bibles* that are not in some newer *Bibles*. (Please see the Chapter titled *'Jesus went to heaven'* for detailed account about what verses are missing and in which Bibles). Some *Bibles* do not even have the 4th *Gospel*, the book of *John*. (Please see the *Bible* titled *The Short Bible*, by *Edgar J. GoodSpeed* & *J.M. Powis Smith* & published by *The University of Chicago Press, Chicago Illinois).* Please remember that people usually say that the meaning of short *Bible* is that it does not have the book of *John*, but if you read the *Preface* of the *Bible* it contains the list of the books which were not included in this *Bible*, but in that list there is no mention of the book of *John*. Please also remember that around *1920* many scholars totally rejected the book of *John* and considered it to be a false book. According to the *'Los Angeles Times' March* 4th 1991 edition it says on page #A-24 *"The only saying of John... Most scholars, if they had worked through the sayings as we had, would tend to agree there is virtually nothing in the 4th Gospel [John] that goes back to Jesus,"* said *Robert Fortna of Vassar college..."* Some *Bibles* are printed without *Old Testament*; some *New Testament Bibles* are printed with *Psalms*. (Please see the chapter *titled "Psalms or the 5th Gospel?"* for the list of those *Bibles* which are appended in the *New Testament* with *Psalms).*

Which one of these *Bibles* is the true and flawless version? Who is more righteous the *Christians* who have six less books in their *Bible*? Or the *Catholics* are more righteous than *Christians* because they have six extra books in their *Bible*? This is very strange

	that *Christians* usually do not respect their *Bible* and often say that respect of *Bible* means nothing. I guess because of all these changes and many more other changes, *God* took their respect away from their hearts. Perhaps for the *Christians* it is more a book of men than the book of *God.*	
12	*Christians* & *Jews* try to convince *Muslims* that *Abraham* tried to sacrifice his son *Isaac* not *Ishmael*. But the *Bible* says: *"The LORD said, "Go get Isaac, your only son"* (Genesis 22:2). I do not know how could *God* forget that *Isaac* was *Abraham's* 2nd son not "ONLY" son. The descendants of *Isaac* (Jews & Christians) have no value for the sacrifice and they do not commemorate it either.	The *Qur'an* says it was *Ishmael*, who was at the sacrifice table. (*Al-Saffat 37:103 to 109*). While the descendants of *Ishmael* (Muslims) have great value for that day called *Eid-Ul-Adha*, and we commemorate it every year.
13	The *Bible* says that *Abraham* took his son and tried to sacrifice him without him being known. *"Isaac said, "Father?" "Yes, my son,"* Abraham replied. "We have the wood and the fire," said the boy, "but where is the lamb for the sacrifice?" "God will provide a lamb, my son," Abraham answered. And they both went on together"* (Genesis 22: 7 & 8 NLT). This denotes *Isaac* was evidently unaware of who was going to be sacrificed.	But the *Qur'an*, on the other hand, says that *Abraham* asked his son it says: *"And when he was old enough to run along with him, he said, 'O my dear son, I have seen in a dream that I offer thee in sacrifice. So consider what thou thinkest of it!' He replied, 'O my father, do as thou art commanded; thou wilt find me, if Allah please, steadfast in my faith"* (Al-Saffat 37:102-103).

This means that not only *Abraham* tried to sacrifice his son with his son's own permission but *Ishmael* also offered his life for the sake of *God*. |

After reading the above few examples from the *Qur'an*, does it seem to you that *Muhammad* copied these verses from the *Bible*? If a person who has ample knowledge to correct an account, then why would he copy to begin with? A long time ago my brother *Amjad* was taking a test in a school, a student next to him was copying what my brother was writing. At the end of the test the teacher asked that boy who was copying my brother, did you copy *Amjad's* test paper? That student was stunned and asked why do you think that? The teacher said because *Amjad* wrote his father's name *Younus* and you wrote your father's name *Younus* as well. That boy was so occupied in copying that he did not even notice what he was copying. While everybody who knows the basics of *Muhammad's* life would know that he could not read and write. Then how did he copy? Another interesting point is that *Torah* was not even translated in *Arabic* until almost the 10th Century. And the *Gospels* were not translated into *Arabic* around the 9th century. Now the question arises that the *Torah* and the *Gospels* which were not even available for another 300 to 400 years after *Muhammad's* life. Where did *Muhammad* get the *Old* and the *New Testament* to read, interpret, comprehend, corrected them and then compiled them in the *Qur'an*?

Most western *Jewish* and *Christian* scholars who ever write about *Islam* always accuse the *Qur'an* about one thing. They allege that the *Qur'an* imposes harsh punishments. Let us put forward the punishments from both books and then analyze which one of these two books of *God* is imposing harsh punishments?

Harsh Punishments of the Qur'an

No.	The Holy Bible	No.	The Holy Quran
1	*"If a man have a stubborn and rebellious son, which will not obey the voice of his father, or the voice of his mother... And all the men of his city shall stone him with stones, that he die..." (Deuteronomy 21:18-21).*	1	The *Qur'an* does not impose any punishment on a disobedient child. Rather, it recommends the parents to pray for them.
2	*"For every one that curseth his father or his mother shall be surely put to death: he hath cursed his father or his mother; his blood [shall be] upon him."(Leviticus 20:9)*	2	The *Qur'an* does not impose any punishment for people who curse their parents. Rather, it admonishes the people not to do that.

3	*"A bastard shall not enter into the congregation of the LORD; even to his tenth generation shall he not enter into the congregation of the LORD"* (Deuteronomy 23:2).	3	*Allah* knows that if a couple has committed a sin, the child who is born out of the wedlock has nothing to do with that sin. Therefore the *Qur'an* does not impose any punishment for the child.
4	*"One day while the people of Israel were in the wilderness, they caught a man gathering wood on the Sabbath day. ... Then the LORD said to Moses, "The man must be put to death! The whole community must stone him outside the camp." (Numbers 15:32-35 NLT).* Please contemplate on this point, that a man who goes to the wilderness to gather some sticks, we do not know if he was hungry and he wanted to set a fire with those sticks, as to cook something. Or he was cold and he wanted to set a fire to get some heat from those sticks but the *Lord* of *Israel* asked *Moses* to stone him to death.	4	*Friday* has been the holy and resting day for *Muslims*. But the *Qur'an* does not impose any punishment if you work all day instead of resting.
5	*"If two Israelite men are fighting and the wife of one tries to rescue her husband by grabbing the testicles of the other man, her hand must be cut off without pity"* (Deuteronomy 25:11-12 NLT). Please contemplate on this point that a woman who tries to save the life of her husband, gets her hand cut off. But the laws of *America* are more sensible in this regard and there is no known punishment in the law of *America* about that.	5	There is absolutely no punishment for any woman who tries to save the life of her husband. Unless, she breaks the law of that country, and get punishment by law of that country. The *Jews & the Christians* usually propagate about the punishment of cutting the hand of a thief man/ woman as a harsh punishment. But that punishment applies only for habitual criminals and it does not apply to a person who was hungry and stole a piece of bread.
6	*"Anyone arrogant enough to reject the verdict of the judge or of the priest who represents the LORD your God must be put to death." (Deuteronomy 17:12 NLT)*	6	There is absolutely no punishment for anyone to disagree with the verdict of the judge. Those people are encouraged to go to the higher judicial system.
7	*"Men and women among you who act as mediums or psychics must be put to death by stoning. They are guilty of a capital offense"* (Leviticus 20:27).	7	There is no punishment imposed on *Muslims* who are psychics.

8	The *Bible* says about the apostasy as follows:	8	There is absolutely no punishment for apostasy or renunciation in *Islam*. The *Qur'an* says:
	"by serving other gods or by worshiping the sun, the moon, or any of the forces of heaven, which I have strictly forbidden. ...Then that man or woman must be taken to the gates of the town and stoned to death" (Deuteronomy 17:3-5 NLT).		*"And say, 'It is the truth from your Lord; wherefore let him who will, believe, and let him who will, disbelieve" (Al-Kahf 18:29-30).*
	"Suppose your brother, son, daughter, beloved wife, or closest friend comes to you secretly and says, 'Let us go worship other gods'—gods...		*"...So he who disbelieves, will himself suffer the consequences of his disbelief" (Al-Fatir 35:39- 40).*
	Stone the guilty ones to death because they have tried to draw you away from the LORD your God, who rescued you from the land of Egypt, the place of slavery."		*"Say, 'Obey Allah and the Messenger;' but if they turn away, then remember that Allah loves not the disbelievers" (Aal-e-Imran 3:32-33).*
	(Deuteronomy 13:6-10 NLT).		In this verse the *Qur'an* simply says that *God* does not love the disbeliever, but does not give right to anyone to kill the disbelievers. I am sure you would have heard on TV many times that many people got killed in *Pakistan* or other *Muslim* countries for leaving *Islam*. But I can assure you that those are the laws of today, based on today's cleric's laws but they are totally against the teachings of *Islam* and the *Qur'an*. That is the reason *God* had to send *Ahmad* to remind them of the original teachings of *Islam*.

| 9 | *"In such cases, [of adultery] the judges must take the girl to the door of her father's home, and the men of the town will stone her to death. She has committed a disgraceful crime in Israel by being promiscuous while living in her parents' home. Such evil must be cleansed from among you."*

(Deuteronomy 22:21 NLT).

"If a man is discovered committing adultery, both he and the other man's wife must be killed. In this way, the evil will be cleansed from Israel"
(Deuteronomy 22:22 NLT). | 9 | The *Qur'an* imposes flogging as a punishment for adultery/fornication. The entire *Qur'an* does not prescribe stoning for any sin committed by anyone. In addition, the *Qur'an* makes the imposition of flogging harder by appending that the accuser must bring four witnesses. Now imagine, what kind of a woman would commit this heinous act in front of four people? In fact, this condition has been imposed by the *Qur'an* to stop people from accusing innocent women for this wicked sin.

All those husbands who want to get rid of their wives for either another woman or for fear of losing wealth in case of divorce, usually accuse their innocent wives for this atrocious sin. In this case, no innocent woman could be punished unless the accuser brings forth four witnesses. But this commandment [bring four witnesses] also implies that this punishment is for habitual sinner (prostitute etc.). *Hadith* the sayings of *Muhammad* tell us another strange aspect in this regard. It says if you are flogging a person, man or woman, and if they run away do not chase them let them get away. This also denotes that this punishment in *Islam* is to scare people from sins and punishments. |
| 10 | *"Take the blasphemer outside the camp, and tell all those who heard him to lay their hands on his head. Then let the entire community stone him to death"*
(Leviticus 24:14). | 10 | There is no punishment for blasphemy imposed in the *Qur'an*.

I am sure you would have heard about *"blasphemy act,"* in *Pakistan* and some other *Muslim* countries. But again, these are the laws of today's clerics (Mullahs) they have nothing to do with the real *Islam*. |

11	*"The penalty for homosexual acts is death to both parties. They have committed a detestable act and are guilty of a capital offense."* (Leviticus 20: 13NLT).	11	The *Qur'an* says: *"And if two men from among you are guilty of obscenity, punish them both. And if they repent and amend, then leave them alone; surely, Allah is Oft-Returning with compassion and is Merciful"* (Al-Nisa 4: 16- 17).
			The *Qur'an* only prescribes punishment, but the method of punishment is up to the authorities. Usually social boycott is practiced by many sects of *Islam*. But in no case stoning to death is imposed by the *Qur'an*.
12	*"But I say that a man who divorces his wife, unless she has been unfaithful, causes her to commit adultery. And anyone who marries a divorced woman commits adultery'* (Matthew 5:32 NLT).	12	Not only that there is no punishment to divorce a woman. But *Islam* encourages the *Muslims to* marry a divorced woman.

According to the above chart, almost all the sins committed by the *Jews* and the *Christians* were punishable by stoning to death.

1. Rebellious children; stone to death

2. People who Curse their parents; put to death

3. Breaking the Sabbath; stone to death

4. Adultery/fornication; stone to death

5. Marrying a divorce women commits adultery, ultimately, stone to death

6. Leaving Judaism (apostasy), stone to death

7. Psychics; stone to death

8. Homosexuals; put to death

9. Blasphemer; stone to death

10. Rejecting the verdict of the judge; put to death

For all those who would read all of the above punishments from the *Bible* and say that those are the *Old Testament* punishments and that they were rescinded after *Jesus*. Since, these punishments are harsh, the *Christians* of today deny having to do anything with the *Law* of *Moses*. Just by denying the law of *God* is not going to solve the problem. If the *Christians* chose to follow *Christ*, they have no choice but to follow the *Law of Moses*, to enter into the heavens. Let me remind here also that *Jesus* said in clear words:

> *"Think not that I am come to destroy the law, or the prophets: I am not come to destroy, but to fulfill, ... you will by no means enter the kingdom of heaven" (Matthew 5:17-20).*

After reading all the above references, can anyone construe from this that the punishments of the *Qur'an* are harsh? While we can see for ourselves that clearly the punishments prescribed by the *Bible* are much harsher than the *Qur'an*.

Fatwa on Your Head?

Recently, a new bus ad campaign was introduced by *Ahmadiyya*, inviting people to the true *Islam*. *Ms. Pamela Geller*, who started her own campaign ads offering *Muslims* safe refuge from *Islam*, if they chose to leave *Islam*. Though many *Muslims* deemed this campaign as *Anti-Muslim* campaign, I personally do not think she is doing anything wrong or that she should be criticized. Saving lives is not only prescribed to *Muslims* by *Islam*, but it is also insisted by it. As I have mentioned above according to the real *Islam*, the religion introduced by *Muhammad* did not have any punishment for apostasy. But unfortunately the *Islam* of today which is the *Islam* of misconceptions insists on killing of an apostate. I wish that these *Muslim* clerics would have studied the *Qur'an* more diligently. The *Qur'an* tells us in clear words that in the time of *Muhammad* people who used to visit *Mecca* would accept *Islam* in the morning so they could receive food, abode and conveniences for free. But they would denounce *Islam* in the evening while returning to their own towns. If the punishment of apostasy was death then why they did not know about it and why they were not killed?

The *Qur'an* says:

> *"And some of the followers of earlier revelation say [to one another]: "Declare your belief in what has been revealed unto those who believe [in Muhammad] at the beginning of the day, and deny the truth of what came later [in the evening]..." (Ale-Imran 3:72-73).*

When *Ms. Pamela Geller* was enlightened by an *Ahmadi* spokesperson, *Dr Waseem Sayed*. He stated that the true *Islam* does not support this view of killing an apostate. She replied that *Ahmadis* are only a small sect who believe that, but most *Muslims* around the world do not agree with them. This means that most people who accept *Islam* and later wish to leave, cannot leave because they get a *Fatwa* of being beheaded and are threatened by other *Muslims*. She is absolutely correct when she says that *Ahmadis* are a small minority in *Islam*, but the fact is if a truth is possessed by a small group of people or a large group of people, the truth always remains the truth. For instance, a group of 10,000 blind people are gathered in a field and there is only one man who could see. The person who could see says that the sun has come out, but the 10,000 blind people say that no, the sun has not come out. Who would you believe? 10,000 blind people because they are a large number of people or you would believe that one person who could see, even though he is the only one person against 10,000 blind people?

My humble request to those who are interested to accept *Islam*, please accept the *REAL Islam*, where there is *"No Fatwa on your head."* You can join whenever you like and if for any reason you wish to leave *Islam*, leave without worries or *Fatwa* on your head. In 120 years of the history of *Ahmadiyya*, no one has ever been killed for apostasy or any other reason within the religion. As the *Qur'an* says:

> *"And say, 'It is the truth from your Lord; wherefore let him who will, believe, and let him who will, disbelieve"* (Al-Kahf 18:29-30).

Ahmadis welcome people to *Islam*, so we can help them guide towards the *Almighty God*, the *God* of *Abraham, Moses, Jesus and Muhammad*, not to take matters into our hands and kill anyone we desire.

If there are two doors, one says: "Welcome to *Islam*, but if you try to escape we will chop your head off," but the other door says: "Welcome to *Islam*, stay as long as you want to stay and leave whenever you wish without worries or *Fatwa* on your head." If one has common sense which door he/she should enter? Obviously, the door which does not coerce you. Like *Ms. Geller*, *Ahmadis* also like to save all those people who are in the danger of *Fatwa* on their heads, but if they went to the wrong door, it is not *Islam's* error, for *Islam* does not prescribe killing for apostasy. In this sense, we are with *Ms. Pamela Geller* to help save lives of innocent victims. As for *"honor killings"* all I can say according to the *Qur'an*, there is absolutely no honor in any kind of killing in real *Islam*.

The *Qur'an* says:

> *"...whosoever killed a person — unless it be for killing a person or for creating disorder in the land — it shall be as if he had killed all mankind; and whoso gave life to one, it shall be as if he had given life to all mankind..." (Al-Maidah 5:32-33).*

Going back to the topic under discussion, there are many things which have been told by *Ahmad*, that are not in the *Bible*, but the people do not want to believe them. For instance, survival of *Jesus* from the cross, the migration of *Jesus* after the crucifixion, and going to *Kashmir, India,* and living with the *'lost tribes of Israel*,' the tomb of *Jesus* in *Kashmir*. All that has been acknowledged by many *Christian* scholars and researchers, with all sorts of tangible & historical evidences, but the people still don't want to believe it. Why? Because it is not written in the *Bible*. Therefore, how can *Holy Spirit* tell you anything more than it is already written in the *Bible*, that you can believe?

Jesus also said in clear words *"he will guide you into all truth.'* This denotes that *Jesus* did not guide people in all the truth; it was the duty of the prophet who would come after *Jesus,* who would guide people in all the truth. *Muhammad* brought the complete book (Qur'an), and the law of *God* was completed in his time. As *Qur'an* says:

> *"Today I have perfected your religion and completed My favors upon you."*[186] Prophet *Muhammad* told us through *Qur'an,* that *Jesus did not die on the cross,*[187] and *"God gave him refuge into a peaceful green valley watered by a fresh spring."*[188]

What about the *New Testament,* is it copied by other religions? The *Jewish* scholars of today openly claim that whatever *Jesus* said in the *New Testament* had already mentioned in the *Torah* (Old Testament). They allege *Jesus* did not introduce anything new.

5th: **He shall not speak of himself,** but whatsoever he shall hear, that shall he speak. Obviously, *Jesus* is talking about a *'man'* inspired by *God.* Simply, because hearing from *God* and then telling people is not very logical for a spirit to do that. *Spirit of God*, according to the *Christians*, is *God* Himself (part of Trinity), then from whom *God* is going to hear from? *Muhammad* on the other hand, was well known as the mouthpiece of *God* and he always started

[186] Please see Qur'an Ch. *Al-Maidah 5:3-4*
[187] Please see Qur'an Ch. *Al-Nisa 4:157-158*
[188] Please see Qur'an Ch. *Al-Mu'minun 23:50-51*

his conversations with the name of *God* all his life. All thirty chapters of the *Holy Qur'an*, starts with "*In the name of God, Most Gracious, Ever Merciful.*" The *Qur'an* does not have a single word of man. Not even the words of *Prophet Muhammad*. It has pure revelations of *God*, received by *Prophet Muhammad*. On the contrary, we read in the *Bible*, words of *Matthew, Mark, Luke, John, Peter, Paul* and so many other people. When *Paul* talked to people, he said: "*I Paul say unto you*" (*Galatians 5:2*), *Peter* said, *Let me speak freely unto you'* (*Acts 2:29*). *Qur'an* confirms the prophecy of *Jesus* in these words:

> "*He [Muhammad] does not speak out of his own desire. It is nothing but pure revelation that has been revealed by God*" (*53:4-5*).

Prophet *Moses* prophesied in the *Bible* about *Muhammad*, in these words:

> "*I [God] will raise them up a Prophet from among their brethren, like unto thee, [like Moses] and I will put my words in his mouth; and he shall speak unto them all that I command him. And it shall come to pass, that whosoever will not hearken unto my words which shall he speak in my name, I will require it of him*" (*Deuteronomy 18:18*).

In this prophecy, *God* said I will raise them up a prophet from among their brethren. When the *Jews* heard this prophecy they thought, '*among their brethren*' means from one of us (*Israelites*). But they forgot that right before *God* promised them a prophet, *God* told them that the prophet will not be from the *Israelites*. Few verses before *Deuteronomy 18:18*, we read that *God* said to them:

> "*According to all that thou desiredst of the Lord thy God in Ho'-reb in the day of the assembly, saying, Let me not hear again the voice of the Lord my God, neither let me see this great fire any more, that I die not*" (*Deuteronomy 18:16*).

In these verses, *God* told *Jews* in lucid words that as per your desire, I would not send any more prophets from *Israelites*. Even *Jesus* reminded them the same promise of *God* saying:

> "*O' Israel thou killest the prophets and stone them, which are sent unto thee. Behold, your house [House of Israel] is left unto you desolate*" (*Matthew 23:37*).

We all know that no prophet of *God* came after *Jesus*, in *Judaism* or in *Christianity*. But believe him a true prophet of *God* or not, no one deny the fact that *Muhammad* came after *Jesus*. None of the *Israelites'* prophets ever claimed that this prophecy of *Moses* is for him, including *Jesus*. Surprisingly, in the *New Testament*, there is not a single commandment of *God* which was given to *Jesus*. If you read the *New Testament*, you will find that *God* did not speak to *Jesus* at all. Then how could *Jesus* be the mouth piece of *God*?

Jesus presented over 35 different prophecies of *Old Testament* for his truthfulness. If this prophecy was about him, as most of the *Christians* contend, then why *Jesus* did not know about it? He never claimed that this prophecy is a sign of his prophet hood. *Jesus* never brought a new law; he also never ever claimed to be a prophet like *Moses*. Ironically, when we show this prophecy of *Moses* to the *Christians* they get very upset and respond very harshly that this prophecy is about *Jesus*, and advise us not to twist the word of *God* and do not try to paste it on *Muhammad*. But when we ask them then tell us the comparison between *Moses* and *Jesus* they say *Jesus* is *God* (God forbid) and *Moses* is just a mere man-prophet there is no comparison between them. They contradict their statement right away. On the other hand, *Muhammad* brought a new law, and the *Qur'an* confirms that *Muhammad* was like unto *Moses*. The *Qur'an* says:

> *"Verily, We have sent to you a Messenger, who is a witness over you, even as We sent a Messenger [Moses] to Pharaoh."*[189]

The *Qur'an* also confirms the prophecy of *Deuteronomy 18:18* in these words:

> *"…a witness from among the children of Israel bears witness to the advent of one like him…"*[190]

Let us see if the history of *Moses* & *Muhammad* has any similarities, and in the same way, if the history of *Jesus* and *Ahmad* has any similarities?

---

[189] Please see Qur'an Ch. *Al-Muzzammil 73:15-16*
[190] Please see Qur'an Ch. *Al-Ahqaf 46:10-11*

Moses & Muhammad

Jesus & Ahmad

	MOSES		MUHAMMAD
1)	*Moses* brought new book *Torah.* (Old Testament)	1)	*Muhammad* brought new book *Qur'an.*
2)	*Moses* brought a *New Law*	2)	*Muhammad* brought a *New Law*
3)	*Moses* had many wars with idol worshippers. Another words, *Moses* was given the permission from *God* to fight against his enemies. (Deuteronomy 3:3-6)	3)	*Muhammad* had many wars with idol worshippers. Another words, *Muhammad* was given the permission from *God* to fight against his enemies
4)	*Moses* prophesied about *Muhammad* (Deuteronomy 33:2)	4)	*Jesus* prophesied about *Ahmad* in the *Bible* (John 14:16) *Holy Quran* confirms this prophecy of *Jesus* (As-Saff 61:6-7)
	JESUS		AHMAD
5)	*Jesus* came about *1400* years after *Moses.*	5)	*Ahmad* came about *1400* years after *Muhammad.*
6)	When *Jesus* came, *Jews* had *72* Sects called *Septuagint* which literally means 70 but it is always referred to *72* sects of *Judaism.*	6)	When *Ahmad* came, *Muslims* had *72* Sects.
7)	*Jesus* did not bring a new law, *Jesus* came to refresh the law of *Moses* (Matthew 5:17-20)	7)	*Ahmad* did not bring a new law *Ahmad* came to refresh the law of *Muhammad.*

8)	When *Jesus* came *Jews* were under the *Roman* government	8)	When *Ahmad* came *Muslims* were under the *British* government
9)	The *Jews* were expecting a *Messiah* who would bring an army or big power and he would fight with *Romans* and set the *Jews* free from the *Roman Empire*. (a common belief among many *Jews*, which is not supported by the *Torah*)	9)	The *Muslims* were expecting a *Messiah* who would bring an army or big power and he would fight with *British* and set the *Muslims* free from the *British Empire*. (a common belief among many *Muslims*, which is not supported by the *Qur'an*)
10)	*Jesus* was not given permission from *God* to fight with a sword. Rather, he was bound to show sacrifices and win the enemy with prayers and peace. (History of Early *Christianity* strongly indicates that *Jesus* did not fight against *Romans*. Instead, he presented, *Message of Peace*)	10)	*Ahmad* was not given permission from *God* to fight with a sword. Rather, he was bound to show sacrifices and win the enemy with prayers and peace. (History of *Ahmadiyya* strongly indicates that *Ahmad* did not fight against the *British Government*. Instead, he presented, *Message of Peace*) *Ahmadiyya* Slogan: *Love for All; hatred for None*
11)	When *Jesus* came *Jews* were expecting an old prophet *Elijah* to descend from heaven bodily. (Malachi 4:5). But *Elijah* never descended, *Jews* are still waiting for *Elijah*	11)	When *Ahmad* came *Muslims* were expecting an old prophet *Jesus* to descend from heaven bodily. But *Jesus* never descended. *Muslims* are still waiting for *Jesus*
12)	The *Jews* tried their best to kill *Jesus* on false charges to crucify him on the cross but they never succeeded.	12)	The *Muslims* tried their best to kill *Ahmad* on false charges to hang him to death but they never succeeded.

13)	The *Jews* did not have their own power to crucify *Jesus*; they had to go through *Roman Empire* to file charges.	13)	The *Muslims* did not have their own government to hang *Ahmad* they had to go through *British Empire* to file charges.
14)	The *Jews* were expecting a *Messiah*, who would speak *Hebrew*, *Jews'* own language. But *Jesus* spoke *Aramaic*, which made them very upset. They argued that he himself cannot understand *Hebrew*, how he can teach us better than what we know the *Torah*?	14)	The *Muslims* were expecting a *Messiah*, who would speak *Arabic*, the *Muslim's* religious language. But *Ahmad* spoke *Urdu*, which made them very upset. They argued that he himself cannot understand *Arabic*, then how can he teach us better than what we know the *Quran*.
15)	*Jesus* is generally known by his native country *Nazareth*, therefore, he is known as *Jesus* of *Nazareth*. Unlike, *Adam*, *Noah*, *Abraham*, *Moses* etc. who were not known by their nativity.	15)	*Ahmad* is also generally known by his native country *Qadian*, therefore, he is known as *Ahmad of Qadian*.
16)	The followers of *Jesus* are known as *Christians* which derives from *Christ*: from *Christ* to *Christians*.	16)	The followers of *Ahmad* are known as *Ahmadi* which derives from *Ahmad*: from *Ahmad* to *Ahmadi*. *But* this name *Ahmadiyya* is based on the *Second Manifestation of Muhammad*.

On the basis of similar events in the life of *Jesus* & *Ahmad* both were prophesied as *Messiahs*. Is it possible for anyone to forge these signs in his favor? Or these signs were designed by *God* in the favor of *Ahmad*?

I have tried my best to comprise only major similarities and events in the lives of both of the *Messiahs*. These can be compared without having a debate over them. Another words, these are the similarities which we all know from the history and there is no mystery about them, you don't need to check archives about them or to refer to the encyclopedias. We all know *Jesus* came about *1400* years after *Moses*. If *Ahmad* came in *1889* he came about *1400* years after *Muhammad*. Similarly, we all know *Jews* are waiting for *Elijah* to descend from heaven bodily. Similarly, we can ask any *Muslim* and they will tell you very proudly that they are waiting for *Jesus* to descend from heaven bodily, etc.

According to *Deuteronomy 18:18, God* wanted to send a universal prophet to the world with complete teachings. But because the *Jews* told *God* that we do not want another prophet, therefore, *God* said *"They have well spoken that which they have spoken" (Deuteronomy 18:17)*. Then *God* said, I will raise them up a prophet from the brother of *Israelites*, as we all know that Prophet *Abraham* had two sons, *Ishmael* and *Isaac*. All the *Arabs* are the descendants of *Prophet Ishmael*, and all the *Israelites* are descendants of *Prophet Isaac*. When *God* said brother of *Israel*, he meant *Ishmael*. We read in *Genesis* about the promise of *God* to *Ishmael*. Thus, the *Bible* says:

> *"And as for Ish'-ma-el, I have heard thee: Behold, I have blessed him, and will make him fruitful, and will multiply him exceedingly; twelve princes shall he beget, and I will make him a great nation" (Genesis 17:20).*

According to the verse mentioned above the descendants of *Ishmael* were to multiply exceedingly and were to become a great nation. If the claims of the *Arabs* to be the descendants of *Ishmael* is false, then equally must these *Biblical* prophecies be considered false also. There is no other nation in the world which claims descent from *Ishmael*. It is only when the claim of the *Arabs* is accepted, that the *Biblical* prophecies relating to *Ishmael* can be proven true; for they all apply to the *Arabs*. Please see the Chapter titled *"Islam in the Bible,"* for the detailed work on the descendant of *Ishmael* and where they actually lived according to the history.

Jesus came for Israelites only

God sent *Jesus* as a prophet to refresh the *Law of Moses* for *Jews* only, not for the whole world, and not with the complete teachings either. As *Jesus* himself clarified this in his own words:

1. *"I have yet many things to say unto you, but you cannot bear them now" (John 16:12).*

2. *"I am not sent but unto the lost sheep of the house of Israel" (Matthew 15:24).*

3. *"These twelve Jesus sent forth, and commanded them, saying: Go not into the way of the Gentiles, and into any city of the Samaritans enter ye not; but go rather to the lost sheep of the house of Israel" (Matthew 10:5).*

    Those twelve disciples, who were trained by *Jesus*, took *Jesus'* word very seriously. As we read in *'Acts,'* even long after *Jesus*, those twelve disciples *'preached none except Jews' (Acts 11:19).*

4. *Jesus* said:*" I pray for them [Jews] I pray not for the world, but for them which God has given me" (John17:9).* This is strange that all good *Muslims* pray for the whole world and not just for themselves. Because *Islam* articulates that in order to get your prayers accepted we suppose to pray for the whole world. But *Jesus*, who according to the *Christian* doctrine came for the whole world would not even pray for the whole world?

5. *Jesus* said: *"...when the son of man shall sit in the throne of his glory, ye also shall sit upon twelve thrones, judging the twelve tribes of Israel" (Matthew 19:28).* (What about the rest of the world?)

6. *"He [Jesus] shall reign over the house of Jacob [Israel] forever" (Luke 1:33).*

7. *Judas* asked *Jesus, "How is it that you manifest yourself to us [Israelites] and not to the world" (John 14:22).*

8. A prophecy about *Jesus"...out of you shall come a Governor, who shall rule my people Israel" (Matthew 2:6).*

9. *"...Blessed is the King of Israel [Jesus] that comes in the name of the Lord" (John12: 13).*

10. One of the disciples said in disappointment, *"But we had hoped that he (Jesus) was the one who was going to redeem Israel" (Luke 24:21).*

11. *"Give not that which is holy unto the dogs, neither cast ye your pearls before swine, lest they trample them under their feet, and turn again and rend you" (Matthew 7:6).* Basically *Jesus* called all the *Gentiles*, dogs and swines.

The *Qur'an* also tells us that *Jesus* was for *Israelites only*, it says:

> *"(Jesus) the prophet for Beni-Israel (children of Israel)" (Aale Imran 3: 49-50).*

There is a verse in the last chapter of Matthew, where the last words of *Jesus* were:

> *"Go ye therefore, and teach all nations, baptizing them in the name of the Father, and of the Son, and of the Holy Ghost" (Matthew 28:19).*

But strange enough, the *Gospel of Luke* reports totally opposite of what *Matthew* reported, it says:

> *"And now I will send the Holy Spirit, just as my Father promised. But stay here in the city [Jerusalem] until the Holy Spirit comes and fills you with power from heaven."*[191]

What did *Jesus* really say? Did he ask them to *go to all nations* as *Gospel of Matthew* reports or he said *stay in the city of Jerusalem* as *Gospel of Luke* reported? Even the book of *Acts* confirms that *Jesus* asked them to stay in *Jerusalem* and not to go to anywhere else. It says:

> *"And, being assembled together with them, commanded them that they should not depart from Jerusalem, but wait for the promise of the Father..."*[192]

Even if *Jesus* commanded them to *'go to all nations'* does not necessarily means all the nations of all the religions, it could only mean all *Jewish* nations. For example, the *Bible* says:

> *"And it came to pass in those days, that there went out a decree from Caesar Augustus, that all the world should be taxed."*[193]

But we all know that *Augustus* was talking about taxing all the *Roman* world and not the actual whole world. Would you like to pay taxes for *Africa*, *China* or *Japan*? Going back to the original question that if *Jesus* came for *Israel* only, then who came for the rest of the world?

---

[191] Please see *Luke 24:49 New Living Translation*
[192] Please see *Acts 1:4*
[193] Please see *Luke 2:1*

The *Hindus* claim that their teachings is for the whole world, so do the *Buddhists, Sikhs, Zoroastrians* and the other religions claim the same. Claiming anything is not significant, the significance is to substantiate that claim. But if you ask them does your book claims to be the book for the whole world? They cannot show even one verse to support their claim. The *Christians* claim that *Christianity* is for the whole world. But if you ask them does your *Bible* claim it is for the whole world? They fail to show any reference. The whole *Bible* is talking about *Israelites* and talking to *Israelites* only. Everything mentioned in the *Bible* is for *Israelites*, then how can they say it is for the whole world?

The *Qur'an* does not refer anything to the *Arabs*; it talks to the whole of mankind. If you ask the *Jews* or the *Christians* do you believe in *Krishna, Buddha, Confucius, Zoroaster or Muhammad or Ahmad* they say absolutely not. How could they claim to be for the whole world when they confine their *God* for *Israelites* only? The *Jews* and the *Christians* believe that all the prophets came to *Israelites* only. This basically denotes that *God* is such an unjust and prejudice *God* (God forbid) that he cares about *Israelites* only, but for the rest of the world, He is not concerned at all.

The total population of the world is about *Seven* billion people, but according to this perception out of seven billion people *God* only cares about 6 million *Jews* and 1.8 billion *Christians*. But for the rest of the world which is about Five billion in number *God* has no concern for them. On the other hand, *Islam* commands the *Muslims* to believe in all the prophets and make no distinction between them in these words:

1. *"Say ye: 'We believe in Allah and what has been revealed to us, and what was revealed to Abraham and Ishmael, and Isaac, and Jacob and his children, and what was given to Moses and Jesus, and what was given to all other Prophets from their Lord. We make no difference between any of them; and to Him we submit ourselves" (Al-Baqarah 2: 136-137).*

2. *"And We bestowed upon him [Abraham], Isaac and Jacob; each of them We guided; and Noah did We guide aforetime; and of his seed (We guided) David and Solomon and Job and Joseph and Moses and Aaron. Thus do We reward the good. And We guided Zachariah and John and Jesus and Elias; each one of them was of the righteous. And We also guided Ishmael and Elisha and Jonah and Lot; and each one did We exalt above the people" (Al-Anam 6: 83 to 88).*

The *Qur'an* is the only book on earth which not only proclaims to be the book for the whole of mankind but also it recognizes all the prophets of *God* as true prophets. The *Qur'an* does not feel any necessity to defame other prophets to glorify *Muhammad*. The *Qur'an* is the *Book of God*, not a comic book that anyone can change in any way they wish. But unfortunately, the scribes of the *Bible* saw the only chance to glorify *Jesus* was by adding shameful acts to all the other prophets. In other words, they probably thought that the only way they could glorify *Jesus* and depict him as a perfect messiah or perfect god, if they make all the other prophets imperfect. For instance,

a) **Adam**: disobeyed *God*

b) **Noah:** *"One day he [Noah] became drunk on some wine he had made and lay naked in his tent"* (Genesis 9:21 NLT).

c) **Abraham:***"And Abraham said of Sarah his wife, She is my sister"* *(Genesis 20:2)*. (please remember *Abraham* lied about his wife after *God* had told him: *"…I am the Almighty God; walk before me, and be thou perfect" (Genesis 17: 1)*.

According to the *Scribes* of the *Bible* even *God* could not make *Abraham* perfect (God forbid). But after he lied to the king, *God* loved him so much that He made him father of all nations. Does it make any sense at all? Could a liar be honored so well by *God*?).

d) **Isaac**: *"And the men of the place asked him [Isaac] of his wife; and he said, She [Rebekah] is my sister" (Genesis 26: 7)*. According to the perception of the *Scribes*, *God* loved *Isaac* for lying like that and He made him father of all the *Hebrews*.

e) **Lot**: *"So that night they [lot's daughters] got him [Lot] drunk again, and the younger daughter went in and slept with him. As before, he was unaware of her lying down or getting up again. So both of Lot's daughters became pregnant by their father" (Genesis 19:35 & 36). (God forbid)*

f) **Jacob**: Isaac answered, *"Your brother [Jacob] tricked me and stole your blessing." (Genesis 27:35 NLT)*. According to this verse *Jacob* lied to his old and blind father and stole the blessing (prophet hood). Can anyone steel prophet hood? Is prophet hood like a car or jewelry that can be stolen? But according to the *Scribes*, *God* was so happy with *Jacob* because of what he did to his old and blind father how he cheated him that *God* appeared to him as a man at a later time and said: *"... Thy name shall be called no more Jacob, but Israel: for as a prince hast thou power with God and with men, and hast prevailed"* (Genesis 32: 28). As a result, *Jacob* became the father of the *12* tribes of *Israel.*

g) **Judah**: *"So he [Judah] stopped and propositioned her to sleep with him, not realizing that she was his own daughter-in-law."How much will you pay me?" Tamar asked"* (Genesis 38: 16 NLT). According to the *Scribes*, *God* was so impressed with *Judah*, how he defiled his own *daughter-in-law* that *God* made him the father of all the *Hebrews.* *Judah* was the only man whose tribe survived out of all the *12* tribes of *Israel.* All the *Jews* left in the world are the descendant of *Judah.* What a great reward for such a shameful crime.

h) **Jacob's son:** *"And it happened, when Israel dwelt in that land, that Reuben went and lay with Bilhah his father's concubine; and Israel heard about it. Now the sons of Jacob were twelve"* (Genesis 35:22 NKJV). In this verse the *Bible* is saying that *Jacob's* son *Reuben* slept with his step mother to give *Jacob* 12 sons. As if having 12 sons was so important and necessary that if the father *Jacob* could not do it his son contributed to get his mother impregnated (God forbid).

i) **Moses:** *"At that time we took all his towns and completely destroyed them—men, women and children. We left no survivors"* (Deuteronomy 2: 34 NIV). Again it says for another country: *"We completely destroyed them, as we had done with Sihon king of Heshbon, destroying every city—men, women and children"* (Deuteronomy 3: 6). *God* loved *Moses* so much after that that he gave him and his followers all the spoils of that country and all the virgins. The *Bible* says: *"But all the livestock and the spoil of the cities we took as booty for ourselves"* (Deuteronomy 3: 7). *"Only the young girls who are virgins may live; you may keep them for yourselves"* (Number 31: 18). After that *God* was so happy with *Moses* that *He* gave him *Torah* and made him the father of all the *Jews.*

j) **David**: *"Late one afternoon David got out of bed after taking a nap and went for a stroll on the roof of the palace. As he looked out over the city, he noticed a woman of unusual beauty taking a bath"* (2 Samuel 11: 2 NLT). Furthermore, the *Bible* says that *David* defiled her and ordered the woman's husband be killed and then he married her against the will of *God.* *(a short summary of 2Samuel 11:2-17)*

According to the scribes of the *Bible, God* honored him exceedingly and made him the forefather of the messiah (Jesus).

According to my research, all these blemishes on the pious, righteous and beloved of *God* prophets were pasted around the *Constantine* era (around 350 CE to 400 CE). Because after the destruction of the *Temple Mount* around 74 CE, the *Jews* were decimated, and the few of the lucky ones who had survived that ordeal, migrated to nearby countries to save their faith. In that wholesale slaughter of the innocent *Jews*, those who survived might not have an opportunity to take their sacred scrolls (scrolls of Torah) with them or at least majority of it. When they did get a chance to compile the *Torah* they probably did not have enough material to go by.

It seems to me that after over 200 years in exile, they had forgotten the original *Torah*, so they probably had no choice but to borrow it from the *Christians*. At that time, since the *Christian* scribes had already decided to portray *Jesus* as *a* god, they had no choice but to put blemishes on the pious, righteous and beloved of *God* prophets. So, they could tell the world about the difference of the *Son of God* (Jesus) in comparison to the other prophets of *God*. How high *Jesus* was spiritually and how low the other prophets of *God* were spiritually (God forbid). These prophets according to them were very sinful and immoral (God forbid). The question is why would the pious *Jewish* scribes assert all that what I have mentioned above about the pious, righteous and beloved of *God* prophets? Because that act of degrading prophets was done by the early *Christians* and not by the early *Jews*.

All the *Christians* of today honor their messiah by correlating him with *King David* and claim proudly that he is the descendant of *David*, while *Jesus* had no father to begin with. As I have mentioned earlier in the chapter titled *"Original Sin,"* that *God* called these prophets righteous and called some even perfect. Righteousness is direct opposite of sin, this means if they were sinners then there is no possible way *God* would contradict *Himself* and tell us that they were sinner righteous. Perfect means *without errors, flaws, or faults* or *excellent or ideal in every way."*[194] How can these prophets who committed all kind of sins were honored by *God* as perfect? This notion is plain and simple erroneous and blasphemous. According to *Islam*, all these prophets became prophets of *God* or messengers of *God* because they were the most righteous and most perfect people in their times.

Please contemplate on this point in another way, in *America*, when a candidate is considered for a president or for a senator, the authorities check

---

[194] Please see *Encarta Dictionary* of msn.com

their backgrounds and make sure that these candidates are not involve in any criminal act now or they were not involve in any criminal act before in their lives. While these candidates apply for a political position and not for spiritual position or prophet hood. They apply for worldly affairs, if we think about this then people of *America* have more wisdom than *God* (God forbid) that they do not even elect criminals and people with bad morals as their political leaders. If they elect them and then they find out that someone had done something bad or had done some criminal act in the past they impeach that person. If the person does something immoral or criminal after he had been elected people usually come out on streets and demand his impeachment or ask for his resignation. But *God* chooses hideous criminals with outrageous sins for the spiritual benefits of his people. Does it make any sense? This is a tremendous favor of *God* that through the *Qur'an, God* restored all the honor, dignity and righteousness of all the prophets. The people who do not believe the *Qur'an* as the flawless word of *God* would always wonder why *God* would appoint those who are worst among us?

Celibacy which was not prescribed by *Jesus* was adopted by *Christians* hundreds of years after him as a tenet of *Christianity*. In fact, it was adopted by *Pope Gregory the Great* in *590 C.E.* If it was the commandment of *God* then it should not have yielded catastrophic results. He tried to go against *God* by rejecting something which was holy permissible and he tried to make it unholy and unacceptable. By adopting the ways that are not prescribed by *God* never yields good results. When the priests were impeded from their basic and religious rights then they were forced to do, what they perhaps did not want to do at all. In my opinion, the reason that *Catholic* priests did not mind molesting all those children was due to the erroneous belief about the sinner prophets (God forbid). Perhaps they think that if the chosen people of *God* did all these heinous crimes then why would they mind? A priest said on his TV interview that it was people's fault who trusted them and left their young girls with them. So he blamed it on the people who called them fathers (priests) and trusted them with their daughters.

Even the nuns could not abide by the rules made by the men. There was a book published in *1985,* titled *Lesbian Nuns: Breaking Silence.*[195] In this book the nuns are proudly telling their stories of how they became lesbians in the church. What is my point for mentioning all this? My point is that the grave mistake was done by the scribes to portray all prophets as sinners, and then the result was that the priests thought if the prophets of *God* could commit

---

[195] Please see *Lesbian Nuns: Breaking Silence* Copyright © 1985 by *Rosemary Curb & Nancy Manahan*

all these heinous crimes then why they cannot? When the nuns heard all that crime is done by the prophets (God forbid) and by the priests then why should they stay behind. That's how the whole church system which is also known as the house of God became the house of sinners. If the house of *God* is not left alone then think about the people who go there, how can they become righteous?

Did you know that *Vatican* paid over 4.5 billion dollars in *Church* abuse scandals by the year 2007. But even after all the mess they had created they still have no remorse. Recently, a church's display board had this message: *"Be Single Be happy."* This denotes, instead of being appalled about what they had done, they are still corrupting people by commanding them to stay single? Another words, they are encouraging people to commit fornication. Because when people cannot get married and live a descent life in accordance with the *Law of God*, then they will obviously commit fornication. As the priests and nuns were not allowed to get married and they did all these heinous sins. The pastor might say that I put that sign just for a joke, I did not mean that. But the truth is that a church is supposed to be a place of worship and a school for learning the *Law of God* and not a circus, where people would come for amusement. Please see the actual photos of the *Church* display.

Disrespecting the holy ones of *God* has become a ritual for many priests. I was talking to a priest, he said that *Baba Guru Nanak,* (founder of the *Sikh* religion) was a hit man, who was hired by the government to go and kill around people. How low these priests go to glorify *Jesus* that they have to demean all the holy people of *God*. While *Baba Guru Nanak* was the most righteous man of his time. He was the only saint in that era that *God* talk to him as he talks to the prophets. But the poor priest, all he could see with his dirty eyes was dirt everywhere.

Another reason, I see in all this mess that *Christians* never acknowledged the fact that *Jesus* was married. To them perhaps marriage is a heinous thing to do. While no religion on earth ever opposed marriage in last 6000 years. In my opinion, *Christians* are paying the price for inventing such hatred for such a holy relationship. The *Christians* who do recognize the importance of this holy relationship they call it *'holy matrimony.'*

Long ago, I was talking to couple of my co-workers, who were very devout *Catholics.* One lady among those co-workers said that when she gets upset with her husband, she sleeps with other guys to take out her anger. I was shocked, I asked her very politely and decently that you go to the church regularly, don't you know that this is called adultery and breaking of the law of *God*, and according to the *Bible* such people will not be able to enter heaven? She said to me that she never heard that by anyone and she never heard that in her church either. The next day she came to me and she seemed very angry, she asked me why did you lie about adultery and all that. She explained that she went to her church and asked her priest, but the priest said your friend (Asad) is lying and trying to destroy your faith. The priest told her that after *Jesus* died on the cross to pay for our sins there is absolutely nothing you can do, which will stop you from entering the heaven.

The other lady said that she is living with the man who is not her husband and nobody ever said anything. She further said proudly that her mom and dad are not married, her uncles and aunts are not married even her grandparents are not married. In addition, she said if there would be any sin involve in it don't you think that my parents or grandparents would know that? She further stated that the area of *Mexico* she is from not too many people get married.

Why do the Muslim women wear head Coverings?

These ladies and many other co-workers always laugh at the *Muslim* women and ask me that why they have to cover their bodies and hide their hair; are *Muslim* women so ugly usually that they have to hide their ugliness? We, the *Christians* women don't have to do that. According to them the *Muslim* women are in bondage and that's abomination in the site of *God*. I asked them that if covering the whole body and hiding the hair is an abomination in the site of *God*, then why do the *Nuns* in your *Catholic Churches* cover their whole bodies and hide their hair? If they are the church leaders and know that they are doing a virtuous deed in this matter, then you should do it as well; don't you want to go to the heaven? And if they are doing wrong then you should try to convince them that they should get rid of all those extra clothing and enjoy the freedom and the love of *God*. Unfortunately, in this age the more women show their bodies, the more they are considered modern and educated and if they show less bodies and wear full clothing the more they considered backward and ignorant. But these women do not know that wearing men's clothing and all that fashion is abomination in the site of *God*. The more they show their bodies the less virtuous they become. Thus, less chance to go to the heaven. Therefore, the *Bible* articulates:

1. *"Yes, if she refuses to wear a head covering, she should cut off all her hair. And since it is shameful for a woman to have her hair cut or her head shaved, then **she should wear a covering**"* (1Corintians 11:6 NLT). (Please remember that in this verse of the *New Testament* the *Bible* is talking about all women and not just nuns)

2. *"Your beauty should not come from outward adornment, such as braided hair and the wearing of gold jewelry and fine clothes. Instead, it should be that of your inner self, the unfading beauty of a gentle and quiet spirit, which is of great worth in God's sight. For this is the way the holy women of the past who put their hope in God used to make themselves beautiful. They were submissive to their own husbands"* (1Peter 3:3-5 NIV).

3. *"A woman shall not wear a man's garment, nor shall a man put on a woman's cloak, for whoever does these things is an abomination to the Lord your God"* (Deuteronomy 22:5 ESV).

When I showed these verses to my *American Christian* friends, most of them say in a disgusted tone that these are the sayings and teachings of old times, these teachings are not for the modern times. This is exactly what *Ahmadis* are trying to teach the world, that the teachings of *Christianity* or the teachings of the *Bible* are for the people who existed two thousand years ago, and only for the *Israelites* of that era. Not for the whole world and definitely not for the modern times. This is the reason the world needs to know more about the teachings and beliefs of *Ahmadiyya*.

The *Qur'an* also urges us about the head coverings of the women in these words:

> *"And say to the believing women that they restrain their eyes and guard their private parts, and that they disclose not their natural and artificial beauty except that which is apparent thereof, and that they draw their head-coverings over their bosoms, and that they disclose not their beauty save to their husbands... And turn ye to Allah all together, O believers, that you may succeed."*[196]

The question arises that why the *Muslim* women wear the head coverings? The answer is all the true religions prescribe the head coverings. The only difference is between the *Muslim* women and the others that the *Muslim* women obey the commandments of *God* and others feel pride in disobeying it.

Almost all the *Christians* I have talked to, beside many strange things they tell me about their beliefs, there is one thing which is on the top. They say "*God* hates the sin but loves the sinner." How preposterous is this belief? I usually ask those who tell me these strange beliefs that when someone kills someone then why do the police catch the killer and put him behind bars? Why they do not catch the sin and put the sin behind bars? When someone robs the bank, why do the police catch the robber and put him behind bars, why they don't catch robbery and put the robbery behind bars? Who comes up with these contradictory and preposterous beliefs? Why would *God* love the sinner, when the history of mankind is telling us that *God* had destroyed all those who were sinners? In fact, *God* does not like sinners, but I guess this belief also is a product of believing sinner prophets. Let us read from the *Bible* how *God Almighty* destroyed those nations who were sinners.

The *Bible* tells us that:

a) *"The nation of Noah was destroyed because they were sinners."*

b) *"Sodom & Gomorrah were destroyed because they were sinners."*

c) *"He who sacrifices to any god, except to the LORD only, he shall be utterly destroyed" (Exodus 22:20 NKJV).*

---

[196] Please see *Al-Nur 24: 31 or 32*

d) *"The Lord listened to Israel's plea and gave the Canaanites over to them. They completely destroyed them and their towns; so the place was named Hormah" (Numbers 21:3 NIV).* Why they were destroyed?

e) *"And we took all his cities at that time, and utterly destroyed the men, and the women, and the little ones, of every city, we left none to remain..." (Deuteronomy 2:34).*

f) *"But the LORD thy God shall deliver them unto thee, and shall destroy them with a mighty destruction, until they be destroyed" (Deuteronomy 7:23). Jesus said: "...Fear only God, who can destroy both soul and body in hell" (Matthew 10:28 NLV).*

Please contemplate on this point, why would *Jesus* say *God* can destroy body & soul if *He* loves the sinner? The next belief I am talking about is so preposterous and so outrageous that I do not understand who are the genius minds behind it? My friend *Mr. Darryl* says that when you read the *Bible*, you don't read the *Bible* the *Bible* reads you. This claim is as preposterous as if someone say that when you eat the food, you don't eat the food; the food eats you. After this I rest my case.

I am not mentioning all this to make fun of *Christianity* or my *Christian* brothers and sisters. All I am mentioning this is to draw your attention to the fact that many churches just to keep their congregation larger and larger do not say anything to their members what the members don't want to hear, and perhaps consequently, they might leave the church. Is this the way they can ever give you the spiritual knowledge? As *Jesus* said:

> *"Let them alone. They are blind leaders of the blind. And if the blind leads the blind, both will fall into a ditch."*[197]

Think about this if a prophet is spiritually blind and a sinner how he can lead anyone towards *God* and why would *God* appoint him anyway?

Going back to the topic under discussion, the scribes assert that all prophets were sinners (God forbid). But on the contrary, the *Qur'an* says:

> *"And We bestowed upon him [Abraham], Isaac, and as a grandson, Jacob, and We made all of them righteous."*[198]

Let us examine, the sayings of the *Qur'an* about the *Torah (Old Testament)* of the *Jews* and the *Gospels* of the *Christians*? And evaluate ourselves if *God*

---

[197] Please see *Matthew 15:14 NKJV*
[198] Please see Qur'an *Al-Anbiya [the prophets] 21: 72-73*

felt any necessity to demean other books in order to prove the holiness of the *Qur'an*?

The *Qur'an* says:

1. *"We gave Moses the Book — completing the favour upon him who did good, and an explanation of all necessary things, and a guidance and a mercy — that they might believe in the meeting with their Lord" (Al-Anam 6:154-155).*

2. *"And verily, We gave Moses the Book and caused after him Messengers to follow in his footsteps; and to Jesus, son of Mary, We gave manifest Signs, and strengthened him with the Spirit of holiness..." (Al-Baqarah 2: 87-88).*

3. *"And they do not make a just estimate of Allah, when they say: 'Allah has not revealed anything to any man.' Say: 'Who revealed the Book which Moses brought, a light and guidance for the people..." (Al-Anam 6:91- 92).*

4. *God* said, *"O Moses, I have chosen thee above the people of thy time by My messages and by My word. So take hold of that which I have given thee and be of the grateful" (Al-A'raf 7: 144-145).*

5. *"And We caused Jesus, son of Mary, to follow in their footsteps, fulfilling that which was revealed before him in the Torah; and We gave him the Gospel which contained guidance and light, fulfilling that which was revealed before it in the Torah, and a guidance and an admonition for the God-fearing" (Al-Ma-idah 5:46- 47).*

6. *"And We gave Moses the Book, and We made it a guidance for the children of Israel, saying, 'Take no guardian beside Me" (Bani-Isra'il 17: 2-3).*

7. *"And relate the story of Moses as mentioned in the Book. He was indeed a chosen one; and he was a Messenger, a Prophet" (Maryam 19: 51-52).*

8. *"And We gave the Book to Moses, after We had destroyed the earlier generations, as a source of enlightenment for men, and a guidance and a mercy, that they might reflect" (Al-Qasas 28: 43-44).*

9. *"And before it there was the Book of Moses, a guide and a mercy; and this is a Book in the Arabic language fulfilling previous prophecies,*

that it may warn those who do wrong; and as glad tidings to those who do good" (Al-Ahqaf 46: 12-13).

10. *"Then We caused Our Messengers to follow in their footsteps; and We caused Jesus, son of Mary, to follow them, and We gave him the Gospel. And We placed in the hearts of those who accepted him [Christians] compassion and mercy..." (Al-Maidah 5:51-52)*

11. *"Among the People of the Book [i.e. the Jews & Christians], there is he who, if thou trust him with a treasure, will return it to thee; and among them there is he who, if thou trust him with a dinar [roughly a dollar], will not return it to thee, unless thou keep standing over him..." (Aal-e-Imran 3: 75-76).*

12. *"They are not all alike. Among the People of the Book [i.e. the Jews & Christians], there is a party who stand by their covenant; they recite the word of Allah [God] in the hours of night and prostrate themselves before Him" (Aal-e-Imran 3: 113-114).*

I would humbly ask the *Jews* and the *Christians* that if they honestly think that they are the followers of true prophets *Moses and Jesus*, and if your books (Torah & Gospels) are true books from true *God*, then why do you call the *Qur'an* a false book (God forbid)? Can we construe from this when *Qur'an* testifies about your prophets and your books that they are from *God*, that testimony is not valid? Would you reject a book which testifies in your favor? If the *Qur'an* is not from *God* (God forbid) then can you bring any religious book which testifies about your book? The fact is that the *Qur'an* not only emphatically proclaims that it is for the whole world, it also recognizes all the holy books of the world as true books from One true *God*. Would *Jews* and the *Christians* get outraged about the *Qur'an* because it testifies your truthfulness? I understand that the *Qur'an* says a few things about the *Jews* and the *Christians* that sound like *Qur'an* is against them, and some people construe from those verses that the *Qur'an* is talking about all the *Jews* and the *Christians*. For instance the *Qur'an* says:

"O ye who believe! take not the Jews and the Christians for friends. They are friends one to another. And whoso among you takes them for friends is indeed one of them. Verily, Allah guides not the unjust people."[199]

---

[199] Please see Qur'an *Al-Maidah* 5:51-52

The *Jews* and the *Christians* get outraged when they hear these verses and even publicize in their books and magazines and say look the *Qur'an* hates them that is the reason it tells the *Muslims* not to be friends with them. But the fact is that the *Qur'an* does not talk about common *Jews* and *Christians* it articulates about only those who make fun of your religion and fight against you, do not make them your friends. Thus, the *Qur'an* says:

"O ye who believe! take not those for friends who make a jest and sport of your religion from among those who were given the Book before you, and the disbelievers. And fear Allah if you are believers."[200]

The *Qur'an* makes the matter clearer by saying:

"Allah [God] forbids you not, respecting those who have not fought against you on account of your religion, and who have not driven you forth from your homes, that you be kind to them and act equitably towards them; surely Allah loves those who are equitable."[201]

This means clearly that the *Qur'an* is not forbidding the *Muslims* to be friends with all the *Christians* and the *Jews*, the *Qur'an* is forbidding to not to be friends of only those *Christians* and the *Jews* who make fun of your religion and they fight with you to destroy *Islam*.

Not only that the *Qur'an* also tells us:

"And if Allah did not repel some men by means of others, there would surely have been pulled down cloisters and churches and synagogues and mosques, wherein the name of Allah is oft commemorated. And Allah will surely help one who helps Him. Allah is indeed Powerful, Mighty" (Al-Hajj 22:40-41).

This means that *God* help those who respect other religions and protect their places of worship. Another words, *God* teaches *Muslims* to respect other religions and protect their places of worship. According to the history of *Islam*, the early *Muslims* did respect other religions and they did protect their places of worship. But unfortunately, when most *Muslim* leaders forgot this peaceful teachings and start killing innocent people of other religions, then *God* had to send *Ahmad the Promised Messiah* to refresh the *Law of Muhammad*.

We believe that all the religions were introduced by all true prophets. But their teachings were distorted after the demise of their prophets and

---

[200]   Please see Qur'an *Al-Mai'dah* 5:57-58
[201]   Please see Qur'an *Al-Mumtahanah* 60:8- 9

they started to worship their prophet as *God*. This belief is supported by the following verse of the *Qur'an*, it says:

> *"They have taken their priest and their monks for lords besides Allah. And so have they taken the Messiah, [Jesus] son of Mary. And they were not commanded but to worship the One God. There is no God but He. Holy is He far above what they associate with Him!"*[202]

Just like what happened in *Christianity* that the *Christians* started to worship *Jesus* instead of *God Almighty*. *Muhammad* had to come for the whole world, to reprove the world of sin, just as *Jesus* prophesied about him. Thus, the *Qur'an* says:

> *"And We have not sent thee [Muhammad] but as a mercy for all the worlds"* [i.e., for all the people, and for all the ages][203]

The *Quran* also says:

1. *"And certainly We raised in every nation a messenger saying: Serve Allah and shun the devil."* (Al-Nahal 16: 36-37).

2. *"And We have not sent any Messenger except with revelation in the language of his people in order that he might make things clear to them"* (Abraham 14:4-5).

This means in almost every major language, there was a prophet of *God* for them. If *Sanskrit* is a language then *Krishna* was definitely a prophet of *God*. If *Persian* is a language then *Zoroaster* was definitely a prophet, if *Chinese* is a language then *Confucius* was definitely a prophet. If *Greek* is a language then *Socrates* is definitely a prophet etc.

3. *"And for every people there is a Messenger. So when their Messenger comes, it is judged between them with equity, and they are not wronged"* (Yunus 10:47-48).

The *Muslims* proclaim that *Islam* is the ultimate religion of the world; it is not an assumption or conjecture. It is based on facts, truth and crucial evidences. As I have mentioned earlier, every religion claims to be the ultimate religion of the world. But their teachings and their sacred scriptures tell us otherwise. *Islam* not only tell us that this is an ultimate religion but also the proclamation of the *Qur'an* about *Muhammad* to be the prophet for the whole

---

[202] Please see Qur'an Ch. *Al-Taubah 9:30-31*
[203] Please see Quran Ch. *Al-Anbiya 21:107-108*

of mankind. Let's compare this belief with other world leading religions. For instance, let's start with *Judaism*, the whole *Bible* is talking about *Israelites* and talking to *Israelites*. None of the *Biblical* prophecy ever says that the messiah, the *Jews* are waiting for would be for the whole world. After that can we infer that the *Judaism* is going to be an ultimate religion of the world?

Let's go to the world's largest religion: *Christianity*. Could *Christianity* be the ultimate religion of the world? Long time ago, I was talking to a *Rabbi*; I asked him, who do you think will be the ultimate religion of the world? He replied, there are only two real contenders for the ultimate religion of the world. Either, *Judaism* or *Islam*. I was stunned; I could not believe what I heard from a *Rabbi*. I asked him why would you think of *Islam* to be the real contender but not *Christianity*? He replied that *Christianity* preaches three gods, a polytheist religion can never be the ultimate religion of the world, and consequently, it does not stand a chance to be the contender. *Islam* however, is a monotheist religion, and it could be a good contender. This view is not just a personal opinion of a *Rabbi*; it is also based on some serious facts.

As I have mentioned earlier, *Jesus* always talked about *Israel* and denied very strongly to be the prophet for the world. Please refer to the article *'Jesus came for Jews only,'* for further detail. Not only that every *Christian* unanimously believes that when *Jesus* will come back he will not touch the ground. Rather, he would stay in the mid air and receive all of his faithful and take them to heaven (Rapture). Please contemplate on this issue, when he will have time to rule the world or to preach the world about *Christianity*? Either the *Christians* of today reject this hypothesis as an erroneous belief or forget the notion that the *Second Coming* of *Christ* will bring the whole world into *Christianity*. They have to choose one or the other, they can't have both ways. Since this is a serious contradiction in their doctrine, and I apologize for saying that.

6th: **He shall show you things to come.** Let us consider, have you been told any prophecies by the *Holy Spirit* that are not in the *Bible*? While *Muhammad* have told *Muslims* hundreds of prophecies about the future. Such as, the inventions of cars, buses, trains, airplanes and ships etc.[204] The use of *Internet* and books will be published in abundance, in these words: *"And when the books are spread abroad" (Qur'an 81:9-10).*

7th: *He shall 'glorify' me.* Glorify means; *"make appear superior"* to cause something more pleasant, more important or more desirable than is actually

---

[204] Please see the books of *Hadiths*, under the title *"Dajjal"* [Antichrist]

the case.[205] How the *Holy Spirit* can glorify *Jesus*, it can only tell you something you already know. But *Muhammad* glorified *Jesus* through *Qur'an*, which says:

> "*I [God Almighty] shall purify thee [O' Jesus] of all the false charges imputed to thee by disbelievers [Jews] (Qur'an 3:55-56).*

In this verse of the *Qur'an*, *God* is promising *Jesus*, that *God* will set you free from all the false charges of the *Jews*. Such as, 1] When they alleged, *we killed Jesus on the cross*, and proved from the *Bible*, that he was the *accursed of God* (God forbid), 2] *Jesus* was an illegitimate son of *Mary* (God forbid), 3] And he was a false *Messiah (God forbid)*. The prophecy further says: '*for he shall receive of mine, and shall shew it unto you.*' That's exactly what *Ahmadis (followers of Ahmad, the 2nd Coming of Christ)* are doing we are showing you from your own *Bible* the teachings, the *Jews* and the *Christians* have forgotten.

8th: *but when the Comforter is come, whom I will send unto you from the father, even the Spirit of truth which proceedeth from the Father (John 15:26).* It has been clarified previously that *Comforter* and the *Spirit of truth* is the name of the same being. What about the *Holy Ghost*? According to the *Bible Lexicon, Spirit of truth* and *Holy Ghost* is the name of the same entity. In fact, the term '*Holy Ghost*' does not even exist in most of the *Bibles*, these *Bibles* refer *Holy Ghost* as *Holy Spirit*.

9th: **He shall testify me**. (*Testify: to be clear evidence of something*). Only a messenger of *God* could testify about *Jesus*, that *Jesus* was a true prophet of *God* and a true *Messiah*. The *Qur'an* clearly states that *Jesus* was a humble *Prophet* of *God* and a true *Messiah*. On the contrary, *Christians* all over the world believe that *Jesus* is *God*, or son of *God*, which he never claimed. There is not a single verse in the entire *New Testament*, where *Jesus* said I am *God*.

10th: *And I will pray the Father, and he shall give* **you** *another Comforter, that he may abide with you forever (John 14:16).* In this verse, *Jesus* is telling us in clear words that *Jesus* would pray to *God* to give his followers another *Comforter*. This could also mean that *Jesus* was a *Comforter* himself. Since we all know that *Jesus* was the *Messiah*, it denotes that the meaning of *Comforter* is *Messiah* also. When *Jesus* said another, how can people say *Jesus* was talking about himself? The reason I especially mentioned it because in another verse after *Jesus* talked about the *Comforter* he said:

---

[205] Please see *Encarta dictionaries of MSN.com*

"Hereafter I will not talk much with you: for the prince of this world cometh, and hath nothing in me" (John 14:30).

When I ask my *Christian* friends who is that *"Prince of the world,"* who suppose to come after *Jesus?* They say *Jesus* was talking about himself. *Jesus* further clarified by saying: *'and hath nothing in me.'* If you read this verse in the *NLT Bible* it says: *'he has no power over me.'* [206] This denotes that he would bring his own law, and he would have no power over the law of *Jesus* or *Moses* and *Jesus* would have no power over his law.

If you look up this word in the *Vine's expository dictionary of the New Testament.* It says:

"In the widest sense, it signifies a "succourer, comforter." Christ was this to His disciples, by the implication of His word "another (allos, "another of the same sort," not heteros, "different") Comforter," when speaking of the Holy Spirit, John 14:16. In John 14:26; 15:26; 16:7 He calls Him "the Comforter." "Comforter" or "Consoler" corresponds to the name "Menahem," given by the Hebrews to the Messiah." [207]

This denotes that *Jesus* articulated about another *Messiah* and did not prophesy about his own return. Therefore, the meaning of original *Greek* word *Parakletos* would be both *Ahmad* and *Messiah*. *Ahmad* who came about 120 years ago proclaims to be the *Messiah*, and *the Second Coming of Christ.*

The *Qur'an* says:

"And when Jesus, son of Mary, said, 'O children of Israel, surely, I am Allah's Messenger unto you, fulfilling that which is before me of the [prophecies] of the Torah [Old Testament] and giving the good news of a Messenger who will come after me, his name being Ahmad, but when he came to them with clear proofs, they said, This is clear magic" (Al- Saff 61:6-7).

According to the *Qur'an*, *Jesus* prophesied in the *New Testament* about the coming of a prophet after *Jesus* and his name would be *Ahmad*. Most *Muslim* scholars contend that this prophecy is about *Muhammad* and not *Ahmad*. They assert that the prophet who came after *Jesus* was *Muhammad*, how could *Ahmadis* fool people by asserting that this prophecy is about *Ahmad*? But when you read this prophecy little further it clarifies itself that this prophecy applies more to *Ahmad* than *Muhammad*. It further says: *"...even as he is being invited to Islam?"*[208]

Islam was introduced to the world by *Muhammad*, then how could anyone has the audacity to invite him to *Islam*? But this is evident from the history of *Ahmadiyya* that the *Mullahs* (Muslim clerics) who deny *Ahmad* as the *Messiah* foretold by *Jesus* and *Muhammad* claim that *Ahmad* has become apostate (God forbid), they further asserted that we invite him to *Islam*. This is a fact which is mentioned in the *Qur'an*.

But not only that the *Qur'an* further states:

> *"Their intention is to extinguish Allah's Light (by blowing) with their mouths: But Allah will complete His Light, even though the Unbelievers may detest it" (Al-Saff 61:8-9).*

If we take the *Arabic* word of the *Qur'an* literally which says: =*"beafwahehim."* Which means *"with rumors"* then the meaning would be *'their (the disbeliever's) intention is to extinguish Allah's Light with the rumors.'* We can also view this verse as the disbelievers would try to prove him false just by spreading the rumors about him. Though, every prophet was defamed by his people, and prophet *Muhammad* was no exception. But the reason this verse of the *Qur'an* does not apply to *Muhammad's* era more than *Ahmad's* era is because in *Muhammad's* life time his oppressors tried to stop his teachings by sword. But in *Ahmad's* era, only rumors were utilized to stop his teachings and no sword was used. That is what we study from the *Ahmadiyya* history that all the *non-Ahmadi Muslim* scholars and clerics, who ever say anything about *Ahmadis* they always lie about *Ahmad* and his message; they have no facts to prove their accusations.

The question is what kind of false prophet has come that to prove him false the scholars and the top pious clerics have to lie day and night to prove him false, but they cannot prove him false by truth? Is there any precedent in the history of mankind? The adversaries suppose that just by lying about *Ahmad* and by spreading rumors about him would destroy him. But they forget what the *Qur'an* says further, it says: *"But Allah will complete His Light, even though the Unbelievers may detest it."*[209] This means their lies and rumors will not deceive anyone but themselves.

---

208 Please see Qur'an *Ch. Al- Saff 61:6 to 9*, translation by *Yusuf Ali*
209 Please see Qur'an Ch. *Al- Saff 61:6 to 9*, translation by *Yusuf Ali*

If you ask any *Muslim* scholar or cleric about *Ahmad* they immediately start lies and rumors about him, by asserting, his prophecies did not fulfill, he does not believe in the *Qur'an*, and he claims to be better than every prophet (God forbid) etc. This is the blessing of *God* that even with all the lies and rumors from our opponents, we are in 184 countries and we are about 200 million strong. Though, it seems a very small number if you compare it to the world population of about seven billion people. But to achieve 200 million in just hundred years is far greater number than any religion on earth in its first hundred years.

Going back to the topic under discussion, when we read the *English New Testament* we will not find the name *Ahmad*. You might think why *Qur'an* talks about something which is not true? But the truth is if you read the book of *John* it mentions a word which is in original *Greek* and in original *Aramaic* is *Ahmad*. The prophecy goes like this:

> *"But when the **Comforter** is come, whom I will send unto you from the Father, even the Spirit of truth, which proceedeth from the Father, he shall testify of me."*[210] Jesus also says in the book of *John*: *"Nevertheless I tell you the truth; It is expedient for you that I go away: for if I go not away, the **Comforter** will not come unto you..." (John 16:7).*

If you read this prophecy in the *Greek Bible*, it says little different. It says *'Parakletos'* not the comforter. According to a *Biblical* scholar, the word *'Parakletos'* mentioned in the *Bible* is very similar to a *Greek* word περικλυτός = *"Periklutos" which means Ahmad and Muhammad*. Mr. *Jack Finegan* is professor emeritus of *New Testament* history and archaeology at the *Pacific School of Religion* and *Graduate Theological Union, Berkeley, California*. Author of over dozen books. *Mr. Finegan* writes in his book about the above mentioned verse of the *Qur'an*, and says: *"The possible basis for this [Qur'an 61:6- 7] is John 16:7 where in Greek the word for Comforter (παράκλητος) ['Parakletos' or 'paraclete']is very similar to the word for "renowned" (περικλυτός),* [Periklutos] *the latter being the meaning of the names Ahmad and Muhammad."*[211]

One may say, he/she does not believe in the *Qur'an* and don't know *Mr. Jack Finegan*. How do these people find out from third reliable source that *Jesus* said *Ahmad* and not *the Comforter*? It's a blessing of *God*, that a scroll has

---

[210] Please see *John 15:26*

[211] Please see the book *The Archaeology of the World Religions the background of Shinto Islam & Sikhism Vol. 3* by *Jack Finegan*, Copyright© 1952, by *Princeton University Press at Princeton, New Jersey page # 494 & #495*

been discovered towards the end of the nineteenth century in *Ezra* synagogue, *Old Cairo*, it describes *Jesus* as having foretold the advent of a *"Holy Spirit,"* named *Emeth: "And by His Messiah, He has made them know His Holy Spirit. For it is he who is Ehmeth, i.e., the Truthful One, and in accordance with his name are also theirs…"*

Ehmeth = אמת in *Hebrew* pronounced as *Eh'-meth*, which means *'the Truth,' the Truthful one and a person of constant goodness.*[212] To find this word in *Hebrew King James Bible*, please go to on-line *Bible* website called blueletterbible.org and type "truth" or "h571" in the search area. This word *Ehmeth* corresponds to *Arabic* name *Ahmad*.

The fourth evidence that *Jesus* prophesied about *Ahmad* is in the book of *John*. It says:

> *"Pilate therefore said unto him (Jesus), Art thou a king then? Jesus answered; Thou sayest that I am a king. To this end was I born, and for this cause came I into the world, that I should bear witness unto the truth… Pilate saith unto him, What is truth?" (John 18:37-38).*

According to the *Syriac Edition Bible, Jesus* told *Pilate* that I came into this world, that I should bear witness to *Ahmad,* because this word *Ahmad* was a foreign word for *Pilate* that made him to repeat the word, what is *Ahmad?* If we suppose as *English Bible* says that *Pilate* asked, *'what is truth?'* It does not make any sense. Since *Pilate* was a *Judge*, and he dealt with lies and truth every day, how he did not know what truth is?

The fifth evidence is the *Gospel of Barnabas*, though it is not a part of the canonical *Bible*, but it is an ancient and authentic *Gospel*. It talks about Prophet *Muhammad* by his very name at least 15 times. The history of this document tells us:

> *"The Gospel of Barnabas was accepted as a Canonical Gospel in the Churches of Alexandria till 325 C.E. Iranaeus (130-200) wrote in support of pure monotheism and opposed Paul for injecting into Christianity doctrines of the pagan Roman religion and Platonic philosophy. He had quoted extensively from the Gospel of Barnabas in support of his views. This shows that the Gospel of Barnabas was in circulation in the first and second centuries of Christianity."*

---

[212] Please see *Strachan's Fourth Gospel, page #141*

In 325 C.E., the Nicene Council was held, where it was ordered that all original Gospels in Hebrew script should be destroyed. An Edict was issued that any one in possession of these Gospels will be put to death. [perhaps this is the reason the early Christians hid the scrolls, which were found in this century, naming, the *Dead Sea Scrolls*, the scrolls of *Nag Hamidi*, the *Gospel of Philips* etc.] *In 383 C.E., the Pope secured a copy of the Gospel of Barnabas and kept it in his private library."²¹³*

Revisiting the topic under discussion, the 11ᵗʰ prophecy of *Jesus* about the *Holy Ghost* says:

"Even the Spirit of truth; whom the world cannot receive because it seeth him not, neither knoweth him: but ye know him; for he dwelleth with you, and shall be in you" (John 14:17).

In this verse *Jesus* said *'whom the world cannot receive because it seeth him not.'* Therefore, the people usually say, we told you that *Jesus* is talking about a spirit and not a man that is the reason people cannot see him, because you cannot see a spirit. But in fact, this mystery was also elucidated by the *Qur'an* in these words:

"And if you [Muhammad] invite them to guidance, they do not hear; and you see them looking towards you, yet they do not see you."²¹⁴

Surprisingly, this verse of the *Qur'an* is talking about *Muhammad* the similar way *Jesus* talked about *Muhammad* on the above mentioned verse of *John.* The verse does not mean that *Muhammad* had become invisible or a spirit that is the reason people could not see him. But it only denotes that the people or the disbelievers see *Muhammad* just as a man, but they do not see him as a prophet or a messenger of *God.* Similarly, when the *Jews* of the time of *Jesus* saw him, they just saw him as an ordinary man, but they did not see him as the *Messiah* or the messenger of *God.*

Jesus also said in above quoted verse that *"and [Holy Spirit] shall be in you"* my *Christian* friends usually contend that read this verse *Jesus* is saying *'he shall be in you'* this clearly means that the *Comforter* would not be a man but a spirit. But they don't realize that that was the figure of speech, *Jesus* did not mean literally *'he will be in you.'* To clarify this concept I present here another verse of the *Bible* where *Jesus* said to his disciples:

²¹³ Please see *www.Barnabas.net* for further detail
²¹⁴ Please see Qur'an Ch. *Al-A'raf 7:198-199*

> *"On that day you will realize that I am in my Father, and you are in me, and I am in you."*[215]

This verse tells us that when *Jesus* said *'I am in you'* he did not mean that he (Jesus) was a spirit. But if you insist that *Jesus* was a spirit that is the reason he mentioned it, then 1st of all, *Jesus* had clearly denied in the book of *Luke* being a spirit, *'For a spirit hath not flesh and bones as ye see me have."*[216] If you still insist that *Jesus* was a spirit then according to above verse *"you are in me'* *Jesus* is saying 'disciples will be in me' is that means that disciples were spirit also. Were they spirits or human beings?

12th: **He shall teach you all things**. As I mentioned earlier, *Jesus* himself said: *I have many things to say, but you cannot bear them now*. It shows that *Jesus* could not tell everything he wanted to tell his disciples, simply because they were not ready for the complete teachings. But the messenger, who supposed to come after him, would come with the complete teachings. As *Qur'an* says:

> *"Today I have perfected your religion and completed My favors upon you"* (Qur'an 5:4).

Prophet Muhammad came not only with *Universal teachings*, but also with complete teachings that covered each & every aspect of human life. *Qur'an* gives a general guidance to every *Muslim* for every situation. It covers every social, civil, commercial, military, judicial, criminal, penal need, and yet it is a religious code. Every situation of a person's life is regulated by it, from the ceremonies of religion to those of daily life. It covers the salvation of the soul, to the health of the body, from the rights of general community to those of society, from morality to crime, from punishment here to that of the life after.

13th: **He shall bring all things to your remembrance**. This is possible through a prophet only, and not with a spirit. After a long time following the passing away of a prophet, people usually forget the original teachings. As it happened in the time of *Jesus*, when the *Jews* forgot the original teachings of *Moses*, and started practicing their own will. When *Jesus* came, he reminded them the original teachings of *Moses*. As *Jews* did not like *Jesus* to correct them in their wrong believes. In the similar way, all the *Jews, Christians* and *Muslims* did not like when *Muhammad* and *Ahmad* reminded them of their original teachings, and corrected them for some of the wrong believes they had. As it happens to all the religions, *Christians* also claim that they are on the right path the path which was shown to them by *Jesus* and they have not forgotten anything. Let us see the next chart if the *Christians* are right in their claim.

22. The Holy Ghost (Part 2)

What did Christians lose?

There are few things I would like to mention here, which were the part of *Torah* (Old Testament) and *Christians* supposed to follow them better than the *Jews* because *Jesus* came to refresh the *Law of Moses*, the *Jews* rejected him and the *Christians* believed in him. But unfortunately, after the early *Christians* were banned to go to *Jewish Synagogues*, they got frustrated and severed all of their ties to *Judaism*. On the top of it, they were extremely misled by a *Jewish* man named *Paul* who changed the entire *Christianity*. All those good deeds which were introduced by *Judaism* were lost by *Christians* but with the mercy of *God* they were brought back again to mankind by *Islam*.

No.	Judaism	Christianity	Islam
1	*'God is One'* (Deuteronomy 6:4) Practiced by majority *Jews*	Three gods (Trinity) Oneness of *God* is not practiced by BIG majority, Only a verbal claim.	*'God is One'* (Qur'an, *Al-Ikhlas 112: 1-2*) Practiced by almost 100% *Muslims* The *'Kalima'* or the declaration of faith, in *Islam* played a crucial role to stop the *Muslims* deviating from the truth. The *Kalima* says: *"There is none worthy of worship except God; Muhammad is the Messenger of God."* This is the back bone of *Islam* which stopped this notion for ever that a man could be *God* or *Muhammad* could be *God*. Otherwise, without this declaration of faith, *Muslims* would have venerated *Muhammad as God* also *(God forbid)*.

| 2 | 'Fear of God' was prescribed by God throughout the Old Testament. The following are just a few examples:

but shalt fear thy God: I am the LORD' (Leviticus 19: 14).

'and fear thy God: I am the LORD' ((Leviticus 19: 32).

'but thou shalt fear thy God: for I am the LORD your God' (Leviticus 25: 17). | Even though, Jesus clearly prescribed fear of God, thus, Jesus said:

"Don't be afraid of those who want to kill you. They can only kill your body; they cannot touch your soul. Fear only God, who can destroy both soul and body in hell" (Matthew 10: 28, NLT). But unfortunately, Christians preach not to fear God and on the contrary, they say God is love. Christians of today have forgotten the teachings of Jesus which is in the Gospels but they adhered to the letter of Paul, which was just a letter, not a commandment of God. They preach and I myself have been told many times by many Christians that fear of God is a false doctrine. The Christians say, if you believe that Jesus died for your sins then there is nothing you can do that will upset God. You will go straight to heaven. | The Qur'an also commands us to fear God and it says throughout the Qur'an. The following are just a few examples of just one chapter:

"and Me alone should you fear" (Qur'an, Al-Baqarah 2: 40-41).

"so fear them not, [who are unjust] but fear Me [your God]" (Qur'an, Al-Baqarah 2: 150-151).

3) "it is an obligation on those who fear God" (Qur'an, Al-Baqarah 2: 180-181). |
| 3 | 'Do not commit adultery' (Exodus 20:14)

Obeyed by the majority | Not practiced by majority | 'Do not commit adultery' (Qur'an, Bani-Isra'il, 17: 32-33).

Obeyed by the majority |

4	*'Do not eat swine (pig)'* (Deuteronomy 14:8) Practiced by the majority	Not mentioned. *Christians* love to eat pig by BIG majority	*'Do not eat swine'* (Qur'an, *Al-Nahl, 16:115-116*) Practiced by the majority
5	*'Must eat Kosher food'* Practiced by the majority	There is no concept of *Kosher* or non-kosher in *Christianity*. They eat any dirty thing even swine and it is fun for many of them.	The *Qur'an* tells us strongly to eat only *Halaal food (Hebrew version of Kosher food)*. The *Qur'an* says: *"O ye men! eat of what is lawful and good in the earth; and follow not the footsteps of Satan; surely, he is to you an open enemy" (Qur'an Al-Baqarah 2:168-169).* The *Qur'an* also says: *"He has made unlawful to you only that which dies of itself, and blood and the flesh of swine, and that on which the name of any other than Allah has been invoked. But he who is driven by necessity, being neither disobedient nor exceeding the limit, it shall be no sin for him. Surely, Allah is Most Forgiving, Merciful"* (Qur'an, *Al-Baqarah, 2: 173-174*).
6	*'Must circumcise'* (Genesis 17:13) Practiced by the majority as a religious duty	*Christians* have been commanded by *Paul* not to circumcise. *"Indeed I, Paul, say to you that if you become circumcised, Christ will profit you nothing"* (Galatians 5:2 NKJV).	*'Must circumcise'* (Al-Hadith) Practiced by the majority as a religious duty

7	*'Obedience to parents'* (Deuteronomy 21:18 -21) Practiced by the majority	*Jesus* disrespected his own mother, how could he teach his disciples not to do that? (John 2:4) Not practiced by BIG majority.	*'Obedience to parents'* (Qur'an *Bani-Isra'il, 17:23-24*). Practiced by the majority
8	*'Do not drink (Alcohol)'* (Leviticus 10:9) Practiced by the majority	*Jesus'* first miracle was to make water into wine, how could he tell his disciples not to taste his biggest miracle? Most *Christians* love to drink on every occasion, it doesn't matter if it is a birthday or a funeral, or wedding or *Baptism*, New years or *Christmas*. If they are home or in their churches they drink everywhere. My Christian friend told me that he knows about fifty Muslims who who drink also. My question was to him that if he found fifty Muslims who drink, whom you consider follower of a false prophet (God forbid). How many can you find who drink among those (Christians) you consider from God? Not practiced by BIG Majority	*'Do not drink (Alcohol)'* (Qur'an, *Al-Ma'idah, 5:91-92*). Practiced by the majority

9	*'Obey the Law of God'* The whole concept of *Judaism* introduced by *God* was to create new order & balance in their religion, and in their society. (Ten commandments, practiced by the majority)	*'Law is curse'* (Galatians 3:13) *Christians* often say it proudly that there is no law for *Christians*. Their favorite saying, *'We are not under the law, we are under the grace.'* Lawlessness in religion and in society is proudly preached in *Christianity*. According to many *Christians*, if they kill, rob, rape or do any of the heinous crimes, they may get punished by the law of the country but *God* would still love them and would not punish them. Again it seems as if the law of the *Christian* countries is better than the law of *God. (God forbid).*	*'Obey the Law of God'* (Hadith) The whole concept of *Islam* introduced by *God* was to create new order & balance in the religion, and in the society. (Practiced by the majority)

| 10 | Divorce was allowed in the *Old Testament* which is a very natural. This denotes that the couples sometimes can't live together because of many different reasons. Thus, the *Bible* says: *"When a man hath taken a wife, and married her, and it come to pass that she find no favour in his eyes, because he hath found some uncleanness in her: then let him write her a bill of divorcement... And when she is departed out of his house, she may go and be another man's wife"* (Deuteronomy 24:1-2 KJV).

(Unfortunately, these two verses have been changed completely *by NKJV, NLT, NIV, ESV* and many other versions. They have omitted *"let him,"* 'let him' denotes the permission from *God.* Similarly, the 2nd verse says in the *King James Version,* 'she may go and be another man's wife.' Here 'she may go,' also denotes to the permission from *God,* but most *Bibles* have omitted that as well. | On the contrary, according to the *New Testament, Jesus* articulated: *"But I say that a man who divorces his wife, unless she has been unfaithful, causes her to commit adultery. And anyone who marries a divorced woman commits adultery"* (Matthew 5:32 NLT). I personally do not believe that *Jesus* prescribed that for his followers. Because when the messengers of *God* prescribe something it is always for the betterment of the believers. It brings goodness and blessings in the lives of the faithful and in the society. But unfortunately, this exhortation brought havoc and promiscuity in the *Christian* societies. People got so frightened of divorce that they stopped marrying. And the people who were barely ten to fifteen percent who did get married have divorce rate more than 70%. The above verse denotes that a man can divorce a woman, but it does not elucidate, if a woman can ask for a divorce from a man as well. Could this be a teaching of *Jesus,* whom you consider god? | The *Qur'an* says: *"And when you divorce women and they reach the end of their period, prevent them not from marrying their [soon-to-be] husbands, if they agree between themselves in a decent manner. This is an admonition for him among you who believes in Allah and the Last Day. It is more blessed for you and purer; and Allah knows but you do not know"* Qur'an, (Qur'an, Al-Baqarah 2:232-233).

The *Qur'an* also exhorts: *"And if they decide upon divorce, then surely, Allah is All-Hearing, All-Knowing"* (Al-Baqarah 2:227-228). In this verse *"they"* denotes that a man or a woman decides. This means a woman has equal right as a man when it comes to divorce. All the women of the *Muslim* world were given right to divorce fifteen hundred years ago. When even today many western countries it is considered to be an abomination. Though they are allowed to divorce through the constitution of the country. This means that the constitution of these countries is better than the law of *God. (God forbid).* |

11	The *Jews* always respect their book *Torah* (Old Testament), because it is not a comic book or a novel it is the word of *God*.	The *Christians* treat their *Bible* worse than a *Jew* or *Muslim* would treat a used napkin. My *Christian* friends often throw their *Bibles* on the floor when they are done reading it. Sometimes they even stand on their *Bibles* with their shoes on to demonstrate that respecting or disrespecting of *God's* book means nothing. I guess they just don't believe that their book is worth respecting.	The *Muslims* always respect their book *Qur'an*, and keep our book on the elevated places of the house and even to carry; most *Muslims* carry *Qur'an* above their navel level because it is not just a book: it is the *Book* of *God*.
12	All the *Jewish Rabbis* always covered their heads, and majority women Even today practiced by the majority	*Christians* Priests don't cover their heads. They don't seem to follow anything what *Jesus* did.	*Muslim* Preachers & majority righteous women always cover their heads
13	*Jewish Rabbis* always have beards. Including *Abraham, Moses,* & *Jesus*	*Christian* Priests don't have beards which is a sign of *Godly* people though they claim to be *Christ-like*, but in reality they have nothing in common with *Jesus*.	*Muslim* Scholars and Preachers always have beards.
14	Covering all body parts is a sign of decency in *Judaism* still practiced by the majority. All prophets always had their whole bodies covered.	Early *Christians*, male & female followers of *Jesus* all covered their whole bodies. But now walking around half naked is a very common practice today, especially women	*Muslim* men & women always have their whole bodies covered. Even today practiced by the majority.

| 15 | *Homosexuality* was condemned in the *Old Testament* and was ordered to put to death

"*The penalty for homosexual acts is death to both parties. They have committed a detestable act and are guilty of a capital offense.*"

(Leviticus 20: 13NLT).

"*Do not practice homosexuality; it is a detestable sin*" (Leviticus 18:22 NLT).

(Homosexuality is practiced rarely; if any) | *Christians* who openly claim to be *Christians*, even *Church* goers, openly declare to be *homosexuals*. The priests are becoming priests even after they openly declared to be *homosexuals*. They have been getting married legally in their churches and growing very rapidly. More and more people are getting out of the closet; one would wonder how big is that closet? | *Homosexuality* is condemned in *Qur'an*.

It says: "*And if two men from among you are guilty of obscenity, punish them both. And if they repent and amend, then leave them alone; surely, Allah is Oft-Returning with compassion and is Merciful*" *(Al-Nisa 4: 16-17).*

(Homosexuality is practiced rarely or we can say that because of the strict laws of the Muslim countries, at least they do not declare it openly.) |
| 16 | *Righteousness* was prescribed by the *Old Testament*.

"*And it will be righteousness for us, if we are careful to do all this commandment before the Lord our God, as he has commanded us*" *(Deuteronomy 6:25 ESV)*

Still practiced by majority | *New Testament* discourages righteousness by saying:

"*Not by works of righteousness which we have done, but according to his mercy he saved us,*" *(Titus 3:5).*

Priests of today use the following verse from *Isaiah* to prove righteousness means nothing, they quote:

"*...and all our righteousnesses are as filthy rags...*"*(Isaiah 64:6).* | *Righteousness* is very essential in *Islam*, the *Qur'an* insists on that, it says:

"*...And furnish yourselves with necessary provisions for your journey and surely, the best provision is righteousness...*" *(Al-Baqarah 2:197-198)*

"*...And help one another in righteousness and in piety...*" *(Al-Maidah 5:2-3).*

"*Verily, for the righteous is a triumph*" *(Al-Naba 78: 31-32).* |

| 17 | *Good works* was prescribed by the *Old Testament.*

(Still practiced by majority) | *The New Testament* discourages good works by saying:

"A man is justified by faith not by deeds" (Galatians 2:16). | The *Qur'an* and the *Hadith* strongly prescribe good deeds.

"Surely, this Qur'an guides to what is most right; and gives to the believers who do good deeds the glad tidings that they shall have a great reward"

(Bani-Israil 17: 9-10).

"Surely, those who believe and do good deeds, will have Gardens of Paradise for an abode"

(Al-kahf 18: 107-108).

"Except those who repent and believe and do good deeds. These will enter Heaven, and they will not be wronged in the least" (Maryam 19: 60-61).

(Still practiced by majority) |
| 18 | *God* commanded the *Jews* to bow down to *Him.* The *Bible* says: *"O come, let us worship and **bow down**: let us kneel before the LORD our maker" (Psalms 95: 6).* A beautiful way of worship to show respect to our *God.* All prophets including *Jesus* did that.

(Practiced by the Majority) | Now a day's *Christians* sit on chairs and use guitars, drum sets and pianos, sing and dance in their churches as they do in their nightclubs. If you get a chance to visit their churches, you will feel like you are in a night club. And they do not practice what was the practice of all Godly people. | *Muslims* all over the world offer 5 times prayers. They pray by bow down to *God.* Like all the previous prophets of *God* had done.

(Practiced by the Majority) |

19	The *Jews* always say to one another "שלום"=*Shalowm*='Peace be unto you.' A beautiful prayer to send blessings on each other. (Practiced by almost 100%)	*Christians* do not care to send peace on each other. They usually say hi, hello, what is that mean anyway? *Jesus* sent blessings on his disciples and it is recorded in the *New Testament*. It says: *"[Jesus] saith unto them, Peace be unto you"* *(Luke 24: 36).* *Jesus and stood in the midst, and saith unto them, Peace be unto you"* *(John 20:19).* *"Then said Jesus to them again, Peace be unto you"* *(John 20: 21).* *d)"[Jesus] said, Peace be unto you"* *(John 20: 26).*	*Muslims* always say '*Salaam Alaikum,*' which is the *Arabic* version of *Hebrew Shalowm.* (Practiced by the majority)

| 20 | The *Bible* commands very strongly: ' *Ye shall make you no idols nor graven image, neither rear you up a standing image, neither shall ye set up any image of stone in your land, to bow down unto it: for I am the LORD your God'* (Leviticus 26:1).

This denotes that *Jews* were commanded by *God* not to make any image, neither standing image nor any image of stone. | The *Christians* should have practiced this commandment too, but unfortunately, their churches are often seen with many images of *Jesus, Mary, Paul or Peter.* When we ask *Christians* about images they usually say that *Catholics* have images or idols of *Mary* or *Peter* in their churches, but we don't, we only have the statues of *Jesus.* But my question is what the difference is? One is worshipping mother and the others are worshipping her son. All have become idol worshippers. *Catholics,* who worship *Mary,* are about 1.2 billion and *Christians* who worship *Jesus* are about 8 hundred million, who is left? Almost the whole *Christian* world is engaged in idol worshipping, except for a minority sect of *Jehovah Witnesses,* who are not idol worshippers. But they are very small group. Let alone all the *Catholic* Churches, which look like an art gallery. If you look at the *Vatican* building alone, it has more statues than any idol worshipping temple of the *Hindus.* (I apologize for this is a little harsh, but true) | By the *Grace* of *God* you will never see any images in any *Muslim Mosque.* |

287

		But *Catholics* insist that Christians are idol worshippers and they are not idol worshippers. Do you find any credibility in their claim?	
21	When *Jewish* people are upset with someone, and they want to disgrace his name they throw his name on the floor and run over under their feet to show their anger and disgust.	Unfortunately, when the *Christians* honor someone they write their name on the floor and let it run over under their feet, and then they announce proudly, he/she was honored on '*Hollywood walk of fame.*' While, actually, it should be *Hollywood walk of shame.*	When Muslims are upset with someone, and they want to disgrace his name they throw his name on the floor and run over under their feet to show their anger and disgust.

Out of all the commandments I have mentioned above, if we take only one commandment which is '*do not eat pork,*' and search the *Bible*. We will see that how strongly *Jews* were told not to eat pork, and *Christians* who came to re-established the *Law of Moses*, how easily they forgot that commandment, and love to eat pork, is surprising. The *Sanskrit* word for swine is '*Soo-er,*' which is made of two words '*soo*' means '*bad*' and '*er*' means *I see [it].* The *Arabic* word for swine is *Khunz-er,* which is very close to the word used in the *Hebrew.* Which again pertains to '*Khunz,* means *bad* and *er,* means *I see [it].* Swine in *Hebrew* is חזיר = *chaziyr,* pronounced as *khaz-ēr,*' *which* could also mean '*I see [it] bad.*' This means that all three ancient and major religions of *God* were given the similar commandment that do not eat swine "*I[God] see it bad for [eating].*" Even the word '*sewer*' pronounced exactly as *soo-er* for water waste or sewerage water is very close to *Sanskrit* or *Urdu* word *soo-er,* for pigs mentioned above. This again has a connotation of something bad, dirty, or waste. Therefore, the *Bible* says:

1. "*And the swine, because it divideth the hoof, yet cheweth not the cud, it is unclean unto you: ye shall not eat of their flesh, nor touch their dead carcase*" (Deuteronomy 14:8).

2. "*And the swine, though he divide the hoof, and be clovenfooted, yet he cheweth not the cud; he is unclean to you. Of their flesh shall ye not eat, and their carcase shall ye not touch; they are unclean to you*" (Leviticus 11:7&8).

3. *"Or if a soul touch any unclean thing, whether it be a carcase of an unclean beast,[swine] or a carcase of unclean cattle, or the carcase of unclean creeping things, and [if] it be hidden from him; he also shall be unclean, and guilty"* (Leviticus 5:2).

4. *"They that sanctify themselves, and purify themselves in the gardens behind one tree in the midst, eating swine's flesh, and the abomination, and the mouse, shall be consumed together, saith the LORD" (Isaiah 66:17).*

5. *"A people that provoketh me to anger continually to my face; that sacrificeth in gardens, and burneth incense upon altars of brick; Which remain among the graves, and lodge in the monuments, which eat swine's flesh, and broth of abominable things is in their vessels" (Isaiah 65:3-4).*

6. *Jesus said:* *"Think not that I am come to destroy the law, or the prophets: I am not come to destroy, but to fulfilFor verily I say unto you, Till heaven and earth pass, one jot or one tittle shall in no wise pass from the law, till all be fulfilled. Whosoever therefore shall break one of these least commandments, and shall teach men so, he shall be called the least in the kingdom of heaven: but whosoever shall do and teach them, the same shall be called great in the kingdom of heaven. For I say unto you, That except your righteousness shall exceed the righteousness of the scribes and Pharisees, ye shall in no case enter into the kingdom of heaven" (Matthew 5:17-20).* This denotes that if the *Christians* want to follow *Jesus,* they have no choice but to follow the *Law of Moses.*

Who are Double Christians?

The main reason for the above comparison is to establish the fact that in my opinion *Ahmadiyya* is the 4th generation of the *Jews;* 3rd generation of the *Christianity* and 2nd generation of the *Islam*. It also means that the *Jews,* the *Christians,* the *Muslims* and the *Ahmadis* are brothers of each other, and descendants of two brothers, *Isaac* & *Ishmael.* In this regard, I consider *Ahmadis* to be *"Double Christians."* Because we are the only religion on earth who believes the *First* and the *Second Coming of Jesus Christ.* The fact is, we (Ahmadis) are the advocates of the *Bible,* we defend *Jesus* and the *New*

Testament from the attacks of those who consider them false on the basis of misconceptions. My book starts with the quotation of *Jesus Christ* about the followers of his *Second Coming*, it says:

> "*I will give you the wisdom to know what to say. None of your enemies will be able to oppose you or to say that you are wrong.*"[217]

Jesus also said about his *Second Coming*:

> "*he shall glorify me for he shall receive of mine, and shall shew it unto you*" *(John 16:12 to 14)*.

That is what *Ahmadis* do all their lives; we glorify *Jesus* by rejecting his accursed death on the cross and we elucidate the misconceptions of *Christianity*. The only reason of my above chart is to tell everyone that when the *Jews* forgot some of the teachings of *Moses*, they were reminded by *Jesus*. And when the *Christians* forgot some of the teachings of *Jesus*, they were reminded by *Muhammad* and when the *Muslims* forgot some of teachings of *Muhammad* they were reminded by *Ahmad*.

Going back to the topic under discussion:

14th: **Peace** *I leave with you, my peace I give unto you: not as the world giveth, give I unto you. Let not your heart be troubled, neither let it be afraid.*[218]

In this verse, which is mentioned right after *Jesus* mentioned about the *Holy Ghost (Muhammad)*. *Jesus* said: *'Peace I leave with you'* Islam means *'peace'* this denotes that *Jesus* said in clear words that *'Islam'* I leave with you. *Jesus* again said "*my peace I give unto you: not as the world giveth, give I unto you.*" This means *Jesus* is talking about giving you religion of peace (Islam). And not just peace in the sense of serenity. *Jesus* is not talking about worldly peace, he is talking about the religion *'peace,'* which is *Islam. Jesus* also said: "*Let not your heart be troubled, neither let it be afraid.*' Which means do not be afraid to accept *Islam*. This prophecy was also mentioned by *Isaiah* in these words:

> "*For ye shall go out with joy, and be led forth with peace the mountains and the hills shall break forth before you into singing, and all the trees of the field shall clap their hands.*"[219]

---

[217] Please see *Luke 21:15 CEV*
[218] Please see *John 14:27*
[219] Please see *Isaiah 55:12*

This prophecy of *Jesus* about the religion named *Islam* was confirmed by *Qur'an* in these words:

"He [Allah] has chosen you [Muslims] and has laid no hardship upon you in the matter of religion; so follow the faith of your father Abraham; He has named you Muslims both before and in this Book" (Al-Hajj 22: 78-79).

This means without any doubt that *Islam* was mentioned in the *Bible* by the prophecies of *Jesus* and it was named *Islam* in the *Qur'an* as well. The *Qur'an* also says: *"Surely, the true religion with Allah is Islam"* (*Aal-e-Imran* 3: 19-20).

The proof of this prophecy is that, all those countries, where *Jesus* personally preached, while he was going to the '*lost tribes of Israel*,' through the *Silk route*. *Jesus* told them about *Muhammad* and *Islam* in clear words. All those countries *Syria*, *Iraq*, *Iran*, *Afghanistan* and *Kashmir* became *Muslim* within a short period of time, right after the dawn of *Islam*. Some *Christians* assert that I have twisted the words to fit these verses on *Muhammad* and *Islam*, while these verses have nothing to do with *Muhammad* or *Islam*. But the strange thing is that when the *Christians* show some of the prophecies of the *Old Testament* to the *Jews* to prove that these prophecies were fulfilled in *Jesus*. The *Jews* always asserted in the similar way, that the *Christians* have twisted the words to fit these verses on *Jesus*, while these prophecies have nothing to do with him.

According to the *Christian* believe *Holy Ghost* or *Holy Spirit* is *God* (Part of Trinity), and direct teaching and guidance for the *Christians* without any man or prophet. If it is true, is that possible that *God* could lie to you? Or could He misguide you? Then how *the Christians* are divided into hundreds of sects and every sect claims that, only they have the real *Holy Ghost*, which dwells among them, and all other sects are wrong. I have talked to *Jehovah's witnesses*, and they say that we are the only one who has the real *Holy Ghost*, and true guidance from *God*, and all others are wrong. I have talked to *Mormons*, and they say that we are the only one who have the real *Holy Ghost*, and true guidance from *God*, and all others are wrong. The *Christians* make the same claim, and so do the *Catholics*. How can the *Holy Ghost* dwell among different people, and different sects of *Christianity*, and tell them different doctrines. Is this the direct teaching and guidance from *God*, which scatter you in many sects and beliefs?

It denotes that the *Holy Ghost* which supposes to come after *Jesus* was not supposed to be a spirit, but a prophet of *God*. As we read in 'Acts,' *Jesus* reminded his followers:

> *"And, being assembled together with them, [Jesus] commanded them that they should not depart from Jerusalem, but wait for the promise of the Father, which, saith he, ye have heard of me. For John truly baptized with water; but ye shall be baptized with the Holy Ghost not many days hence."*[220]

According to the above verses, *Jesus* is leaving his disciples, and reminding them that, they should not depart from *Jerusalem*, but wait for the promise of *God*. It clearly means that until *Jesus* should leave, the *Holy Ghost* would not come upon the disciples. Are we to believe that for all those three years when *Jesus* was with his disciples, he was without *Holy Ghost*? It means that whosoever was supposed to come was not really a spirit, but a prophet.

But if you still insist that *Jesus* said in clear words 'Holy Ghost' or 'Holy Spirit', then it supposed to be *Holy Ghost*, or *Holy Spirit* and nothing else, let me elucidate, according to the *Bible*, *Holy Spirit* was there, when *God* was creating the earth. The *Holy Spirit* was there when *David* was there, when *Isaiah* was there, when *Jesus* was not even born, *Holy Ghost* was with *Mary* mother of *Jesus*, *Holy Ghost* was with every righteous men and women. Let us read the following:

The Holy Ghost

1. *"The Spirit of God moved upon the face of waters"* (Genesis 1:2).

2. *Isaiah* said: *"The Spirit of God is upon me, because the Lord has anointed me"* (Isaiah 61:1).

3. *"The Spirit of the Lord came upon David from that day forward"* (1Samuel 16:13).

4. *"This scripture must needs have been fulfilled, which the Holy Ghost by the mouth of David spake before concerning Judas"* (Acts 1:16).

---

[220] Please see *Acts1: 4-5*

5. An angel told *Joseph: "Mary thy wife, for which is conceived in her is of the Holy Ghost" (Matthew 1:20).*

6. *Jesus* said: *"For it is not you that speak, but the Spirit of your Father which speaketh in you" (Matthew 10:20).*

7. *"But I [Jesus] cast out devils by the Spirit of God" (Matthew 12:28).*

8. *"David himself said by the Holy Ghost the Lord said to my Lord sit thou on my right hand" (Mark12: 36).*

9. *Jesus* said: *"You [disciples] in that hour, that speak ye; it is not ye that speak but the Holy Ghost" (Mark13: 11).*

10. *"he [John the Baptist] shall be filled with the Holy Ghost even from his mother's womb" (Luke 1:15).*

11. *"An angel said to Mary the Holy Ghost shall come upon thee" (Luke 1:35).*

12. *"Elisabeth was filled with the Holy Ghost" (Luke 1:41).*

13. *"Zacharias was filled with the Holy Ghost" (Luke 1:67).*

14. *"Simeon was waiting for the consolation of Israel and the Holy Ghost was upon him" (Luke 2:25).*

15. When *Jesus* was baptized the *Holy Ghost* descended in a bodily shape like a dove upon him *(Luke 3:22).*

16. *"Jesus being full of the Holy Ghost returned from Jordan" (Luke 4:1).*

17. *"Jesus breathed on them [disciples] and said; Receive ye the Holy Ghost" (John 20:22).* If the disciples had already received the *Holy Ghost* then what was *Jesus* promising after his departure?

18. *"Until the day in which he [Jesus] was taken up, after that he through the Holy Ghost had given commandments unto the apostles he had chosen" (Acts 1:2).*

After reading all 18 verses of the *Bible*, is it not apparent that the *Holy Ghost* or *Holy Spirit* was always there, from day one? When the earth was created, to all the way till *Jesus* left for the *lost tribes of Israel*. Then what *Jesus* was talking about? When he said:

> "*I go away: for if I go not away, the comforter will not come unto you; but if I depart, I will send him unto you.*"[221]

That was no one else but the *Holy Prophet* of *Arabia* "*Muhammad*" (Peace and blessings of God be on him) who came after *Jesus*.

John the Baptist and the Gospel of Barnabas

There is a prophecy in the *Gospel of Matthew*, which says *John the Baptist* prophesied about *Jesus* and said:

> "*I indeed baptize you with water unto repentance: but he that cometh after me is mightier than I, whose shoes I am not worthy to bear: he shall baptize you with the Holy Ghost, and with fire.*"[222]

Ironically, even after this lucid prophecy; *Jesus* always baptized with water all his life and all the *Christians* followed him in the same manner after him, even today. Most surprisingly, *Jesus* says in *Acts* that he prophesied about this prophecy. Therefore, it says:

> "*And, being assembled together with them, commanded them that they should not depart from Jerusalem, but wait for the promise of the Father, which, saith he, **ye have heard of me**. For John truly baptized with water; but ye shall be baptized with the Holy Ghost not many days hence.*"[223]

As you can see *Jesus* said in clear words "*ye have heard of me.*" Not only that even *St. Peter* affirms, that *Jesus* said that. He said:

> "*Then remembered I the word of the Lord, [Jesus] how that he said, John indeed baptized with water; but ye shall be baptized with the Holy Ghost*" (Acts 11:16).

---

[221] Please see *John 16:7*
[222] Please see *Matthew 3:11*
[223] Please see *Acts 1:4-5*

The third evidence takes the mystery out utterly. The *Gospel of Barnabas* confirms that *Jesus* said those great words about *Muhammad,* please evaluate:

The Gospel of John (New Testament)	The Gospel of Barnabas
And this is the record of John, when the Jews sent priests and Levites from Jerusalem to ask him, Who art thou?	"Wherefore they sent the Levites and some of the scribes to question him, saying: "Who are you?"
And he confessed, and denied not; but confessed, I am not the Christ.	Jesus confessed, and said the truth: "I am not the Messiah."
And they asked him, What then? Art thou Elias? And he saith, I am not. Art thou that prophet? And he answered, No. Then said they unto him, Who art thou? that we may give an answer to them that sent us. What sayest thou of thyself?	They said: "Are you Elijah or Jeremiah, or any of the ancient prophets?" Jesus answered: "No." Then said they: "Who are you? Say, in order that we may give testimony to those who sent us."
He said, I am the voice of one crying in the wilderness, Make straight the way of the Lord, as said the prophet Esaias.	Then Jesus said: "I am a voice that cries through all Judea, and cries: "Prepare you the way for the messenger of the Lord," even as it is written in Esaias."
And they which were sent were of the Pharisees. And they asked him, and said unto him, Why baptizest thou then, if thou be not that Christ, nor Elias, neither that prophet?	They said: "If you be not the Messiah nor Elijah, or any prophet, wherefore do you preach new doctrine, and make yourself of more account than the Messiah?"

John answered them, saying, I baptize with water: but there standeth one among you, whom ye know not; He it is, who coming after me is preferred before me, **whose shoe's latchet I am not worthy to unloose.** (Gospel of John 1: 19 to 27).	**Verses from chapter 42:** Jesus answered: "The miracles which God works by my hands show that I speak that which God wills; nor indeed do I make myself to be accounted as him of whom you speak. **For I am not worthy to unloose the ties of the hosen or the ratchets of the shoes** of the Messenger of God whom you call "Messiah," who was made before me, and shall come after me, and shall bring the words of truth, so that his faith shall have no end." (The Gospel of Barnabas chapter 42). **Verses from chapter 44:** "O blessed time, when he shall come to the world! Believe me that I have seen him and have done. Him reverence, even as every prophet has seen him: seeing that of his spirit God gives to them prophecy. And when I saw him my soul was filled with consolation, saying: **"O Muhammad;, God be with you, and may he make me worthy to untie, your shoe latchet;,** for obtaining this I shall be a great prophet and holy one of God." And having said this, Jesus rendered his thanks to God." (The Gospel of Barnabas chapter 44).

Many scholars reject the *Gospel of Barnabas* as a medieval forgery, but the question is if it was forged around medieval times then how this gospel was quoted by the second century scholar named *St. Irenaeus*? Some scholars try to resolve this intricate problem by asserting, *St, Irenaeus* did mention the *Gospel of Barnabas* but he only mentioned it to disprove it. But my point is even if he mentioned it to disprove it, at least it proves that the *Gospel of Barnabas* existed in the first and second centuries and it was not a medieval forgery or forged by the *Muslims*. *Islam* came into existence around 6th century CE, there is no possible way *Christian* scholars can prove that *Muslims* forged a document which existed four to five hundred years before them.

To me it is easy for anyone to reject the truth and manipulate the verses in their favor. As I have quoted earlier and the following chapters will prove that too that *Jesus* prophesied about *Muhammad*. You be the judge and decide for yourself, if *John the Baptist* said that about *Jesus* or *Jesus* said that about *Muhammad*? If you put together the *Holy Ghost* (Muhammad) and baptizing with fire, with the *Fiery law*[224] you will get the whole picture, who was talking about who?

Many modern *Biblical* scholars strongly suggest that *John the Baptist* did not say that for *Jesus*, because except for two, none of the followers of *John the Baptist* ever became the followers of *Jesus*. Is that possible if *John the Baptist* regarded *Jesus* highly and uttered such great words about him, but most of his followers did not believe him and not believing is something negligible, but they curse him, use abusive language for him, and call him a liar and a false messiah? This denotes that the followers of *John the Baptist* never heard the above quoted verses from him about *Jesus*. The history of mankind is denying that *John the Baptist* said that for *Jesus*. On the contrary, according to this evidence, if *Jesus* said that for *Muhammad*, then it makes more sense, because if you look at the history of *Christianity*, all those areas where *Jesus* preached personally after the crucifixion they all became *Muslim*. What makes more sense, a mere verbal claim which was pasted on to *Jesus* but in history there is no proof? Or the history of *1,400* years which proves beyond any doubt that *Jesus* said those words for *Muhammad*?

The people who are the followers of *John the Baptist* are called *Mandaeans*. They believe *John the Baptist*, called Yahya in their book *'Sidra D Yahya'* (Book of John), was the last and greatest of the prophets. While *Mandaeans* agree that *John the Baptist* baptized Yeshu (Jesus), but they reject *Jesus* as either a savior or a prophet. They viewed *John* as the only true *Messiah*. According to the *Dead Sea Scrolls*, the followers of *John the Baptist* called *Jesus* wicked teacher and wicked priest. How can they refer *Jesus* with these insulting titles, if their *Messiah* (John the Baptist) regarded *Jesus* as *'whose shoes I am not worthy to bear'*? If *Holy Spirit* is *Muhammad*, then it is most certain that *Jesus* said that for *Muhammad*. Since *Jesus* said in clear words *'...but he that cometh after me.'* *John the Baptist* came before *Jesus* while *Muhammad* came after him. *Jesus* also said that about the *Holy Ghost*:

> *"And whosoever speaketh a word against the Son of man, it shall be forgiven him: but whosoever speaketh against the Holy Ghost [Muhammad], it shall not be forgiven him, neither in this world, neither in the world to come."*[225]

Muhammad and *Ahmad* both were mentioned in the *Bible* by their names. But the *Christians* who did want people to know about them, they took out

---

[224]   Please see *Deuteronomy 33:2*

[225]   Please see *Matthew 12:32 & Mark 3:29*, bracketed text is not the part of the *Gospel*

both names from the *Hebrew* and the *Greek Bibles*. But all the prophecies in the current *Bibles* about *Muhammad* and *Ahmad* are still there. One of the most favorable verses in the *Bible* about *Muhammad* is:

King James Version	Revised Standard Version
"The Lord came from Si'-nai, and rose up from Se'-ir unto them; he shined forth from mount Pa'-ran, and he came with ten thousands of saints: from his right hand went a fiery law for them"(Deuteronomy 33:2).	*"The Lord came from Sinai and dawned from Seir upon us; he shone forth from Mount Paran. With him were myriads of holy ones; at his right, a host of his own"* (Deuteronomy 33:2).
The same prophecy you can see in the *Catholic Bibles* as follows: *"The Lord came from Sinai and dawned on his people from Seir; He shone forth from Mount Paran and advanced from Meribath-kadesh, While at his right hand a fire blazed forth and his wrath devastated the nations"* (Deuteronomy 33:2 The *New American Bible* (St. Joseph medium size Edition) Copyright © 1992 by *Catholic Book Publishing Co.* New York.	

As you can see above, the same prophecy in three different versions of the *Bible*. The *King James Version*, the *Revised Standard Version* and *New American Bible*. How this prophecy has been changed from, *'ten thousands of saints'* of the *King James Version* to *'myriads of holy ones'* of the *New Revised Standard Version*. The *Catholic Bible* does not even mention any saints at all. From the *'fiery law'* of *King James Version* to *'host of his own'* of the *New Revised Standard Version*. Instead, of *'fiery law'* of *King James Version*, *'a fire blazed forth'* is mentioned in *New American Bible*. Coming from *Sinai* refers to the appearance of *Moses*, and rising up from *Seir* refers to the advent of *Jesus*.

The prophet who shone forth from *Mount Paran* could be no other than the *Holy Prophet of Arabia, Muhammed*. As *Paran* is one of the ancient names of *Mecca*, the birthplace of the *Holy Founder of Islam (Muhammad)*. If it was not him, then could you name anybody else who came from *Mount Paran*? Also, at the conquest of *Mecca*, *Muhammad* came with ten thousands of holy men (*his disciples*) and he had "*a fiery law*," the *Holy Quran*. This event of *Prophet Muhammad's* coming with ten thousands of his disciples is also mentioned by a book titled *Great Religions of the World*.[226]

When *Ahmad* (*The Promised Messiah*), proclaimed that he is the *Second Coming of Jesus*, and presented many references from the *Bible*, then a group of top *Christian* scholars perhaps realized that they cannot win with *Ahmad*, unless they change the *Bible*. Above two columns show the change of prophecy, from *'Ten Thousand'* to *'Myriads'* and from *'Fiery Law'* to *'a host of his own.'* Mr.

---

[226] Please see *Great Religions of the World* Copyright © 1978 by *National Geographic Society*. ISBN # 087044-140-X page # 236

Bruce M. Metzger, and *Mr. Roland E. Murphy* wrote in their *Revised Standard Version* of *Bible,* and I quote:

> *"Yet the King James Version has serious defects. By the middle of the nineteenth century, the development of biblical studies, and the discovery of many biblical manuscripts, more ancient than those on which the King James Version was based, made it apparent that these defects were so many as to call for revision..."*

What were the serious defects of *King James Version?* I have provided two references above. Would you like to change the word of *God* just because you do not agree with *Muslims* that this prophecy refers to *Prophet Muhammad?*

There is another conversation reported by *John.* It says:

> *"...When the Jews sent priests and Levites from Jerusalem to ask him, [John the Baptist] Who art thou? And he confessed, and denied not; but confessed, I am not the Christ. And they asked him, What then? Art thou E-li'-as? And he saith, I am not. Art thou that prophet? And he answered no." (John 1:19-21).*

According to these verses, *Jews* were waiting for three prophets. First, as we all know, is *Jesus Christ.* Second, according to *Jesus, John* the *Baptist* is the *(Second Coming)* of *Elias (Matthew 11:14).* Then what happened to the third prophet? Who was known as *"that Prophet,"* whom all the *Jews* were waiting for? If you do not believe *Muhammad* is *"that Prophet,"* then where is he? About three thousand four hundred years have passed, and *"that Prophet"* never appeared?

Another prophecy of the *Bible* talks about *Muhammad* in these words:

> *"The burden upon **Arabia**. In the forest in Arabia shall ye lodge,. ...For they fled from the swords, from the drawn swords, and from the bent bow... For thus hath the Lord said unto me: Within a year... all the glory of Ke'dar shall fail: And...the mighty men of the children of Ke'dar, shall be diminished: for the Lord God of Israel hath spoken it."*[227]

Firstly, 'Arabia' (modern day Saudi Arabia) is referred in this prophecy, *Muhammad* appeared in *Arabia.* Secondly, the prophecy mentions '*him that fled.*' The migration of *Muhammad* is a historical event of *Islam* it was upon

---

[227] Please see *Isaiah 21:13-17*

that migration from *Mecca* that the *Muslim* calendar began. Thirdly, *'fled from drawn swords'* conclusively proves the fulfillment of the prophecy of *Muhammad*, when his house was surrounded by his deadly enemies. The enemies stood there with drawn swords, thirsty for his blood. Fourthly, the prophecy states that: *'Within a year...all the glory of Ke'dar will fail...the mighty men of Ke'dar shall be diminished.'* This was fulfilled in the battle of *'Badr,'* which occurred within a year after the migration of *Muhammad*. In that battle, *Quraish of Mecca* also known as, *Ke'dar*[228] sustained a crushing defeat, when most of their mighty men died in that battle.

Another prophecy of *Bible* in the *Song of Solomon 5:9-16*. The person, who is spoken of is the *'Beloved of God'*. Which is one of the titles of *Muhammad*. People can contend that *'Beloved of God'* could be anyone, why are you saying that it is written for *Muhammad* only? Let me clarify it further, which will explain clearly why it applies to *Muhammad* only and no one else. It also says: *"My beloved is white and ruddy"* which was the color of *Muhammad*. Thirdly it says: *'Chiefest among ten thousand.'* I have already mentioned on above prophecy that, *Muhammad* on the conquest of *Mecca* led an army of ten thousand followers. The fourth and most convincing point in this prophecy, which explains why *Muslims* believe that this prophecy belongs to *Muhammad* only and no one else in the entire world, is the name *"Muhammad"* mentioned in verse 16. But unfortunately, the word *"Muhammad"* has been deleted in the *English Bible*. The prophecy used to read מחמד = *Machmad* but it now says, *"altogether lovely"* (Song of Solomon 5:16). But in the *Hebrew Bible*, it still says *"Muhammad"*. (Please see the next page for the *Original Version of Hebrew King James Bible*, by *Blue Letter Bible.org*). Please remember when you read *Muhammed's* name in *Hebrew*, you will see *'Machmad'* you might think it says *'Machmad'* not *Muhammad*, but in *Hebrew 'Ch'* is pronounced as *'Kh-a'* or *'Ha'* as throat clearing. As we see in *'Chanukkah'* but we pronounce it *'Hanukkah'*.

---

[228] *Kedar* is the previous name of *Koraish* of *Mecca, Koraishis* are notorious enemies of *Prophet Muhammad*. Please See *The Historical Geography of Arabia*, by *Rev. C. forster*, pp. 244-265

K C L
I V D Sgs 5:16 His mouth [is] most sweet: yea, he [is] altogether
lovely. This [is] my beloved, and this [is] my friend, O
daughters of Jerusalem.

Information on Hebrew Scroll

16 חכו ממתקים וכלו מחמדים זה
דודי וזה רעי בנות ירושלם.

English		Strong's	Hebrew (Root form)	Tense
(Click on any item below for Concordance)				(Click)
His mouth	Phr	[02441]	חך chek	
[is] most sweet:	Phr	[04477]	ממתקים mamtaq	
yea, he [is] altogether lovely.	Phr	[04261]	מחמד machmad	
This [is] my beloved,	Phr	[01730]	דוד dowd	
and this [is] my friend,	Phr	[07453]	רע rea`	
O daughters	Phr	[01323]	בת bath	
of Jerusalem.	Phr	[03389]	ירושלם Y@ruwshalaim	

Another prophecy of the *Bible*, says:

> *"God came from Te'-man, and the Holy One from mount Pa'-ran. His glory covered the heavens, and the earth was full of his praise."*[229]

As I have mentioned earlier, there is only one who ever came from mount *Paran* in the history of mankind, who is known to 1.5 billion people in the world, as *'Holy'* and that was *Muhammad*. If you do not believe *Muhammad* as holy, then at least believe the *Bible*, where it says *Holy One came from mount Paran*. And remember what *God* said about him (Muhammad) that his glory covered the heavens, and the earth was full of his praise.

"For unto us a child is born"

There is a prophecy in *Isaiah*, which has been pasted on *Jesus*. Ironically, if you read the prophecy sincerely, it has nothing to do with *Jesus*. The prophecy says:

> *"For unto us a child is born, unto us a son is given: and [1] the government shall be upon his shoulder: and [2] his name shall be called Wonderful, [3] Counsellor, [4] The mighty God, [5] The everlasting Father, [7] The Prince of Peace. [8]Of the increase of his government and peace there shall be no end, upon the throne of David, and upon his kingdom, to order it, and to establish it with judgment and with justice from henceforth even forever. The zeal of the LORD of hosts will perform this"* (Isaiah 9:6-7).

[1] **the government shall be upon his shoulder:**

Has he (Jesus) ever had a government to rule, even for an hour? According to the *Gospels*, *Jesus* did not even have a roof on his head. *Jesus* mentions this in despair:

> *"...The foxes have holes, and the birds of the air have nests; but the Son of man hath not where to lay his head."*[230]

---

[229]   Please see *Habakkuk 3:3*
[230]   Please see *Matthew 8:20 & Luke 9:58*

Jesus was arrested within the first three years of his ministry; he was beaten, spitted on his face and mercilessly crucified. *Jesus* also said: *"A prophet is not without honour, save in his own country and in his own house" (Matthew 13:57 & Mark 6:4).* When did he become a ruler? *Christian* scholars contend that when *Jesus* comes back, then he will become a king or ruler. But the problem is according to their own belief, when *Jesus* will come back, he would not touch the ground. Half way down from the sky he would receive his righteous people and take them back to heaven (Rapture). When would he have time to rule the people? On the contrary, *Muhammad* became king of *Arabia* and he had a government to rule. He remained king until his demise due to old age.

[2] *his name shall be called Wonderful:*

Some scholars assert that because *Jesus* was born without father that's why he was called *'wonderful.'* But unfortunately, that became the biggest hindrance for *Jews* to accept *Jesus* because they believed *Jesus* was born out of wedlock (God forbid). *Jews* openly called *Jesus* illegitimate child (God forbid) and they call him that even today, then how could he be called wonderful? On the other hand, the way *Muhammad* lived his life so perfectly his enemies even called him wonderful.

[3] *Counsellor:* there is no evidence from the *Bible* that *Jesus* ever became a counselor. On the contrary, people of *Arabia* even before the ministry of *Muhammad* came to him for counseling. After he had become a great power and ruler people came more often for counseling. The *Qur'an* testifies this in these words:

> *"O ye who believe! when you consult the Messenger in private, give alms before your consultation. That is better for you and purer. But if you find not anything to give then Allah is Most Forgiving, Merciful."*[231]

[4] *The mighty God:* If you read the prophecies I have mentioned above about *Muhammad* many of those prophecies refer *Muhammad* as god, not in literal sense but as a universal prophet, as *God Almighty* is universal God. a) *Lord* came from *Sinai* also talks about the same *Lord* shone forth from *Mount Paran.* b) *Lord* came from Tema, c) In a parable of vineyard the one who would come after the son (Jesus) is slain (metaphorically) is *Lord* (Muhammad) came himself (Matthew 21:33-40) etc.

---

[231] Please see Qur'an Ch. *Al-Mujaadilah 58:12-13*

[5] ***The everlasting Father:*** *Jesus* himself prophesied about the one who would come after him, *'he will abide with you forever.'* *Jesus* never claimed that he would be forever. Instead, he said *'I go to my Father, and ye see me no more (John 16:10). Jesus* also said: *"As long as I am in the world, I am the light of the world"* *(John 9:5).* Most devout *Christians* also hold the notion that when *Jesus* will return, he will not touch the earth. My question to those *Christians* is when he will have time to rule forever? This denotes beyond any doubt that when *Jesus* goes away, someone else (Muhammad) will be the light of the world, who will be the *Everlasting Father.*

The *Christians* usually claim that *Jesus* is the everlasting father and in this regard they usually present the verses of the *Book of Revelation*, which says: *"... I am Alpha and Omega, the first and the last."*[232] If these *Christians* would have studied the *Bible* carefully, they would have never say that this is the claim of *Jesus* and no one else ever claimed that before. Because if you read the *Proverbs,* you will not only find a similar claim, but much more powerful claim than that of *Revelation.* It is said by *Solomon*:

> *"The LORD possessed me in the beginning of his way, before his works of old. I was set up from everlasting, from the beginning, or ever the earth was. When there were no depths, I was brought forth; when there were no fountains abounding with water. Before the mountains were settled, before the hills was I brought forth: While as yet he had not made the earth, nor the fields, nor the highest part of the dust of the world. When he prepared the heavens, I was there: when he set a compass upon the face of the depth: When he established the clouds above: when he strengthened the fountains of the deep: When he gave to the sea his decree, that the waters should not pass his commandment: when he appointed the foundations of the earth: Then I was by him, as one brought up with him: and I was daily his delight, rejoicing always before him..."*[233]

Did *Jesus* ever say any of this? If not, then *Solomon's* claim is stronger than that of the claim of *Jesus.* Even the *New Testament* says similar words for *Melchisedec, king of Salem,* it says:

> *"Without father, without mother, without descent, having neither beginning of days, nor end of life; but made like unto the Son of God; abideth a priest continually"* (Hebrews 7:3).

---

[232] Please see *Revelation 1: 11*
[233] Please see *Proverbs 8: 22 to 30*

If *Jesus* said *I am Alpha and Omega, the first and the last*, and it convinces you to worship him as *God*, then reconsider worshiping *Solomon* or *Melchisedec*, because they have more compelling claim, if you desire to worship a man. Did you know that *Lord Krishna* also made a similar claim 2000 years before *Jesus*? He says: *"Of all the creations, I am the beginning and the end, and the middle. I am unborn, and without beginning."* (*Bhagavad Gita*). Who really is the first and who really is the last? Too many people are making the similar claim.

[6] **The Prince of Peace:** People usually paste this verse on *Jesus* immediately and say that *Jesus* was the only man who was the prince of peace. But *Jesus* was never called in the entire *Bible* as *Prince of Peace*. If you look at the history of *Jesus'* ministry, he was not able to show his mercy against his enemies at all. *Jesus* was put on the cross mercilessly right after he started his ministry. He had no time to show if he could forgive his enemies.

On the other hand, *Muhammad* and his followers were persecuted severely for thirteen years. But when *Muhammad* had the opportunity to take the revenge against his enemies, on the conquest of *Mecca* (which was also mentioned in the book of *Deuteronomy 33:2*). That was the perfect time for *Muhammad* to fill the streets of *Mecca* with the blood of his enemies who persecuted him so severely. But what does he do? He forgives every one regardless of what they had done to harm *Muhammad*, his wife, his children and his followers. That was praised in the history of mankind even by his enemies as *'the prince of peace.'* Many honest *Jewish* and *Christian* scholars who wrote the history of *Arabia* about the time of *Muhammad*, praised him for showing the highest level of mercy.

Jesus the king of peace

In the entire *New Testament, Jesus* was never praised as 'prince of peace or the 'king of peace' by any *Gospel* writer even a single time. If you still think *Jesus* was king of peace let us read what *Jesus* says about the peace:

1. *"Think not that I am come to send peace on earth: I came not to send peace, but a sword"* (Matthew 10:34).

2. *"...and he that hath no sword, let him sell his garment, and buy one"* (Luke 22: 36).

3. *"I am come to send fire on the earth; and what will I, if it be already kindled?" (Luke 12:49).*

4. *" For I am come to set a man at variance against his father, and the daughter against her mother, and the daughter in law against her mother in law" (Matthew 10:35).*

5. *"And a man's foes shall be they of his own household" (Matthew 10:36).*

6. *"If any man come to me, and hate not his father, and mother, and wife, and children, and brethren, and sisters, yea, and his own life also, he cannot be my disciple" (Luke 14:26).*

7. *"But Jesus said unto him, Follow me; and let the dead bury their dead" (Matthew 8:22).*

8. *" For from henceforth there shall be five in one house divided, three against two, and two against three" (Luke 12:52).*

God says in the Old Testament: *"The prophet which prophesieth of peace, when the word of the prophet shall come to pass, then shall the prophet be known, that the LORD hath truly sent him" (Jeremiah 28:9).* This means if the prophet does not talk about the peace, then he is not from God. Did Jesus really say all that?

My Christian friends usually refer this verse *'prince of peace'* in the event of Jesus' crucifixion. They say when Jesus was crucified mercilessly by his enemies, being on the cross; Jesus still forgave them that is the reason he was known as prince of peace. But let me give you a scenario and then you decide who is the prince of peace. If a man is defeated by his enemy and the enemy is sitting on his chest and about to kill him and the person underneath him helplessly says, I forgive you, would that be considered prince of peace, or the person who defeated his enemy who persecuted him for a long time then finally he got a chance to kill him and he is sitting on the chest of his enemy and about to kill him, but instead, he says I forgive you. Obviously, the person who had the power to kill but he did not use it is more likely to be called the prince of peace, rather than a defeated man who is helpless. Correct?

[7] *"Of the increase of his government and peace there shall be no end, upon the throne of David, and upon his kingdom, to order it, and to establish it with judgment and with justice from henceforth **even forever**."* In this verse the prophecy says that the person addressed in this verse will have *'increase of*

his government and peace there shall be no end.' As I have mentioned above *Jesus* did not even have a government therefore, he did not have an increase of the government either. The prophecy also says: *'there shall be no end, upon the throne of David.'* The book of *Psalms* tells us who would rule *Palestine*. It says:

a) *"The righteous shall inherit the land, and dwell therein forever" (Psalms 37:29).*

b) The *Qur'an* also tells us that: *"And We have already written in the Book of David, [Psalms] after the reminder, that My righteous servants shall inherit the Land."*[234]

The *Old Testament* tells us that the *Jews* will be expelled from *Palestine* twice. *Moses* tells us:

"And it shall come to pass, that as the LORD rejoiced over you to do you good, and to multiply you; so the LORD will rejoice over you to destroy you, and to bring you to nought; and ye shall be plucked from off the land whither thou goest to possess it. And the LORD shall scatter thee among all people, from the one end of the earth even unto the other..." (Deuteronomy 28:63-64).

But *God* also told *Moses* that if your people (Jews) became humble and good, *God* will have mercy on them again, therefore it says:

"That then the LORD thy God will turn thy captivity, and have compassion upon thee, and will return and gather thee from all the nations, [which happened when *Israel* became nation in 1948] *whither the LORD thy God hath scattered thee."*[235]

The *Bible* also says:

"They provoked him to jealousy with strange god, with abominations provoked they him to anger... And he said, I will hide my face from them, I will see what their end shall be: for they are a very froward generation, children in whom is no faith. They have moved me to jealousy with that which is not God; they have provoked me to anger with their vanities: and I will move them to jealousy with those which are not a people; I will provoke them to anger with a foolish nation.

---

[234] Please see Qur'an Ch. *Al-Anbiya 21: 105 or 106*
[235] Please see *Deuteronomy 30:3*

> For a fire is kindled in mine anger, and shall burn unto the
> lowest hell, and shall consume the earth with her increase,
> and set on fire the foundations of the mountains. I will heap
> mischiefs upon them; I will spend mine arrows upon them. They
> shall be burnt with hunger, and devoured with burning heat,
> and with bitter destruction: I will also send the teeth of beasts
> upon them, with the poison of serpents of the dust. The sword
> without, and terror within, shall destroy both the young man
> and the virgin, the suckling [babies] also with the man of gray
> hairs. I said, I would scatter them into corners, I would make
> the remembrance of them to cease from among men. For they
> are a nation void of counsel, neither is there any understanding
> in them" (Deuteronomy 32:16- 26).

According to the above quoted verses of *Deuteronomy*, *God* will punish *Jews* twice and will expel them twice from *Palestine*. These verses are supported by the *Qur'an* in these words:

> "And We gave (Clear) Warning to the Children of Israel in
> the Book, that twice would they do mischief on the earth and
> be elated with mighty arrogance (and twice would they be
> punished)!"[236]

We all know that *Palestine* was not only the birth place of *King David* it is also known as the throne of *King David*. From the time, when *Jesus* claim to be the *Messiah*, until he was crucified, *Jesus* had no government on his shoulder, not even for a minute. The *Throne of David* which is mentioned here was not ruled by *Christians* until 325 C.E. This denotes that the first time *Christians* ever ruled *Palestine* or *Bethlehem*, was 325 years after *Jesus*. But in 638 C.E., a little over 300 years, *Islam* came into existence and ruled the throne of *King David* until 1098C.E. Almost 460 years, but in 1099 C.E., the *Crusaders* took *Jerusalem* from *Muslims* by killing thousands of innocent *Muslim*, men, women and children. But for only 88 years, in 1187C.E. *Muslims* repossessed *Jerusalem* & ruled for another 761 years until 1948. This means that the total time *Christians* ruled over *Israel* in their 2000 years of history was about 300 years. But *Muslims* ruled *Israel* for sure for 1,221 years. Even though *Jerusalem* is now under control by the *Jews* but the 'Temple Mount,' the holiest site in *Judaism* is still under control by *Muslims*. Who seems to be fulfilling the prophecy of *Isaiah*? The *Qur'an* asks the *Jews* an important question:

---

[236] Please see Qur'an Ch. *Bani-Isra'il 17: 4-5*

"The Jews and the Christians say, 'We are sons of Allah [God] and His loved ones.' Say, 'Why then does He punish you for your sins? Nay, you are only human beings among those He has created.' He forgives whom He pleases and punishes whom He pleases. And to Allah belongs the kingdom of the heavens and the earth and what is between them, and to Him shall be the return."237

This basically means that no one is beloved of *God* just because he belongs to a certain religion, nation, color or tribe. The only beloved of *God* are those who are righteous. Hence, to clarify this exhortation, the *Qur'an* says:

"O mankind, We have created you from a male and a female; and We have made you into tribes and sub-tribes that you may recognize one another. Verily, the most honorable among you, in the sight of Allah, is he who is the most righteous among you. Surely, Allah is All-knowing, All-Aware."238

Did you know that *Israel* has been destroyed 17 times? If *Jews* were the only beloved people of *God* and they were the only chosen people of *God*, then, why they were punished so severely? I do agree that when *Hebrews* accepted *Moses* as the prophet of *God* then they did become *God's* only beloved people and *God's* only chosen people. But as soon as they rejected *Jesus* they were no longer beloved of *God* or chosen people of *God*. This is the reason that they were destroyed in *74 C.E.*, because of the rejection of the *Messiah* (Jesus) sent by *God*. Then *Christians* became the beloved of *God* and chosen people of *God*, because they accepted the *Messiah* sent by *God*. But when they rejected *Muhammad* they were no longer beloved of *God* or chosen people of *God*. Then *Muslims* became the beloved of *God* and chosen people of *God*. But when even they rejected *Ahmad* the *Promised Messiah* sent by *God* they were too no longer beloved of *God* and chosen people of *God*. Now only *Ahmadis* are the beloved of *God* or chosen people of *God*, as long as they remain righteous and stay at the right path of *God Almighty*.

Going back to the original question who deserves more for the title *"there shall be no end, upon the throne of David."* Who ruled the *Palestine* the longest? Or who seems to be fulfilling the prophecy of *Isaiah*? Does three hundred years of *Christianity* ruling *Jerusalem* seems *'forever'*? Or *1,221* years of *Muslims* ruling *Jerusalem* seems *'forever'* of the prophecy of *Isaiah*? Who

---

237 Please see Qur'an Ch. *Al-Maidah 5:18-19*
238 Please see Qur'an Ch. *Al-Hujurat 49: 13-14*

you really think fulfilled the prophecy, *Jesus* or *Muhammad*? *Christianity* or *Islam*?

I have tried my best to prove from the *Bible*, that *Muhammad* came to fulfill the prophecies of the *Bible*. From the country he would come from (Arabia), to the city he would be born (Paran), to the fiery law he would bring (Qur'an), to the success of his mission in his lifetime (ten thousands saints), to the description of his appearance (white and ruddy), to the exact very name (Muhammad) is mentioned in the *Bible*. Accordingly, the people of our time should not be confused if these prophecies are about *Muhammad* or someone else. As *God* exhorted us in the *Bible*: *Whosoever will not hearken unto my words which he shall speak in my name, I will require it of him.*

23. Islam in the Bible

The important question is, was *Jesus* mentioned in the *Old Testament*, as if *God* said, there will be a man named *Jesus*, he will be the *Messiah*, you must accept him? No, right? Only some of the main events of his life were mentioned. When you compare those events you can say yes, he is the one who was promised. In the similar way, many main events of the life of *Muhammad* were also mentioned in the *Bible* too. Therefore, when he came, people could recognize him by comparing these events from the *Bible*. If these events were not about *Muhammad* and *Islam*, then, is this a mere coincidence that many of these holy places, people, & main events of the *Islamic* history were mentioned in the *Bible?*

1. ALLAH (*the creator of universe, one and only God*):

Allah is mentioned 4,473 times in all the *Bibles* printed in the *Arabic* language. These *Bibles* are in use daily by millions of *Christian Arabs* all over the world. If *Allah* is a false *God* (God forbid), as most *Christian* scholars claim, then what a false god is doing in the true *Bible?* Even today, all *Arab Christians* consider *Allah* as the only *God*, and creator of the universe. Some *Christians* try to resolve this issue by asserting that the *Arabic Bible* was translated by *Arab Muslims* and this is the reason they translated *God* into *Allah*. How lame is this claim? Are they saying that in last thousand years or so, no *Arab Christian* was educated enough who would come forward to correct the *Bible?* They do not even have to be educated to fix the alleged problem, all they had to do is to replace the name *Allah* with *God* and print the *Bible* again. But I guess according to those who claim that no one was smart enough to even do that. But the fact is contrary to this, the fact is all

Arab Christians unanimously believe that *Allah* is the real *God*, creator of heaven and earth.

Allah written in Arabic

Allah written in Arabic

التكوين

Genesis
Chapter One

الأصحاح الأول

١ فِي ٱلْبَدْءِ خَلَقَ ٱللهُ ٱلسَّمَوَاتِ وَٱلْأَرْضَ • ٢وَكَانَتِ ٱلْأَرْضُ خَرِبَةً وَخَالِيَةً وَعَلَى وَجْهِ

٢ ٱلْغَمْرِ ظُلْمَةٌ وَرُوحُ ٱللهِ يَرِفُّ عَلَى وَجْهِ ٱلْمِيَاهِ •٣وَقَالَ ٱللهُ لِيَكُنْ نُورٌ فَكَانَ نُورٌ •٤وَرَأَى

٥ ٱللهُ ٱلنُّورَ أَنَّهُ حَسَنٌ •وَفَصَلَ ٱللهُ بَيْنَ ٱلنُّورِ وَٱلظُّلْمَةِ •٥وَدَعَا ٱللهُ ٱلنُّورَ نَهَارًا وَٱلظُّلْمَةَ

دَعَاهَا لَيْلًا •وَكَانَ مَسَاءٌ وَكَانَ صَبَاحٌ يَوْمًا وَاحِدًا

٦ ٦وَقَالَ ٱللهُ لِيَكُنْ جَلَدٌ فِي وَسَطِ ٱلْمِيَاهِ •وَلْيَكُنْ فَاصِلًا بَيْنَ مِيَاهٍ وَمِيَاهٍ •٧فَعَمِلَ ٱللهُ

٨ ٱلْجَلَدَ وَفَصَلَ بَيْنَ ٱلْمِيَاهِ ٱلَّتِي تَحْتَ ٱلْجَلَدِ وَٱلْمِيَاهِ ٱلَّتِي فَوْقَ ٱلْجَلَدِ •وَكَانَ كَذَلِكَ •٨وَدَعَا

ٱللهُ ٱلْجَلَدَ سَمَاءً •وَكَانَ مَسَاءٌ وَكَانَ صَبَاحٌ يَوْمًا ثَانِيًا

٩ ٩وَقَالَ ٱللهُ لِتَجْتَمِعِ ٱلْمِيَاهُ تَحْتَ ٱلسَّمَاءِ إِلَى مَكَانٍ وَاحِدٍ وَلْتَظْهَرِ ٱلْيَابِسَةُ •وَكَانَ

١٠ كَذَلِكَ •١٠وَدَعَا ٱللهُ ٱلْيَابِسَةَ أَرْضًا •وَمُجْتَمَعَ ٱلْمِيَاهِ دَعَاهُ بِحَارًا •وَرَأَى ٱللهُ ذَلِكَ أَنَّهُ

١١ حَسَنٌ •١١وَقَالَ ٱللهُ لِتُنْبِتِ ٱلْأَرْضُ عُشْبًا وَبَقْلًا يُبْزِرُ بِزْرًا وَشَجَرًا ذَا ثَمَرٍ يَعْمَلُ ثَمَرًا كَجِنْسِهِ

١٢ بِزْرُهُ فِيهِ عَلَى ٱلْأَرْضِ •وَكَانَ كَذَلِكَ •١٢فَأَخْرَجَتِ ٱلْأَرْضُ عُشْبًا وَبَقْلًا يُبْزِرُ بِزْرًا كَجِنْسِهِ

١٣ وَشَجَرًا يَعْمَلُ ثَمَرًا بِزْرُهُ فِيهِ كَجِنْسِهِ •وَرَأَى ٱللهُ ذَلِكَ أَنَّهُ حَسَنٌ •١٣وَكَانَ مَسَاءٌ وَكَانَ صَبَاحٌ

يَوْمًا ثَالِثًا

١٤ ١٤وَقَالَ ٱللهُ لِتَكُنْ أَنْوَارٌ فِي جَلَدِ ٱلسَّمَاءِ لِتَفْصِلَ بَيْنَ ٱلنَّهَارِ وَٱللَّيْلِ •وَتَكُونَ لِآيَاتٍ

١٥ وَأَوْقَاتٍ وَأَيَّامٍ وَسِنِينَ •١٥وَتَكُونَ أَنْوَارًا فِي جَلَدِ ٱلسَّمَاءِ لِتُنِيرَ عَلَى ٱلْأَرْضِ •وَكَانَ

١٦ كَذَلِكَ •١٦فَعَمِلَ ٱللهُ ٱلنُّورَيْنِ ٱلْعَظِيمَيْنِ •ٱلنُّورَ ٱلْأَكْبَرَ لِحُكْمِ ٱلنَّهَارِ وَٱلنُّورَ ٱلْأَصْغَرَ

٢

This is the actual picture of the first page, of the book of Genesis from the Arabic Bible. Circled is the name ALLAH, used for God, 16 times on just one page. If anyone supposes that I have played any trick to manipulate the Arabic Bible, then please ask any Arab Christian, there are thousands of them living in America and elsewhere in the world. (Please see Arabic Bible 40 series, ISBN# 1 903865 00 X)

2. *Muhammad (the holy prophet of Islam):*

There is a prophecy of the *Bible* in the *Song of Solomon 5:9-16.* The person, who is mentioned here is the *'Beloved of God.'* This is one of the titles of *Muhammad.* Let's go further with the prophecy, which will explain clearly why it applies to *Muhammad* only and no one else. It also says: *"My beloved is white and ruddy"* which was the color of *Muhammad.* Thirdly it says: *'Chiefest among ten thousand.'* *Muhammad* on the conquest of *Mecca* led an army of ten thousand followers. The fourth and most convincing point in this prophecy, which explains why *Muslims* believe that this prophecy belongs to *Muhammad* only and no one else in the entire world, is the name *"Muhammad"* mentioned in verse 16. But unfortunately the word *"Muhammad"* has been deleted in the *English Bibles.* The prophecy used to read "מחמד" = *'Machmad'* meaning *Muhammad,* but it now says, *"altogether lovely"* (Song of Solomon 5:16). But in the *Hebrew Bible,* it still says *"Muhammad."* Please remember when you read *Muhammed's* name in *Hebrew,* you will see *'Machmad'* you might think it says *'Machmad'* not *Muhammad,* but in *Hebrew 'Ch'* is pronounced as *'Kh-a'* or *'Ha'* as throat clearing. As we see in *'Chanukkah'* but we pronounce it *'Hanukkah.'*

K C L **Sgs 5:16** His mouth [is] most sweet: yea, he [is] altogether
I V D lovely. This [is] my beloved, and this [is] my friend, O
daughters of Jerusalem.

```
Information on Hebrew Scroll
16 חכו ממתקים וכלו מחמדים זה
דודי וזה רעי בנות ירושלם.
```

English		Strong's	Hebrew (Root form)	Tense
(Click on any item below for Concordance)				(Click)
His mouth	Phr	[02441]	חך chek	
[is] most sweet:	Phr	[04477]	ממתקים mamtaq	
yea, he [is] altogether lovely.	Phr	[04261]	מחמד machmad	
This [is] my beloved,	Phr	[01730]	דוד dowd	
and this [is] my friend,	Phr	[07453]	רע rea`	
O daughters	Phr	[01323]	בת bath	
of Jerusalem.	Phr	[03389]	ירושלם Y@ruwshalaim	

Did John the Baptist say that about Jesus or did Jesus say that about Muhammad?

There is a prophecy in the *Gospel of Matthew*, which says *John the Baptist* prophesied about *Jesus* and said:

> *"I indeed baptize you with water unto repentance: but he that cometh after me is mightier than I, whose shoes I am not worthy to bear: he shall baptize you with the Holy Ghost, and with fire"* *(Matthew 3:11)*.

Ironically, even after this prophecy; *Jesus* always baptized with water all his life and all the *Christians* followed him in the same manner after him, even today. Most surprisingly, *Jesus* says in *Acts* that he prophesied about this prophecy. Therefore, it says:

> *"And, being assembled together with them, commanded them that they should not depart from Jerusalem, but wait for the promise of the Father, which, saith he, ye have heard of me. For John truly baptized with water; but ye shall be baptized with the Holy Ghost not many days hence"* *(Acts 1:4-5)*.

As you can see *Jesus* said in clear words *"ye have heard of me."* Not only that even *St. Peter* says, that *Jesus* said that. He said:

> *"Then remembered I the word of the Lord, [Jesus] how that he said, John indeed baptized with water; but ye shall be baptized with the Holy Ghost"* *(Acts 11:16)*.

The third evidence takes the mystery out utterly. The *Gospel of Barnabas* confirms that the above quoted prophecy was from *Jesus*, and not from *John the Baptist*, please evaluate:

The Gospel of John (New Testament)	The Gospel of Barnabas
And this is the record of John, when the Jews sent priests and Levites from Jerusalem to ask him, Who art thou?	*"Wherefore they sent the Levites and some of the scribes to question him, saying: "Who are you?"*
And he confessed, and denied not; but confessed, I am not the Christ.	*Jesus confessed, and said the truth: "I am not the Messiah."*

And they asked him, What then? Art thou Elias? And he saith, I am not. Art thou that prophet? And he answered, No. Then said they unto him, Who art thou? that we may give an answer to them that sent us. What sayest thou of thyself?	They said: "Are you Elijah or Jeremiah, or any of the ancient prophets?" Jesus answered: "No." Then said they: "Who are you? Say, in order that we may give testimony to those who sent us."
He said, I am the voice of one crying in the wilderness, Make straight the way of the Lord, as said the prophet Esaias.	Then Jesus said: "I am a voice that cries through all Judea, and cries: "Prepare you the way for the messenger of the Lord," even as it is written in Esaias."
And they which were sent were of the Pharisees. And they asked him, and said unto him, Why baptizest thou then, if thou be not that Christ, nor Elias, neither that prophet?	They said: "If you be not the Messiah nor Elijah, or any prophet, wherefore do you preach new doctrine, and make yourself of more account than the Messiah..."
John answered them, saying, **I baptize with water**: but there standeth one among you, whom ye know not; He it is, who coming after me is preferred before me, **whose shoe's latchet I am not worthy to unloose.** (Gospel of John 1: 19 to 27).	***Verses from chapter 42:*** Jesus answered: "The miracles which God works by my hands show that I speak that which God wills; nor indeed do I make myself to be accounted as him of whom you speak. **For I am not worthy to unloose the ties of the hosen or the ratchets of the shoes** of the Messenger of God whom you call "Messiah," who was made before me, **and shall come after me**, and shall bring the words of truth, so that his faith shall have no end." (The Gospel of Barnabas chapter 42). ***Verses from chapter 44:*** "O blessed time, when he shall come to the world! Believe me that I have seen him and have done. Him reverence, even as every prophet has seen him: seeing that of his spirit God gives to them prophecy. And when I saw him my soul was filled with consolation, saying: "**O Muhammad;, God be with you, and may he make me worthy to untie, your shoe latchet;,** for obtaining this I shall be a great prophet and holy one of God." And having said this, Jesus rendered his thanks to God." (The Gospel of Barnabas chapter 44).

Many scholars reject the *Gospel of Barnabas* as a medieval forgery, but the question is if it was forged around medieval times then how this gospel was quoted by the second century scholar named *St. Irenaeus*? Some scholars try to resolve this intricate problem by asserting, *St, Irenaeus* did mention the *Gospel of Barnabas* but he only mentioned it to disprove it. But my point is even if he mentioned it to disprove it, at least it shows that the *Gospel of Barnabas* existed in the first and second centuries and it was not a medieval forgery or forged by the *Muslims. Islam* came into existence around 6th century C.E., there is no possible way that the *Christian* scholars can prove that *Muslims* forged a document which existed five to six hundred years before them. To me it is easy for anyone to reject the truth and manipulate the verses in their favor, as I have quoted earlier and the following chapters will prove that too. You be the judge and decide if *John the Baptist* said that about *Jesus* or *Jesus* said that about *Muhammad*? If you put together the *Holy Ghost* (Muhammad) and baptizing with fire, with the '*Fiery law*' you will get the whole picture, who was talking about who?

The scholars of today strongly suggest that *John the Baptist* did not say that about *Jesus*, because except for two, none of the followers of *John the Baptist* ever became the followers of *Jesus*. Is that possible if *John the Baptist* regarded *Jesus* highly and uttered such great words about him, but most of his followers did not believe him and not believing is something insignificant, but they curse him, use abusive language for him, and call *Jesus* a liar and a false messiah? This denotes that the followers of *John the Baptist* never heard the above quoted verses from him about *Jesus*. The history of mankind is denying that *John the Baptist* said that about *Jesus*. On the contrary, according to this theory, if *Jesus* said that about *Muhammad*, then it makes more sense, because if you look at the history of *Christianity*, all those areas where *Jesus* preached personally after the crucifixion they all became *Muslim*. What makes more sense, a mere verbal claim which was pasted on to *Jesus* but in history there is no proof? Or the history of *1,500* years which proves beyond any doubt that *Jesus* said those words about *Muhammad*?

3. *Ahmad in the Bible:*

The *Qur'an* says:

> "*And when Jesus, son of Mary, said, 'O children of Israel, surely, I am Allah's Messenger unto you, fulfilling that which is before me of the [prophecies] of the Torah [Old Testament] and giving the good news of a Messenger who will come after me, his name being Ahmad, but when he came to them with clear proofs, they said, This is clear magic.*"[239]

---

[239] Please see Qur'an *Al-Saff* Ch. *61:6-7*

According to the *Qur'an, Jesus* prophesied in the *New Testament* about the coming of a prophet after *Jesus* and that his name would be *Ahmad*. But when you read the *English New Testament,* you will not find the name *Ahmad*. You might think that why *Qur'an* mentions something which is not true? But the truth is if you read the book of *John* in *Greek Bible*, it mentions *Ahmad.* The prophecy states:

> *"But when the* **Comforter** *is come, whom I will send unto you from the Father, even the Spirit of truth, which proceedeth from the Father, he shall testify of me."*[240] In another verse of the book of *John, Jesus* said: *"Nevertheless I tell you the truth; It is expedient for you that I go away: for if I go not away, the* **Comforter** *will not come unto you; but if I depart, I will send him unto you."*[241]

If you read this prophecy in the *Greek Bible*, it says little different. According to the historians, the word *Parakletos* mentioned in the *Greek Bible* is very similar to a *Greek* word περικλυτός = *"Periklutos"* which means *Ahmad* and *Muhammad. Mr. Jack Finegan is professor emeritus of New Testament history and archaeology at the Pacific School of Religion and Graduate Theological Union, Berkeley, California.* He is author of over a dozen books. *Mr. Finegan* writes in his book about the above mentioned verse of *the Qur'an,* and says:

> *"The possible basis for this [Qur'an 61:6] is John 16:7 where in Greek the word for Comforter (παράκλητος) ['Parakletos' or 'paraclete'] is very similar to the word for "renowned" (περικλυτός), [Periklutos] the latter being the meaning of the names Ahmad and Muhammad."*[242]

One may say that he/she does not believe in the *Qur'an* and don't know *Mr. Jack Finegan.* How can these people verify from a third reliable source that *Jesus* said *Ahmad* and not *the Comforter?* It's a blessing of *God* that a document discovered towards the end of the nineteenth century in *Ezra synagogue, Old Cairo, Egypt,* known as *"The Damascus Document"* describes *Jesus* as having foretold the advent of a *"Holy Spirit,"* named *Emeth:*

---

[240] Please see *John 15:26*
[241] Please see *John 16:7*
[242] Please see the book *The Archaeology of the World Religions: the background of Shinto Islam & Sikhism Vol. 3* by *Jack Finegan,* Copyright © 1952, by *Princeton University Press at Princeton, New Jersey. Pages 494 & 495*

> *"And by His Messiah, He has made them know His Holy Spirit. For it is he who is Emeth, i.e., the Truthful One, and in accordance with his name are also theirs…"*

Therefore, the *Holy Spirit, Comforter* and *Ehmeth* are one, and the name of Prophet *Ahmad.* אמת = *Emeth in Hebrew* is pronounced as *"Eh'-meth"* which means *"the Truth," "the Truthful one and a person of constant goodness."* The *Arabic* name *"Ahmad"* also means *'Truth'* in *Arabic.* To find this name in *Hebrew King James Bible,* please go to on-line *Bible* website called blueletterbible.org and type "truth" or "h571" in the search area. This word *Ehmeth* corresponds to the *Arabic* name *Ahmad.* In *Hebrew,* there is no vowels, so the first alphabet "א" = *"Alef"* serves the purpose of all the vowels, *A, E, I, O* and *U.* The strange thing is when *Hebrew* scholars write *Adam, Abel, Aaron* and *Abraham,* they write with *"A"* which is the *Hebrew* alphabet *"Alef."* But when they write *"Eh-meth"* they write it with *"E"* with the same alphabet *"Alef."* I guess they know if they write *'Eh-meth'* with *'A'* = *'Ahmeth,'* it would be too close to the name of the prophet of *Islam* (*Ahmad*).[243]

John has also reported a conversation between *Jesus* and *Pontius Pilate.* It says:

> *"Pilate therefore said unto him (Jesus), Art thou a king then? Jesus answered; Thou sayest that I am a king. To this end was I born, and for this cause came I into the world, that I should bear witness unto the truth… Pilate saith unto him, What is truth?"* (John 18:37-38).

According to the *Syriac Edition Bible, Jesus* told *Pilate* that I came into this world, that I should bear witness to *'Eh-meth'* (Ahmad) because this word *'Eh-meth'* was a foreign word for *Pilate* that made him to repeat the word, what is *Eh-meth*? If we believe as *English Bible* says that *Pilate* asked, *'what is truth?'* It does not make any sense. Since *Pilate* was a Judge, and he dealt with lies and truth every day, how could he not know what truth is?

4. **Qur'an** (the holy book of Muslims): There are very clear prophecies in the *Bible* about the *Holy Book of Muslims,* the *Qur'an.* It says:

> *"For precept must be upon precept, precept upon precept; line upon line, line upon line; here a little, and there a little: For with stammering lips and another tongue will he speak to this*

---

[243] I apologize to my readers for writing this part again, but I honestly think this is the demand of this chapter as well

people... but the word of the Lord was unto them precept upon precept, precept upon precept; line upon line, line upon line; here a little, and there a little..." (Isaiah 28:10 -13).

In these verses, prophet *Isaiah* is talking about a word of *God* which would be revealed to the people in another tongue. It denotes that a tongue other than *Hebrew, Aramaic or Greek,* languages commonly spoken in ancient *Israel.* As you might know, that the *Holy Qur'an* was revealed in *Arabic.* Here *Bible* is talking about '*precept upon precept, line upon line, here a little there a little*' that is how exactly the *Qur'an* was revealed to our prophet *Muhammad.* Since it was revealed very slowly, it took twenty-three years to reveal the whole *Qur'an.* This prophecy of *Isaiah* was confirmed by the *Qur'an* in these words:

> *"And it is a Qur'an which We have revealed in portions so that you may read it to the people by slow degrees, and We have revealed it, revealing in portions" (Bani-Isra'il 17: 106-107).*

Not only the *Bible* talks about how *Qur'an* was revealed slowly, little by little, but the *Bible* also talks about the first revelation of *Muhammad* received from *God,* in the form of angel *Gabriel.* It says:

> *'And the vision of all is become unto you as the words of a book that is sealed, which men deliver to one that is learned, saying, Read this, I pray thee: and he saith, I cannot; for it is sealed: And the book is delivered to him that is not learned, saying, Read this, I pray thee: and he saith I am not learned' (Isaiah 29:11-12).*

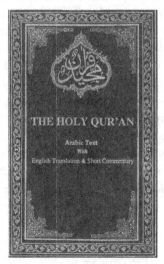

Qur'an the Holy book of Muslims

This is how the *Qur'an* was revealed to our *Prophet Muhammad*. When angel *Gabriel* asked *Muhammad* to *'Read,'* but he said, I cannot read, because I do not know how to read. *Angel Gabriel* asked him again to read, and again his answer was the same. The third time angel *Gabriel* asked *Muhammad* to read, and he said, I cannot read, because I am not learnt. Then angel *Gabriel* asked *Muhammad* to repeat after him the verses of the *Qur'an*. Another very interesting point in this prophecy of *Isaiah* is that it is talking about a book, which is sealed. The *Qur'an* was prophesied in the *Bible* by prophet *Isaiah* about 742 years before *Jesus*. *Muhammad* came 600 years after *Jesus*, total of 1,342 years, even before *Muhammad* was born, *Isaiah* prophesied about the *Qur'an* that it would be a sealed book. It denotes a book that cannot be altered. The *Qur'an* confirms this prophecy in these words:

> "And recite that which hath been revealed unto thee of the scripture of thy Lord. There is none who can change His words… "[244] *God* also says in the *Qur'an*: "Surely, I have sent down this book, and I will most surely safeguard it."[245]

The *Qur'an* is over fourteen hundred years old. It has only one version, which is in use everywhere in the world. It has never been altered.

Some *Christians* claim that the *Bible* is the most read book in the world. It could be true I do not contend that, but it is also a fact that the *Qur'an* is the most memorized book in the world. This means that even today there are thousands of people in this world who have committed the whole of the *Qur'an* into their memory. This also denotes that if (God forbid) the *Qur'an* disappears from the world somehow, then even one person out of those thousands of people who have put into their memory the whole of the *Qur'an* will be able to dictate the whole of the *Qur'an* and it will be available within days again. But if the *Bible* disappears (God forbid) from the world it might take years to compile the whole of the *Bible* again and they might need thousands of people to put together different chapters. Since I never heard in my life that any *Christian* has memorized the whole *Bible*, which I am specially referring to the *Old* and the *New Testaments* combined. I am not denying the fact that the *Qur'an* is a much shorter book than the *Bible*. The *Qur'an* has only thirty books all together while the *Bible* has sixty-six books according to the *King James Version*. I myself never heard of any *Christian* or a *Jewish scholar* who has memorized completely even the ten books of the *Bible*.

---

244   Please see Qur'an Ch. *Al-Kahf 18:27-28*
245   Please see Qur'an Ch. *Al-Hijr 15:9-10*

In this regard, the *Qur'an* is much easier to memorize, but there lies another huge fact which makes the *Qur'an* distinguished among all the other books of *God*, that the *Qur'an* is in *Arabic* language which is still a living language. Unfortunately, the *Old* and the *New Testaments* both are in languages which are not in use. I am referring to the *Hebrew* and the *Aramaic* languages in which the *Old* and the *New Testaments* were written originally, or even *Greek* for that matter.

The reason I did not say I never heard of a *Jewish* person memorizing the whole of the *Bible* is that since they do not believe the *New Testament* as a word of *God* then why would they put efforts to memorize it? The reason I have mentioned all this is that this was one of the main reasons of the *Old Testament* seemingly have contradictions is that the *Bible* has been destroyed many times, especially in the time of *King Nebuchadnezzar*. Every time when they tried to compile the *Bible* they found differing versions about the same subject, but they had no choice since they did not know which version is more accurate than the others, so, they comprised both versions and in some cases they comprised many versions of the same subject. The *Book of Revelation*, also talks about the *Qur'an* and the first chapter of the *Qur'an* in these words:

> *"And I saw in the right hand of him that sat on the throne a book written within and on the backside, sealed with seven seals. And I saw a strong angel proclaiming with a loud voice, Who is worthy to open the book, and to loose the seals thereof? And no man in heaven, nor in earth, neither under the earth, was able to open the book, neither to look thereon. And I wept much, because no man was found worthy to open and to read the book, neither to look thereon. And one of the elders saith unto me, Weep not: behold, the Lion of the tribe of Juda, the Root of David, hath prevailed to open the book, and to loose the seven seals thereof" (Revelation 5:1-5).*

The most interesting part in this prophecy is that it is talking about a book and on the backside of the book has **seven seals**. As we all know that the book of *Revelation* is the final book of the *New Testament*. Therefore, the book mentioned here cannot be any of the books of the *New Testament*. The book which came after the *New Testament* was the *Qur'an*. Surprisingly, the name of the first chapter of the *Qur'an* is *"Fatihah,"* which literally means *"to open,"* or to *"open up."* The *Qur'an* opens up from the back side, this means unlike any other book which opens from left hand and ends at the right hand. The *Qur'an* opens up from right hand and ends at the left hand. Because *Qur'an* was revealed in *Arabic* language. *Arabic* language, unlike *English*, is written from right to left.[246]

---

[246] Please see the picture of the first chapter of the *Qur'an* named *'Fatihah,'* or to *'Open up,'* with seven verses or seven seals.

324

 سُوۡرَةُ الۡفَاتِحَةِ مَكِّیَّةٌ

1. ^aIn¹ the name² of Allāh,³ the Gracious, the Merciful.⁴

2. ^aAll⁵ praise^{5A} belongs to Allāh *alone*, Lord⁶ of all the worlds,^{6A}

3. ^aThe Gracious, ^bthe Merciful,⁷

4. ^cMaster⁸ of the ^dDay⁹ of Judgment.¹⁰

5. ^aThee alone do we worship¹¹ and ^bThee alone do we implore for help.¹²

6. Guide us in ^cthe straight path,¹³

7. The path of ^athose on whom Thou hast bestowed *Thy* favours,¹⁴ those who have not ^bincurred *Thy* displeasure and those who have not ^cgone astray.¹⁵

Picture of the First Chapter of Qur'an, Arabic verses have been concealed to protect Qur'an from desecration

Not only that more surprisingly, the first chapter of the *Qur'an* has seven verses. Some *Qur'ans* do not have 1st verse marked as 1st verse and they start counting from the 2nd verse. Only in those *Qur'ans* you may see only six verses marked. This is the main reason I have included double verses throughout my book, for example: *Baqarah 2: 35-36,* instead of just writing *Baqarah 2: 35.* But including 1st verse every *Qur'an* has seven verses in the 1st chapter. When *Muhammad* came and started to receive revelations of the *Qur'an* then he was able to interpret it or according to the *Bible* he was able to *open the book.* Same was done by *Ahmad,* he interpreted the *Qur'an* in our time the way that no *Muslim* scholar of today was able to do. He also interpreted the *Bible* in a way that no *Jewish* or *Christian* scholar was able to do. As we all know that when *Jesus* came and interpret the *Torah* none of the *Jewish* scholars was able to do. My whole book is the result of the teachings of *Ahmad.* But I have only written my understanding of *Ahmad's* teaching. I do not represent *Ahmad* or the *Ahmadiyya* sect.

5. Sacrifice of Abraham:

The incident of *Abraham,* when he took his son *Ishmael* to sacrifice for the will of God *(Genesis 22:2-13).* Surprisingly, the *Bible* says that it was *Isaac,* who was sacrificed by *Abraham.* The question is, if it was *Isaac* not *Ishmael,* then why this event is only commemorated by *Muslims* (descendants of Ishmael), and not by the *Jews* or the *Christians* (descendants of Isaac). Millions of animals are slaughtered every year, by *Muslims,* in the memory of *Ishmael's* sacrifice, and it the biggest religious event in *Islam.*

6. Hagar and Ishmael and the sacred water; (Aab-e-Zam Zam)

According to the *Muslim* traditions, *Hagar* and *Ishmael* were brought to *Paran* (one of the ancient names of the *Valley of Mecca*) by *Abraham.* The water *Hagar* brought with her ran out within a few days. Her son *Ishmael,* a little child, started to cry for water. There was no water anywhere near, since they were in between tow rocky hills of *Safa* and *Marwah,* (מוריה = *Moriah* in *Hebrew, Genesis 22:2*). By the grace of *God,* a spring broke out from the rocks miraculously. *Hagar* gave her son that water which saved their lives. This incident was told by *Jesus* in these words:

> *"He [Ishmael] turned the rock into pools of water; yes, springs of water came from solid rock."*[247]

---

[247] Please see *Psalms 114:8 New Living Translation* Copyright © 1996 by *Tyndale Charitable Trust*

That water is called '*Aab-e- Zum Zum,*' which means '*Water stop stop.*' This water is still springing out for over four thousand years. *Muslims* all over the world not only use this water during their stay in *Mecca*, but also they take this water home for blessings.

This narrative of *Hagar* and sacred water is mentioned in *Hadith*. Surprisingly, almost in the similar way this story of *Hagar* and sacred water is mentioned in the *Bible* in these words:

> *"And Abraham rose up early in the morning, and took bread, and a bottle of water, and gave it unto Ha'-gar, putting it on her shoulder, and the child, [Ishmael] and sent her away: and she departed, and wandered in the wilderness of Beersheba. And the water was spent in the bottle, and she cast the child under one of the shrubs. And she went, and sat her down over against him a good way off, as it were a bowshot: for she said, Let me not see the death of the child. And she sat over against him, and lift up her voice, and wept.*
>
> *And God heard the voice of the lad; and the angel of God called to Ha'-gar out of heaven, and said unto her, What aileth thee, Ha'-gar? fear not; for God hath heard the voice of the lad where he is. Arise, lift up the lad, and hold him in thine hand; for I will make him a great nation. And God opened her eyes, and she saw a well of water; and she went, and filled the bottle with water, and gave the lad drink. And God was with the lad; and he grew, and dwelt in the wilderness, and became an archer. And he dwelt in the wilderness of Paran: and his mother took him a wife out of the land of Egypt"* (Genesis 21:14- 21).

The *English Bibles* says, a *"well of water"* which is quite different from the *Muslim* traditions, because it says '*spring of water*' in *Muslim* traditions. But when I checked the *Hebrew* version of this narrative, it says: באר = *Beayer* means '*Well*' or '*Spring,*' this means it was only translated as a '*well,*' but original *Hebrew* word also means *"Spring,"* or water spring.

7. *'Kaaba' (The Holy Shrine of Mecca):*

According to the *Muslims*, the foundations of '*Kaaba*' were laid by *Adam 6000* years ago. Then the whole building was rebuilt by *Abraham* and his son *Ishmael*. The book of *Genesis* says: *Abraham* went to "בית–אל" = *Beyth-El* (*Beyth* means House and *El* refers to *Elohiym* = *God* in *Hebrew*) '*Kaaba*' which is also known as '*Bait-ulah*' or *Beyth of Elohiym* or *Beyth of Allah*. All *Bibles* printed in *Arabic* language still say *'Bait-ulah' instead of Beyth-el.* The *Bible* further says:

> *"And he [Abraham] removed from thence unto a mountain on the east of Bethel, and pitched his tent, having Bethel on the west, and Hai on the east: and there he builded an altar unto the LORD, and called upon the name of the LORD" (Genesis 12:8).*

Not only *'Kaaba'* is mentioned, but the *'Hajr-al- Aswad' (the black stone),* which was installed on the corner pillar of *Kaaba* is also mentioned in the *Bible,* in these words:

> *"Then Jacob awoke from his sleep and said, "Surely the Lord is in this place, and I did not know it." And he was afraid and said, How awesome is this place! This is none other than the house of God, and this is the gate of heaven." Then Jacob rose early in the morning, and took the stone that he had put at his head, set it up as a pillar, and poured oil on top of it [to anoint it]. And he called the name of that place Beyth'-El: but the name of that city had been Luz previously. "And this stone, which I have set as a pillar, shall be God's house..."*[248]

New King James Version Bible says: And he called the name of that place Beth'-el: but the name of that city had been Luz previously. But the The Living Bible,[249] says "He [Jacob] named the place Bethel (House of God), though the previous name of the nearest village was Luz" (Genesis 28:19).* This means that the name of *Bethel* was not previously called *Luz,* but the name of nearest town was previously called *Luz.*

Some scholars contend that *'Beyth-El'* is a city of *Jerusalem.* According to them, *Jacob* is talking about that city of *Jerusalem* and not the *Kaaba,* (the holy shrine of Muslims). But the strange thing is *Jacob* is talking about *"House of God"* not the *"city of God."* Where *Jacob* put that historical stone, no scholar knows. But as we can see that that stone was installed on the corner pillar of *Kaaba* and it is still there. That historical stone has been touched thousands of times a day, as a ritual of *Hajj.*

---

[248] Please see *Genesis 28:16 - 22* in *New King James Version* Copyright 1982 by *Thomas Nelson & sons Inc.*

[249] Please see *Genesis 28:19* in *The Living Bible, Paraphrased* by *Kenneth N. Taylor,* Copyright © 1971 by *Tyndale House Publishers*

Picture of Holy Shrine Kaaba, (black cubicle) with thousands of people circuiting around. (Photo by M. Arshad)	*Picture of Holy Shrine Kaaba close-up (Photo by Shazia Khan)*

8. *Ishmael will become a great nation:*

God promised *Hagar* about her son *Ishmael*, the *Bible* says:

> "And God heard the voice of the lad; and the angel of God called to Ha'-gar out of heaven, and said unto her, What aileth thee, Ha'-gar? fear not; for God hath heard the voice of the lad where he is. Arise, lift up the lad, and hold him in thine hand; for I will make him a great nation" (Genesis 21:18).

God made a similar promise with *Abraham* and said:

> "And as for Ish'-ma-el, I have heard thee: Behold, I have blessed him, and will make him fruitful, and will multiply him exceedingly; twelve princes shall he beget, and I will make him a great nation."[250]

[That is to say, the descendants of *Ishmael* were to multiply exceedingly and were to become a great nation. If the claims of the *Arabs* to be the descendants of *Ishmael* is false, equally must these *Biblical* prophecies be false. For there is not another nation in the world which claims descent from *Ishmael*. It is only when the claim of the *Arabs* is accepted, that the *Biblical* prophecies relating to *Ishmael* can be proven true; for they all apply to the *Arabs*.

The strongest historical evidence consists of stable national traditions. For thousands of years a people have regarded themselves as descendants of *Ishmael* and no other people in the world so regard themselves. There is

---

[250] Please see *Genesis 17:20*

no better evidence than this. According to the *Bible*, the *Ishmaelites* lived in *Paran*, and *Paran*, according to *Arab* geographers, is the territory extending from *Mecca* to the northern border of *Arabia*. *Paran*, therefore, is part of *Arabia* as certainly as the *Quraish [Biblical Kedar]* are the descendants of *Ishmael*. The divine glory which was to rise from *Paran* was, therefore, to rise from *Arabia*. The *Ishmaelites* had settled in *Arabia* is proved by further evidence from the *Bible*. According to *Genesis*:

> *"And these [are] the names of the sons of Ishmael, by their names, according to their generations: the firstborn of Ishmael, Nebajoth; and Kedar, and Adbeel, and Mibsam, And Mishma, and Dumah, and Massa, Hadar, and Tema, Jetur, Naphish, and Kedemah: These [are] the sons of Ishmael, and these [are] their names, by their towns, and by their castles; twelve princes according to their nations (Genesis 25:13-16).*

1. **Nebajoth:** The first son of *Ishmael*, the territory peopled by his descendants, according to geographers is between 30 and 38 degrees *North*, and 36 to 38 degrees *East*. The descendants of *Nebajoth* occupied the territory between *Palestine* and *Yanbu*, the port of *Madina*.

2. **Kedar:** The second son of *Ishmael*, the literal meaning of *Kedar* is *'of camels,'* which points to their *Arabian* habitation. They are to be found in the territory between *Hijaz* and *Medina*. There are *Arabs* even today who claim descent from *Kedar*.

3. **Adbeel:** The third son of *Ishmael*, according to *Josephus*, the *Adbeels* also lived in *Hijaz* and *Medina*.

4. **Mibsam:** The fourth son of *Ishmael*, no traces are found in ordinary geography books

5. **Mishma:** The fifth son of *Ishmael*, the *Mishmas* are still to be found today in *Arabia*.

6. **Dumah:** The sixth son of *Ishmael*, a well known spot in *Arabia* is still called *Dumah*, and the *Arab* geographers have always traced this name to that of the sixth son of *Ishmael*.

7. **Massa:** The seventh son of *Ishmael*, whose name is to be found intact in a *Yemenite* tribe.

8. **Hadar** *or* **Hadad:** The eighth son of *Ishmael,* after whom, the famous town of *Hudaida* in *Yemen.*

9. **Tema:** The ninth son of *Ishmael,* from *Najd* to the *Hijaz* the territory is called *Tema* and it is all peopled by the descendants of *Tema.*

10. **Jetur:** The tenth son of *Ishmael,* in *Arabic Jetur* is pronounced as *Yatur.* The *Jeturs* can also be traced in *Arabia* and are known as *Jedurs.* The sounds *'J'* and *'Y'* often interchange, as do *'T'* and *'D.'*

11. **Naphish:** The eleventh son of *Ishmael, Rev. C. forster, thinks* that the authority of *Josephus* and the *Old testament* supports the view that the descendants of *Naphish* lived in the wilds of *Arabia.* (Please see *The Historical Geography of Arabia* By *Rev. C. forster).*

12. **Kedemah:** The twelfth son of *Ishmael,* the habitations of the descendants of *Kedemah* is known to lie, according to the famous geographer, *Masudi,* in *Yemen.* The tribe known as *Ashab al-Rass* and mentioned also in the *Qur'an* are the descendants of *Ishmael,* and they were two tribes one called *Kedamah* and the other *Yamin.*

How beautifully this prophecy of the *Bible* has been fulfilled is amazing. Denying of the fulfillment of this prophecy would be as bad as denying the *Bible].*[251]

9) *Arabia* ערב=Arab & Paran of the Bible (the country where *Muhammad* was born):

The divine glory which was to rise from *Paran* = פארן, pronounced in *Hebrew* as *Pa'ran,* but in *Arabic* it is pronounced as Faran, which is still in use by all *Arabs.* Ironically, just like *Ahmad* in *Arabic* is written with A and same word *Ahmad* in *Hebrew* is written with E= *Ehmeth.* When the scribes write פנים =*paniym, (Genesis 32:30),* they used the same *Hebrew* character פ=P or Ph or a sound of F. When they write *Pharez,* or Farez, they used the same *Hebrew* character פ=P or Ph or a sound of F, thus, the word sounds פרץ =*Pharez.* While you can see that it has only three *Hebrew* characters P, R and Z, and there is no H & E. But those scribes who wrote *Faran* they used the same

---

[251] Excerpts from *The Tafseer-e-Kabir,* (The Grand Interpretation) by *Hadhrat Mirza Bashir-ud-Din Mahmood Ahmad the Second Successor* of the *Promised Messiah*

Hebrew character פ=P or Ph or a sound of F, but wrote *Faran* with P and made it sound like *Paran* or *Pa'ran*.

The mere explanation for this behavior is that they did not want to write *Faran* with F sound. So, the people would not associate this name *Faran* with the *Mount Faran* or the *Koh-e-Faran* of *Arabia*, the birthplace of *Muhammad* and *Islam*. First, they try to eradicate all the verses or names about *Muhammad* and *Islam*. Or, they even translated some *Islamic* names like *Muhammad* is translated in *English Bible* as 'altogether lovely.' While anyone who has a basic knowledge of translation knows that a name cannot be translated in the religious scriptures. If that is not true, then why the *English* translators of the *Bible* did not translate *Moses* to *Mosheh* in *Hebrew* which means 'drawing out,' in the *English Bibles*? Why they did not translate *Abraham* which means 'father of nations,' and referred to him that way? They emphatically claim that there is no mention of *Islam* or *Muhammad* in the *Bible*. I remember, an evangelist was saying on a famous *Christian TV* channel that *Jesus* was prophesied throughout the *Bible* from *Genesis* to *Malachi*. But *Muhammad* was not prophesied in any book, he just said, I am here accept me.

The *Bible* talks about *Muhammad* in these words:

> *"The burden upon **Arabia**. In the forest in Arabia shall ye lodge,. ...For they fled from the swords, from the drawn swords, and from the bent bow... For thus hath the Lord said unto me: Within a year... all the glory of Ke'dar shall fail: And...the mighty men of the children of Ke'dar, shall be diminished: for the Lord God of Israel hath spoken it."*[252]

Firstly, *'Arabia'* (modern day Saudi Arabia) is referred in this prophecy, *Muhammad* appeared in *Arabia*. Secondly, the prophecy mentions *'him that fled.'* The migration of *Muhammad* is a historical event of *Islam* it was upon that migration from *Mecca* that the *Muslim* calendar began. Thirdly, *'fled from drawn swords'* conclusively proves the fulfillment of the prophecy of *Muhammad*, when his house was surrounded by his deadly enemies. The enemies stood there with drawn swords, thirsty for his blood. Fourthly, the prophecy states that: *'Within a year...all the glory of Ke'dar will fail...the mighty men of Ke'dar shall be diminished.'* This was fulfilled in the battle of *'Badr,'* which occurred within a year after the migration of *Muhammad*.

---

[252] Please see *Isaiah 21:13-17*

In that battle, *Quraish of Mecca* also known as, *Ke'dar*[253] sustained a crushing defeat, when most of their mighty men died. *Kedar* is the previous name of *Koraish* of *Mecca [Koraishis* are notorious enemies of *Prophet Muhammad.]*[254] In this prophecy not only it talks about *Arabia* the birth country of *Muhammad*, but also it talks about the deadly attack of *Muhammad's* enemies. In this attack *God* saved him miraculously and sent him away from *Mecca* safely.

10) *Mecca,* בכא = *Baca in Hebrew (the city where Muhammad was born):*

The *Old Testament* mentions the *Kaaba* and the pilgrimage in these words:

> *"How lovely is your dwelling place, [Kaaba] O LORD Almighty! My soul yearns, even faints, for the courts of the LORD; my heart and my flesh cry out for the living God... Blessed are those who dwell in your house; they are ever praising you. Selah Blessed are those whose strength is in you, who have set their hearts on pilgrimage. As they pass through the Valley of Baca, [an ancient name of the Valley of Mecca] they make it a place of springs; the autumn rains also cover it with pools. They go from strength to strength, till each appears before God in Zion. Hear my prayer, O LORD God Almighty; listen to me, O God of Jacob. Selah Look upon our shield, O God; look with favor on your anointed one [Your Messiah] Better is one day in your courts than a thousand elsewhere; I would rather be a doorkeeper in the house of my God than dwell in the tents of the wicked."*[255]

Because *Kaaba* was built by *Abraham* that is the reason it was honored by most *Hebrew* prophets. *Jesus* praised *Kaaba* in the above quoted verses. Even *Moses* went to *Paran* or *Mecca*, which is clearly evident from the following verses of the *Old Testament*, please read:

a) *"And afterward [Moses &] the people [of Israel] removed from Hazeroth, and pitched in the wilderness of Paran" (Numbers 12:16).*

---

[253] Please See *The Historical Geography of Arabia*, by *Rev. C. forster*, pp. 244-265
[254] Ibid.
[255] Please see *Psalms 84: 1-10 New International Version* Copyright © 1973-1984 by *International Bible Society*

b) *"And Moses by the commandment of the LORD sent them from the wilderness of Paran: all those men were heads of the children of Israel" (Numbers 13:3).*

As I mentioned earlier that the book of *Psalms* was mainly written by *Jesus* and not by *David*, as we have traditionally believed for centuries. In this passage of *Psalms, Jesus* is telling us that *'How lovely is your dwelling place, O LORD Almighty* (Which he was referring to Kaaba). *Jesus* is praising the place of *Mecca (Baca)* and the Holy Shrine of *Muslims Kaaba,* in the similar way *Prophet Jacob* praised it in *Genesis."[256] Jesus* further says: *'Blessed are those who dwell in your house; they are ever praising you' (Psalms 84:4).* You might know that since *Mecca* and *Kaaba* have been under the care of *Muslims* it has been the place of worship 24 hours a day, and seven days a week. Thousands of *Muslims* from around the world visit this place every day and worship here day and night. But especially in the time of *Hajj*, every year nearly three million people perform *Hajj* (annual pilgrimage to Mecca). As *Jesus* mentioned this pilgrimage in these words:

> *"Blessed are those whose strength is in you, **who have set their hearts on pilgrimage**. As they pass through the Valley of Baca, they make it a place of springs…"[257]*

The *Qur'an* confirms that the ancient name of *Mecca* was *Baca* in these words:

> *"Surely, the first House founded for all mankind is that at Becca, [Baca in Hebrew] abounding in blessings and a guidance for all peoples."[258]*

Some modern *Biblical* scholars have translated the *'Valley of Baca'* as a *'Valley of Weeping'* or *'Valley of lack of streams,'* in the newer *Bibles*. Perhaps, to cover up any association of *Baca* with *Mecca*. Although both translations are correct, as it was told in the *Genesis: "for she [Hagar] said, Let me not see the death of the child. And she sat over against him, and lift up her voice, and wept."[259]*

---

[256] Please see *Genesis 28:16-22, New King James Version'* Copyright 1982 by *Thomas Nelson & sons Inc*

[257] Please see *Psalms 84: 5-6 New International Version* Copyright © 1973-1984 by *International Bible Society*

[258] Please see Qur'an Ch. *Aale-Imran 3: 96-97*

[259] Please see *Genesis 21:16*

Hagar did weep, and the valley did lack water. But I personally think that the names should not be translated, it confuses people. In the newer *Bibles* you will see *Baca* is replaced by *Valley of Weeping*. Please see the following *Bibles, Psalms 84:6*, in *New Living Translation, Robert Young Literal Translation, American Standard Version* and *'Hebrew Names Version' Bibles)*. How blessed is the place *Kaaba* built by *Abraham*, and praised by *Jacob* and *Jesus*.

11) *Ten thousand saints (the biggest victory of Islam in the time of Muhammad):*

King James Version	New Revised Standard Version
"The Lord came from Si'-nai, and rose up from Se'-ir unto them; he shined forth from mount Pa'-ran, and he came with ten thousands of saints: from his right hand went a fiery law for them"(Deuteronomy 33:2).	"The *Lord* came from *Sinai* and dawned from *Seir* upon us; he shone forth from *Mount Paran*. With him were *myriads* of holy ones; at his right, a host of his own" (Deuteronomy 33:2).
The same prophecy you can see in the *Catholic Bibles* as follows:	
"The Lord came from Sinai and dawned on his people from Seir; He shone forth from Mount Paran and advanced from Meribath-kadesh, While at his right hand a fire blazed forth and his wrath devastated the nations" (Deuteronomy 33:2 The *New American Bible* (St. Joseph medium size Edition) Copyright © 1992 by *Catholic Book Publishing Co.* New York.	

As you can see above, the same prophecy in three different versions of the *Bible*. The *King James Version*, the *New Revised Standard Version* and *New American Bible*. How this prophecy has been changed from, *'ten thousands of saints'* of the *King James Version* to *'myriads of holy ones'* of the *New Revised Standard Version*. The Catholic Bible does not even mention any saints at all. From the *'fiery law'* of *King James Version* to *'host of his own'* of the *New Revised Standard Version*. Instead, of *'fiery law'* of *King James Version*, *'a fire blazed forth'* is mentioned in *New American Bible*.

Unfortunately, the *Qur'an* tells us that the *Jews* and the *Christians* will continue to interpolate in the *Bible*. Therefore, the *Qur'an* says:

> *"But on account of their breaking their covenant We cursed them and made their hearts hard; they altered the words from their places and they neglected a portion of what they were reminded of; and you shall always discover treachery in them excepting a few of them; so pardon them and turn away; surely Allah loves those who do good (to others)."*[260]

---

[260] Please see *Qur'an Al-Mai'dah 5:13-14*

But at the same time *God* tells us the glad tiding that whatever these scholars hide and change in the *Bible* the Messenger of *God* has come to clarify those changes. The *Qur'an* says:

> *"O' People of the Book [Jews and Christians] there has come to you Our Messenger who makes clear to you much of what you have kept hidden of the Book [Bible] and forgives many of your faults. There has come to you indeed from Allah a light [Muhammad & Ahmad] and a clear book [Qur'an]."²⁶¹*

Revisiting the topic under discussion, the interpretation of the prophecy of *Moses,* coming from *Sinai* refers to the appearance of *Moses,* and rising up from *Seir* alludes to that of *Jesus.* The prophet who shone forth from *Mount Paran* could be no other than the *Holy Prophet of Arabia, Muhammad.* As *Paran* is one of the ancient names of *Mecca,* the birthplace of the *Holy Founder of Islam Muhammad.* If it was not him, then could you name anyone else who came from *Mount Paran?* Also, at the conquest of *Mecca, Muhammad* came with ten thousands of holy men (*his disciples*) and he had *"a fiery law,"* the *Holy Qur'an.* This incident of *Prophet Muhammad's* coming with ten thousands of his disciples is also mentioned by a book titled *Great Religions of the World.*²⁶²

*12) **Islam** is also mentioned in the Bible (Islam means **Peace**):*

> *"Peace I leave with you, my peace I give unto you: not as the world giveth, give I unto you. Let not your heart be troubled, neither let it be afraid.' (John 14:27).*

In this verse, which is mentioned right after *Jesus* mentioned about the *Holy Ghost (Muhammad). Jesus* said: *'Peace I leave with you' Islam* means *'peace'* this means, *Jesus* said in clear words that *'Islam'* I leave with you. *Jesus* again said *"my peace I give unto you: not as the world giveth, give I unto you."* This means he is giving you *Islam,* not as the world give you, which means *Jesus* not talking about worldly *peace,* he is talking about the religion *Islam. Jesus* also said: *"Let not your heart be troubled, neither let it be afraid.'* Which means do not be afraid to accept *Islam.* This prophecy was also mentioned by *Isaiah* in these words:

> *"For ye shall go out with joy, and be led forth with peace the mountains and the hills shall break forth before you into singing,*

---

²⁶¹ Please see Qur'an *Al-Mai'dah 5:15-16*
²⁶² *Great Religions of the World* Copyright © 1978 by *National Geographic Society* ISBN # 087044-140-X page # 236.

and all the trees of the field shall clap their hands"(Isaiah 55:12).

The proof of this prophecy is that, all those countries, where *Jesus* personally preached, while he was going to the *'lost tribes of Israel,'* through the *Silk route. Jesus* told them about *Muhammad* and *Islam* in clear words. All those countries *Syria, Iraq, Iran, Afghanistan* and *Kashmir* became *Muslim* within a short period of time, right after the dawn of *Islam*. Some *Christian* friends told me that I have twisted the words to fit these verses on *Muhammad* and *Islam*. While these verses have nothing to do with *Muhammad* and *Islam*. But the interesting part is that when *Christian* scholars present the prophecies of the *Old Testament* to the *Jewish* scholars to prove that these prophecies were fulfilled in *Jesus. The Jewish* scholars always respond in the similar way that *Christians* have twisted the words to fit these verses on *Jesus* while these prophecies have nothing to do with *Jesus*.

Why do Muslims kill other Muslims?

Most of the *Christians* I have conversed within the last 20 years or so, they always ask me that why all the *Muslims* of the world fighting and killing each other? Additionally, they say that you will never hear *Christians* fighting or killing each other. I usually smile at this naïve question and ask them very nicely have you ever studied the history of the early churches? If we glance at the history of the *Christianity*, we see that there were dozens of sects existed around first, second and third centuries. There were some who were called *Ebionites* who were the most pure form of *Christianity*, who believed in one *God* and obeyed the *Law of Moses*. Then there were some who were the followers of *St. Paul* who portrayed *Jesus* as a god and rejected the *Law of Moses*.

Around the second century when the followers of *St. Paul* seems to be growing larger and larger in number a sect called *Gnostics* came into existence. The word *Gnostics* came from a *Greek* word γν□σις = *Gnosis*, which means *'inner knowledge'* or *'hidden knowledge.'* The question arises that what inner knowledge or hidden knowledge they possessed that they named their sect *Gnostics*? If you study them little more you would come to know that this sect was the one who had found out the truth about *Jesus*. That he was just a messenger not a god as the other sects were portraying *Jesus*, they also found out that he did not die on the cross, he was married just like all other prophets and regular people were married. They also knew that he did not go to heaven (bodily). How do we know all of this? Almost all the scrolls have been discovered anywhere in *Israel, Egypt, Syria* etc. they all elucidate these topics. Apparently, when they feared that all the true *Gospels* will be eradicated by the *Catholic Church*, they put their lives in danger and concealed these documents, hoping to be found by the *Christians* of the later times when the persecution would have seized.

This is the reason that around the time of the third century, as soon as *Christianity* gained power through the support of the *Emperor Constantine*, they started persecuting those who did not believe on the *Nicene Creed*. The poignant part is that those who believed in one *God* and did not partake in any sinful act were severely persecuted and they were forced to believe in *Trinity, Jesus* as god and all the misconceptions we see today. Thousands of those innocent *Christians* were killed and their holy book which was *Bible* indeed were burnt or destroyed. Then in 391 C.E. *Theodosius* the heir of *Constantine* outlawed all religions. This means that not only the *Christians* killed the *Christians* but the *Christians* killed all the followers of all other religions in that region. In this wholesale slaughter of the innocent people, the followers of *Mithras, Dionysus, Osiris, Apollonius, Simon Magus* and *Isis* all were killed, their holy books were burnt and their churches were either converted into the *Christian* churches or destroyed. After the *Gnostics* it was the turn of the *Cathars* (a righteous sect of *Christianity*) who became the target in the 13th century. Thousands of *Cathars* were killed by the *Christian* dominants of that time.

Then in *1478 Catholic Monarchs Ferdinand II* of *Aragon* and *Isabella I* of *Castile*, started the inquisition in *Spain* which is known in the history as the *"Spanish Inquisition."* Thousands of *Jews* & *Muslims* were forced to convert to *Christianity*. Those who did not want to be converted were either killed or forced to leave the country. Those *Jews* who were compelled to convert to *Christian*ity, were called *"Maranos,"* which means *'pigs.'* This means that even those innocent *Jewish* people, who were forced to become Christians, were still detested by the *Christians* of that era and were called pigs. These innocent *Jews* and *Muslims* were forced to eat pork publicly to prove that they are not surreptitiously practicing their previous religion.

Then in *1606* a group of *Christians* in *England* disagreed with the *Church of England*. They were also severely persecuted and thousands of *Protestants* were killed. This is the reason pilgrims came to *America*. I do not want to go into the details, and I am not mentioning all of this to accuse anyone. All I am trying to do is to draw your attention to the fact that every religion which gained power, always tried to convert all minorities to their religion, even if they had to use coercion. In fact, throughout the history of the *Christianity*, there always have been some minorities who were called heretics because they differ with the *Orthodox Church* and they have been persecuted by the dominants of that time. What is the difference between the *Muslims* killing the *Muslims* or the *Christians* killing the *Christians*? The only difference is that the *Muslims* are killing now and the *Christians* killed in the past. There is no other difference or reason. All the dominant religions always try to convert people by force, doesn't matter if they were *Muslims, Christians* or others. But one thing we all have to remember that all of this persecution and killings is the product of ignorance and nothing more. It has nothing to do with the teachings of that religion. Why always *Islam* is to blame? Simply because the *Christians* are done with their persecutions, long ago, while the *Muslims* are still enjoying persecuting other religions.

24. Jesus in the Qur'an

The picture of *Jesus* presented in the *Bible*, is not a pretty picture, rather, it's a grotesque image if you look at it sincerely. *Christians* regard *Jesus* as *Holy, Perfect, Righteous* and a *true Messiah*. *Muslims* also regard *Jesus* as *Holy, Perfect, Righteous*, and a true *Messiah*, according to the teachings of the *Holy Qur'an*. Let's have a fair mind, and compare the teachings of the holy *Bible* and the *Holy Qur'an* about *Jesus*, and see which one of these two books of *God* is really glorifying *Jesus*.

Jesus in the Bible		*Jesus in the Qur'an*
1) Descendant of Evildoers:		
Matthew 1:1 talks about the grandparents of *Jesus*. Beside many people, it shows three people, 1) *King David* (Matthew 1:6) 2) *Judah*, (Matthew 1:3) 3) *Ra'-hab* or *Ra'-chab* (Matthew 1:5) According to the *Old Testament*, *King David* committed adultery with *Beth-she'-ba*, wife of *Uriah* and had an illegitimate son name *Solomon*. In other words, prophet *David* was an adulterer and his son *Solomon* was an illegitimate son, and *Jesus* was the descendant of that adulterer & illegitimate son. *(2 Samuel 11:3-5)*, (God forbid). *Judah*, who committed adultery with his *daughter-in-law* and had an illegitimate son name *Pha'-rez*, an ancestor of *Jesus*. *(Genesis 38:16)*. *Ra'-hab* or *Ra'-chab* was a harlot (prostitute), *(Joshua2: 1)*. *Jesus* was the descendant of that prostitute (God forbid).	a) b)	The *Qur'an* says: *"Mary's father was not a wicked man, nor was her mother an unchaste woman"* *(Maryam 19:28-29)*. The *Qur'an* also says: *"Mary mother of Jesus was a **righteous** woman'"* (Al- Maidah 5:75-76).
The *Bible* says: *"The seed of evildoers shall never be renowned"* (Isaiah 14:20). According to the genealogy of *Jesus*, he was the descendant of evil doers (King David) and he was the descendant of an illegitimate man (Solomon). (God forbid) *Bible* also says: *"A bastard shall not enter into the congregation of the Lord; even to his tenth generation..."* (Deuteronomy 23:2).	c)	The *Qur'an* says: *"Mary, Allah has made you high in character and purified you, and chosen you from among all the women of your time"* (Al-Imran 3:42-43).

341

2) *Disobedient to his Mother*		
a)	According to *Matthew* 12:46: *Mary* mother of *Jesus* did not accept *Jesus* as a *Messiah* that's the reason *Jesus* said: *"Who is my mother? Who is my brother? Whosoever shall do the will of my father... is my brother, and sister, and mother."* This implies that his mother was not the believer. This is very strange that the angel of *God* told *Mary*: *"therefore also that holy thing which shall be born of thee shall be called the Son of God" (Luke 1:35).* But even after learning from the angel of *God*, *Mary* still did not believe in her son.	a)	The *Qur'an* says: *"Mary, who guarded her chastity and We sent Our Word to her, and she fulfilled the words of her Lord and His Books and (Mary) was one of the obedient" (Al-Tahrim 66:12-13).* It denotes that *Mary* was a believer
b)	The *Bible* portrays *Jesus*, as a cruel and rebellious towards his mother, when she told him *"they have no wine"*. *Jesus* said to his mother, ***"Woman, what have I to do with thee?" (John 2:4).* According to *Romans 1:30-32*, *"Disobedient to parents... are worthy of death."* Thus, *Jesus* becomes worthy of death according to his own *Bible*.	b)	According to the *Qur'an:* *"Jesus said Allah has made me obedient towards my mother and I am not harsh and bad mannered" (Maryam 19:32-33).*
3) *Man of bad character* (God forbid)		
	According to the *Bible*: *Jesus* had a bad character (God forbid). *Gospel of Luke* says, **a)** *"A woman, who was a harlot (prostitute) she kissed Jesus' feet washed them with her tears, put oil on them and wiped them with her hair" (Luke 7:37 to 50).* **b)** Same women *"kept on kissing Jesus' feet and would not stop" (Luke 7:45). "The Pharisee... he said to himself that if he* [Jesus] *were a prophet, would have known, who and what manner woman this is who is touching him" (Luke 7:39).* The heading in *New International Version* says: *"Jesus Anointed by a Sinful Woman"* Could any righteous be anointed by a sinner?		The *Qur'an* says: *"And We bestowed upon him [Abraham]... And We guided Zachariah and John and Jesus and Elias; each one of them was of the righteous..." (Al-Anam 6: 83 to 88).*

4) Cursing people (God forbid)		
a)	The *Bible* says *"do not curs"* *(Romans 12:14)*. But *Jesus* cursed prevalently. *"Evil and adulterous generation"* (Matthew 12:39). *"Ye serpents, ye generation of vipers"* (Matthew 23:33). *Jesus* said: *"If you say 'you fools' you'll be in danger of hell fire" (Matthew 5:22).* Then he turns around and calls them *"you fools"* in (Matthew 23:17); (Matthew 23:19); (Luke 11:40) and (Luke 24:25).	a)	The *Quran* says: *"Jesus was only a servant of Ours, on whom we presented Our favor, and We made him an **example** for the children of Israel" (Al-Zukhruf 43:20).* But according to the verses on the left he was not a good example.
b)	What would you think of a man who came to fulfill the prophecies of thieves and robbers? Would you not think that he would be a bigger thief and robber, and a bad person? According to the *Bible Jesus* fulfilled 35 prophecies of many thieves and robbers, such as *Abraham, Jacob, King David, Isaiah, Jeremiah* and *Moses. Jesus* said: *"All that ever came before me are thieves and robbers…" (John 10:8).* But on the other hand, *Jesus said:* *"Do not think I have come to destroy the law or the prophets…but to fulfill"* (Matthew 5:17).	b)	*Qur'an* not only recognizes all the prophets before *Muhammad,* but it requires all *Muslims* to honor all prophets, and believe in them as true prophets in order to become *Muslim.* Thus, the *Qur'an* says: *"Say ye: 'We believe in Allah and what has been revealed to us, and what was revealed to Abraham and Ishmael, and Isaac, and Jacob and his children, and what was given to Moses and Jesus, and what was given to all other Prophets from their Lord. We make no difference between any of them; and to Him we submit ourselves"* *(Al-Baqara 2:136-137).*

5) Prophecies did not fulfill (God forbid)		
Jesus said: a) *"There be some of them that stand here, which shall not taste of death till they have seen the kingdom of God come with power" (Mark 9:1).* It is imperative to mention here that because of this prophecy, followers of *Jesus* did not feel any urgency to write the *Bible*, since they thought *Jesus* would come back soon. But when *Jesus* did not come back, and over thirty years had passed and some of the most devout followers of *Jesus* had died, then they started to write *Bible*. In about 65 C.E. is believed to be the time by some scholars, that the first gospel, Mark, was written. *Jesus* said: b) *"...verily I say unto you, There shall not be left here one **stone** upon another, that shall not be thrown down" (Matthew 24: 2).* If you look at the *Jewish* sacred *wailing wall*, or *Western Wall*, the whole wall is intact, thus it appears that this prophecy did not fulfill entirely. (God forbid)		The *Qur'an* says: *"Allah reveals not His secrets to anyone, except to him whom He chooses from among His Messengers" (Al-Jinn 72:28).* Which means if *Jesus* is the true messenger of *God* (which he is), then what ever he prophesied should have come true. Since it was not him who prophesied, but it was *God* who revealed to him.
Jesus told the thief on the cross: c) *"Today you will be with me in paradise" (Luke 23:43).* But according to the *Christian* doctrine, *Jesus* did not go to *Paradise* that day instead; He went to hell for three days. (God forbid)		

	Jesus told *Peter*: d) *"I will give you the keys of the kingdom of heaven" (Matthew 16:19).* But four verses later called him *Satan*, and said *"you are an offence unto me" (Matthew 16:23). Peter* also showed his unfaithfulness with *Jesus* when he cursed him to save his own skin. The *Bible says:* *"Then began he [Peter] to curse and to swear, saying, I know not the man" (Matthew 26: 74).*		
	Jesus said: e) *"Other sheep I have, which are not of this fold: them also I must bring, and they shall hear my voice; and there shall be one fold, and one shepherd" (John 10:16).* But according to the *Christian* doctrine, *Jesus* went to heaven after crucifixion, and did not go looking for the lost tribes of *Israel* as he promised.		
	Jesus told *Mary Magdalene*: f) *"Do not touch me; for I am not yet ascended to my father" (John 20:17).* If she could not touch him while he was on earth, then how she could have touched him when he would have gone to his father? Was *Jesus* planning to take *Mary Magdalene* bodily to heaven?		
6) Jesus was accursed (God forbid)			
a)	*"Christ…being made a curse for us"* (Galatians 3:13). On the other hand, the *Bible* also says: *"No man speaking by the Holy Spirit call Jesus accursed" (1Corinthians 12:3).*	a)	The *Qur'an* says: *"His name shall be Messiah, Jesus son of Mary,* **honored** *in this world and in the hereafter" (Al-Imran 3:46).*

b)		b)	
	"For he that is hanged is accursed of God" (Deuteronomy 21:23). Let us review all these verses of the *Bible*, we find: 1. *Jesus* was the descendant of evildoers (Prostitutes, adulterers) 2. *Jesus* was born in a generation of illegitimate people (being the son of Solomon) (God forbid). 3. Disobedient to his mother (Becomes worthy of death) 4. Man of bad character (Letting a prostitute to kiss his feet) 5. Cursing people frequently 6. Prophesies did not fulfill (Makes him a false Messiah & worthy of death by *Old Testament* (Deuteronomy 13:5)). 7. Being an accursed, becomes rejected from *God's* heaven, a false messiah and again worthy of death by *Old Testament*. After reading the above comparison, can we construe that the *Bible* was written by the people who were sincerely writing to glorify *Jesus*? Is this a pretty picture? On the other hand, read the verses of the *Qur'an* and see for yourself, if the *Qur'an* is against *Jesus* and his mother, and is trying to give them a bad name? Now my question is, if the *Qur'an* is glorifying *Jesus* and his mother, then why the *Christians* do not respect *Qur'an* as much as they should. As you can see, the *Qur'an* is not against your *Jesus*, and *Christianity*?		The *Qur'an* says: *"[The Jews allege]We did kill the Messiah, Jesus son of Mary, the messenger of Allah; whereas they slew him not, nor did they crucify him, but he was made to appear to them like one crucified to death; and those who have differed in the matter [of his having been taken down alive from the cross] are certainly in a state of doubt concerning it, they have no definite knowledge about it, but only follow a doubt; they certainly did not kill him; indeed, Allah exalted him to Himself..."* (*Al-Nisa 4:157-159*).

This is the reason *Bible* says that *Jesus* was handed over to the authorities by the *Jews* to be crucified, *"because he was an evildoer" (John 18:30 NKJV)*. But the *Qur'an* totally denies these charges against *Jesus*, and calls him a holy, righteous and a humble prophet. This is the fact which was prophesied by *Jesus* about the *Holy Ghost* that *"He shall glorify me: for he shall receive of mine, and shall shew it unto you"* (John 16:14). I apologize to my readers, if I mentioned anything which offended them. The purpose of the above comparison is not to offend my brothers and sisters in *Christ*; but to glorify *Jesus*.

Jesus in the Qur'an

This is unfortunate, that some of the *Scribes of the Bible,* in order to glorify *Jesus* they degraded other prophets and many messengers of *God.* I do not believe this is the way people should glorify their messengers of *God* by throwing trash on other messengers of *God.* But the early *Christians* especially around the time of *Constantine* had no choice but to present him as a god, because the theory of a human accursed messiah would not work. Therefore, they started saying that *Jesus* was son of *God* some even said he was *God* himself (God forbid). Then the early *Christians* had another unusual task to handle. How could they prove that their messiah is really a god and not a human? They started to scribe demeaning things about all other prophets; so they can explain that their messiah is way better than any other human being. *a) Abraham* was called liar by them.

Would *God* make a liar his friend and also call him righteous? But unfortunately, some one wrote in *Genesis* that he lied about his wife and told the King of *Egypt* that *Sarah* was his sister so he could get some conveniences in *Egypt.* (God forbid). *b) Bible* says about *David,* when *Samuel* anointed him then *'The 'Spirit of the Lord' came upon David from that day forward'* (1Samuel 16:13). The *Bible* also says, *David* was adulterer and rapist, who raped his neighbor's wife and got her husband killed. How could *Bible* testify about *David* that *'The 'Spirit of the Lord' was on David*? This means he was beloved of *God,* and at the same time he was a murderer, rapist and adulterer? (God forbid) Would *God* love a sinner who had broken most of the *Ten Commandments*? If you remember what the *Bible* says about the *Second Coming of Christ*:

1. *He shall bring all things to your remembrance (John 14:26).*

2. *He shall reprove the world of sin (John 16:8).*

3. *But the "Spirit of truth" is come he will guide you into all truth (John 16: 13).*

4. He shall show you things to come (John 16: 13).

5. He shall glorify me (John 16:14).

Now it is totally up to you, one may believe what the *Qur'an* says that all the prophets were righteous, and perfect in their generations. Then this belief will lead you to *Jesus* as a descendant of righteous people. Or you may believe the *Bible* that all the prophets were sinners, rapist adulterers, murderers and liars and *Jesus* was the descendant of those sinners. After *God* sent his messengers, *Muhammad* and *Ahmad* and their book *Qur'an*, He did not give you much choice. As the Qur'an emphatically claims:

> "O' People of the Book [Jews and Christians] there has come to you Our Messenger who makes clear to you much of what you have kept hidden of the Book [Bible] and forgives many of your faults. There has come to you indeed from Allah a light [Muhammad & Ahmad] and a clear book [Qur'an]" (Al-Mai'dah 5:15-16).

You can catch the work of those people (whoever changed the Bible) by catching the contradictions in the *Bible*. This is not possible that *God* would tell one thing to someone and forget that and then say something totally different to another prophet. The later scribes are the one who are fully responsible for all the contradictions in the *Bible* not *God*. This is the reason that *Jesus* has become a mystery. Because the people who came much later tried to depict him as *God* and in the process they lost the real *Jesus*. Please read the following:

Jesus: A Mystery?

1. What was the real name of *Jesus*? No one knows for sure, *Arabic* and *Urdu* Bibles say *Yesu*, *Hebrew* Bible say *Joshua* and *Greek* Bible say *Iesous* {ee-ay-sooce'}. 2,000 years old scriptures found in *Buddhist* monastery talks about a *mathea (messiah* or messiah) who was crucified and the name mentioned is *Isa. Hindus'* holy book name *Purana*, talks about a man who survived a cruel punishment (crucifixion) and came to *India*, 2000 years ago his name is mentioned *"Isa." Qur'an* calls *Jesus "Isa."*

2. Did he die on the cross or not? The *Jews* assert that they killed *Jesus* on the cross and thus, proved from the *Bible* that he was accursed, liar and not the true messiah. *Christians* however, say that he did die on the cross but he died voluntarily to pay for our sins. Mainstream *Muslims* believe that when *Romans* came to arrest *Jesus, God* made *Judas Iscariot's* face look like *Jesus* and they crucified him not *Jesus*. *Ahmadis* say that *Jesus* was put on the cross, but he was fainted and appear to be dead but he survived miraculously. As he predicted his survival in the prophecy about the sign of *Jonah*, (Matthew 12:38).

3. When *Jesus* was born? Was *Jesus* born according to *Matthew 2:1* around King *Herod's* time, while *King Herod* died 4BC? Or *Jesus* was born according to *Luke 2:2-4* in the time of *Cyrenius* 4C.E. almost 10 years after what *Matthew* reported? Was *Jesus* 30 years old when he started his ministry or 40 years old?

4. Was *Jesus* god or a man? (*Jesus* prayed, ate, drank like regular people)

5. Was *Jesus* the son of god? (*Jesus* called himself son of man 84 times in the four Gospels).

6. Did *Jesus* go to the heaven with his body or not? ('... *that flesh and blood cannot inherit the kingdom of God' (1 Corinthians 15:50)*. Most *Bibles* older than thirty years do not have the verse *Jesus* went to heaven.

7. Did he show miracles or not? *Jesus* denied all the miracles pasted on him by the later scribes by saying:

   "...*there shall no sign be given to it, but the sign of the prophet Jonas*" *(Matthew 12:38)*. *Jesus* also said:

   '*He that believeth on me, the works that I do shall he do also; and greater works than these shall he do...*' *(John 14:12)*.

   According to this verse if you believe in *Jesus* you can walk on water, bring dead people to life and heel the blinds. Can anyone in the whole *Christian* world do that? If not, then either *Jesus* did not do these miracles literally, as *Christians* believe or *Jesus* was lying about that (God forbid).

349

8. Was he born fatherless? Why the *Gospels* of *Matthew* & *Luke* show his father & forefathers? Did you know that *Krishna, Buddha, Osiris, Dionysus* & many more were also born without father? *Buddha* came 500 years before *Jesus*, *Krishna* came 2000 years before *Jesus*, it is not possible that they would have adopted the *Christian* idea. They blame *Christians* for plagiarizing and to adopt their articles of faith as *Christian* articles of faith.

9. Where was *Jesus* between the ages of 12 to 29?

10. Did *Jesus* have brothers and sisters? *Gospel* of *Mark* says he did (Mark 6:3).

11. Was *Jesus* married and had children? *Dead Sea Scrolls* say *Jesus* was married to *Mary Magdalene* and had three children.

12. Was *Jesus Palestinian Arab*, a *Nazarene*, or from *Bethlehem*, white, *Black* or *Chinese*? If *Jesus* was born in *Bethlehem* according to *Matthew 2:1*, then why he was known all his life as *Jesus of Nazareth*?

13. Did *Judah* betray *Jesus* or not? Gospel of *Judah* says he did not betray *Jesus*.

14. Was *Jesus* born on *December 25th* or some other month?

15. Did *Jesus* rise from the dead the 3rd day or one and a half day? He was crucified *Friday* afternoon. From *Friday* afternoon to *Saturday* afternoon one day (24 hours) from *Saturday* afternoon to *Sunday* early in the morning (Mark 16:2). This makes it only one and a half day not the 3rd day.

16. Did *Jesus* advise his disciples to go to *all nations* (Matthew 28:19). Or did he tell them to *stay in Jerusalem*? (Luke 24:49 and Acts 1:4).

17. Did *Jesus* go up the Mountain to deliver the sermon (Matthew 5:1) or as the *Gospel* of *Luke* mentions *Jesus* went down the mountain to deliver the sermon (Luke 6:17).

18. Everybody knows *Jesus* had twelve disciples, but no one knows who were they since, *Mark* & *Luke* the Gospels writers are not even mentioned in the list of disciples in Matthew 10:2-4, Mark

3:16-19 & Luke 6:13-16. Who really wrote the gospels and when?

19. Did *Jesus* deliver a sermon of 110 accounts of the *Lord's Prayer* on the mountain top as *Matthews* recorded? Or did he deliver just over 30 accounts on a leveled ground according to *Luke*?

20. Did *Jesus* go to paradise on the day of his crucifixion (Luke 23:43). Or did he go to hell according to the book of *Revelation 1:18*?

21. Did *Jesus* bring final book? Why did he say *"I have yet many things to say unto you but you cannot bear them now"* (John 16:12).

22. Did *Jesus* guide *Christians* into all truth? Why did he say that the *Holy Spirit* will guide you into all truth?

23. When *John the Baptist* said, *"I indeed baptize you with water... he [Jesus] shall baptize you with the Holy Ghost and with fire" (Luke 3:16).* Then why *Jesus* still baptized people with water? And even today *Christians* all over the world baptize with water. Why *Jesus* did not fulfill the prophecy of *John the Baptist*?

24. The prophecy of *Isaiah* says:

"Therefore the Lord himself shall give you a sign; Behold, a virgin shall conceive, and bear a son, and shall call his name Immanuel" (Isaiah 7:14).

But how the angel forgot the prophecy of *Isaiah* and said to *Mary* it says in *Luke*

"And the angel said unto her, thou shalt conceive in thy womb, and bring forth a son, and shalt call his name JESUS" (Luke 1:30-31).

Because of all these mysteries, many faithful *Christians* have left *Christianity* and have become atheists. *Mr. Timothy Freke and Peter Gandy* wrote a book a few years ago, and in this book they emphatically claimed that *Jesus* of the *Bible* never existed. They even ask on the book Cover, "WAS THE ORIGINAL JESUS" A PAGAN GOD? Because of the misconceptions of *Christianity*, these two authors wrote a book which will cause more confusion in *Christianity*. They write in the dust cover leaflet:

"This astonishing book completely undermines the traditional history of Christianity that has been perpetuated for centuries by the church. Drawing on the cutting edge of modern scholarship, authors Tim Freke and Peter Gandy present overwhelming evidence that the Jesus of the New Testament is a mythical figure.

Far from being eyewitness accounts, as is traditionally held, the Gospels are actually Jewish adaptations of ancient Pagan myths of the dying and resurrecting godman Osiris-Dionysus. The supernatural story of Jesus is not the history of a miraculous Messiah, but a carefully crafted spiritual allegory designed to guide initiates on a journey of mystical discovery."[263]

Even the right hand of *Mr. Billy Graham; Mr. Charles Templeton*, left *Christianity* and wrote a book titled *Farewell to God: My Reasons for Rejecting the Christian Faith.* Did you know that the most people who become atheists come from *Christianity*? I am talking about leaving their birth religion; I am not talking about the people who are born atheists. In this regards unfortunately, *Christianity* is the leading religion, who loses its followers more than any religion of the world.

If all the clues I have presented under the heading *"Clues in the Bible,"* make sense then I would encourage *Hollywood* directors especially, *Mr. James Cameron* who was courageous enough to put all the traditions behind and made the movie, *"The Aquarian Gospel."* To make a movie based on facts, how *Jesus* was arrested, how he survived miraculously, how he met his disciples in secret, then left *Israel* to go to the lost sheep of the house of *Israel,* how he was accepted by the lost sheep in *Kashmir* and finally died like a king. Instead of making a movie like *"The passion of the Christ,"* by *Mr. Mel Gibson* which was made on the misunderstanding of the scriptures.

---

[263] Please see the inner leaflet of *The Jesus Mysteries*, by *Timothy Freke* and *Peter Gandy,* Published by *Harmony Books* New York, ISBN# 0-609-60581-X

Which of the Following Statements are we supposed to follow?

	(King James Version & common Christian beliefs)	(Taken from King James Version)
1	Law is **holy** (Romans 7:12).	*Law is **curse*** (Galatians 3:13).
2	Jesus was made **accursed** (Galatians 3:13).	*Jesus was **not accursed*** (I Corinthians 12:3).
3	**Love** your wife (Colossians 3:19).	*Hate your wife* (Luke 14:26).
4	**Honor** your mother and father (Luke 18:20).	*Hate your mother and father* (Luke 14:26).
5	A man is justified by **faith** not by deeds (Galatians 2:16).	*A man is justified by **deeds** and not by faith alone.* (James 2:24).
6	Jesus was the only one, who was born without a father (A common Christian belief).	*"Mel-Chis'-e-dec was born without father & mother, no ancestry, no beginning of his days, no end of his life"* (Hebrews 7:3) [Does it qualify him to be the God?]
7	Jesus, only begotten son of God (John 3:16).	David, begotten son of God (Psalms 2:7). Since David was the First begotten son of God, we can call him only Begotten son of God of his time.
8	Jesus was the only "PERFECT" man ever. (A common Christian belief. But All four Gospels, Matthew, Mark, Luke and John never called Jesus "Perfect").	God called Job "PERFECT" 4 times in his book (Job 1:1 - 1:8 - 2:3 - 8:20). Abraham was "PERFECT" (Genesis 17:1). Noah was "PERFECT" (Genesis 6:9). Asa was Perfect (1King 15:14)

9	Jesus was the only "Righteous" man ever. All other	a) *Mel-chis'-e-dec was "King of Righteousness"* (Hebrews 7:2).
	Messengers of God were sinners (God forbid).	b) *Zacha-ri'-as and his wife both were "Righteous"*
	(A common Christian belief).	(Luke 1:6).
		c) *Simon was "Righteous"* (Luke 2:25).
		d) *Abel was "Righteous"* (Hebrew 11:4).
10	Jesus died for our sins (1Corinthians 15:3).	*"Father shall not die for children, neither shall the children die for the father, but every man shall die for his own sin."*
	(A common Christian belief)	(2Chronicles 25:4), (Deuteronomy 24:16),
		(Jeremiah 31:30), (Ezekiel18:20) & (2Kings 14:6).
11	Jesus came for the whole world.	Jesus said *" I am not sent but unto the lost sheep of*
	(A common Christian belief).	*the house of Israel"* (Matthew 15:24)
12	Jesus the "KING OF PEACE."	Jesus said *" Think not that I am come to send peace on earth: I came not to send peace, but a sword"*
	(a common Christian belief)	(Matthew 10:34).
	[Jesus was never called King of Peace in the entire Bible. Instead, Melchisedec was called King of Peace (Hebrews 7:2)]	Jesus said *"Sell your garments and buy a sword"*
		(Luke 22:36).
13	Jesus descendant of **Solomon,** who was son of David	Jesus descendant of **Nathan** who was son of David (Luke 3:31).
	(Matthew 1:6).	
	(Solomon and Nathan both were sons of David then how could Jesus be son of 2 brothers at the same time?)	

14	Mary's husband Joseph was son of Jacob (Matthew 1:16).	Mary's husband Joseph was son of He'-Li (Luke 3:23).
15	Jesus was born 40 generations after Abraham. (Matthew 1:2 to 16).	Jesus was born 55 generations after Abraham (Luke 3:23 to 34).
16	Father, Son and Holy Ghost [Trinity] (Matthew 28:19).	*One God and there is none, but He.* (Mark 12:32).
17	Jesus was the only man ever, who walked on water (A common Christian belief).	Elisha walked on water (2Kings 2:14).
18	Elijah went up to heaven in a chariot of fire and horses of fire (2 Kings 2:1).	No man has ascended up to heaven, but he that cometh down from heaven, even the son of man... (John 3:13).
19	Jesus [bodily] went to heaven (Mark 16:19).	*Flesh and blood cannot inherit in the kingdom of God* (1Corinthians 15:50).
20	God told Adam, if you eat from this tree, you'll surely die (Genesis 2:17).	On the contrary, Satan told Adam, if you eat from this tree you'll never die. Adam ate that fruit and he did not die (Genesis 3:4).
21	*Jacob said I have seen God face to face* (Genesis 32:30). *And the LORD spake unto Moses face to face, as a man speaketh unto his friend"* (Exodus 33:11).	*No man hath seen God at any time (John 1:18)* *No man can see God and live* (Exodus 33:20).
22	Judah slept with his daughter-in-law (God Forbid) (Genesis 38:16-18)	If you sleep with your daughter-in-law you should be put to death. (Leviticus 20:12) [Instead, God blessed him and made him a Prophet and a father of all the Jews]
23	Man shall live 120 years (Genesis 6:3)	Noah lived 950 years (Genesis 9:29)

These contradictions are apparently caused by the people who came many years after *Jesus* and tried to include their own beliefs in the *Bible*. Ironically, the *Jews* and the *Christians* who consider the *Qur'an* not from God has no contradictions in it at all. Not only that, the *Qur'an* emphatically declares it in these words:

> "*Will they not, then, try to understand this Qur'an? Had it issued from any but God, they would surely have found in it many an inner contradiction!*" *(Al-Nisa 4:82-83).*

And the book (Bible) the *Jews* and the *Christians* consider from *God* is in front of you. But in no case I am implying that the *Bible* is not from *God*, but all I mean is that the *Jews* & the *Christians* should think before they contend the authenticity of the *Qur'an*.

List of a few books written Jesus in India

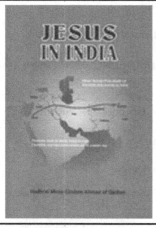	
1. **Jesus in India** by *Hadhrat Mirza Ghulam Ahmad* of *Qadian* (the Second Coming of Jesus Christ Published in 1908). Printed in U.K. at: Raqeem Press Tilford, Surrey.	2. **Jesus lived in India** by Holger Kersten (Germany, Published in 1984, Reprint 1986, 1987, 1993, 2002) ISBN: 0906540909 Amazon.com)
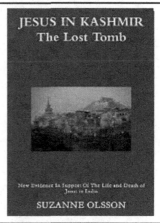	
3. **Roza Bal: the tomb of Jesus** by Ms Suzanne Olsson & Dr. Fida Hassnain (Amazon.com)	4. Jesus in Kashmir The Lost Tomb by Ms Suzanne Olsson, (Amazon.com)

5. **Jesus in India** by James W. Deardorff Published by International Scholars Press, 2002. ISBN # <u>1883255368</u>

6. **Jesus of India** by Maury Lee

7. **Jesus in Heaven on Earth** by Khwaja Nazir Ahmad

8. **Jesus tomb in India** by Pappas Paul C.

9. **The Unknown life of Jesus Christ** by Nicholai Notovitch

10. **Jesus & Moses are buried in India** Birthplace of Abraham and the Hebrews By Gene D. Matlock

11. **Saving the Savior** by AbuBakr Ben Ishmael Salahuddin

12. **Christ in Kashmir** by Aziz Kashmiri

13. **Jesus died in Kashmir** by A. Faber Kaiser

Summary

The reason that I have mentioned all the misconceptions of the Christianity, because all the Christians I have talk to claim that they are following exactly the teachings of Jesus; Why do we need another messiah? The reason I have mentioned all those sins of many Christians because they say we are living according to the Bible, we will go straight up to the heavens. Then why do we need to change our lives & follow 2nd Coming of Christ? The reason, I have mentioned all the contradictions and interpolations in the Bible, not to upset my Jewish and Christian brothers and sisters, but to clear their minds about the necessity of a flawless book (Qur'an), because all the Christians unanimously claim that our Bible is a flawless book; why do we need another book or Qur'an for that matter? The reason I have mentioned all the wars and killings by Christian countries because most Christians honestly believe that they are the most peaceful people on earth and all Muslims are the culprits, who are destroying the world's peace.

What's the reason to mention all of this? Not to wreak havoc in the world but to invite very humbly the whole world to the Messiah (Ahmad) who has been long awaited by the whole world by many different names. Such as, 'Kalki Autar,'by Hindus, this means the final visit of god Vishnu, which corresponds to the final visit of World Savior or Messiah. 2nd Coming of Lord Krishna, 2nd Coming of Buddha, Maharaja by Sikhs, Mashiyekh or Messiah awaited by the Jews. Christ or Messiah by the Christians and Mahdi (guided one by God) or Masih or Messiah by Muslims. The whole world is complaining about the turmoil, destruction, immorality, discord, confusion, disruption and chaos. But when God showed his mercy to end all of that and sent his Messiah, but people are making all kinds of excuses not to accept him.

Summary

I hereby, humbly request all the people of the world to please contemplate on this issue and at least try to understand Ahmadiyya. At least try to examine the evidences I have put forward to see, what if he is the real messiah, what if by not accepting him we lose all the blessings of God? In the same manner how Jews rejected Jesus because of many misunderstandings especially his misunderstood accursed death and lost all the mercy and blessings of God.

At the end I would like to say special thanks to a few people who did everything in their capacity to help me publish this book. Mr. Amir Idllbi, Mr. M. Amjad Sahab, Mr. M Arshad Sahab,

Mr. Ather Sahab, Ms. Seema Farooq Sahiba. Dr. Aslam Daud Sahab,
Shamshad A. Nasir Sahab,
Ms. Suzanne Olson
and Mr. George Cardiel
May God Bless them all

The people who read my manuscript before it was published, asked me that why do you say your book does not represent *Ahmadiyya* sect, while the whole book is an attempt to prove the truthfulness of *Ahmadiyya* sect? It is true that the only reason for publishing this book is to invite the whole world to the *Promised Messiah* (Ahmad). But since this book is not authorized by the *Ahmadiyya* administration and many claims I have made in this book which do not represent *Ahmadiyya* sect, therefore, I cannot openly say that this book represents *Ahmadiyya* believes.

To Contact the Author Directly: Please send an email to

asad@jesusandmosesinindia.com (please no spaces)

(i.e. Jesus and Moses in India.com (I have separated the words to show the email words clearly))

To visit Ahmadiyya website

www.alislam.org

Watch 24 hours seven days a week Ahmadiyya programs in English, German, French, Arabic, Urdu & other languages. www.mta.tv

Biblical References

	THE NEW TESTAMENT	
	Islam in New Testament	
	PROPHESIES (bracketed text is not in the Bible)	
1)	a) KINGDOM OF GOD will BE TAKEN AWAY FROM You & given to another nation [MUSLIMS]	(Matthew 21:43)
	b) YOU WILL NEVER SEE ME AGAIN UNTIL YOU SAY BLESSED IS HE [MUHAMMAD] WHO COMES IN THE NAME OF THE LORD [which means 2nd Coming of Jesus will be after Muhammad]	(Matthew 23:39)
	c) AS LONG AS I am in the world, I am the light of the world [Which means after Jesus, someone else would be the light of the world]	(John 9:5)
	d) THE HOUSE OF ISRAEL WILL BE LEFT DESOLATE [meaning, there will be no more prophets coming in Israel]	(Matthew 23:38) & (Luke 13:35)
	e) BLASPHEMY AGAINST HOLY GHOST [MUHAMMAD] SHALL NEVER BE FORGIVEN	(Matthew 12:32) (Mark 3:29)
	f) COMFORTER [MUHAMMAD] WILL ABIDE WITH YOU FOREVER	(John 14:16)
	g) COMFORTER WILL TEACH YOU ALL THINGS; BRING ALL THINGS TO YOUR REMEBRANCE	(John 14:26)
	h) PEACE (ISLAM) I LEAVE WITH YOU, MY PEACE I GIVE YOU	(John 14:27)

363

	i) WHEN THE COMFORTER COME HE SHALL TESTIFY OF ME	(John 15:26)
	j) IT IS GOOD FOR YOU THAT I GO AWAY FOR IF I GO NOT AWAY THE COMFORTER WILL NOT COME	(John 16:7)
	k) HE SHALL REPROVE THE WORLD OF SIN	(John 16:8)
	l) I HAVE YET MANY THINGS TO SAY UNTO YOU, BUT YOU CANNOT UNDERSTAND THEM NOW	(John 16:12)
	m) HE SHALL GUIDE YOU INTO ALL TRUTH	(John 16:13)
	n) HE SHALL GLORIFY ME	(John 16:14)
	o) HE SHALL SEND JESUS [Second Coming] WHICH BEFORE WAS PREACHED TO YOU [which means 2nd coming of Jesus will be after the appearance of Muhammad]	(Acts 3: 20-23)
	1) BIBLE SAYS: JOHN the Baptist SAID "I BAPTIZE YOU WITH WATER, ONE WILL COME AFTER ME WILL BAPTIZE YOU WITH HOLY GHOST"	(Matthew 3:11)
	2) BUT JESUS SAID: YOU HEARD FROM ME, "For John truly baptized with water; but ye shall be baptized with the Holy Ghost not many days hence."	(Acts 1:4-5)
	3) PETER SAID "I REMEMBER JESUS SAID; JOHN INDEED BAPTIZE WITH WATER"	(Acts 11:16)
	Jesus and God are 2	
	1) 1st of all Commandments Lord our God is ONE LORD	(Mark 12:29)
	2) In your law, the TESTAMONY of TWO MEN IS TRUE	(John 8:17)

3) I thank you Father Lord of Haven & Earth	(Matthew 11:25)
4) God is Spirit	(John 4:24)
5) Jesus said: I am not Spirit	(Luke 24:39)
6) I am God not man	(Hosea 11:9)
7) God is not a man	(Numbers 23:19)
8) BORN of FLESH is FLESH , born of SPIRIT is SPIRIT	(John 3:6)
9) No man has seen God at any time	(1John 4:12) (John 1:18)
10) God CANNOT be TEMPTED Jesus was tempted (Matthew 4:1, Mark 1:13 & Luke 4:2). Could Jesus be God? (James 1:13)	
11) Eternal, Immortal INVISIBLE God	(1Timothy 1:17)
12) I thank you Father Lord of Heaven & Earth	(Matthew 11:25)
13) He that abides in the doctrine of Christ HE HAS BOTH FATHER & SON	(2John 1:9)
12) Anti Christ is he who denies Jesus & God	(1John 2:22)
13) One mediator between God & men Jesus	(1Timothy 2:5)
14) I am not alone, because the Father is with me.	(John16:32)
15) GOD is GREATER than Jesus	(John 14:28)
16) Jesus prayed to God, and he continued to pray all night.	(Luke 6:12)
17) My DOCTRINE is not mine, but his that sent me.	(John 7:16)
18) Not U speak but SPIRIT of YOUR FATHER speak in U	(Matthew 10:20)

	19) IT IS NOT YOU SPEAK BUT THE HOLY SPIRIT	(Mark 13:11)
	20) MY FATHER & YOUR FATHER MY GOD YOUR GOD	(John 20:17)
	21) I AM IN MY FATHER AND YOU IN ME & I, IN YOU	(John 14:20)
	22) I CAN DO NOTHING OF MYSELF	(John 8:28)
	New Testament	
1)	THERE BE SOME STANDING HERE shall NOT TASTE DEATH	(Matthew 16:28)
2)	I COME IN MY FATHERS NAME	(John 5:43)
3)	1) FLESH & BLOOD cannot inherit in the Kingdom of God	(I Corinthians 15:50)
4)	2) No man has ASCENDED up to HEAVEN	(John 3:13)
5)	**No** man call **JESUS ACURSED**	(I Corinthians 12:3)
6)	Jesus said BE PERFECT as your father is perfect	(Matthew 5:48)
7)	a) If you DO NOT HONOR YOUR PARENTS you DIE	(Matthew 15:4)
	b) JESUS SAID: "WHO IS MY MOTHER?" [HE WAS BEING REBELLIOUS AGAINST HIS MOTHER]	(Matthew 12:48)
	c) HATE YOUR PARENTS	(LUKE 14:26)
	d) REBELLIOUS CHILD SHOULD BE STONE TO DEATH	(Deuteronomy 21:18)
8)	IF you say **YOU FOOL**, you will be in danger of hell fire	(Matthew 5:22)
9)	a) DIVORCE WOMEN MAY RE-MARRY	(Deuteronomy 24:2)
	b) If U Marry DIVORCE WOMAN U commit ADULTRY	(Matthew 5:32)
10)	ABOUT FASTING	(Matthew 6:16)
11)	Jesus will be CRUCIFIED, the 3RD DAY he will rise again	(Matthew 20:19)

12)	Miracle of FIG TREE	(Matthew 21:19)
	a) IF YOU HAVE FAITH, you tell Mountain to fall in Sea	(Matthew 21:21)
	b) DISCIPLES CAN DO GREATER MIRACLES THAN JESUS	(John 14:12)
	c)IF YOU HAVE FAITH AS LITTLE AS MUSTARD SEED	(Matthew 17:20)
13)	NOT GONE thru CITIES of ISRAEL B/4 Jesus comes	(Matthew 10:23)
	Jesus said Obey the Law of Moses	
14)	a) Do Not think I come to DESTROY the LAW or Prophets	(Matthew 5:17)
	b) ONE JOT OF LAW SHALL NOT PASS TILL ALL BE FULFILLED	(Matthew 5:18)
	c)WHOSOEVER BREAKS LEAST OF THESE COMMANDMENTS	(Matthew 5:19)
	d) EXCEPT your RIGHTIOUSNESS EXCEED RIGHTIOUSNESS OF SCRIBES & PHARISEES, You cannot enter Heaven	(Matthew 5:20)
	e) SCRIBES AND PHARISEES SIT IN MOSES SEAT	(Matthew 23:2)
	f) Man is JUSTIFIED by DEEDS and NOT BY FAITH ALONE	(James 2:24-26)
	About PETER	
15)	a) JESUS SAID TO PETER, SATAN YOU ARE AN OFFENCE UNTO ME	(Matthew 16:23)
	b) PETER WAS AMONG THOSE WHO FLED TO SAVE THEIR LIVES WHEN JESUS GOT COUGHT	(Matthew 26:56)
	c) PETER DENIED JESUS UNDER OATH	(Matthew 26:72)
	d) PETER CURSED JESUS 3 TIMES	(Matthew 26:74)
16)	a) BIBLE SAYS: EVEN IF AN ANGEL PREACH YOU DIFFERENT GOSPEL LET HIM BE ACCURSED	(Galatians 1:8)

	b) JESUS SAID: WHOSOEVER BREAK ONE OF THESE LEAST COMMANDMENTS AND TEACH MEN SO SHALL BE CALLED LEAST IN THE KINGDOM OF HEAVEN (SATAN is least in the Kingdom of Heaven)	(Matthew 5:19)
	c) WHEN PETER made EVERY UNCLEAN FOOD CLEAN (NO CHRISTIAN ASKED PETER HOW CAN YOU BRAEK THE COMMANDMENTS?)	(Acts 11:6-9)

Sayings of Paul

17)	a) PAUL SAID: you are DEBTOR TO DO the WHOLE LAW	(Galatians 5:2-4)
	b) PAUL named Jesus' followers CHRISTIANS	(Acts 11:26)
	c) PAUL KILLED CHRISTIANS	(Acts 26: 9-11)
	d) PAUL SAYS: JESUS RAISED FROM THE DEAD, ACCORDING TO MY GOSPEL	(1Timothy 2:8)
	e) PAUL SAID YOU ARE NOT UNDER THE LAW, BUT UNDER THE GRACE	(Romans 6:14)
	f) PAUL SAID YOU DON'T HAVE TO BE CIRCUMCISED [BECAUSE OF PAUL, CHRISTIANS LOST THE PROMISED LAND 4 EVER, because the token to live in the Promised land (circumcision) was rejected by Paul]	(Galatians 5:2)
	g) PAUL DECIDED to preach to GENTILE	(Acts 13:46)
	h) GOD PROMISED ABRAHAM THAT IF YOU KEEP MY COMMANDMENT OF CIRCUMCISION I WILL GIVE YOU THE PROMISED LAND FOR EVER [BUT MUSLIMS HAVE THE PROMISED LAND FOR 1,221 YEARS, BECAUSE THEY KEPT THE COMMANDMENT OF CIRCUMCISION]	(Genesis 17:7-13)

	Jesus for the Jews	
18)	a) I PRAY NOT for the World. I pray for them [Jews]	(John 17:9)
	b) OTHER SHEEP I have which are not in this fold	(John 10:16)
	c) JESUS SENT 12 TO PREACH. BUT TOLD THEM "DO NOT GO to GENTILE, go to lost sheep of Israel	(Matthew 10:5)
	d) THOSE 12 Apostles NEVER WENT TO GENTILE	(Acts 11:19)
	e) I AM NOT SENT but to the LOST SHEEP of Israel	(Matthew 15:24)
	f) TO Take CHILDREN'S BREAD & CAST TO DOGS	(Matthew 15:26)
	g) DO NOT CAST YOUR PEARLS TO SWINES (for Jews only)	(Matthew 7:6)
	h) JESUS shall reign over the house of JACOB forever	(Luke 1:33)
	i) THE KING OF ISRAEL comes in THE name of Lord	(John12: 13)
	j) WHO SHALL RULE MY PEOPLE ISRAEL	(Matthew 2:6)
	k) You Manifest yourself TO US but NOT to WORLD	(John 14:22).
	l) We had HOPED Jesus would REDEEM ISRAEL	(Luke 24:21)
	m) PAUL DECIDED to preach to GENTILE	(Acts 13:46)
19)	JESUS as a child was SAVED by a DREAM of JOSEPH	(Matthew 2:13)
20)	WHY CALL ME GOOD? There is no GOOD but GOD	(Matthew 19:17)
21)	Blessed are the peace makers, they are children of God	(Matthew 5:9)

22)	Jesus said DO NOT TELL anyone I am Jesus CHRIST (also in Mark 1:44; Mark 8:30; and Luke 9:21)	(Matthew 16:20)
23)	1) Jesus told PETER I will GIVE YOU KEYS OF HEAVEN	(Matthew 16:19)
24)	2) Jesus told PETER GET BEHIND ME SATAN, you are an OFFENCE unto ME	(Matthew 16:23)
25)	a) DO NOT CALL ANY ONE YOU FOOL or you'll be in hell fire	(Matthew 5:22)
	b) Jesus called "YOU FOOL" in many places (Matthew 23:17; 23:19), (Luke 11:40; 24:25)	
	c) DO NOT CURSE	(Romans 12:14)
	d) EVIL and adulterous generation	(Matthew 12:39)
	e) You SERPENTS you generation of VIPERS	(Matthew 23:33)

Jesus king of Peace

a) JESUS WAS NEVER CALLED KING OF PEACE IN THE ENTIRE BIBLE	
b)ONLY MELCHISEDEC WAS CALLED KING OF PEACE IN ENTIRE BIBLE	(Hebrew 7:2)
c)Do not think I have come to bring PEACE but SWORD	(Matthew 10:34)
d)He that hath no sword, let him sell his garment, and buy one	(Luke 22: 36).
e)I am come to send fire on the earth	(Luke 12:49).
f)Jesus come to set a man at variance against his father	(Matthew 10:35).
g)Man's foes shall be his own household	(Matthew 10:36).
h)If any man come to me, and hate not his father & mother he is not worthy of me	(Luke 14:26).
i)Jesus said unto him, Follow me; and let the dead bury their dead	(Matthew 8:22).
j)There shall be five in one house divided, three against two,	(Luke 12:52).

	k)The prophet which prophesieth of peace, the LORD hath truly sent him	(Jeremiah 28:9).

JOHN THE BAPTIST IS ELIJAH

26)	a) John the Baptist will BORN WITH THE POWER OF ELIJAH	(Luke 1:17)
	b) JOHN THE BAPTIST IS ELIJAH	(Matthew 11:14)
	c) JOHN THE BAPTIST IS ELIJAH	(Matthew 17:11)
	d) JOHN THE BAPTIST IS ELIJAH	(Mark 9:11-13)

JOHN THE BAPTIST

27)	a) ALL THAT EVER CAME BEFORE ME WERE THIEVES & ROBBERS	(John 10:8)
	b) JOHN the BAPTIST greater than any man BORN of WOMEN	(Matthew 11:11)
28)	GOD PROMISED ABRAHAM : "I WILL BLESS THEM THAT BLESS YOU AND CURSE THEM THAT CURSE YOU" (Old Testament)	(Genesis 12:3)
29)	No man can SEE GOD and Live (Old Testament)	(Exodus 33:20)
30)	Melchisedec KING OF RIGHTIOUSNESS	(Hebrew 7:2)
31)	JEWS didn't want Jesus to preach, Jews might STAY IN Slavery	(John 11:48)
32)	If a SON ask for BREAD, would a father give him STONE?	(Matthew 7:9)
33)	If a SON ask for BREAD, would a father give him STONE?	(Luke 11:11)
34)	I PROPHESIED IN YOUR name, Jesus said I don't know YOU	(Matthew 7:22)
35)	PROPHET CANNOT BE PERISH out of JERUSALEM	(Luke 13:33)
36)	VIRTUE HAD GONE FROM JESUS	(Mark 5:30)

37)	NO PROPHET IS ACCEPTED IN HIS OWN COUNTRY (Also in Mark 6:4; and John 4:44)	(Luke 4:24) (Matthew 13:57);
38)	JESUS DID NOT WALK OPENLY AMONG JEWS (John 7:10; Mark 1:45)	(John 11:54)
39)	JESUS HID HIMSELF FROM JEWS BEFORE CRUCIFIXION	(John 8:59)
40)	Prophecy of ISAIAH Jesus WILL SURVIVE THE CROSS (Matthew 13:57)	(Isaiah 53:8-11)
41)	SIGN OF JONAS	(Matthew 12:39)
42)	Jesus prays to God to TAKE AWAY the CUP (Also in Luke 22:42)	(Matthew 26:39)
43)	Jesus' SWEAT as DROPS of BLOOD	(Luke 22:44)
44)	Jesus said MY SOUL is exceeding sorrowful unto DEATH	(Mark 14:34)
45)	ANGEL APPEARED to Jesus, STRENGHTHENING him	(Luke 22:43)
46)	JESUS CURSED JUDAS for BETRAYING him	(Matthew 26:24)
47)	WHO DELIVERED ME TO YOU HAS GREATER SIN	(John 19:11)
48)	JUDAS feels bad throws the money and HANGS himself	(Matthew 27:3)
49)	JUDAS lives & buys a land with the betrayal money	(Acts 1:18)
50)	Pilate's WIFE saw a VISION	(Matthew 27:19)
51)	JESUS as a child was SAVED by a DREAM of JOSEPH (Matthew 2:13)	
52)	Pilate finds Jesus INNOCENT	(Luke 23:14)
53)	Pilate, WASHES HANDS not to do anything with Jesus	(Matthew 27:24)
54)	Crucifixion was DELAYED 6 HOURS	(John 19:14)

55)	Jesus was on the cross for 6 HOURS [But originally 2 Hrs]	(Mark 15:33)
AFTER CRUCIFIXION		
56)	Jesus was brought to GOLGOTHA, means 'place of skull'	(Mark 15:22)
57)	CHIEF PRIEST MOCKED at Jesus Let him come down	(Mark15:31-32)
58)	(CLOUD covers the sky), makes the DAY INTO NIGHT	(Matthew 27:45)
59)	a) Earth Quake & WIND (shows anger of God, not happiness) b) Psalms says God was angry earth was shook [earth quake]	(Matthew 27:54) (Psalms 18:7)
60)	GRAVES were opened and many SAINTS AROSE	(Matthew 27:52)
61)	JESUS DRINKS VINEGAR	(John 19:29-30)
62)	Jesus TALKS briefly after drinking vinegar	(Luke 23:43)
63)	Right after drink Jesus gave up the ghost	(John 19:30)
64)	Pilate was MARVELED, if Jesus was already dead	(Mark 15:44)
65)	Blood and water GUSHED OUT (see "The Message" Bible by Eugene Peterson)	(John 19:34)
66)	[Body of Jesus was not buried], but placed in a CHAMBER	(Matthew 27:60)
67)	Chamber like tomb was big for people to enter & exit	(Luke 24:3)
68)	Door of the tomb was OPEN	(Luke 24:2)
69)	2 ANGELS in the tomb [Actually 2 men helped Jesus (Luke 24:4)]	(John 20:12)
70)	Mary Magdalene did NOT RECOGNIZE Jesus	(John 20:14)
71)	Mary Magdalene thought that Jesus was a GARDENER	(John 20:15)
72)	Disciples did not RECOGNIZE JESUS	(Luke 24:18)

73)	Other disciples did not RECOGNIZE JESUS	(John 21:4)
74)	ANGELS told disciples that Jesus is ALIVE, [not revived]	(Luke 24:23)
75)	ANGELS told disciples, why seek LIVING among DEAD	(Luke 24:5)
76)	JESUS GETS UPSET, why thoughts arise in your heart?	(Luke 24:38)
77)	Jesus shows his HANDS and FEET, & says: I am not a ghost	(Luke 24:39)
78)	Jesus said to Thomas be not FAITHLESS but BELIEVING	(John 20:27)
79)	Jesus EATS MEAT [to show, he is not a SPIRIT but human]	(Luke 24:43)
80)	a) IDLE TALES that Jesus is alive	(Luke 24:11)
	b) Followers didn't know Jesus would RISE AGAIN from dead	(John 20:9)
	c) PAUL SAYS: JESUS RAISED FROM THE DEAD, ACCORDING TO MY GOSPEL	(2 Timothy 2:8)
81)	Jesus gave INFALLABLE PROOFS THAT HE IS ALIVE	(Acts 1:3)
82)	Jesus appointed disciples to MEET HIM at a MOUNTAIN	(Matthew 28:16)
83)	a) JESUS SAID GO TO ALL NATIONS	(Matthew 28:19)
	b) BUT IN LUKE JESUS SAID: "STAY IN JERUSALEM" (which one of these statements is true?)	(Luke 24:49)
	c) ACTS SAYS "THEY SHOULD NOT DEPART JERUSALEM"	(ACTS 1:4)
84)	PAUL SAYS: ADAM WAS NOT A SINNER BUT EVE WAS A SINNER	(1 Timothy 2:14)
	2nd COMING OF JESUS	
85)	FALSE PROPHETS will come [Would they come from sky?]	(Matthew 24:11)

86)	I will come from the EAST, [INDIA IS IN EAST which also means not from SKY]	(Matthew 24:27)
87)	JESUS SAID: 1ST, I WILL BE REJECTED AND SUFFER [HOW CAN JESUS SUFFER IF HE IS NOT GOING TO TOUCH THE GROUND (Rapture)]	(Luke 17:25)
88)	SUN & MOON will ECLIPSE. 1) Matthew 24:29, 2) Mark 13:24, 3) Luke21:25, 4) Acts 2:20, 5) Revelations 6:12, 6) Revelations 8:12, 7) Isaiah 24:23, 8) Isaiah 13:10, 9) Isaiah 60:19, 10) Ezekiel 32:7, 11) Joel 2:10,12) Joel 2:31 13) Joel 3:15, & 14) Amos 8:9	
89)	There will be EARTH QUAKES [1,900 people died in India 1905 in the time of Second Coming of Jesus Christ (Ahmad)]	(Matthew 24:7)
90)	Jesus would NOT FIND FAITH	(Luke 18:8)
91)	Nation will rise against nation [1st World War 1914]	(Matthew 24:7)
92)	YOU'LL BE HATED BY ALL NATIONS FOR MY NAME SAKE	(Matthew 24:9)
93)	YOU SHALL NOT GONE through the CITIES of ISRAEL B/4 Jesus comes [ISRAEL BECAME STATE IN [MAY 14TH 1948, WHERE IS THE MESSIAH?]	(Matthew 10:23)
94)	JESUS SAID I WILL GIVE YOU MOUTH AND WISDOM	(Luke 21:15)
95)	DAYS WILL BE SHOTENED	(Matthew 24:22)
96)	GOSPEL SHALL BE PRAECHED TO ALL NATIONS [Today almost every nation has been preached by Missionaries. Where is the Messiah?]	(Matthew 24:14)
97)	PICURE OF LAST DAYS	(2 Timothy 3:1-5)

	Part 2 References of the Old Testament	
1	God created the Heaven and Earth	(Genesis 1:1)
2	Spirit of God moved upon the face of the waters	(Genesis 1:2)
3	God create man in his own image	(Genesis 1:27)
4	Four rivers of Garden of Eden	(Genesis 2:10)
5	Gold of that land is good	(Genesis 2:12)
6	God made Adam to cultivate the land & keep it.	(Genesis 2:15 NASB Version)
7	God created Adam on 6th day Friday	(Genesis 1:31)
8	a) God: If you eat that tree "you will surely die."	(Genesis 2:17)
9	b) Satan said, "you will not surely die."	(Genesis 3:4)
10	Punishment of Adam and Eve	(Genesis 3:14-19)
11	Man is become one of us (God)	(Genesis 3:22)
12	God called their name Adam(Many Adams lived)	(Genesis 5:2)
13	a) Man shall live 120 years	(Genesis 6:3)
	b) Noah lived 950 years	(Genesis 9:29)
	c) Adam lived 930 years	(Genesis 5:5)
	d) Seth lived 812 years	(genesis 5:8)
	e)Shem and his Children lived 400 to 500 years	(Genesis 11:11)
	f) Terah lived 205 years	(Genesis 11:32)
	g) Abraham lived 175 years	(Genesis 25:6)
14	a) Cain will be fugitive and a vagabond	(Genesis 4:14)
	b) Cain's wife was pregnant [How can Cain get a wife, he was the only man on Earth?]	(Genesis 4:17)
15	Sons of God saw the daughters of men	(Genesis 6:2)
16	a) Noah was perfect	(Genesis 6:9)
	b)Abraham walked with God and became perfect	(Genesis 17:1)

	c) Job was perfect 1) (Job 1:1); 2) (Job 1:8); 3) (Job2:3)	
17	Noah was righteous	(Genesis 7:1)
18	God promised. No more flood to destroy all flesh	(Genesis 9:13)
19	a) Whole Earth was populated by the sons of Noah.	(Genesis 9:19)
	b)Names of cities were the names of sons of Noah	(Genesis 10:5)
20	A) Abraham lied about his wife and said, "She is my sister." (God Forbid)	(Genesis 12:13)
	B) Abraham obeyed God's commandments	(Genesis 26:5)
	C) God's Promise to Abraham: I will bless them that bless you	(Genesis 12:3)
	D) Abraham had a mistress (God Forbid)	(Genesis 25:6)
	E)Isaac lied about his wife and said, "She is my sister"	(Genesis 26:6)
21	Covenant of circumcision with Abraham	(Genesis 17:1)
22	Daughters of a lot got pregnant by their fathers [God forbid]	(Genesis 19:36)
23	Mandrakes [Natural Anesthetic: called Hyacine]	(Genesis 30:14)
24	Jacob became Israel	(Genesis 32:28)
25	a) Jacob saw God face to face	(Genesis 32:30)
	b) Man cannot see God and live	(Exodus 33:20)
	c) God talked to Moses face to face	(Deuteronomy 5:4)
26	Jacob returned to Bethel	(Genesis 35:13-16)
27	a)Judah slept with his daughter-in-law (God Forbid)	(Genesis 38:16)
	b)If you had sex with your daughter-in-law you should be put to death [Instead God blessed him and made him Prophet & father of all the Jews]	(Leviticus 20:12)
28	a)Jacob had two Illegitimate kids: (Pharez & Zarah) (Great Great Grand Fathers of Jesus) (God Forbid)	(Genesis 38:29-30)

	b) A bastard shall not enter into Heaven to his 10th generation	(Deuteronomy 23:2)
	c) Seed of evil doers shall never be honored	(Isaiah 14:20)
	d)David committed adultery: with the wife of Uriah (God Forbid)	(2 Samuel 11:3)
	e) Amnon son of David raped his sister Tamer	(2 Samuel 13:14)

References of the Old Testament
Islam in the Bible

Note: Bracketed text is not in the Bible

1	Abraham built altar in the east of Bethel [Kaaba]	(Genesis 12:7-8)
2	Abraham went on his journey south to Bethel [Kaaba]	(Genesis 13:3)
3	Hagar became wife of Abraham	(Genesis 16:3)
4	God promised Hagar, Ishmael, multiply exceedingly	(Genesis 16:10)
5	Ishmael will be a wild man	(Genesis 16:12)
6	God made covenant with Abraham [circumcision]	(Genesis 17:2-14)
7	a) Abraham was 99 years old: when he was circumcised	(Genesis 17:24)
8	b) Ishmael was 13 years old: when he was circumcised	(Genesis 17:25)
9	c) Abraham & Ishmael: Both circumcised the same day	(Genesis 17:26)
10	a) God promised Abraham, Ishmael, will multiply exceedingly,12 princes shall he beget	(Genesis 17:20)
11	b) God promised Abraham: Ishmael will become a nation	(Genesis 21:13)
12	Hagar, Ishmael & Aabe Zam, Zam:[The sacred water]	(Genesis 21:19)
13	Sacrifice of Abraham of Ishmael	(Genesis22:2-13)
14	Abraham dwelt at Beersheba	(Genesis 22:19)

15	Sons of Ishmael 12 princes	(Genesis 25:12)
16	Isaac dwelt at Beersheba	(Genesis 26:23)
17	Jacob put stone in (Hajre Aswad)	(Genesis 28:18)
18	Jacob returned to Bethel (Kaaba)	(Genesis 35:13-16)
19	Jacob put stone [Hajre Aswad on Kaaba]	(Genesis 28:16-22)
20	Jacob returned to Beth-el [Kaaba]	(Genesis 35:13-16)
21	Elijah and Elisha went to Beth-el [Kaaba]	(2 KINGS 2:2)
22	Kaaba was praised by Jesus in Psalms	(Psalms 84:1-10)
23	Mecca was mentioned: by old name Baca (see NIV)	(Psalms 84:6)
24	Burden upon Arabia [birth country of Muhammad]	(Isaiah 21:13-17)
25	Muhammad is mentioned in Hebrew King James Version of Bible (see blueletterbible.org) go to 5: 16 then go to Hebrew concordance	(Song of Songs 5:16)
26	God will name [Islam] in Gentile	(Isaiah 62: 2)
27	Ahmad is mentioned in Syriac edition of Bible	(John 18: 37)
28	[Quran] is mentioned as revealed, verse by verse	(Isaiah 28 :10-11-13)
29	[Quran] as a sealed book [cannot be altered]	(Isaiah 29:11-12)
30	[Quran]: backside of the book 7 seals	(Revelations 5:1-5)
31	Unto us a child is born [Prophecy about Muhammad not Jesus]	(Isaiah 9 : 6-7)
32	Holy One [Muhammad] from Mount Paran	(Habakkuk 3:3)
33	All nations call him [Muhammad] the blessed: daily shall he be praised	(Psalms 72:7-17)
34	Lord [Muhammad] came from Mount Paran (old name of Mecca)	(Deuteronomy 33:2
35	God will raise up [Muhammad] a prophet among thy brother [Ishmael, which was brother of Isaac]	(Deuteronomy 18:15-22)
36	God will raise unto David a righteous branch of king	(Jeremiah 23:5) (Jeremiah 33:15

	Commandments of Torah (Old Testament)	
37	Adultery : stone to death	(Deuteronomy 22: 22-24)
38	God is one (Mark 12:29)	(Deuteronomy 6:4)
39	God is not a man, I'm god not man (Hosea 11:9)	(Numbers 23:19)
40	There is no God before me: or after me	(Isaiah 43:10)
41	a)Man cannot see God and live	(Exodus 33:20)
	b)No one has seen God at any time	(John 1:18)
	c)No man has seen god at any time	(1John 4:12)
42	Do not make image of anything: on earth to worship	(Deuteronomy 5:7-9)
43	Jews have changed the law	(Isaiah 24:5)
44	False prophet should be put to death	(Deuteronomy 13-9)
45	Keep the Sabbath holy	(Deuteronomy 5:12)
	Man who breaks Sabbath should be put to death	(Exodus 35:2)
46	Do not drink wine you or your sons forever	(Jeremiah 35:6)
47	Love thy neighbor as thyself	(Leviticus 19:18)
48	Bodily Discharges: Men & Woman	(Leviticus whole ch.15)
49	God reveals himself to prophets	(Numbers 12:6)
50	First born has the right of inheritance	(Deuteronomy 21:15)
	Miracles of the Biblical People	
1)	Elisha walked on water	(2 Kings 2:14).
2)	Elijah went up to heaven in a chariot of fire and horses of fire'	(2Kings 2:11).
3)	Paul raised a dead man to life	(Acts 20:9 to 12).
4)	Elijah raises a dead child alive	(1 Kings 17:21-22).
5)	Elisha raises a dead child alive	(2 Kings 4:29 to 35).

6)	Elisha cures Naaman of leprosy	(2 Kings 5:1 to 14).
7)	Elijah heals a blinded army and restores the eyesight of its men	(2Kings 6:20).
8)	A dead man's body touches Elisha's bones, the man comes to life and stands up on his feet	(2Kings 13: 21).
9)	Moses makes darkness for three days	(Exodus 10:22).
10)	Moses makes sea to go back by a strong wind and makes sea a dry land	(Exodus 14:21).
11)	Moses turned water throughout the land of Egypt into blood	(Exodus 7:17 to 20).
12)	Joshua ordered the sun and moon to stay still 'and the sun and moon stopped'	(Joshua 10:13)
13)	The priests make the whole nation pass Jordan by making a dry passage in Flooded River	(Joshua 3:17).
14)	Ezekiel raises up a slain army, from dry, scattered bones into life	(Ezekiel 37:10).
15)	Four men were thrown into fire and were not burnt	(Daniel 3:25).
16)	Paul cured a cripple	(Acts 14:8-10).
17)	Ananias restored eyesight of Paul	(Acts 9:17-18).
18)	Phillip healed palsies and lamed	(Acts 8:5-7).

Index

A

Aab-e-Zam Zam 326
Abba Yahyah 31, 167
Absalom 95
Abu Hurairah 90, 199
Adbeel 330
Africa 125, 126, 156, 252
Aish Muqam 194
Akmal-ud-din 218
Al-Ahqaf 231, 246, 264
Al-An'am 230, 233
Al-Anfal 148
Al-A'raf 263, 273
Alexander Dowie 213
Alexandria 128, 272
Al-Fath 148
Al-Fatir 239
Al-Hajj 265, 291
Al-Ikhlas 229, 277
Al-Jathiyah 231
Al-Jinn 230, 344
Al-Kahf 233, 239, 243, 322
Al-Momin 190
Al-Mujaadilah 303
Al-Mu'minun 89, 110, 244
Al-Mumtahanah 265
Al-Muzzammil 246

Al-Naba 284
Al-Naml 228
Al-Nur 261
Alpha and Omega 304, 305
Al-Qasas 161, 263
Al-Qiyamah 217
Al-Saffat 125, 236
Al-Taubah 57, 66, 266
Al-Zukhruf 343
Amber xv, 154, 155
Amir Idllbi xv, 361
Amjad xv, 236, 237, 361
Ananias 48, 160, 381
Anne Besant 215
Anwer Mahmood Khan 27
Apollonius of Tyana 65
Archbishop Ussher 216
Arias 128
Ark of the Covenant 84, 94, 95
Arsenio Añoza 13
Arshad xv, 329, 361
Art gallery 287
Ashab al-Rass 331
Asim xv, 144
Athanasius 128
Ather xv, 361
A thief in the night 208
Attis of Phrygia 66

Augustus 33, 252
Aurangzeb 88
Awantipur 197

B

Baal 157, 196, 197
Baca 333, 334, 335, 379
Badr 300, 332
Bait-ulah 327, 328
Bait-Ul-Futuh 221
Balakh or Balkh 83
Barabbas 9
Baramoulay 88, 94
Baramula 88, 94
Barbara Thiering 163
Bar-jo'-na 142
Barnabas 182, 234, 272, 273, 294, 295, 296, 316, 317, 318
Basharat Saleem 42
Beafwahehim 270
Beards 283
Becca 334
Bethany 69, 104, 198, 216
Bhabishya Purana 110
Bhagavad Gita 305
Bibi Injeel 100, 104
Billy Graham 156, 157, 352
Black stone 328
Bokhara 83
Born of a woman 120
Breaking news 88
Broiled fish 17
Bruce M. Metzger 172, 299

C

Cabul 82
Cain 113, 376
Capernaum 41
Castile 338
Cathars 338
Celibacy 226
Charles Templeton 352
Chaziyr 288

Chickens 124
China 100, 104, 124, 252
Cleopas 23
CNN 106
Coins 15, 32, 33, 150, 164
Col. G. B. Malleson 111
Couch 198
Crucifixion: By an Eye Witness 163
Crusaders 308
Cyrenius 349

D

Damascus 44, 47, 48, 319
Daniel Smith Christopher 34
Darryl 262
Dead Sea Scrolls 16, 17, 25, 41, 79, 163, 164, 188, 194, 196, 198, 273, 297, 350
Dionysus 64, 89, 157, 338, 350, 352
Divi Filius 33
Divine Son 33, 66
Double Christians 215, 289
Dr. Alan Meenan 54
Dr. George Moore 111
Dr. James Deardorff 27
Dr Jyotsna 39
Dr. Michael Tite 166
Dr. Muhammad Aslam Nasir 219
Dr Waseem Sayed 243
Dumah 330

E

Ebionites 58, 337
Edgar J. GoodSpeed 235
Edward T. Martin 79, 110, 168
E. Grimm 46
Eid-Ul-Adha 236
El, El, azab 182, 186
Elijah 1, 2, 3, 4, 89, 156, 157, 159, 202, 206, 209, 210, 211, 248, 250, 295, 317, 355, 379, 380, 381
Eliphaz 42

Elisha 1, 89, 159, 253, 355, 379, 380, 381
Elohiym 327
Emmaus 23
Entrust 226
Ernest Renan 231
Essene 15, 188
Every eye shall see 208
Ezra synagogue 272, 319

F

Fatihah 323, 324
Fatwa 242, 243
Ferdinand 338
Fida M Hassnain 162
Filipinos 13
Filthy rags 284
First lady 114
First World War 135, 213, 217
F. Overbeck 45
Fragrance 197, 198
Francois Bernier 88, 94
Friday 13, 18, 25, 66, 188, 238, 350, 376
Fr. James Bruce 57

G

Galilee 69, 70, 167, 189
Gambling 227
GARDENER 373
G. B. Malleson 111
Gene D. Matlock 162, 358
Genetic Anthropology 111
Gharib 32
Glorified body 15, 21
Gnosis 337
Goats 124
Golgotha 9, 37, 110, 164
Good Friday 13
Gospel of Philip 35, 42, 163
GUSHED OUT 373

H

Hadad 331
Hajr-al- Aswad 328
Halaal 279
Ham 83, 124, 125, 126, 196, 197
Hanjis 125
Harmony Books 64, 65, 352
Hazara 82
Head covering 260
He keeps all his bones 169, 192
Heli 150, 152
Hematohydrosis 19
Henry Lincoln 197, 198
Herat 31, 83, 111, 167
Hermas 234
Herod 18, 33, 34, 54, 62, 229, 349
High tide 154, 155
Hijaz 330, 331
Hilal 218
Hiroshima 135
Hitler 206
Hollywood 352
Holocaust 135
Holy Land 90
Honeycomb 17
Horses 1, 124, 159, 202, 355, 380
Horus 62, 89, 157
Hosen 296, 317
Hud 155
Hudaida 331
Hyacine 20, 22, 167, 377

I

Ian Plimer 127
IDLE TALES 374
I had fainted 186, 187, 200
Immanuel 27, 351
Injeel 100, 104, 163
Iran 29, 291, 337
Iranaeus 272
Isabella 338
Isa Khel 194
Island of Patmos 54, 164

J

Jack Finegan 271, 319
James Bryce 111
James Cameron 352
James Orr 173
James Polster 42
Japan 124, 252
J.D. Shams 19, 48
Jedurs 331
Jeff Salz 110, 168
Jehovah Witnesses 287
Jesus Seminar 165
Jetur 330, 331
Jhelum 93
Jiddu Krishnamurti 215, 216
J.M. Powis Smith 235
John Keay 122
John Kitto 231
John nelson Darby 207
John Richard 173
John the Baptist 2, 3, 4, 53, 54, 55, 90,
    131, 145, 164, 202, 206, 209, 211,
    217, 293, 294, 296, 297, 299, 316,
    318, 351, 371
Jonas 26, 27, 28, 32, 158, 187, 189,
    190, 349
Jonathan Reed 33
Jop'-pa 28
Jos 156
Joseph of Arimathaea 15, 21
Josephus 34, 330, 331
Joses 40
Joshua 43, 151, 159, 348, 381
Judas 15, 71, 150, 157, 251, 292, 349
Judea 5, 295, 317
Julius Caesar 33

K

Kabul 82
Kadambani 39
Kaduna 156
Kalima 277
Kalki Autar 217, 359

Kano 156
Kashgar 100, 104
Kashi 104
Kashtiye-Nooh 215
Kedemah 330, 331
Kenya 156, 157
Khunz-er 288
Khyber 82
Kindled 306, 308
Kingdom of God shall be taken 209,
    210
Kingdom of the Cults 216
KING OF PEACE 354, 370
Kohath 82
Koh-I-Hama 124
Kosher 279
Kunzul-A'maal 32, 37
Kurt Berna 167
Kutud 13

L

Ladakh 83
Lamb 196, 223, 236
Last Supper 25
La Verne 33
Lazarus 145
Leonardo Da Vinci 25
Lesbian Nuns: Breaking Silence 257
Let them be confounded 190
Lhasa 83
Lineage 119, 150
Lion 206
Lord's Prayer 351
Luz 328

M

Machmad 165, 300, 314
Maharaj 217
Mahatma Surdasji 217
Majid Hussain 125
Mandaeans 297
Mandrake 20, 167
Manoravataranam 123

Maranos 338
Marham-i-Isa 166, 188
Marjan 104
Marriage supper 39, 198
Marwah 326
Mary 3, 16, 18, 22, 24, 32, 33, 37, 40,
   41, 42, 59, 60, 62, 69, 70, 89, 90,
   97, 98, 99, 104, 106, 110, 119,
   128, 130, 131, 144, 145, 150, 152,
   163, 164, 190, 196, 197, 198, 208,
   229, 230, 263, 264, 266, 268, 269,
   287, 292, 293, 318, 341, 342, 345,
   346, 350, 351, 355, 373
Mary Magdalene 16, 22, 24, 41, 42,
   69, 70, 90, 163, 164, 196, 197,
   198, 345, 350, 373
Massa 330
Masudi 331
Maulana Noor-Ud-Din 204
Medina 330
Melchisedec 304, 305, 354, 371
Mel Gibson 352
Menahem 269
Metaphoric light 27
Metaphoric light Literal darkness 27
Mibsam 330
Michael Baigent 197, 198
Michael D. Coogan 172
Microfiche department 213
Midian 85
Mirza Bashir-Ud-Din Mahmood
   Ahmad 204
Mirza Masroor Ahmad 205
Mirza Nasir Ahmad 204
Mirza Tahir Ahmad 204
Mishma 330
Mithras 89, 157, 338
Mohammed Zaman Khokhar 96, 125
Monday 25
moon shall not give her light 213
Moriah 326
Mosaic Law 6, 58
Mount Carmel 157
Muhammad bin Ali 217

N

Nagasaki 135
Nag Hammadi 167
Nahkalank 217
Najd 331
Nancy Manahan 257
Naphish 330, 331
Nard 197, 198
Nation will rise against nation 212,
   217, 375
Neanderthal 112, 118
Nebajoth 330
Neb-u-chad-nez'-zar 28
New Delhi 99, 125
New Heaven and New Earth 214
Nicaea 128
Nicene Creed 58, 128, 338
Nicodemus 20, 170, 188
Niel Bradman 111
Nightclubs 285
Nin'-e-veh 28
Noe 206

O

Ointment of Jesus 166, 188
Old Cairo 272, 319
Omar Khan 200
O. M. Burke 167
Osiris 63, 89, 157, 338, 350, 352

P

Pacific School 271, 319
Padre Pio 57
Pakistan 82, 96, 98, 111, 125, 164,
   239, 240
Pali 32, 164
Pamela Geller 242, 243
Pampanga 13
Parakletos 3, 269, 271, 319
Pass over 18
Paula Fredriksen 72
Paul Davids 79
Paul J. Achtemeier 172

Pentecostals 157
Persia 29
Peshawar 82
Pestilence 215
Peter Gandy 64, 65, 351, 352
Pha'-rez 341
Philip 35, 42, 71, 163
Philippines 13
Platonic philosophy 272
Pneuma 13
Pontius Pilate 18, 320
Pope Gregory the Great 257
Pope John Paul II 79
Princeton University 271, 319
Professor Majid Hussain 125
Protestants 338
Punjab 32, 97, 126

Q

Qadian 249, 357
Qaf 231
Qamar 218
Qarabadin-i-Rumi 166, 188

R

Rabbi 92, 267
Radiocarbon dating 166
Ra'-hab 341
Rajatarangini 94
Ramadhan 218, 219
Rapture 84, 207, 267, 303, 375
Ratchets of the shoes 296, 317
Rawalpindi 97
Rebekah 254
Rev. C. forster 300, 331, 333
Richard Leigh 197, 198
Rija xv, 154, 155
Rishis 92
Robert Fortna 235
Rosemary Curb 257
Royal Funeral 37
Roza-Bal 39

S

Saba xv, 37
Sabbath 18, 58, 69, 201, 238, 241, 380
Safa 326
Sahibzada Basharat Saleem 42
Salaam Alaikum 286
Salem 304
San Fernando 13
San Pedro 13
Satapatha Brahmana 123
Saturday 25, 350
Sea of the Reeds 153
Second World War 135
Seema xv, 361
Septuagint 247
Seven seals 323, 324
Shaka 39
Shalibahan 110
Shalowm 286
Shankacharaya 94
Shazia Khan 329
Sheikh Mubarak Ahmad 156
Shining garments 15, 70
Shinto 271, 319
Shoe's latchet 296, 317
Show us a sign 160
Sialkot 96, 125
Sidra D Yahya 297
Simon 5, 10, 24, 40, 71, 119, 142,
    223, 338, 354
Simon Bar Kokhba 5
Sinakulo 13
Single Christians 215
Sirkap 111
Sir William Jones 111
Skardu 100
Slaughter of the Innocents 33
Soo-er 288
Soviet Union 195
Spanish Inquisition 338
Sri Guru Garanth 217
Staff of Moses 194
Star of Bethlehem 33
St. Francis of Assisi 56

Stigmata 56, 57
Stone's throw 90
Strachan's Fourth Gospel 272
Sudan 156
Sunan-Dar-Qutni 218
Sun be darkened 213
Sundance Channel 79, 110, 168
Sursagar 217
Suttee 138
Suzanne Olsson iii, xv, 87, 93, 94, 95,
    96, 98, 99, 101, 109, 125, 162,
    357
Sweating blood 19
Sydney 164
Syriac Edition 16, 164, 272, 320

T

Tafseer-e-Kabir 331
Ta Ha 120
Taklamakan 104
Talmud of Immanuel 27
Tanda 96, 125
Tanuk 99
Tar'-shish 28
T'atirul-Anam 20
Taxila 111
Tema 303, 330, 331
Te'-man 302
Temanite 42
Temple Mount 84, 256, 308
Theodosius 338
Theosophical Society 215, 216
The Ten Yard Graves 96, 125
Thhatta 82
Thief in the night 208, 209
Thomas 16, 22, 23, 71, 75, 77, 79,
    126, 163, 164, 176, 328, 334, 374
Tiberias 69
Tibet 83, 110
Timothy Freke 64, 65, 351, 352
Tocharian 104
Touhfa-e-Gulervia 163, 217
Tudor Parfitt 111

U

University of La Verne 33
Unloose the ties 296, 317
Urdu 180, 230, 249, 348, 362
Uriah 341, 378

V

Vassar 235
Vatican 166, 258, 287
Vedas 122, 123
VICT'RY UNTO VICT'RY 156
Vietnam 135
Vikramaditya 110

W

Walking on water 153, 155, 156, 208
Wall Street Journal 111, 166
Washington Times 106, 107
Water of life 155
Wicked priest 297
Wicked teacher 297
William Martin 156, 157
William Miller 216

Y

Yahyah 31, 54, 167
Ya-Sin 89
Yatur 331
Yemen 331
You kept me alive 187
Younus xv, xvii, 237
Yusuf Ali 89, 270

Z

Zabur 172, 199, 200